MALE RAGE
FEMALE FURY

Gender and Violence in Contemporary American Fiction

Marilyn Maxwell, Ph.D.

University Press of America, Inc.
Lanham · New York · Oxford

Copyright © 2000 by
University Press of America,® Inc.
4720 Boston Way
Lanham, Maryland 20706

12 Hid's Copse Rd.
Cumnor Hill, Oxford OX2 9JJ

All rights reserved
Printed in the United States of America
British Library Cataloging in Publication Information Available

Library of Congress Cataloging-in-Publication Data

Maxwell, Marilyn
Male rage female fury : gender and violence in contemporary
American fiction / Marilyn Maxwell.
p. cm.
Includes bibliographical references and index.
1. American fiction—20th century—History and criticism. 2. Violence
In literaure. 3. Gender identity in literature. 4. Masculinity in literature.
5. Femininity in literature. 6. Sex role in literature. I. Title.
PS374.V58M38 2000   813'.5409355—21   00-057756 CIP

ISBN 0-7618-1803-0 (cloth: alk. ppr.)

The paper used in this publication meets the minimum
requirements of American National Standard for Information
Sciences—Permanence of Paper for Printed Library Materials,
ANSI Z39.48—1984

To Virginia, my sister and friend
to Pat, Bentley and Devon, my family
and to my students

Contents

Acknowledgments	vii
Introduction	xi

Chapter I—Donald Barthelme	1
Woman as Textual/Sexual Prisoner: The Short Stories	1
Bitch vs. Witch: *Snow White*	22
Dying Fathers and Emerging Daughters:	
Barthelme, Didion and *The Dead Father*	36
Chapter II—Joan Didion	51
Stagnant River Matrons: *Run River*	58
Female Bondage: *Play It As It Lays*	66
Female Bonds: *A Book of Common Prayer*	80
Female Bonding: *Democracy*	94
Chapter III—Thomas Pynchon	115
Woman as Mystery: *V.*	119
Woman's Place in the *Raketenstadt*: *Gravity's Rainbow*	158
Chapter IV—Toni Morrison	189
Male-Initiated Violence: *The Bluest Eye* and *Jazz*	197
Female-Initiated Violence: *Sula* and *Beloved*	230
Concluding Remarks	263
Notes	265
Bibliography	291
Index	303

Acknowledgments

The successful completion of this project is the result of the collaborative efforts of many people who provided me with both intellectual guidance and spiritual encouragement. I am indebted to Dr. Frederick Karl, my faculty advisor at New York University, for having inspired me to pursue my interest in women and violence in contemporary American fiction. His salient comments and continual support served to minimize the various obstacles encountered along the way; to him I owe everything that is good about this project.

I also gratefully acknowledge the many other people who patiently saw me through this rather arduous process: Dr. Ruth Formanek, who has always encouraged me to believe in myself; Alice Federico, who generously gave up many hours of her own time to convert the manuscript to a readable format; Stephanie Brudner, my colleague, and Jason Loew, my student, who helped me unravel the complexities of the computer program; C. J. Morrissey, the "Poet Laureate" of Hewlett High School who contributed his "Syllables" to this project; Ruth Goldenberg, my friend, who vigorously secured the necessary copyright permissions; Margery Kashman, my friend and colleague, who painstakingly proofread the text; Nancy H. Fenton, who brought an editor's eye to the text and clarified my corrections; Peggy Maday and Marlene Morris, who, with my sister, Virginia, and her husband, Paul, reminded me of the importance of laughter; Nechama Liss-Levinson, who provided me with emotional support; and Walter and Dana Scheirer who provided an inspiring title. To my family—Pat, Virginia, Paul, Bentley and Devon—and to my dear friends, Nancy P. Burton, Beverly Matthews and Myrna Omang, I owe my sanity.

Finally, I would like to thank Janet Cooper, who magically transformed the manuscript into a book, and Peter Cooper, from The University Press of America, for believing in this project.

Male Rage/Female Fury

The author gratefully acknowledges permission to reprint material from the following sources:

From *Gravity's Rainbow* by Thomas Pynchon, copyright © 1973 by Thomas Pynchon, used by permission of Viking Penguin, a division of Penguin Putnam, Inc.;

From *City Life*, copyright © 1970 by Donald Barthelme and *Sixty Stories*, copyright © 1982 by Donald Barthelme, used by permission of The Wylie Agency, Inc.;

From *Slow Learner* by Thomas Pynchon, copyright © 1984 by Thomas Pynchon and *Vineland* by Thomas Pynchon, copyright © 1990 by Thomas Pynchon, used by permission of Little, Brown and Company;

From *Invisible Man* by Ralph Ellison, copyright © 1972 by Ralph Ellison, used by permission of Random House, Inc. and International Creative Management, Inc.;

From *Tropic of Cancer* by Henry Miller, copyright © 1961 by Henry Miller, *Tropic of Capricorn* by Henry Miller, copyright © 1961 by Henry Miller and *Sexus: The Rosy Crucifixion* by Henry Miller, copyright © 1965 by Henry Miller used by permission of Grove/Atlantic, Inc;

From *Last Exit to Brooklyn* by Hubert Selby, Jr., copyright © 1964 by Hubert Selby, Jr., used by permission of Grove/Atlantic, Inc.;

From *Jazz* by Toni Morrison, copyright © 1992 by Toni Morrison, *The Bluest Eye* by Toni Morrison, copyright © 1970 by Toni Morrison, *Beloved* by Toni Morrison, copyright © 1987 by Toni Morrison, *Sula* by Toni Morrison, copyright © 1973 by Toni Morrison and *Song of Solomon* by Toni Morrison, copyright © 1977 by Toni Morrison. Used by permission of International Creative Management, Inc.;

Reprinted by permission of Farrar, Straus and Giroux, LLC: excerpts from *The Dead Father* by Donald Barthelme, copyright © 1975 by Donald Barthelme; excerpts from *Play It As It Lays* by Joan Didion, copyright © 1970 by Joan Didion; excerpts from *Slouching Towards Bethlehem* by Joan Didion, copyright © 1966, 1968, renewed by Joan Didion; excerpts from *The White Album* by Joan Didion, copyright © 1979 by Joan Didion;

Reprinted with the permission of Scribner, a Division of Simon and Schuster, from *Snow White* by Donald Barthelme, copyright © 1967 by Donald Barthelme;

Acknowledgments

Reprinted by permission of HarperCollins Publishers, Inc: specified excerpts from *Native Son* by Richard Wright, copyright © 1940 by Richard Wright, copyright© renewed 1968 by Ellen Wright; Lines 14-17 from "Howl" from *The Collected Poems 1947-1980* by Allen Ginsberg, copyright © 1955 by Allen Ginsberg; lines 15-21 from "A Birthday Present" from *Ariel* by Sylvia Plath, copyright © 1963 by Ted Hughes; excerpts from *V.: A Novel* by Thomas Pynchon, copyright © 1961, 1963 by Thomas Pynchon;

Reprinted by permission of the author: excerpts from *Salvador* by Joan Didion, copyright © 1983 by Joan Didion; excerpts from *Democracy* by Joan Didion, copyright © 1984 by Joan Didion; excerpts from *Run River* by Joan Didion, copyright © 1963 by Joan Didion; excerpts from *A Book of Common Prayer* by Joan Didion, copyright © 1977 by Joan Didion.

Introduction

In the introduction to the 1984 edition of his early short stories entitled *Slow Learner*, Thomas Pynchon issues an "apology" for the "unacceptable level of racist, sexist and proto-Fascist talk" that informs the narrative voice of "Low Lands": "I wish that I could say that this is only Pig Bodine's voice, but, sad to say, it was also my own at the time."[1] Observing the historical authenticity of a narrator whose prejudices reflected the racist and sexist attitudes endemic to the America of the 1960's, Pynchon, in retrospect, characterizes the voice in the story as "that of a smart-assed jerk who didn't know any better"(SL12). While the author apologizes for both his own and Bodine's failings, he also advises us that Bodine remained for him a very likeable character, so likeable that he "brought the character in a time or two since in novels"(SL11).

The "likeable sexist/racist," if not an oxymoron, certainly captures the ambivalence of a postmodern writer. Although later sensitive to and aware of the insidious effects of prejudice as a means of "keeping us divided and so relatively poor and powerless," Pynchon could not fully let go of the "smart-assed jerk" who kicks "third-world people around" and who reduces women to "babes" and sex toys (SL12). Emblematic of an ambivalence toward women that informs some pivotal works of American postmodernist fiction, Pynchon's qualified apology foregrounds the ideological tension and ambiguity that arise in those experimental texts that display innovative structural devices while simultaneously invoking traditional, if not reactionary, attitudes towards women. More specifically, the clash between technical innovation, on the one hand, and conventional sex-stereotyping (e.g. passive female and aggressive male), on the other, seems to have unleashed a sexualized rage so virulent that it has spawned some of the most horrific and brutal images of violence against women to appear in American fiction.

Male Rage/Female Fury

This work explores the phenomenon of women and violence in selected works of postmodern American fiction. While I concentrate primarily upon the concept of woman as the recipient of masculine rage, I also explore the image of the "violent" woman, particularly in the final chapter dealing with the texts of Toni Morrison. As I will argue, however, "violent" women are by far less overtly aggressive and less comfortable with their momentary gestures of fury than are their male counterparts. Each of the authors considered in this study—Donald Barthelme, Joan Didion, Thomas Pynchon and Toni Morrison—participates in the American literary trend known as postmodernism, which for purposes of this study, will denote the experimental fictional texts that have appeared between the 1960's and the early 1990's and that display a variety of innovative technical strategies with regard to narrative voice, temporal sequence, and self-reflexivity, as well as a re-examination of gender roles. As Larry McCaffery notes, the term "experimental postmodernism" eludes exact definition and within the three-decade span that I have chosen as a means of identification, this literary trend has splintered off into many directions.[2] Critics have sub-divided this time period into first and second-wave postmodernist fiction[3] or referred to the experimental texts written after 1975 as "post-postmodernist" fiction to denote more of a blend of realism and experimentalism.[4] Acknowledging the existence of a variety of experimental techniques among the authors selected, I have, for the purposes of simplicity, used the term "literary postmodernism" to denote the emergence of innovative American fiction in the thirty-five year period since 1960 and the term "postmodern America" as an historical label to signify approximately the same era.

Like McCaffery who designates the cultural upheaval of the 1960's as a line of demarcation between the socio-political optimism of the post-World War II years and the spiritual malaise of the years to follow,[5] I have embraced the 1960's as the pivotal point at which much of America experienced a shift in sensibility with regard to the individual's autonomy in the vast network of the military-industrial complex. While campus rebellions and second-wave feminism of the 1960's seemed to herald the rise of effective political coalitions, the fragility of all human life on this planet was brought home to us daily not only in the horrifying images of the Vietnam War, with its numbing statistics of the wounded and dead flashed on the evening news screen, but also in the ever-present and ubiquitous threat of nuclear holocaust. The rising number of violent crimes against women in America in the ensuing years also underscored the continued

Introduction

vulnerability of members of an emerging vocal minority to male-dominated cultural institutions of control, from the military and the justice system to organized religion and education. Many of the texts considered in this study generate images of psychological impotence and spiritual torpor, of the individual dwarfed by cultural institutions that seemingly have eclipsed personal autonomy. Invoking the theories of Jürgen Habermas and Jean François Lyotard, Deborah Madsen, in her analysis of Pynchon's texts, points out that this "postmodernist malaise"—the sense that the individual is manipulated often unknowingly by pervasive societal structures of control—accounts for much of the tension that informs postmodernist novels as writers rail against succumbing to "dominant institutionalized versions of Truth."[6] The extent to which the texts selected for discussion include women in their rebellion against institutional control—for example, the extent to which they attempt to liberate women from the old prison houses of sexual stereotypes and cultural myths about female masochism and passivity—will prove to be a critical factor in the following analyses of postmodernist images of sexual violence.

While each of the four authors employs his/her own unique innovative strategies, they all share an experimental impulse to subvert various staples of the traditional novel. Barthelme and Didion—representatives of the literary "school" of minimalism—and Pynchon and Morrison—members of the "school" of expansive mythicism—all question the legitimacy and efficacy of traditional formal possibilities regarding temporal linearity, univocal narrative perspective, closure, characterization and identity; they all manifest a textual self-consciousness that highlights the novel as artifact and that invites the reader into the process of co-creating the text. While Barthelme and Pynchon also rely upon the literary postmodernist staples of parody and the collapsing of a distinction between high and low culture, all four novelists, to varying degrees, subvert conventional, linear narrative strategies and raise questions concerning the concept of gender/sexual identity.

The troubling ambiguity that attends the images of women and violence in the experimental works of these four novelists is not solely a result of the textual disparity between innovative technical strategies and conventional sex-stereotypes; it also reflects the ambiguous position of women in a society that pays lip service to ameliorating their status as second-class citizens but in actuality still harbors myths about female sexuality that implicitly perpetuate and often sanction abuse. Clustered around the 1960's women's movement, that is, second-wave feminism, many of the texts that I have targeted for discussion seemingly rely upon the hackneyed stereotypes of the "woman-as-willing-victim" and "woman-as-sexual-object," suggesting that the experimental impulse that brazenly challenges the hegemony of conventional discourse and techniques of mimetic realism does not always guarantee a parallel subversion of sex stereotypes. Rita Felski has compellingly argued that there is no necessary connection between feminism and experimental form and that often technically innovative texts can be quite inimical to the interests of women while traditional realist texts can be quite compatible with the advancement of feminist agendas.[7] Sandra Gilbert and Susan Gubar have even suggested that the "rhetoric of innovation may camouflage regressive or nostalgic sexual ideologies."[8] Felski's dismissal of a purely feminist aesthetic as chimerical and her contention that "the political values of literary texts from the standpoint of feminism can be determined only by an investigation of their social functions and effects in relation to the interests of women in a particular historical context"[9] underscore the necessity of viewing these literary texts, and specifically their images of violence and women, against the socio-political backdrop of their era. One of the premises of this study is that the textual ambiguity that arises when the liberating impulse of technical experimentation does not extend to a concomitant re-envisioning of the roles of women and men aptly reflects the ambivalence with which women have been perceived in postmodern America, that is, in the twenty-five year period ushered in by the significant political and social disruptions of the late 1960's.

Women: A Population at Risk

Our pop culture is inhabited by many "likeable sexists," from the charismatic but perhaps lethal O. J. Simpson to the "comedic" Andrew Dice Clay, from the vituperative Rush Limbaugh to rock groups like "Guns n Roses" that enjoy gold and platinum record sales with albums that shout forth misogynistic lyrics. Second-wave feminism may have raised the collective cultural consciousness with regard to the socio-economic oppression of women in postmodern America and succeeded perhaps in providing women with professional and educational opportunities denied their mothers and grandmothers; however, statistics also reveal an alarming rise in the rate of both impersonal "hate crimes" against women (i.e. those crimes which the FBI maintains are committed against women simply because they are members of a group)[10] and more intimate assaults (i.e.

Introduction

those crimes, such as domestic abuse, rape, sexual harassment and murder, which are leveled at women for more personal reasons):

> A 1990 Senate committee report indicates that three out of four women will be victims of violent crime during their lifetime. According to a national crime survey, since 1974 assaults against women have risen 50 percent, while assaults against men have declined by 12 percent. The Bureau of Justice Statistics says that 95 percent of the victims of domestic violence are women.[11]
>
> The 1990 Senate Judiciary Committee found that rape increased four times as fast as the overall crime rate over the previous decade and that a woman is raped every six minutes while only half the rapes are ever reported.[12]

Additional findings support the idea that contemporary women are living in an ever-increasingly hostile environment. Social workers, psychologists, and attorneys who confront woman-abuse victims substantiate the general perception that women constitute a population at risk in postmodern America:

1) one out of every six wives is beaten each year;
2) one of six teenage girls will be abused by the time she is eighteen years of age;
3) one woman in the United States is beaten every eighteen seconds;
4) between 2000-4000 women die every year from abuse;
5) 30% of all women killed every year are slain by partners;
6) domestic violence is the leading cause of injury to women in the U.S.[13]

American women have found themselves in the rather awkward position of living in a society that seemingly both respects and degrades them. While some women are perhaps reaping the economic and professional benefits of second-wave feminism, all women in postmodern America appear to remain vulnerable to an often lethal masculinist hostility. The statistics reveal not only that "violence against women is a grave and frequent problem"[14] but also that women often feel themselves living in a state of siege, afraid to walk in their neighborhoods after dark and constantly fearful of rape and violent assault.[15] Recent psychological studies suggest that postmodern American women view themselves as vulnerable to sexual attack and thus experience a higher degree of fear and anxiety than their male counterparts.[16]

Male Rage/Female Fury

The proliferation of sociological, psychological and legal studies concerning crimes against women has produced a body of research aimed at elucidating the personal and social causes of male aggression against females. There is a general consensus among many researchers that while there is no clear-cut reason as to why men assault women,[17] one of the contributing factors in rape[18] and in partner-precipitated violence is the desire to exercise power and control over the victim.[19] Psychologist Matthew Campbell argues that men continue to abuse their wives "not because they lose their tempers or have money or job problems or a masochistic or annoying wife or because the family is an arena of violence" but rather because they need to control others.[20] Furthermore, Campbell's argument that abuse is used as a mechanism of individual male control over a woman can be extended to include the more general social domain; Pynchon's portrayal of the complex web of control strategies at work in the military-industrial state in *Gravity's Rainbow*, while not limited to the manipulation of women, confirms what psychologists have discovered, namely, that male-initiated violence against women "functions as a mechanism of social control and serves to reproduce and maintain the status quo of male dominance and female subordination."[21] Psychologists point out that the fear of rape, for example, serves to control women's lives by restricting their freedom at home, work, and community and, as is comically portrayed in *The Dead Father* and tragically depicted in the Sarah-episode of *V.*, by perpetuating their dependence upon male others as a form of protection from male predators.[22]

Issues of power and control are critical factors influencing the expression of violence against women both in the personal domain and in the more general arena of society. However, the belief that as a male one is entitled to exercise control over one's partner and the idea that often women invite their own sexual degradation by men are myths that continue to be perpetuated by American cultural institutions. Although the exact reasons why men assault women may elude researchers at this time, many psychologists agree that such ubiquitous and tenacious, aggressive behavior must be understood in its socio-cultural context; for many of our cultural institutions continue to bolster misogynistic attitudes that create a social environment conducive to the commission and often to the sanctioning of violence against women. The family, the work place, the military, the legal system and the media continue to serve as vehicles of socialization by which all of us, particularly the young, are taught to embrace traditional gender

Introduction

stereotypes that depict the male as "naturally" dominant and aggressive and the female as passive, nurturing and submissive.

In her study *The War Against Women*, Marilyn French outlines the insidious strategies employed by various cultural institutions to enforce the subordination of women. While her analysis is not limited to that of the United States, many of French's observations provide insight into the nature of America's institutional control of women's continued inferior economic status, their discrimination by police departments, the legal system, religion and the arts. Many of French's contentions have been borne out by psychological research that reveals women's vulnerable position when having to deal with the police, hospitals, the courts, and the education system. The "systemic prejudice" against women manifested by the police department, particularly in "domestic abuse" cases, reflects not only the police's fear of the "unpredictability of the male batterer"[23] but also their own masculinist attitude that women often instigate and provoke their husbands and deserve to be hit. That the police often themselves are batterers, a reality comically alluded to in Barthelme's "The Policeman's Ball," compounds the woman's victimization and sense of helplessness. A 1984 study found that the police responses to wife-beating calls were neglectfully inadequate and stemmed in part from the still deeply-ingrained belief that women are the property of their husbands and that wife abuse is a "private" matter occurring within the sacrosanct family unit over which the husband exercises unquestioned hegemony.[24] Those battered women who do arrive at the emergency rooms often encounter a medical system that continues to trivialize their plight, as another study found that medical personnel categorized the battered women as social rather than true medical cases.[25] Those women who do fight back, who kill their abusive husbands, for example, confront a judicial system informed by many of the same masculinist prejudices that fail to consider female aggression, even when it is self-defensive, as a legitimate mechanism of survival. Criminologist Anne Campbell points out that while an abusive man kills his wife in order to make her "behave properly," an abused wife kills her husband to "make the madness stop;" however, the abuser's motive, from the perspective of the American justice system, is apparently more "reasonable" than the abused's motive, for statistics show "proportionately more wives than husbands being convicted of spousal murder."[26]

The American military also aids and abets the perpetuation of traditional gender stereotypes that contribute to the societal acceptance of male aggression and female passivity as "natural" and genetically-determined hierarchies of behavior. While Pynchon plays with the possibility of destabilizing these stereotypes in the vast military-industrial complex of *Gravity's Rainbow*, such experimentation is ultimately eclipsed by the insidious forces of economic control which have a vested interest in maintaining the *status quo*. Although Didion does not focus primarily on the military machine as the overriding presence in her novels, she does, particularly in *A Book of Common Prayer* and *Democracy*, succeed in subtextually exposing the machinations of military and paramilitary personnel who pull the strings of power in postmodern America. The "Tier Park" episode in *Gravity's Rainbow* limns the socialization process of priming young boys for militaristic aggression. In what could be viewed as a "feminist" companion piece, Susan Griffin's *A Chorus of Stones* marshalls a vast array of sources, including diary entries of Nazi leaders, her own personal narratives of her childhood, art work, and historical and psychological research to suggest that learned gender roles, primarily the acting out of the acceptable role of the sexually-aggressive male, contribute significantly to both the genesis and devastating conclusion of war: "A connection between violence and sexuality threads its way through many histories,"[27] Griffin argues, as she proceeds to imagine the evolution of the sadistic Reichsführer SS Heinrich Himmler from the young boy Heinrich, a frail child "favored by his mother," who probably could not when young live up to the standards set by a society "that gave inordinate significance to masculinity."[28] Perhaps, as Griffin maintains, to compensate for his perceived inadequacy, Himmler assembles an image of himself as the masculine warrior and proceeds to pursue a career in the military that allows him to display his manhood by sadistically controlling others. One is reminded of the sadistic rocket technician, Blicero, in *Gravity's Rainbow*. Randy Shilts, in his comprehensive analysis of gays and lesbians in the American military system, has similarly argued that the need for the latent male homosexual to prove his manhood in a masculinist culture often led to his camouflaging his sexual orientation beneath a set of army fatigues. "Boys go to war to prove they are men," Shilts maintains, and those who most vigorously pursue the "calling" to serve are often those who harbor the greatest doubt about their own "manliness," that is, those who are homosexual.[29] Both Griffin and Shilts, in their discussions of the military as a socializing agent of traditional gender dichotomies, reveal not only a celebration of an often lethal masculinity but also a devaluation of the "feminine" in contemporary culture. The exultation expressed by the male cadets and the administration of the

Introduction

Citadel following Shannon Faulkner's "voluntary" withdrawal underscores a still deeply-seated rejection and debasement of the feminine in this culture. It is not surprising then to hear drill sergeants still referring to their new recruits, those who have not been transformed into real men yet, as "ladies"; nor is it difficult to conclude, as psychologists have, that "the recent Tailhook scandal is but a recent, highly publicized example of a long history of U.S. military contributions to male violence against women."[30]

Like the military, the legal system and the family, the American education system also contributes to rendering American women vulnerable to male abuse. Despite all the research that has, over the last thirty years, disclosed the glaring inequities concerning the treatment of boys and girls in the classroom, the hallway and the counseling centers, the educational system has failed to root out those sexist practices and attitudes among its personnel that still contribute to low female self-esteem in the areas of math and science and to a silencing of the female voice in the classroom. Myra and David Sadker have documented the discrimination that girls and young women have had to combat in American schools throughout the twentieth century, ranging from sexual harassment from peers and teachers to exclusion from various academic programs and scholarships.[31] While Didion does not overtly embrace the issue of the intellectually disenfranchised young woman, her novels display a subtextual acknowledgment of the often displaced daughters of a traditional American culture that generally viewed the education of women as frivolous and secondary to that of men. Many of Didion's female characters—the youthful Lily Knight and the lost daughters of Charlotte Douglas and Inez Victor—are all products, in part, of an educational system that trained women to be ornamental appendages to more academically serious and more powerful males.

The images of women in advertising and in the media often persist in their commodification of the female, in their sexual objectification of the body and in their trivializing of the feminine. Reflecting perhaps a "cannibalistic male psyche,"[32] media images which dismember the female and which encode a not-so-subtle male hatred of women have become almost the required staple of the postmodern cinema. Whether or not "pornography" requires legislative control is an issue that continues to divide not only constitutional scholars but also contemporary American feminists.[33] It is difficult to deny, however, that the proliferation of media images which display the degradation of women—if not a contributing factor toward the establishment of an environment conducive to the violent treatment of women—certainly produces effective emblems of the cultural wars leveled against women in postmodern America. The authors targeted here all tangentially raise the troubling issue of such "pornographic" images of victimized women, as the reader must decide whether such images are being exploited to induce male sexual fantasies or to reflect a misogynistic culture, or perhaps, both.

The perpetuation of traditional gender stereotypes by the various cultural institutions in postmodern America contributes, some psychologists argue, to an atmosphere conducive to the eruption of male-directed violence against women and to the suppression of woman-enunciated anger. Anne Campbell argues that both male and female aggressive behavior must be understood in terms of the gender expectations of society:

> Women cry rather than hit not because of their hormones...or their role as carers but because they see aggression as a personal failure; and the safest release for their anger, when they deny themselves blows, is tears.
>
> Men hit not because their testosterone makes them or because their mothers didn't punish them enough or because they are account executives but because when they are humiliated...they believe that aggression will restore the status quo.[34]

Men have been socialized into believing that aggression is an effective means of "taking control," while women have been raised to view anger as a display of "losing control" that must be suppressed or expressed in more socially accepted ways.[35] Didion's early protagonists, Lily McClellan and Maria Wyeth, provide fitting examples of women who manifest the stereotypic silencing of anger, that is, the suppression of any outwardly-directed fury against hurtful men in favor of more internalized expressions of rage. Yet, Morrison's Violet, Eva, Sula and Sethe serve to raise the seemingly inscrutable phenomenon of the violent woman who, as Anne Campbell points out, presents a theoretical enigma to male-defined schemas of aggression and flies in the face of women's alleged innate passivity: "As long as men hold positions of power it is their beliefs that count, and they tend to see women's aggression—because it remains inexplicable in male terms—as comic, hysterical or insane."[36] Chapter Four focuses most clearly on the violent women in Morrison's postmodernist novels and provides an analysis that challenges patriarchal definitions of female aggression by citing recent feminist theories aimed at elucidating female fury as an instrumental

Introduction

means of announcing and establishing female subjectivity in scripts that have traditionally erased the woman as subject.

Looking at "gendered scripts"—the enactments of socio-cultural expectations and norms for women and men—one researcher argues that the "basic heterosexual script in our culture reflects an androcentric heterosexuality that eroticizes sexual inequality and supports male dominance as normal and natural."[37] Women are expected to have relationships with men who are smarter, taller, older, more educated, more talented and more highly paid than they are. Furthermore, such scripts also display "a male-centered objectification of women that emphasizes their physical attractiveness and ability to stimulate and satisfy men's desires."[38] Such objectification and denial of female subjectivity give rise to some of the most gruesome images of violence in the postmodernist novels analyzed in this study. Barthelme, Didion, Pynchon and Morrison each constructs a landscape of sexually victimized women, some of whom seemingly contribute to their own degradation by masochistically "choosing" to submit to male brutality. Finally, the pernicious myth of female masochism has often served to excuse the eruption of male violence against women both in the home and in the social arena. Despite extensive research that undermines the validity of the concept of an innate female masochism, society frequently continues to invoke such an idea when explaining why battered women remain with their husbands. Aside from the societally-enforced position of economic dependence thrust upon many women that relegates them to the "acceptance" of abuse in exchange for basic survival needs, the "fear of disapproval from family or friends, the concern about losing their children, and the fear of retaliation by a violent partner" are additional factors that influence a woman's "choice" to remain in a dangerous environment.[39] Far from reflecting a "typically-female" proclivity for pain, the inertia of the abused woman points both to a very realistic concern for her own welfare and to a conformity to gender expectations that dictate female self-sacrifice. Many of the postmodern literary works of fiction targeted in my study present images of men who attempt to exercise a sadistic control over women and of women who seemingly comply by engaging in their own masochistic submission. Barthelme's Snow White and the "wife" from "The Captured Woman," Didion's early protagonists, Lily McClellan and Maria Wyeth, and many of Pynchon's women from *V.* and *Gravity's Rainbow* display behavior that initially suggests their welcoming acceptance of male brutality. These fictional images, to varying degrees, both endorse and indict the myth of female masochism, giving rise to a troubling ambiguity in the texts considered. That is to say, they both employ and call into question what psychologists have labelled a "fundamental attribution error" which incorrectly attributes an abused woman's ostensible inertia to her own personality traits rather than to "situational causes."[40]

Women and Literary Postmodernism

Whether or not the ambivalence toward women in postmodern culture reflects a masculinist backlash to the advancements of second-wave feminism, as Susan Faludi argues in her analyses of sexual hostilities of the 1980's,[41] is subject to debate. However, the critical issue for this study is that the troubling ambiguity that attends the images of women and violence in certain postmodernist texts is emblematic of the ambivalence with which women are still perceived in a postmodern, patriarchal culture. Moreover, the proliferation of graphic images of female mutilation, rape and mass femicide that punctuate these texts is both a by-product of the liberating impulse of experimentation and a commentary on the increased rate of violence against women in postmodern America. As Felski maintains, "Literature does not merely constitute a self-referential and metalinguistic system...but is also a medium which can profoundly influence individual and cultural self-understanding in the sphere of everyday life."[42] Consequently, while this study is not a sociological tract aimed at analyzing the phenomenon of violence against women in contemporary America, I cite recent psychological theories and data dealing with male aggression and female response, so that the discussion of the fictional images in the selected texts will perhaps facilitate "individual and cultural self-understanding."

While literary innovation may not logically entail a feminist aesthetics, the historical juxtaposition of the advent of second-wave American feminism and the appearance of experimental American fiction during the turbulent sixties initially suggests a basic philosophical compatibility between feminism and literary postmodernism. Linda Hutcheon has argued for the existence of "overlapping agendas between philosophical postmodernism and "ex-centrics, blacks, women and other traditionally marginalized groups."[43] Gilbert and Gubar have even suggested that the early postmodernist texts of Donald Barthelme, Kurt Vonnegut and John Barth that "ridicule notions of male biological primacy and female fetishization,"

Introduction

thus disclosing the performative nature of gender roles, assisted the feminist agenda that sought to dismantle the concept of gender hierarchy.[44] Second-wave feminist theorists such as Simone de Beauvoir, Carolyn Heilbrun, Kate Millett, Andrea Dworkin, Betty Friedan, Mary Daly, Adrienne Rich, Susan Griffin and others, along with the more recent French post-structuralist feminist theorists—Hélène Cixous, Luce Irigaray and Julia Kristeva—have seized upon the implications for women and men inherent in the "movement away from sexual polarization and the prison of gender toward a world in which individual roles and the modes of personal behavior can be freely chosen."[45]

Yet, while the parodic subversion of the gender hierarchy appearing in the early phases of literary postmodernism may have served the political needs of second-wave feminism and served as a springboard for later feminist theorists, the graphic images of sexual aggression against females in many of these postmodernist texts have also prompted many American critics to express their aversion to embracing literary postmodernism as an enterprise consonant with the concerns of women as an often violently oppressed minority. Bonnie Zimmerman, for example, argues that the 1960's women's movement did not blanketly endorse literary postmodernism because women who looked to avant-garde fiction for emancipatory plots and characterizations found instead "the same old stereotypes, sexual violence, or avoidance of the female that they found in representational fiction."[46] Acknowledging the contributions made by writers such as Barth, Barthelme, Pynchon and others to the toppling of gender hierarchies, Gilbert and Gubar also interpret the sexualized aggression encoded in many of the images in the works of writers like Pynchon, Norman Mailer and William Carlos Williams to be a thinly-veiled masculinist backlash against the socio-political demands of second-wave feminism. They, too, characterize many of these experimental texts as manifesting "ambivalent attitudes" toward male sexual aggression and female victimization.[47]

Yet, it is not only the prevalence of images detailing violent objectification and sexual degradation that alienates many women from the postmodernist literary camp. One of the main tenets of postmodernist philosophical theory is the deconstruction or destabilization of the concept of identity or self. Jean-François Lyotard's refusal of the "grand narratives" of the Western philosophical tradition, expounded in his seminal essay *The Postmodern Condition*, forever called into question the validity of the unitary ego of Enlightenment humanism and led to the positing of a decentered self and an epistemological tentativeness regarding truth claims. Jacques Derrida jettisoned Western metaphysics as an oppressive metaphysics of male self-presence—a phallocentrism—and in its place posited a "self" that arises as a textual construct whose meaning is not one of static coincidence but rather of a fluid and "open-ended play between the presence of one signifier and the absence of others."[48] Lyotard's revolutionary dismantling of the foundations of Western epistemology and Derrida's subversion of the binary opposites of conventional Western metaphysics (e.g. self/other, male/female, etc.) provided the experimental novelist with a philosophical foundation for the innovative technical strategies that would call into question the old staples of narrative "truth," plot, characterization, identity and temporal sequence. Some American feminist theorists, such as Peggy Kamuf and Mary Jacobus, following the lead of the French feminists, Cixous, Kristeva and Irigaray, celebrate the deconstructionist dissolution of the self, particularly of female identity, as a necessary prelude to the emergence of a subversive feminine voice within the confines of patriarchal discourse.[49]

Other American feminists, however, have pointed out that such a hasty dismissal of the unified subject may prove inimical to the needs and momentum of a previously marginalized group that has just begun to cohere as a viable coalition. As Christine Di Stefano argues, "Postmodernism expresses the claims and needs of a constituency (white, privileged men of the industrialized West) that has already had an Enlightenment for itself" and can more comfortably call into question the concepts of "self" and "truth" from which women have traditionally been alienated.[50] Patricia Waugh similarly notes that while postmodernism is deconstructing the sense of self-presence and identity—the humanist's self of liberalism, "feminism is assembling its cultural identity in what appears to be the opposite direction." Acknowledging the similarities between postmodernism and second-wave feminism—their historical coincidence, the rejection of modernism and New Criticism and the dissolution of boundaries between high and low culture—Waugh aptly points out that unlike their male counterparts, "women were for the first time in history beginning to construct a sense of a potent agential self to fight for change."[51] Far from embracing the postmodernist view that the ideas of Self, Truth and Unity were stale, "exhausted" concepts from which one felt alienated, the 1960's feminist, as Zimmerman notes, felt "angry and energized,"[52] poised to enter the arena of political action as an advocate for the community of women. Consequently, as Frederick Karl observes, literary texts that reflect the "deconstructionist tenet that the ego must be eradicated, or dismembered," and that "discourse must be held at the level of language alone" would be viewed by some women as a "form of death for the female experience."[53]

In her critique of the mainstream postmodernist philosophies of Lyotard and Derrida, Jane Flax also warns us about the dangers for feminism of eradicating the concept of Self. While she agrees that the traditional (male) ego of Enlightenment humanism has only served to oppress women throughout modern history, she is equally suspicious of the deconstructionist movement to embrace a purely "textually constituted" subject. Speaking from a feminist psychoanalytic perspective, Flax maintains that the postmodernist rejection of selfhood is "self-deceptively naive" and contrary to women's experience of subjectivity and to the sense in all of us of a basic psychological/emotional cohesion over time, that is, a "core self" that denotes not the unitary, masterful and oppressive male ego of humanism but rather our undeniable sense of continuity or "going-on-being."[54] Like Zimmerman, Gilbert, Gubar and others, Flax is suspicious of the "motives" of those who would outrightly repudiate any form of selfhood at a time when women have just begun to re-assemble their identities and to assert an "agentic subjectivity" previously available only to a "few privileged white men."[55]

The issues of identity, gender and sexuality figure prominently in the literary strategies of the four postmodernist authors discussed in this study and inform the many images of violence that punctuate their texts. To varying degrees and with seemingly varying agendas, each novelist both invokes and destabilizes traditional categories of self, of masculinity and femininity, and calls attention to what psychologists now recognize as almost axiomatic, namely, that "gender is a *social construct*, and not a personal attribute or particular behavior."[56] Feminist theorists such as Judith Butler, Marjorie Garber and Sally Robinson have investigated the performative nature of sex-roles as societal constructs, targeting the "foundational categories of sex, gender and desire" as the effects, rather than the causes, of patriarchal institutions,[57] and have elucidated the implications inherent in positing such ideas of masculinity and femininity as not existing "prior to their articulation in historically specific, and situational, discursive contexts."[58] Citing recent sociological and genetics research, Martine Rothblatt, in *The Apartheid of Sex*, has suggested there is "no socially meaningful characteristic that defines humanity into two absolute groups, men and women," and that like racial apartheid, the legal division of people into males and females serves the pernicious designs of a white, patriarchal culture.[59] While not explicitly focused on the debates in the theoretical community concerning the origin and causes of identity and gender, the works of Barthelme, Didion, Pynchon and Morrison manifest a subtextual tension inherent in the ambiguous images of women and violence that often tangentially challenges the traditional dichotomy between masculinity and femininity.

As minimalists given to sparse images and a profusion of textual silences, Donald Barthelme and Joan Didion both display a troubling ambiguity concerning women and violence in their texts, Barthelme through his parodic depiction of the victimization of women and Didion through a tension inherent in her early female protagonists between their suffering at the hands of men and their self-indulgent inertia.

The four short stories and two novels by Barthelme, discussed in Chapter One, exploit and condemn the victimization of women by mocking both the male aggressor and the female victim through "comic" images, a technique that elicits from the reader an uncomfortable blending of laughter and disgust. Presenting us with a litany of "likeable sexists" and female masochists, Barthelme constructs parodic caricatures of both men who engage in exaggerated fantasies of female decapitation and mutilation, and women who invite their own degradation. The reader is not only amused by the comic posturings of men working so hard at being "masculine" and women at being "feminine" but is also uncomfortable with the tragic realities in postmodern America that underlie such parody. Furthermore, while Barthelme very consciously invokes the deconstructionist subversion of the ontological primacy of any system of discourse, he seems ultimately to remain trapped within traditional male and female discursive registers. Paul-the-Prince, Snow White and the evil Jane fail to break free from conventional sex-stereotypes; while their imprisonment in traditional gender-categories serves to illuminate the performative nature of "typical" male and female behavior, such confinement also suggests the lack of desire to envision alternative modes of being-in-the-world. Through the characters of Emma and Julie, *The Dead Father*, unlike the other Barthelme texts considered in this chapter, does provide both an alternative to traditional phallic discourse and an image of woman as rebellious against patriarchal rule. However, Julie and Emma's paratactic playfulness, while cleverly revealing the arbitrary nature of conventional discourse, fails to take seriously the pragmatic problems inherent in female alienation and reflects, instead, this postmodern writer's agenda to deconstruct not only the concept of phallocentric speech but also the concept of self-identity. Barthelme has, perhaps, cleverly brought to the foreground the controversy that has divided feminist theorists concerning the political efficacy of a uniquely feminine mode of discourse, the subversive linguistic *jouissance* of Kristeva's "semiotic" or Cixous' *l'écriture féminine*, for example. While Jacobus and Kamuf embrace the feminine voice as a potentially subversive intrusion into phallic discourse, Butler, Felski and others question the pragmatic effectiveness of such an "emancipatory ideal" that can never be maintained within culture[60] or that cannot "provide an adequate basis for feminist politics."[61] In what may be a critique of the linguistic *jouissance* of the French post-structuralist theorists, Barthelme's "female speech" in *The Dead Father* presents the reader with a seemingly disconnected series of fragmented utterances rather than any meaningful exchange of ideas between two women; that is to say, one hears "voices" and not "characters."

In considering the four novels of Joan Didion, the focus of Chapter Two, I discovered that her earlier and less technically experimental works, *Run River* and *Play It As It Lays*, overtly rely upon the traditional female stereotype of the woman-as-willing-victim but also display a subtext of compassion and sensitivity to female oppression. Lily McClellan and Maria Wyeth manifest a profound lack of imagination and initiative with regard to extricating themselves from psychologically abusive relationships with men; yet, when considered against the socio-political context of a sexist culture, their inertia, ostensible complicity and appalling absence of "self-empowerment" emerge as the societally ingrained expectations for young women. When turning to her later texts, *A Book of Common Prayer* and *Democracy*, I found Didion employing an innovative technical device by which the narrator/author attempts to "re-collect" the fragmented pieces of a female character's shattered identity through the emotional bonding of two women. Whereas Barthelme deconstructs the concept of identity, Didion reconstructs the notion of the self, the latter writer painfully aware, however, that all such constructions reflect an "identity" that is both tentative and continuous; similar to the notion of the "core self," female identity in Didion's later novels, while not a replication of the unitary, static self of traditional humanism, displays an agential coherence necessary for women to confront the exigencies of the everyday world. Didion also seems to suggest that female identity is relational, that one constructs a sense of self in relation to others, so that, as Gayle Greene and Coppelia Kahn have argued, the "I" emerges in connection to the "we."[62] For, both Charlotte Douglas and Inez Victor, with the aid of a compassionate woman, strive to reassemble a viable sense of self that will enable them to endure the psychological assaults of men and of patriarchal institutions that relentlessly continue to objectify women and deny them their status as subjects.

The troubling ambiguity that characterizes the texts of Barthelme and Didion also attends the novels of Thomas Pynchon and Toni Morrison that are discussed in Chapters Three and Four, respectively. More expansive in their imagery and development of plot and character, these "mythicists" nonetheless display a reluctance to let go completely of traditional assumptions concerning sex stereotypes.

Concentrating on *V.* and *Gravity's Rainbow*, the most challenging and violent Pynchon texts, Chapter Three discloses the graphic images of femicide, rape and mutilation that suggest both a thinly-disguised release of aggression and a critique of our culture's deeply ingrained misogyny. The pathological strategies adopted by Pynchon's female and male characters to survive in the dystopic wasteland of America, as depicted in both *V.* and *Gravity's Rainbow*, spawn kinky, "pornographic" images that belie a profound despair. The ironies inherent in the self-destructive behavior of Mondaugen, Esther Harvitz, Benny Profane, Blicero, and the majority of the Pynchon "crew," receive a rather sardonic and at times scathing and scatological treatment by the author, who, despite his sensitivity to the plights of the weaker members of the corporate State, projects a dark vision of hopelessness in which lust and the sexual degradation of women run rampant. Whereas Barthelme parodically and minimalistically summons forth "comic" images of the cultural subordination of women, particularly of women's bodies as territory to be appropriated by more powerful men, Pynchon graphically details the reification of women in the extreme and tragic circumstances of modern warfare, and by extension, illuminates the plight of the female in the masculinist, military-industrial state. Under siege, women and children, for Pynchon, occupy the tenuous status of that of "prisoners of war" who must ingratiate themselves with their captors and often devise masochistic strategies of survival. Pynchon's depictions of such women in *V.* are far more troubling in their ambiguity as the author seems to have remain tethered to the conventional sexual "myths" about female passivity and masochism. It is in *Gravity's Rainbow* that Pynchon comes to apprehend the seeming complicity of women in their own subordination as exemplifying not an innate female masochism but rather a last-ditch attempt to survive their own commodification by both individual men and cultural institutions. Like Barthelme, however, Pynchon suggests that the possibility of a unique

Introduction

female vision—manifested in characters such as the witch, Geli Tripping, and Leni Pökler, the political rebel—does not possess the stamina necessary to be a viable political weapon in toppling phallic rule.

Chapter Four tackles Morrison's uncomfortable blending of a sensitivity to female victimization and a forgiveness of black male aggression in *The Bluest Eye* and *Jazz* that informs her images of violence against women and that stems, perhaps, from her loyalty to both her gender and her race. Such an ambiguity serves to blur the underlying violence of the crime, as the reader, through Morrison's technical strategies, is lured into aligning herself with the plight of the aggressor rather than with the humiliation of the victim. Morrison seems to suggest that black women remain doubly susceptible, victims not only of the brutal treatment of their white male colonizers but also of the displaced aggression of emotionally and economically impoverished black men who have adopted the sexist mores of their white male counterparts. The discussion of *Sula* and *Beloved* focuses upon the image of the woman as the initiator of violence and concludes that Morrison's images contain a complex blending of intentionality and "accident," of sacrifice and murderous love. Citing recent theories of maternal anger as the strategy by which traditionally silenced and objectified women strive to claim their own discourse and to be heard,[63] I also investigate the ambiguity inherent in the act of infanticide and the paradoxical behavior of a mother, whether it be Eva from *Sula* or Sethe from *Beloved*, who would challenge the societally sanctioned hierarchy of motherhood over selfhood by murdering her own child, that is, by destroying that which is both part of and separate from her being. Furthermore, Morrison employs at times a strikingly innovative discourse in *Beloved* that disrupts the semantic and syntactic order of traditional speech, suggesting to some critics that she may be celebrating the *jouissance* of Kristeva's feminine "semiotic" as a potentially subversive weapon for challenging the masculine linguistic order of the "symbolic." While effectively conveying the prediscursive bonding among the women of Sethe's community—a community of women that rescues Sethe from the vampiric consumption of an angry child—the sporadic eruption of "feminine" discourse serves also to reflect the potentially deleterious, regressive withdrawal of the mother and child into the imaginary and insular realm of a primal unity. Morrison, I maintain, harbors serious reservations about the effectiveness of feminine discourse as a weapon in combating the problems that women face in the everyday world.

Barthelme, Didion, Pynchon and Morrison openly challenge many of the structural devices of the traditional novel. Yet, their innovative strategies, while at times subverting conventional notions of narration, identity, closure and authorial distance, also generate some troubling ambiguities concerning the portrayals of women and violence. Although technical experimentation may not logically entail an aesthetic consonant with a feminist political agenda, a reliance upon traditional gender stereotypes and cultural myths about male aggression and female masochism in otherwise innovative works of fiction gives rise to an interesting ideological tension that emerges most clearly in the images of women and violence that punctuate these texts.

Chapter I
ഊരു
Donald Barthelme

Woman as Textual/Sexual Prisoner: The Short Stories

In one of Donald Barthelme's most popular stories, "The Glass Mountain," a young artist attempts to scale a glass mountain on the corner of Thirteenth Street and Eighth Avenue in order to discover a "beautiful enchanted symbol" that sits in a room of a castle of pure gold at the summit. Equipped with only climbing irons on his feet and a plumber's friend in each hand, the artist begins his ascent amidst the taunting jeers of the crowd and the dying moans of those fallen knights who have failed in their quest before him. At an altitude of 206 feet, he pauses to evaluate his motives, recall his fallen friends and observe the crowd stripping the dying knights of their "rings, wallets, pocket watches and ladies' favors and their gold teeth."[1] Discouraged by the cruel behavior of the crowd and unsure of his chances of success, the young artist opts for a fairy tale solution to his plight by which he is lifted into the air by an eagle and carried to the summit of the mountain. There he discovers the "beautiful enchanted symbol with its layers of meaning" only to find that when he "touched it, it changed into only a beautiful princess" (CL 65). In what would seem to be a moment of rage, the young artist "threw the beautiful princess headfirst down the mountain" to his acquaintances "who could be relied upon to deal with her" (CL 65).

This particular story has elicited many responses from those critics who see it as paradigmatic of both Barthelme's minimalist techniques and his reflexive concerns with the modern writer's quest to create an artistic form that will speak to a contemporary audience. Comprised of one hundred numbered fragments, the "Glass Mountain" exemplifies Barthelme's use of collage whereby he juxtaposes incongruous elements (e.g. chivalric knights and a Manhattan street corner) to create a new reality through what Jerome Klinkowitz calls "the shock of contrast."[2] Larry McCaffery argues that this story reflects "the artist's frustration at not being able to create a new form,"[3] while Alan Wilde maintains that Barthelme is attempting to "demythify or disenchant" all enchanted symbols of American culture from "Batman to the American Dream" so that we come to apprehend the world, as does the crowd, as "pure, disenchanted, phenomenal reality."[4] Rather than seeing the story as an attempt to "deflate the authority of symbols in contemporary narrative," Wayne Stengel argues that "The Glass Mountain" points to the modern artist's quest to create symbols that "mediate between its former lofty perspectives" (e.g. a glass mountain) and a harsh modern world," to create an artistic vision that transforms "the sidewalks full of dogshit to the rainbow of color of the artist's palette."[5]

While "The Glass Mountain," like so many of Barthelme's stories, raises structural issues that reflect upon its very own creation as an artistic endeavor in the contemporary world, it also casts a revealing light upon a thematic dimension that informs many of Barthelme's most important texts, namely the pervasive violence in American culture and, in particular, the violent treatment of women in the contemporary world, whether they be enchanted symbol or everyday housewife. Critics have argued in favor of the dual function of much postmodern fiction. Rita Felski points out that "literature does not merely constitute a self-referential and metalinguistic system" but is "also a medium which can profoundly influence individual and cultural self-understanding in the sphere of everyday life."[6] Linda Hutcheon also acknowledges a form of contemporary fiction which she identifies as "historiographic metafiction" as being both "intensely self-reflexive" and yet paradoxically grounded in historical events and personages."[7] And Larry McCaffery, in a defense against those critics, such as Gerald Graff and John Gardner, who would indict postmodernist fiction for its allegedly "self-indulgent narcissism and escapist tendencies," maintains that "for all their experimentation, metafictional impulses, self-reflexiveness, playfulness and game playing," postmodern fiction has "much more to say about history, social issues and politics than is generally recognized."[8] Despite the fact that Barthelme himself expressed a lack of "enthusiasm for fiction about fiction,"[9] many critics have focused their attention upon the purely reflexive aspects of Barthelme's texts and have ignored thematic content or denied any referential function of language in his fiction. Consequently, a story such as "The Glass Mountain" is often discussed at length without any mention, let alone detailed analysis, of the societal implications for women of its violent ending.

Even those critics who warn us against making too much of the formal aspects of Barthelme's works remain curiously silent in their content analyses about the hostility directed towards women in some of his fiction. Critics such as William Peden,[10] Charles Molesworth,[11] Paul Bruss,[12] R.E. Johnson,[13] and Wilde,[14] all concur that Barthelme's fiction remains *both* reflexive *and* referential, a type of "midfiction," to use Wilde's term, between "mimetic naive realism" and a more radical reflexive metafiction;[15] yet none chooses to locate the hostile treatment of women as a significant thematic issue. One of the premises of this chapter is that much of Barthelme's fiction unfolds against the backdrop of a violent, contemporary America, that often his ludic reflexivity and ironic parodying of traditional aesthetic forms and male misogyny simultaneously evoke realistic images of aggression that have come to characterize postmodern American society and that also exploit female victimization for comic purposes. Both reflexive and referential, Barthelme's fiction, as Roland Barthes pointed out about all writing in *Writing Degree Zero*,[16] playfully calls attention to itself as writing, that is, as artifact, while it also tries, as Wilde states, to perceive obliquely "the moral complexities of inhabiting an ontologically contingent world."[17] This chapter will consider four of Barthelme's short stories and two novels as they illuminate, and perhaps re-envision, one of those "moral complexities:" the abiding vulnerability of women in a culture that often imprisons them in oppressive, patriarchal texts.

What do we make of a short story that ends with the violent expulsion of a princess from a glass mountain, hurled to a seething mob below by an artist who is angry at her being "only a beautiful princess"? Viewed from the perspective of the frustrated artist whose attempts to scale the mountain are met with obscene jeers from his acquaintances, the violence committed against the princess could reflect his inability to create an aesthetic symbol appropriate for the quotidian world of modern existence. The symbol of a beautiful princess in a world where the streets are lined with "dogshit" and where the struggling artist is pelted with such epithets as "dumbmotherfucker," "shithead" and "asshole," is just not "plausible, not at all, not for a moment" (CL 65). From a purely formal standpoint, one can conclude, as does Stengel, that the narrator's final anger "suggests the failure of the artistic process to fulfill either the contemporary artist or his audience."[18]

Yet the fact remains that the artist's frustration and anger are directed toward the princess, the only female mentioned in the story, and that ironically his quest to mollify the belligerent crowd below with an aesthetic vision has ended in his succumbing to the very violence he had hoped to transcend. As this chapter will show, the eruption of anger and hostility in Barthelme's fiction often reflects the frustration and despair that his characters experience when signs and symbols, often created and perpetuated by the media (e.g. movies, magazines, books and advertising), promote romantic expectations that fail to be realized in the everyday world.

Among those lingering romantic symbols is the culture's sexual stereotype of the "enchanted woman," the "woman of mystery" whose haunting, ethereal beauty, cloaked in "its layers of meaning" (CL 64), defies rational explanation and invites pursuit and adoration. It is precisely this fairy tale symbol of female perfection, employed in "The Glass Mountain," that the advertising industry exploits in a gamut of Madison Avenue campaign ads, ranging from skin cream to diet fads, and that informs many of the popular romances of today. Presupposing what Derrida has termed a "Metaphysics of Presence," the media's promotion of a romantic expectation of female perfection that can never be achieved by women living in the everyday world represents, in effect, a form of cultural violence against women: if the fullness or total presence of the female ideal remains an elusive, unattainable goal in reality, the media's claim to have "found" it can rest only upon a false and violent objectification or consumption of women. "The Glass Mountain" is emblematic of other Barthelme texts in that the failure of a female sign or symbol to coincide with the everyday realities of the modern world or the expectations of a more powerful male figure—whether he be an artist, a "dead father," a policeman, a bored husband, or seven dwarfs—elicits expressions of male anger and rage that are often directed against women. What unites the artist/narrator and the crowd in "The Glass Mountain," what dehumanizes the artist and makes him one of the gang below, is the shared violence perpetrated against the beautiful princess. For it is the artist who flings her down the mountain to *his* acquaintances "who could be relied upon to deal with her."

Far from clearly sanctioning such outbursts of hostility against women, Barthelme often seems to mock the arrogant, power-wielding male figures that populate his fiction. Unlike McCaffery, I do not see Barthelme's works as a whole indicting "words, *women* and society at large"[19] for issuing signs that lie and plunge us into despair and rage. Nor would I be too quick simply to place Barthelme in that group of male writers who, according to Sandra Gilbert and Susan Gubar, responded to the societal eruption of claims for female equality by often unleashing a "phallic retribution" against aggressive women.[20] If it is even true that the "most liberated intellectual by the 1970's felt threatened" by the second wave of feminism,[21] such intimidation and perceived threat of emasculation did not always result in an unqualified hostility towards women on the part of all postmodern American writers. On the contrary, Barthelme, like the other experimental writers who are the focus of this work, displays an unexplored (unconscious?) ambiguity towards women and second-wave feminism at times that de-centers his texts and renders unstable any interpretive agenda that seeks to reduce his works to a consistent *either* pro- *or* anti-woman agenda; such ambiguity ultimately allows him to dismiss feminist slogans and rhetoric as so much "dreck" while at the same time sympathetically depicting some of his female characters as victims of a more insidious conspiracy to manipulate language and symbols, a conspiracy that, in effect, shackles women to primarily male-authored textual and sexual expectations that are doomed to fail, and that threatens women with violence when they resist conformity. The enchanted princess of "The Glass Mountain" is, after all, a male-created female symbol of fairy tale fame, dense with layers of patriarchal meaning, whose fate, like her origin, is wholly determined by men: she is pursued by knights, "captured" and touched by the artist, transformed by him into another female symbol (a beautiful princess), is found wanting and then is violently dispatched to the hands of the mob. She is indeed a prisoner who is expendable once that text becomes obsolete.

Barthelme heightens the sense of violence through his minimalistic techniques of implying, but not explicitly describing, the actions of his characters and of using fragments that, as Leland notes, "presuppose totalities."[22] "The Glass Mountain," like many of Barthelme's texts, parodies the traditional short story form by employing a fragmentary, episodic structure, filled with ominous silences and white spaces that de-emphasize linear plot movement and character development. For example, fragments 53-57 read as follows:

53. And reached out.
54. It was cold there at 206 feet and when I looked down I was not encouraged.

55. A heap of corpses both of horses and riders ringed the bottom of the mountain, many dying men groaning there.
56. "A weakening of the libidinous interest in reality has recently come to a close." (Anton Ehrenzweig)
57. A few questions burned in my mind. (CL180)

Barthelme's radical innovative strategies appear here in: 1) his use of collage, whereby he juxtaposes incongruous elements and wrenches familiar objects from their common contexts, thus forcing the reader to "re-view" these objects in unfamiliar settings—as Patricia Waugh notes, Barthelme always calls attention to the "materiality of writing" and "undermines semantic coherence" by taking words out of context so that "meaning is continuously deferred as a condition of detextualisation;"[23] 2) his parody of traditional narrative in which he arbitrarily numbers the plot elements so as to reveal a highly self-conscious act of writing, and thereby to incorporate the "situation of writing itself into the text"[24] and indulge in a "flaunting of artifice;"[25] 3) his use of voluminous white space or visual silences that resonate with the murmurings of what is not being said; 4) the concomitant, tacit invitation to the reader to enter into the text to supply a "totality" of meaning, thereby undercutting both the ontological primacy of any one "totality" or system and the assumed authorial/authoritative presence to dispense such meaning. As Carl Malmgren notes in his discussion of the concept of compositional space in the postmodern novel, when the text "deconstructs conventional notions of textuality and demands that the reader assume a more active role in narrative management," the reader is "invited to step in" and fill in the gaps and the silences between the fragments.[26]

What does it mean for a female reader to step in and fill in the silences of "The Glass Mountain" or to complete the missing, presupposed totality? That is to say, how does a feminist reader begin to confront what Waugh refers to as "the violent face" of postmodernist fiction when that violence more often than not is directed against female characters?[27] Are female readers faced with what Sally Robinson states are two equally unappealing alternatives when confronting texts that bifurcate male subjectivity and female objectification, namely, identifying either with "the active male subject or with the passive objectified woman"?[28] Or can feminist readers suspend identification and instead interrogate aesthetic structures that we historically have been asked to accept on good faith? Barthelme's usurpation of traditional narrative conventions invites such an interrogation and fosters a discomfort among feminist readers that serves to illuminate the oppressive nature of traditional literary discourse. Turning to "The Glass Mountain," such interrogation requires the reader to suspend or bracket the uncomfortable contradiction inherent in the very invitation itself, for she is, in effect, being asked to assert her *active* creativity and artistic *freedom* by *speaking* through the silences of a story about a female aesthetic symbol that is *denied autonomy* and rendered completely *passive* and *mute* by external male forces and is ultimately violently destroyed.

It is precisely at this juncture that one encounters a tension between structure and content that often appears in both Barthelme's and Didion's texts. Committed to structural innovation—to a freeing of literary forms from the old prison houses of linear plot, characterization and closure—both writers, at times, still retain the traditional gender dichotomies that have imprisoned women within worn-out stereotypes of passivity, dependence and sexual vulnerability. While Felski convincingly argues that structural innovation in *avant-garde* fiction does not entail a corresponding feminist aesthetic, that is, that there is no necessary connection between experimental form and feminism,[29] the conjunction of "subversive" technical strategies and "reactionary" gender stereotypes creates an interesting ideological tension in the texts considered in this work. Didion does combine textual experimentation with strong, assertive female characters in her later fiction, primarily in *Democracy*; yet her earlier novels, while not relying upon a Barthelme-like parody to encode an ambivalence toward women, manifest a tension within the many images of violence that evokes both a *sympathy for* and an *impatience with* the woman-as-victim. Barthelme, despite his radical dismantling of traditional literary forms and his sympathy, at times, for the woman-as-victim, does not, except perhaps in *The Dead Father*, envision a concomitant transformation of sex stereotypes.

Barthelme does, however, through his parodic caricatures of male abusers and female victims, illuminate the instability of gender roles as cultural "impersonations" rather than "natural" or "biological" consequences of sexual identity, thereby anticipating a 1994 conclusion of a sub-division of the American Psychological Association that "gender is a social construct" and not a personal attribute or particular behavior.[30] Men work so hard at being aggressive or "masculine" and women at being passive or "feminine" in much of Barthelme's works that one begins to understand the "performative" dimension of gender role-playing and that, as Judith Butler argues, "feminine" and "masculine" are socialized ways of "acting" rather than genetically determined modes of "being" in the world.[31] While not overtly concerned with a revisioning of gender constructs, Barthelme does succeed in underscoring the "fictive" quality of gender categories—what Marjorie Garber has labelled the "theatricality" of gender and gender differences[32]—and calls into question one of those "normalizing" discourses that, Jane Flax argues, serve to "legitimate pattern[s] of domination." Flax's argument that Fouçault's and Lyotard's "preference for play and fragmentation" is, in effect, a "strategic device meant to disrupt and erode oppressive Western narratives"[33] could indeed be applied to Barthelme's parody of traditional, oppressive gender discourses. Enclosing his male characters' misogyny within a parodic structure, Barthelme decenters his own texts by simultaneously mocking the validity of male chauvinism and exploiting female subjugation for comic purposes. Despite the parodic destabilization of gender categories, Barthelme's texts still project an ambiguity towards female abuse, a curiously unstable blending of sympathy for and exploitation of victimized women. This ambiguity derives, in part, from the simultaneous mockery of and reliance upon gender stereotypes and the failure to re-envision alternative ways of being in the world for women and men.

Consequently, when the female reader is invited to step in and fill in the silences that appear in a story like "The Glass Mountain," she is being asked not only to overlook the subtle affront to her own autonomy but also to participate in completing the images of violence against the princess, a female stereotype, that are only hinted at in the text. It would be difficult to imagine any female reader, or perhaps any reader, in today's American society, assuming an active role in "narrative management" and *not* filling in the silences that surround the implied acts of violence committed against the beautiful princess by the mob with graphic, realistic images of mutilation and rape. Barthelme's minimalistic suggestion that the crowd "could be relied upon to deal with her" triggers such violent images, for it tacitly invokes the all-too-familiar aggressions against women that have come to be an integral part of contemporary American society.

Part of the totality implicit in the fragmentary structure of "The Glass Mountain," then, entails the violent degradation and violation of the princess by the mob, acting in consort with the artist. Serving as the realistic backdrop to the story's reflexive commentary on the efficacy of traditional symbols in contemporary art forms, the fate of the woman as determined by more powerful male figures reappears as a theme in several other Barthelme tales. This combination of a ludic reflexivity and a referential appeal to crimes against women discloses an ambivalence toward women in his texts. His attitude toward a re-evaluation of aesthetic forms is one of light-hearted, playful experimentation, but his stance concerning acts of aggression against women in his texts is far more complex. While the structure of parody enables Barthelme, at times, to maintain an ironic distance from the textual images of male violence, thereby shielding him from accusations of outright misogyny, it also requires him to incorporate and transform tragically realistic images of female subjugation into fictional, comic episodes, thereby opening him up to charges of an insensitive trivialization, if not implicit sanctioning, of female victimization. In other words, the use of parody seemingly enables Barthelme simultaneously to indulge in and to mock fantasies of male aggression against women, and accounts, in part, for the *aporia* regarding female victimization that destabilizes his texts. Does his work ever take on the gruesomely detailed, fantasized releases of rage against women that will appear in some of Pynchon texts? Or is there a sincere attempt to free women from patriarchal texts, to re-envision their role and the role of men in society? That is to say, if Barthelme's texts represent, as Tanner maintains in his analysis of "The Balloon," an invitation to the reader to play, to engage in a "sportive fantasy floating free above the rigidities of the environment,"[34] does this fantasy encourage an unbridled license to hurt women or a re-evaluation of their traditional subjugation?

Again, any attempt to reduce his stories to an "either/or" logic of critical interpretation that is dependent upon binary opposites, that is, to apprehend his works as either purely "sexist" or basically "feminististic" does not serve to illuminate the structural and moral complexities inherent in his texts or the ambivalence with regard to women that allows him simultaneously to exploit and condemn misogyny in American culture. In attempting to defend the author's moral seriousness, one critic concedes Barthelme's general ambivalence:

> Beneath the clowning and cutting-and-pasting...Barthelme is a conventional moralist *alternatively attracted, amused* and *appalled* by what he sees as the sadness of his times, by its dullness and insipidity, by its indifference to art and the things of the imagination, by its affronts to individual life and dignity.[35]

If Barthelme is "alternatively attracted, amused and appalled" by the violent degradation of women in America, do his texts also invite the reader to experiment with alternative modes of being for men and women in society?

"The Glass Mountain" does not leave much room to play with traditional sex-role stereotypes. It is a short story permeated by violence directed against both males and females, for the fallen knights too are subjected to the atrocities of the crowd. Yet, the violence committed against the men, the fallen knights, is explicitly stated in segments 63-65, as if the reader, in not being asked to identify with the mob, could not be "relied upon" to know the fate awaiting the unsuccessful male climbers; however, the violence enacted against the princess, implied in fragment #99 (the crowd could be "relied upon to deal with her") entails the more active participation of the reader who, in collusion with the mob, can be "relied upon" to reflect a societally-ingrained misogyny. Barthelme "comically" exploits a violence against women which reflects the *status quo*. Unlike the unsuccessful knights and artist, the princess has been denied autonomy and a voice, and her failure is not the failure of a chosen quest but the failure to coincide with the desired expectations of the mob below and the artist atop the mountain. Furthermore, since the young artist of the tale is one who is struggling to find an aesthetic symbol that will placate the crowd below, he, in one respect, reflects the author who is struggling to find a new aesthetic form symbolic of the fragmentation and enervation of contemporary existence. Here, then, it would seem that the author *does* (as frustrated artist) and *does not* (as self-conscious parodist) coincide with the angry protagonist.

Given the possible absence of ironic distance between the author and narrator, then, it would seem that the reader, from the very beginning of the story, has been subtly coerced into complicity with the author/narrator to fill in the implied closure of "The Glass Mountain" with explicit images of violence against the princess. While the narrator's cruelty may serve to heighten the reader's compassion for the victim, at no time is the reader encouraged to envision the possibility of the princess' escaping the brutality of the mob or coming to symbolize a new image of a strong, independent and articulate woman, that is, one that would resonate with feminist implications. Again, Barthelme's use of parody saves him from falling into the abyss of an unqualified misogyny. At times, he seems to be able to get away with his experimental blending of sexism and humor because he combines his images of violence against women with hyperbolic depictions or "caricatures" of male perpetrators and female victims. Caricature or exaggeration often invokes humor but, when blended with a dimension of misogynistic aggression that is all too real and familiar to contemporary readers, gives rise to a textual ambiguity that may elicit an ambivalent response from some readers: we may laugh but it is a discomforting laugh. Perhaps it is through such discomfort that Barthelme seeks to puncture the *status quo* and reveal the sexism still so endemic to American society. Like Mark Twain, who, in his earlier writings, used humor as a vehicle to nudge the reader gently to reform, Barthelme may realize that societal change can be effected more easily through laughter than through straight, moral didacticism. Yet, as Waugh notes with regard to the postmodernist's impulse toward fragmentation: "It is often difficult to know if extreme fragmentation or dehumanization is being used parodically as a mode or critique or as an extension of a dehumanised world."[36] While Barthelme's dismantling of the traditional short story format results in his re-creating a new, minimalist aesthetic form, his destruction of the beautiful princess does not invite a corresponding re-creation of the role of women in art or reality. The parodic structure of the story mocks the behavior of a man who would destroy a woman because she fails to meet his (symbolic) expectations; yet, it also relies upon a demeaning stereotype of woman as the passive, mute victim to heighten the humor. It is precisely this inability of women to break free from their role as textual and sexual prisoner that informs some of Barthelme's other short stories.

In the same volume, *City Life*, there appears a story entitled "The Policeman's Ball," that immediately precedes "The Glass Mountain." Centered around a policeman named Horace and his strategy to lure his girlfriend Margot to bed following the annual policemen's banquet, "The Policeman's Ball" is pervaded by a sense of fear and imminent violence that is represented by some vague, unspecified force lurking outside in the streets. Inside the banquet hall, decorated as Camelot, are twenty-thousand contemporary "knights" or policemen and their "ladies" along with their leader, the "Pendragon" or commissioner. Following a pep talk in which the commissioner implores these modern defenders of the peace to restrain themselves in the use of force when confronting the anarchic crowds outside, Margot decides to give her hero what he wants, to reward his courageous defense of her from the horrors of the outside world with her sexual submission. In a cliché-ridden deliberation, she concludes:

> I will give him what he wants, she decided. Tonight. His heroism deserves it. He stands between us and them. He represents what is best in society: decency, order, safety, strength, sirens.... (CL 56)

The story ends with the narrator's speaking the thoughts of the "horrors," the collective violence of contemporary America. The predatory force that has haunted the story from the beginning has found its voice and has articulated the imminent demise of all who remain within the false security of apartments and banquet halls: "Not even policemen and their ladies are safe, the horrors thought. No one is safe. Safety does not exist. Ha ha ha ha ha ha ha ha ha ha" (CL 56).

Far from constituting an "absurdly melodramatic final sentence," as Stengel asserts,[37] the conclusion to "The Policeman's Ball" presents an appropriate ending to a very frightening tale about the ubiquity of a destructive, repressive force in contemporary America. Without assuming a judgmental posture, Barthelme accurately captures the very real but paradoxical problem confronting postmodern, urban America, wherein police forces often resort to excessive violence in order to stem the so-called "rising tide of violence in the streets." The absurdity inheres in the use of violence to quell violence, so that all of us become potential victims of "the force," whether it be the random "criminal" violence of the streets or the sanctioned violence by the uniformed officer in the apartment house. For, as was the case in "The Glass Mountain," what unites the empowered male figure in "The Policeman's Ball" with the hostile street mobs is the threatened use of violence against a woman, in this case, Margot.

A closer look at the scant but significant images in "The Policeman's Ball" reveals that Margot occupies the traditional role of woman-as-sexual-prey (prisoner), the lowest rung of a hierarchical arrangement of adult power and potential exploitation. First of all, her decision to submit to Horace is predicated upon her having assimilated into her thought processes the male-authored propaganda that maintains that since the Horaces of the world constitute the only protection there is "between us and them," they deserve female sacrifice and compliance. To use Barthelme's language, Margot's mind has been filled with the "dreck and sludge" of patriarchal slogans. Furthermore, if she were to resist his sexual advances, then, as the text suggests, she too would become his prey.

Throughout this minimalist tale Margot comes to be associated with the Rock Cornish game hens that Horace has prepared for Margot and himself as "a special supper." In a comic scene that parodies male strategies of "sexual conquest," Horace has defrosted the frozen birds as he hopes to melt her resistance and frigidity; in an obvious phallic pun, he has used his needlepoint pliers to "pull out" the giblets from the bird's interior and wonders if Margot will "put out" tonight. Anticipating Margot's resistance, Horace comically considers but quickly dismisses the idea of tearing her neck off as he did the hens'. Again, the allusion to potential male violence, while the subject of parody, invokes the not-so-comic realities of female degradation and also discloses a metaphoric "point of intersection" in Western culture between sexual violence and meat-eating, that is, the "butchering" of women and the "rape" of animals. As feminist theologian Carol Adams argues, "when violence against women is talked about" (or envisioned as it is by Horace), "the referent point is slaughtered animals."[38]

Aside from these rather obvious analogies between Margot and the hens, there is the more ominous image of the "little gold frills." Early in the story, Horace, having removed the hens from the oven, "slipped little gold frills which had been included in the package, over the ends of the drumsticks" and then, as he serves Margot the dinner, has the following thought:

> This is a town without pity, this town. For those whose voices lack the crack of authority. Luckily the uniform...Why won't she surrender her person? Does she think she can resist the force? The force of the force? (CL 54)

It is quite clear to Horace that those most vulnerable to oppression, to a surrender not only of sexuality but of personhood, are the Margots of the world, those whose voices lack the power to author(ize) their own texts and destinies in a town ruled by patriarchal force. Horace consumes the gold-frilled drumsticks, and when, toward the end of the story, we read that a "gold frill was placed on (Margot's) pearl toe," we can only conclude that Margot's "voluntary" surrender is, in effect, a coerced abdication to the "force" or an attempt to "civilize" what is, in this hierarchical arrangement, a potentially brutal subjugation of women by men.

One could argue that by submitting to Horace, Margot clearly plays her safest hand within this system of power that denies her voice "the crack of authority." Unlike the beautiful princess of "The Gold Mountain" who is denied any voice at all, Margot speaks two lines that seem to suggest her complicity with the very system that oppresses her. When asked by Horace, at the ball, if she will submit to him tonight, she replies: "Horace, not now. This scene is brilliant. I want to remember it." And of the Pendragon, the ultimate symbol of male authority at the ball, she states: "He is a handsome older man" (CL 55). Taken with the spectacle of her surroundings, Margot articulates a sense of awe when viewing a twenty-thousand-member show of male force. But because Barthelme's minimalist technique includes a flattening out of his characters and a jettisoning of conventional forms of psychological motivation, it is not clear, even within the parodic structure of the text, as to the impetus behind Margot's professed awe. Do her lines reflect a masochistic titillation with the very force that subjugates her; does she succumb, perhaps, to what Sartre would call the lure of "bad faith," futilely attempting to achieve a self-presence by coinciding with the gaze of the Other which perceives women-as-victims; or do her lines point to a strategic ploy on her part to achieve a modicum of self-preservation within a system that threatens women with various forms of enslavement?

The very absence of traditional modes of characterization in Barthelme's texts requires the reader to step in and play with such possibilities and also intensifies the sense of ambiguity toward women that informs some of his works. "The Policeman's Ball" bears the characteristic stamp of what Susan R. Suleiman calls the "first wave of postmodernist fiction," namely the replacement of traditional characters with "disembodied voices."[39] Consequently, the text of "The Policeman's Ball" does not help us to decide whether to feel disdain or sympathy for Margot's vulnerable position, nor does it resolve the tension inherent in the parodic depiction of male violence against women as pointing to an indictment of brutality or as indulging male fantasies of rage. However, whatever motive the reader assigns to Margot's remarks within the compositional "play" space left open by the author, her voice speaks the traditional text of female submission within the patriarchy. The use of an omniscient narrator in "The Policeman's Ball" enables Barthelme to achieve a sense of ironic distance from the text, for it explicitly focuses upon the creative "force" of the author as consciously shifting from one voice to another. By dismantling the traditional short story form and forging a new minimalist tale, the "destructive/creative force" of the author ironically calls attention to itself as "other than" the purely malevolent force of "the horrors." This ironic distance, in conjunction with the ambiguity surrounding the psychological meaning behind Margot's remarks, allows Barthelme to: 1) avoid endorsing Margot's subjugation by a potentially destructive male force; 2) present the possibility of a sympathetic portrayal of the plight of the woman-as-victim.

"The Policeman's Ball" clearly discloses the vulnerability of women in a system that solidifies sex stereotypes into dichotomous camps of male power and female impotence. Imprisoned within the societally-sanctioned image of the "woman-as-sexual-prey," Margot anticipates another Barthelme woman—the unnamed and perhaps universal female in "The Captured Woman." This particular short story is perhaps an allusion to the popular James Thurber cartoon sequence of 1945 entitled "The War Between Men and Women," which, as Gilbert and Gubar note, parodically portrayed various modes of antagonism erupting between the sexes, but which also revealed a more fundamental desire on the part of male authors to re-assert a male potency that they perceived had been vitiated with the disappearance of global masculine exploits of world combat.[40] One such frame in Thurber's comic sequence involves men and women taking each other hostage and anticipates Barthelme's parodying of marital strife and possible role reversal in "The Captured Woman." Yet, in what might be termed a "meta-parody," Barthelme appropriates the comical dimension of Thurber's 1945 marital "war" sequence and through a rather self-conscious "caricaturing" of the masculine and feminine stereotypes, not only foregrounds the performative/fictive dimension of gender roles but also reveals the comic/tragic underpinnings of male domination and female subservience. Barthelme is able to sympathize with and to condemn the woman as "compliant victim." "Criminally abducted" by the narrator, the female seems to succeed in reversing the sex roles of men and women when, assuming the role of the aggressor, she manages to "capture" her captor by arousing his jealousy over another man. This story could be seen as a contemporary marital version of O. Henry's "The Ransom of Red Chief" in that the abductor falls prey to the power of the prisoner. It is initially tempting to view this tale as a re-envisioning of female and male roles in adult relationships and as a humorous attempt to subvert the traditional male hegemony of the American household; however, a closer look at the complexities of the power-plays within the story reveals that the woman, like Margot, employs her wiles within the very system that oppresses her as a possible means of survival, and that far from re-shaping sex stereotypes, she is conforming to a very traditional image of the woman-as-sexual-manipulator and shrew.

Like other Barthelme texts that parody male misogynistic attitudes, "The Captured Woman" includes a number of conversations among the narrator and his male friends, all of whom are holding women as hostages in their homes. Their stereotypic male talk reflects a comically competitive "mine-is-better-than-yours" mentality of ownership as they compare their respective prey and their modes of capture, ranging from "tranquilizing darts" to a "lasso" to "Jack Daniels."[41] While these conversations may be intended as a mockery of such flagrant male chauvinism and serve as a humorous commentary on the strategies of courtship and marriage, they belie a more fundamental antagonism, a state of "war between the sexes" that the traditional culture has socialized us to view as a natural state of affairs in human relationships.

This "war between the sexes" takes a bizarre turn in the story when the woman, upon hearing that her husband will not pay the ransom and does not want her back, invites her own degradation at the hands of her oppressor: "Take me to my room and tie me up," she demands of her captor (SS 292).

Her desire to be "enchained," along with her request to be surrounded by photographic enlargements of her staring rather than smiling, implies that she willingly submits to her role as the subjugated housewife. When she is informed by her captor that she may leave at any time, her reluctance would seem to confirm her voluntary status within the relationship. To cajole her into remaining with him, the "captor" assumes some of the domestic, "feminine" chores, again, as a strategy of control:

> I go into the kitchen and begin washing the dishes—the more scutwork you did, the kindlier the light in which you are regarded, I have learned. (SS 293)

While perhaps mocking the concept of the traditional family, Barthelme creates a tension in the depiction of the woman's subjugated role, presenting it as a position of voluntary submission to which women masochistically cling.

Sounding less like the man in charge and more like the hen-pecked husband who tries to tiptoe around the temperamental needs of the demanding wife, the narrator begins to emerge as the stereotypic "emasculated husband," reduced to the ultimate marital indignity of doing "scutwork." While he assumes the role of the "oppressed" husband, she emerges as the "castrating bitch" who berates him for his weakness, excessive drinking and lack of initiative, who uses the possibility of walking out on him as a means of coercing him into doing what she wants him to do, whether it be "scutwork" or dressing differently. Her ultimate ploy is to assume the role of the aggressor and "capture" one of his friends, L. Although the connection is brief, she has succeeded in using L. to arouse her captor's jealousy and, in effect, enslave her captor further to her whims and desires.

Far from breaking out of traditional sex role stereotypes, as one critic argues,[42] the woman in the story merely exchanges one traditional female sex stereotype for another, both of which are reductive and restrictive. Although she is initially presented as the "captured woman," as the prisoner of the marriage institution that has been assailed by some radical feminists, the woman's apparent complicity in her own victimization serves to vitiate the reader's sympathy for her. In what could be argued to be a rejection of contemporary feminist rhetoric, she is portrayed as inviting her own humiliation. Furthermore, when the woman assumes the role of the aggressor, as the one who "wears the pants" in the family, she is not establishing a new, liberating persona for fictional women but rather taking her place in a long-standing literary heritage that has produced such characters as The Wife of

Bath, Lady Macbeth and others. The so-called "shrew" who controls her husband through devious means, through emotional strategies that manipulate him into relinquishing some of his power, does not, in effect, subvert the traditional marriage hierarchy, for her co-opting of masculine control is at best tenuous and often short-lived. Like the Wife of Bath who had suffered physical abuse at the hands of one of her husbands, the female in "The Captured Woman" remains vulnerable to the more powerful force of the captor whose authority in the household is bolstered by a patriarchal society. If the woman's voice in "The Captured Woman" takes on "the crack of authority," it does so as the stereotypical whining, nagging bitch, not as an autonomous adult female.

"The Captured Woman" best exemplifies the author's ambivalence toward women in his texts. Seemingly critical of the feminist stance that depicts marriage as a male-controlled institution, this particular short story comically invokes a stereotypical, unflattering portrait of the woman-as-shrew, thereby implying that women exercise a degree of leverage within the contemporary marriage arrangement. However, to infer that this story is aimed at defusing the feminist concern for the safety of the woman within the marriage institution is to fail to take into account the threat of male violence that concludes the story and that *tragically* lurks as a societally-sanctioned mode of re-asserting the more traditional voice of authority in the household:

> A week later she is still with me...*If I tore her hair out, no one but me would love her.* But she doesn't want me to tear her hair out.
>
> I wear different shirts for her: red, orange, silver. We hold hands through the night. (SS 294, emphases mine)

Like Horace who contemplates breaking Margot's neck, the narrator considers inflicting physical harm on the woman to insure his exclusive control over her. That the story relies upon comic stereotypes to comment upon power-plays in marriage does not nullify the text's acknowledgment of the fundamental and abiding vulnerability of women in the contemporary marriage arrangement. The tender image of the man and woman holding hands through the night seems to sit incongruously on the same page with the preceding threat of male violence, just as the accounts given by the rising number of abused women in American households paradoxically reveal brief intervals of domestic harmony.

On one level, the captured woman "comically" reveals the plight of the woman whose inability to authorize a new female text of autonomy within the traditional institution of marriage leads her to borrow the conventional male text that equates autonomy with aggression and subjugation, to turn the tables on her oppressor and become temporarily masculine in her quest for control. On another less comic level, the beautiful princess, Margot and the captured woman each represents a variation on the theme of the female prisoner in a sexual/textual hierarchy that denies female voices the "crack of authority." These characters are gradations on a scale of female enslavement that range from a total silencing of the female voice to a temporary co-opting of male sexual/textual domination.

While each of the women discussed so far is the victim of explicit or threatened acts of violence, Barthelme's minimalist reduction of conventional plot and characterization and his blending of parodic humor with female subjugation impart a degree of moral ambiguity to his presentation of such violence. Purchased primarily at the expense of women's victimization, such humor itself might appear as a form of disguised aggression. Yet, while "The Glass Mountain" seems quite harsh in its expulsion of a particular female symbol in contemporary aesthetic formulations, it, like "The Policeman's Ball" and "The Captured Woman," also manages not only to acknowledge the woman's susceptibility to brute male force in postmodern America but also to convey sympathy for the plight of women. Through his use of parodic irony, Barthelme disrupts the prevailing misogyny by undermining the pretentious assumptions of the empowered male figure in each story so as to diminish his humanity and thereby expand the reader's sympathy for the female victim. For all three stories involve the ironic subversion of a male quest for power over women, whether she be an aesthetic symbol, a girlfriend or a captured "housewife": the young artist's attempt to elevate himself above the destructive mob through artistic creation ironically confirms his connection with the riotous crowd when he destroys the female symbol that he set out to liberate; the policeman's threatened use of force to conquer Margot ironically renders him vulnerable to the very violence he fosters; and the wifenapper's quest to enslave a woman leaves him enslaved to her shrewish machinations. Through irony and humor, Barthelme allows himself to be "alternatively attracted and appalled" by the culture's violent treatment of women, so that in a story like "The Captured Woman" he can simultaneously mock those feminists who impugn marriage as an oppressive patriarchal institution and display a sensitivity to the battered housewife. Such ambivalence about women appears in yet another short story entitled "A City of Churches" in which a young woman threatens to authorize a new text that will topple the established patriarchy of the town.

"A City of Churches" is the story of Cecilia, a young woman who arrives in the town of Prester to serve as its car rental agent. Greeted by Mr. Phillips, one of the town fathers and a local real estate agent, Cecilia is immediately instructed in the pious customs of Prester, a town where all the buildings are churches and where all the residents are expected to conform to an ecclesiastical way of life. Since she is "not especially religious," Cecilia doubts whether she will "fit in" in such a town. When she is informed by Mr. Phillips that she will have to rent an apartment in a church, preferably with other women, Cecilia rebels by demanding a place of her own and thereby contravening the local custom of living with others:

> "I don't want to share," Cecilia said. "I want a place of my own."
> "Why?" the real estate man asked curiously. "For what purpose?"
> "Purpose?" asked Cecilia. "There is no particular purpose. I just want—"
> "That's not usual here. Most people live with other people. Husbands and wives. Sons with their mothers. People have roommates. That's the usual pattern." (SS 211)

Cecilia resists conforming to the repressive, provincial mores of a town where solitude is held suspect and where sons live out unresolved oedipal dramas into their adulthood. When asked by Mr. Phillips about her religious denomination, Cecilia replies, "I can will my dreams," which are "mostly sexual" dreams. And when she discovers that her business presence in Prester is superfluous, since every citizen owns a car and no one travels anywhere at all, she threatens to leave. However, Mr. Phillips informs her that she is needed to stand behind the counter to make the town complete, that is, to offset the psychological discontentment of a sexually repressed community. Physically restraining her, Mr. Phillips engages in an exchange of ominous threats with Cecilia that ends the story:

> "I'll dream the Secret," she said. "You'll be sorry....I'll dream the life you are most afraid of," Cecilia threatened.
> "You are ours," he said gripping her arm. "Our car-rental girl. Be nice. There is nothing you can do."
> "Wait and see," Cecilia said. (SS 213)

Lured to Prester under false pretenses, Cecilia becomes the town's newest resident, a "captured woman" who thinks she can use her sexuality to upset the established order.

Again, Barthelme in "A City of Churches" radically undercuts the staples of the traditional short story not only by employing seemingly disembodied voices rather than fleshed-out characters but also by refusing to supply a sense of closure. As Suleiman notes in her analysis of postmodernist fiction, "Where the reader expects an ending, [the text] offers merely a stop."[43] Like many of Barthelme's minimalist tales, "A City of Churches" resonates with a variety of interpretive possibilities. It has been viewed by one critic as a "conceit about the proliferation of ecclesiastical structures and rabid real estate developers in certain mid-Western American cities,"[44] and by another as an "identity story" in which the protagonist Cecilia struggles to resist the oppressive provincialism and "stifling conformity" through her sexuality.[45] While neither critical approach focuses upon the female protagonist as an enslaved woman within the patriarchal structure of the town, each calls attention to a pivotal element in our analysis of the woman-as-sexual (textual)-prisoner. Moleworth's emphasis on the proliferation of ecclesiastical structures underscores the ubiquity of patriarchal power whose steeples and spires eclipse the figure of Cecilia in shadows of insignificance, while Stengel's reference to Cecilia's sexuality illuminates the ambivalence with which female sexuality is viewed in American culture.

As the story of a young woman who travels alone to an inordinately religious town, "A City of Churches" recalls Hawthorne's *The Scarlet Letter* and its female protagonist, Hester Prynne, whose very name may have been partially conflated to form the town name—Prester. For like *The Scarlet Letter*, "A City of Churches" is a tale about the confrontation between female sexuality and patriarchal, ecclesiastical power. Both women—Hester, perhaps unconsciously, but Cecilia very intentionally—employ their sexuality to rebel against the repressive strictures of the Church fathers and to flout the established religious authority of their respective towns. While Hester is initially required to wear the scarlet letter "A" to symbolize her *adulterous* affair with the Reverend Dimmesdale, Hawthorne's use of symbolic alternatives, discussed by F. O. Matthiessen,[46] opens up the textual possibility of the scarlet letter's coming to stand for a multiplicity of choices, among them "*Artist*" and "Angel"; for it is Hester who, through her many years of redemptive service as the town's seamstress and nurse, artistically infuses color and vitality into an otherwise dour Puritan existence. Whereas Hawthorne's technique of symbolic alternatives gives rise to a textual density, Barthelme's minimalism spawns a textual sparseness that leaves the reader groping for explanatory symbols. Interestingly enough, however, both Hawthorne and Barthelme, one through a profusion of symbolic alternatives and the other through a paucity of symbolic references, create a textual ambiguity that is never quite resolved and that requires the active participation of the reader to bring into being any form of textual meaning, though tentative, that may apply. While Hawthorne's ambiguity leans toward the potential resolution of all the possible meanings of the "A" as coming together to suggest the essence of the concept of "being marked," Barthelme's ambiguity reflects the strategy of a postmodern writer who is intent upon undermining closure and breaking up unified meaning or "essences" into multiple perspectives. Consequently, "A City of Churches" leaves open the possibility that Cecilia, whose very name *may* allude to the patron saint of music, will, through her dream texts, artistically weave her sexual fantasies into the very text(ure) of Prester's ecclesiastical fabric. Both Cecilia and Hester prefer to live alone and are, therefore, held suspect by a culture that fears solitude, especially the solitude of the female artist who exists on the periphery of male institutional control.

The phallic power to control and master female sexuality that, according to Leland Person, constitutes the central thematic issue in *The Scarlet Letter*,[47] also informs "A City of Churches." Citing references from the Adam and Eve story and the Pandora myth and tracing the evolving idea of the *femme fatale*, scholars have long noted Western culture's ambivalence toward female sexuality, its celebration of fecundity and exploitation of female eroticism and, as Freud made known, its inveterate fear of the female libido. As Carroll Smith Rosenberg and H. R. Hays note, the culture's apprehension of "the sometimes ominous force of female sexuality"[48] has led to a perception of the woman "as dangerous because of her sexuality,"[49] a perception that views female sexuality as threatening chaos and irrational abandon. Both *The Scarlet Letter* and "A City of Churches," in uniquely different ways, reflect the culture's ambivalent attitude toward female sexuality. Contrary to Carolyn Heilbrun's contention that Hawthorne created an "autonomous female character,"[50] each text allows the desired female sexuality to pulsate only under the *aegis* of male control so that both Hester and Cecilia, despite their respective bids for rebellious, autonomous identities, remain "captured women," ironically serving the needs of the patriarchy that has entrapped them.

Both Hester Prynne and Cecilia are to perform important psychological functions in their towns, functions that have little to do with the professed claims of the town fathers. While Hester is pressured into remaining in Boston ostensibly to face her retribution and seek forgiveness for her act of adultery, she more importantly serves as a socially-acceptable acknowledgment of the town's repressed sexuality, a living projection of their collective, stifled eroticism whom they can simultaneously hate as the town pariah and safely embrace as "our Hester, the town's own Hester";[51] that is to say, Salem needs Hester Prynne as its sexual scapegoat. Similarly, but on a more conscious, almost parodic level, Cecilia is pressured into staying in Prester not because they need a car rental agent but because the town both wants and fears her sexual energy; they require her imaginative vitality to enliven their otherwise enervated, deadly "perfect" existence. Like Hester, Cecilia, who is greeted with jeers and derision from the residents (SS 212), is needed to break the town's sexual taboos, to serve as the socially sanctioned outlet for the town's repressed libido and to end the discontentment in Prester. They will be able to scorn her while simultaneously embracing her as "our car rental girl" (SS 213).

Again, as in "The Captured Woman," Barthelme seems to offer the possibility of breaking free from one female stereotype only to fall into affirming another equally restrictive role for women. While Cecilia's rebellious stance at the beginning of the story suggests her desire to resist conforming to male-imposed expectations, her recourse to dangerous sexual dream texts not only conforms to traditional images of female licentiousness but also serves to meet the psychological needs of the town that has "captured" her. Can her sexuality topple the town's oppressive order of existence as her final warning would seem to predict, or will she, like Hester Prynne, wither away among the people who once both scorned and required her? Still yet, does she have the means to effect a "get away": acutely sensitive to the subliminal suggestions of media symbols, Barthelme associates his protagonist with a car, a vehicle of potential escape. By depicting her as both "free" and "entrapped," the author undermines the possibility of any comfortable sense of closure. Barthelme's attitude toward Cecilia, as a postmodernist's version of Hawthorne's attitude toward Hester Prynne, remains cloaked in ambiguity.

Bitch vs. Witch: *Snow White*

While our analysis of four Barthelme women—the enchanted princess, Margot, the captured woman and Cecilia—suggests a progression toward more articulate, rebellious females, it also reveals the author's fundamental reliance upon conventional gender stereotypes that, in effect, undermine female autonomy and confine women to traditional positions of subservience and physical vulnerability. Turning toward his novel of the 1960's, *Snow*

White, we find what is perhaps the author's response to and evaluation of the culture's organized bid for liberation, the late 1960's women's movement. Of particular interest in our study of women and violence are the portraits of both Snow White and Jane, both substantially revised versions of the Grimm and Disney characters, Snow White (or Snow Drop, as it is frequently translated from the German, *Schnee Witchen*) and the evil queen/witch. Although Barthelme's depictions of both female characters deviate from their original portrayals, they still conform to what psychologist Anne Campbell, in her recent study of the interrelationship between aggression and gender differences, calls "the two equally unattractive roles of witch or bitch."[52]

Labelled by one critic as an "avatar of the women's movement"[53] and by another as a collagist's combination of the traditional Disney/Grimm character and the postmodern Gloria Steinem,[54] Barthelme's Snow White emerges as a far more complicated female presence than her fairy tale predecessor. In the original Grimm depiction and the subsequent Disney script, Snow White is clearly portrayed as the quintessential innocent female victim who is graced with an unparalleled beauty and who lives in a household ruled over by a vain and viciously jealous queen-stepmother. Dispatched by the queen to the woods to be put to death by the queen's huntsman, Snow White is rescued by seven dwarfs, hardworking protocapitalists who mine the earth for gold, copper and ore. Snow White is subjected to three additional attacks by the queen, each employing the queen's evil magic. Snow White is finally rescued by her prince and all live happily ever after, except the queen, of course, who, in Grimm, is forced to dance to her death in red-hot shoes,[55] and in Disney, falls off a cliff.

Clearly the innocent victim of forces outside her control, the traditional Snow White evokes unquestioned sympathy for her plight and hatred for the evil machinations of the queen. Relying upon antithetical female stereotypes—virginal innocence vs. "the cold, tiger-woman type"[56]—the traditional version practically guarantees such clear-cut reactions from its readers. However, Barthelme's postmodern, minimalist adaptation, in rejecting such a simplistic bifurcation of female good and evil, complicates the reader's response and again raises the issue of his attitude toward feminism. For Barthelme's Snow White is a twenty-two year old 1960's woman, living in a Greenwich Village apartment with seven other middleclass businessmen who wash windows, produce Chinese baby food and drink a great deal of beer. Far from exhibiting the sweet, ethereal innocence of her traditional counterpart, this Snow White is a young, sexually active woman who is clearly living in the material world, enjoying the goods and services provided to her by the seven men in exchange for her domestic chores and her sexual favors—she willingly makes herself available to them in frequent "gang bangs" during their morning shower.[57] The fairy tale heroine has become a "sextoid," a "romance robot" in this comic anti-romance.[58] Barthelme's comic reduction of Snow White to a sex-automaton, and his later depiction of Paul as the Prince who tries so hard yet fails to coincide with a masculine ideal of royalty both underscore the fictive quality of gender stereotypes, and as Gilbert and Gubar argue, reveal that eroticism has become a "contaminated linguistic system."[59] When Snow White begins to manifest signs of discontent and boredom with her life style, threatening to rebel against her role in their living arrangement, what begins to emerge is a clashing juxtaposition of the passivity of the traditional Snow White and the activism of the 1960's feminist. If it is the intention of the collagist to bring together discordant elements so as to create a new reality, then we must ask: what female image is born from such a clashing of different perspectives? A closer look at Barthelme's Snow White reveals a spoiled, pretentious young woman, given to spouting feminist clichés and rhetoric; that is to say, she reflects the much-maligned stereotype of the white middleclass feminist of the 1960's who supposedly voiced her dissatisfaction with her role but remained economically secure within its confines, the kind of woman whom Didion impugns in *The White Album*.

Barthelme's Snow White expresses her dissatisfaction with: *the marital text* that requires her to perform the same old chores or "scutwork" and to hear the same old words that constitute her role as maid and sexual object to the dwarfs—"Oh I wish there were some words in the world that were not the words I always hear," she exclaims to the baffled dwarfs (SW 6); and *the fairy tale text* that requires her to *wait* passively for her prince, Paul, to come when she claims that she would rather be out in the world, actively engaged in *doing* something:

> "Well it is terrific to be anticipating a prince—to be waiting and knowing that what you are waiting for is a prince, packed with grace—but it is still waiting...I would rather be doing a hundred other things." (SW 77)

If Snow White is indeed beginning to rebel against the society's reduction of women to either a "horsewife" (i.e. a domesticated beast of burden) or a "cunt" (i.e. a piece of flesh or sexual object), both terms the subject of much discourse in the novel, and if she is, as Leland contends, "locked within the texts she attempts to transcend,"[60] she should emerge as a sympathetic character, despite her contemporary situation. However, Barthelme simultaneously undercuts our compassion for her by mocking her predicament and by implying her complicity with the very system that she verbally attacks. Barthelme may indeed be criticizing women's imprisonment within male-authored textual/sexual arrangements, but he is also indicting "women's complicity in their own commodification."[61] Her rebellious stance, which sounds more like a superficial posturing that she picked up from some book at the library than an expression of her own inner turmoil, is presented as a parody of pop feminist thinking:

> "From now on I deny myself to them. These delights. I maintain an esthetic distance. No more do I trip girlishly to their bed in the night, or after lunch, or in the misty mid-morning. Not that I ever did...And no more will I chop their onions, boil their fettucini, or marinate their flank steak. No more will I trudge about the house pursuing stain...I am not even going to speak to them, now, except through third parties, or if I have something special to announce—a new nuance of mood, a new vagary, a new extravagant caprice. I don't know what such a policy will win me. I am not even sure I wish to implement it. It seems small and mean-spirited. I have conflicting ideas. But the main theme that runs through my brain is that what is, is insufficient. Where did that sulky notion come from? From the rental library, doubtless." (SW 135)

Sounding more like a "small, mean-spirited" bitch than a serious, politically committed activist, this Snow White, like Margot and the captured woman, is also attracted to male brutality. Pursued by Hogo, evil Jane's former boyfriend and biker who views women as replaceable "cunts," Snow White confesses to him that although his brutality has made "its impression" upon her, she cannot accept his "love" because his blood is not "purple" enough for her royal expectations. She is, after all, waiting for her prince. Not only does this so-called feminist enjoy being victimized but she also is an elitist and a dependent female who looks forward to the arrival of her prince to elevate her above the lower classes. Snow White's seemingly self-chosen passivity, her apparent absence of motivation and her desire to wait rather than to act to extricate herself from a dissatisfying situation are qualities that are further exaggerated by Barthelme's highly self-conscious foregrounding of the "materiality of language," which, as Waugh notes, serves to undermine "personal assertion and human agency."[62] Throughout the text of *Snow White*, Barthelme continually interrupts any semblance of narrative continuity and human agency with questionnaires (SW 82), lists (SW 61, 181), diagrams (SW 3) and pop slogans that sit alone on a page in a typographical format different from the format of adjacent pages (SW 54, 178).

Barthelme also trivializes Snow White's imprisonment within patriarchal texts by punctuating the story with a variety of pop psychological and philosophical slogans, which, when taken out of their formal contexts, sound rather pretentious and ridiculous. Parodying the existentialist category of "being-in-the-world," for example, Barthelme classifies Snow White's waiting for her prince as her living "her own being as 'not with' and experiencing an "ache capable of subduing all other data presented to consciousness," namely her "being with" seven other men (SW 70). That is to say, in addition to her whining, "mean-spirited" self-indulgence, Barthelme's Snow White emerges as an emotionally dishonest nag who claims to suffer the ache of male absence while living with "Bill, Kevin, Clem, Hubert, Henry, Edward and Dan."

Despite her professed dissatisfaction with marital and fairy tale texts, Barthelme's Snow White appears, at times, to be a weak and hypocritical version of the 1960's feminist, and at other times, a woman, not clearly defined, who is caught between an awareness of her own oppression and an inability to transcend it. She is a character who lacks the imaginative vision to create a new mode of being-in-the-world and the courage to walk away from the system which she claims is oppressing her. When asked by the seven dwarfs why she does not leave them, Snow White, invoking and parodying her literary precursor, Brett Ashley, from Hemingway's *The Sun Also Rises*, replies, "It must be laid, I suppose, to a failure of the imagination. I have not been able to imagine anything better" (SW 59). Furthermore, in keeping with the general tone of enervation and exhaustion that pervades this minimalist tale, Snow White's rebellion can only muster enough energy to express itself in the form of a four-page dirty poem—"Bandagedandwounded"—which she keeps hidden from the seven men and which is itself a parody of existentialist philosophy. Depleted of energy, Snow White is tired, and her bid for autonomy, as presented by the author, is a rather paltry effort, resulting in a pretentious and vacuous creative writing exercise that allows her to vent her libidinous stirrings of the imagination while remaining, as one critic notes, "embedded in the context of slight men" and "stuck in the fairy tale past of waiting for a prince."[63]

Issuing the poem as a warning to the seven men, Snow White, like Cecilia, threatens to use her imagination to unleash chaos in the household.

Prior to her arrival, the seven dwarfs led smug, unreflective middleclass lives "stuffed with equanimity." The introduction of female sexuality into this all-male household initially presented no threat, for it was controlled by the dwarfs who, in keeping with their capitalist perspective, reduced it to a business arrangement and an exchange of goods and services. However, now that Snow White's imagination is stirring "like the long sleeping stock certificate suddenly alive in its green safety deposit box" (SW 59-60), the dwarfs feel threatened: "Something was certainly wrong, we felt" (SW 60). The dwarfs are, as Graff notes, "self-estranged Babbits" once Snow White punctures their bourgeois self-complacency.[64] While Barthelme's comic, figurative reduction of the female imagination to a monetary transaction undermines the validity and seriousness of Snow White's artistic/sexual stirrings, the simile does serve to awaken the fears of the seven capitalist businessmen: she is, after all, speaking their language. It also serves to illuminate the degree to which postmodern American ideology, what critic Paul Maltby labels "late-capitalistic" society, perpetuates restrictive modes of discourse that "preclude conceptions of an alternative way of life,"[65] that is, to use Snow White's words, of "something better."

Perplexed and frightened by the "rebellious" Snow White and the imminent disruption of their household, the seven dwarfs release their frustration through fantasies of violence directed at women. On one occasion, immediately following one of Snow White's expressions of discontent, the dwarfs go off to work, "hi ho," to wash the buildings:

> [The buildings] are good places to look at girls from... Viewed from above they are targets, the plum colored head the center of the target, the wavy navy skirt the bold circumference... We are very much tempted to shoot our arrows into them, those targets. You know what that means. (SW 8)

Indeed we do know what that means. For all of us who have been blanketed by the psychoanalytic jargon of phallic and vaginal dream texts, the above fantasy is undoubtedly intended as a comic gloss on Freudian symbolism. While this thinly disguised imaginative excursion into sexualized aggression mocks the pop culture's unreflective immersion in such theories, it also serves to trivialize the underlying tragic reality of male sexual violence against women: pop Freudianism may be funny but rape is not. If, as Barthelme implies, the culture has become so jaded by the proliferation of interpretive theories, whether they be Freudian, Jungian, Sartrean, Husserlian or feminist, and if all such examples of "cultural sludge" are to be comically cleared away through parody, as they are in *Snow White*, how are we to view the tragic realities that these theories were intended to explain? For, although tempered, perhaps, by the parodic structure of the short story, the phenomenon of female victimization remains an essential thematic/plot element that cannot be completely defused through humor.

A similar uncomfortable blending of the tragic and the comic informs the dwarf's second fantasy of violence, one aimed at their primary "target," Snow White herself. It is a collective dream in which all the dwarfs participate in the agonizingly slow murder and mutilation of Snow White:

> We dreamed we burned Snow White. Burned is not the right word, cooked is the right word. We cooked Snow White over the fire, in the dream. Snow White was horizontal. She was spitted on a spit. The spit was suspended over the big fire. Kevin threw more wood on the fire, in the dream. Hubert threw more wood on the fire. Clem basted the naked girl with sweet and sour sauce, Dan made the rice. Snow White screamed. Edward turned the crank which made the meat revolve. Was she done enough? She was making a lot of noise. The meat was moving toward the correct color, a brown-red...Snow White asked if we would remove the spit. "It hurts," she said. "No," Bill said. "You are not done. It is supposed to hurt." Jane laughed. "Why are you laughing Jane?" "I am laughing because it is not me burning there. "For you," Henry said, "we have the red hot iron shoes. The plastic red hot iron shoes." (SW 109-110)

Like Horace in "The Policeman's Ball," the seven dwarfs respond to a female's resistance to stereotypic expectations through fantasies of violence. Perhaps a parody of those "fantasies of femicide" that punctuate the writings of Eliot, Lawrence, Hemingway, Nathaniel West and Faulkner,[66] the dwarves' dream sequence captures that typically uncomfortable satiric blending of condemnation and humor that characterizes so many of Barthelme's texts. Emerging as a "comic" rendition of what Carol Adams has argued is a denigration of both animals and women in patriarchal society,[67] all the dwarfs participate in preparing a tasty meal of "meat" and rice, as Horace prepared his Rock Cornish hens and Margot for "consumption." Usurping the role of Grimm's evil queen who mistakenly believes she is eating Snow White's lungs and liver in a pickled stew, Barthelme's seven dwarfs fantasize about consuming Snow White so as to eliminate the disruption she has introduced into their little "kingdom." Whereas Grimm elicits horror with such a tragic image of cannibalism, Barthelme intends, it seems, to evoke a chuckle with his comic image of seven middleclass businessmen barbecuing a woman on a spit on their Greenwich Village apartment fire-escape, while threatening to kill another with "*plastic*, red hot iron shoes" (emphasis mine). It is, however, a chuckle that might stick in the throat of some of his readers, particularly female readers.

The reduction of Snow White from "horsewife" to "horsemeat" is an image that tries to negate or ignore the underlying horror of the situation. If Barthelme's juxtaposition of a traditional fairy tale text and a contemporary urban cookout (immolation) represents, as McCaffery argues, his "use of the myth for comic purposes,"[68] it engenders a humor that is purchased at the expense of the episode's tragic underpinnings, namely the mutilation and death of a young woman. As Mary Gordon observes in her discussion of Faulkner's so-called "comic anti-feminism," "The definition of the comic has always depended upon who is doing the laughing."[69] The murder and consumption of Snow White, although intended perhaps as a "comic" subtext that mocks male fantasies about women in this parodic version of Grimm's fairy tale, presuppose the not-so-comic postmodern reality of women's increasing vulnerability to an avenging male rage. Purchased at the expense of a woman's violent subjugation, such humor emerges as a thinly veiled form of male aggression. Not everyone is laughing.

It is not only the parodic nature of this minimalist tale but also the very portrait of Snow White herself that encourages the reader's humorous response to the dwarfs' violent fantasy. Quite unlike her fairy tale counterpart, Barthelme's Snow White is a "fallen woman," a piece of "white trash," who has willingly "shacked up" with seven other men and become their "old lady," that is, their "horsewife" and "cunt," as Hogo labels her. As the culture has demonstrated so many times in its reaction to and perception of male violence against women, whether they be housewives, prostitutes or date-rape victims, any woman who voluntarily places herself in a vulnerable position to male sexual power somehow deserves what she gets. As a woman who "willingly" gets "gangbanged" every morning in the shower, Snow White, according to this line of thought, deserves a violent ending to her life. Consequently, we are to feel less uncomfortable when laughing about her gruesome demise, for her voluntary status in the male household has somehow vitiated the tragic import of her situation.

The traditional Snow White arouses our sympathy and compassion, for she represents the virginal, naive and passive "damsel in distress"; consequently, her "fairy tale ending"—consisting of marital bliss and economic prosperity—has been applauded as a fitting conclusion by Disney audiences since the movie premiered in 1937.[70] In contrast, Barthelme's

Snow White elicits a condemning smirk, for she comes across as a spoiled, sexually-soiled, malcontented housewife with nymphomaniacal tendencies. The 1960's middleclass feminist was often viewed by her supporters as a serious activist who, at the inception of the 1960's women's movement, was struggling to find a political voice and agenda to articulate her concerns and the collective complaints of all women in America. As portrayed in Barthelme's *Snow White*, this middleclass feminist emerges as a whining nag whose self-proclaimed consciousness belies her own solipsistic desires and self-indulgent fantasies.

A far more compelling character is Jane, Barthelme's postmodernized version of the evil witch/stepmother. For Jane displays a *vitality* and a *unity of purpose* in her devotion to the capricious dissemination of evil that are absent in the lives of Snow White, Paul and the seven dwarfs. Dedicated to the violent elimination of Snow White and very much aware of her own power to effect evil in the world, Jane initially appears to be a woman whose voice resonates with the "crack of authority." However, to conclude that Jane employs her energy to author(ize) her own text is to ignore the traditional, patriarchal stereotypes to which she remains confined. As Betty Flowers observes, of all the characters in the tale, Jane alone manifests the energy to fulfill two roles—that of "a modern psychological type" and that of a "narrative, mythical expectation"—for she is the only character "not plagued by modern, psychological introspection."[71] Energized but not liberated, Jane represents: 1) the jealousy of the "older, other woman"—a modern psychological type that, despite Barthelme's distaste for Freudian categories, resonates, as Bettelheim argues, with unresolved oedipal rage;[72] 2) a 1960's woman who, like her fairy tale precursor, has found a voice to articulate her agenda to introduce the *expected female evil* into the world. While Snow White remains relatively unenthusiastic about the stirrings of her imagination, Jane actively investigates the nature of her role as the agency of evil in the story, leading one critic to conclude that she, along with Hogo, provides alternatives to the other characters who "remain frozen in the past."[73] Again, however, a closer look at this so-called contemporary female rebel will reveal a woman who remains very much entrapped within traditional texts.

Like her fairy tale counterpart, Jane manifests a potentially lethal sexual jealousy, for she competes with Snow White for Hogo's affection and participates in the dwarfs' cannibalistic cookout. Her attraction to Hogo reveals that Jane, like Snow White, the captured woman and Margot, has internalized the culture's reduction of women to sexual objects whose emerging claims for political and economic autonomy are greeted with scorn and derision by many men. Hogo's comic discourse on women as replaceable "cunts," delivered to assuage the dwarfs' anxiety over Snow White, reflects the culture's degradation of women, which Jane, by her attraction to Hogo, implicitly accepts:

> The main thing I wanted to point out is that the world is full of cunts, that they grow like clams in all quarters of the earth, cunts as multitudinous as cherrystones and littlenecks burrowing in the mud in all bays of the world. The point is that the loss of any particular one is not to be taken seriously...Because something is always being cast up on that beach, as new classes of girls mature...But of course with the spread of literacy you now tend to get girls who have thought and feeling too...and some of them will probably...have their own "thing" which must be respected, and catered to and nattered about, just as if you gave a shit about all this *blague*." (SW 74-75)

Women have devolved in this tale from "housewife" to "horsewife" to "horsemeat" to "clam." Hogo's "cunt" speech is undoubtedly a parody of Henry Miller's *idée fixe* in the *Tropic of Cancer*—his "eternal preoccupation" with the "cunt," and to his misogynistic reduction, in *Tropic of Capricorn*, of women to their ovaries and his simile comparing the vagina to an oyster, an "oyster with soft teeth."[74] Gilbert and Gubar argue that Miller's "theology of the cunt" reifies women so as to neutralize the power of female sexuality, a power which for writers like Miller, Mailer and Lawrence, represents a threat to male potency.[75] Clearly, Barthelme parodies Miller's sexual "humor"—which is, as Kate Millet notes, the "humor of the men's house, more specifically, the men's room,"[76]—in Hogo's vituperative outburst and condemns the univocal stance of Miller's virulent misogyny. Barthelme indeed "critiques a male imagination that fetishizes women."[77] Yet, while clearly mocking such an outburst, Barthelme seems unable to resist infusing Hogo's speech with a linguistic energy and poetic vitality that no one else, except Jane perhaps, can sustain; that is to say, Barthelme's most diabolical male character is also his most clever, articulate speaker, who, as a "comic" proponent of female degradation, is given the freedom to engage in a dazzling display of male chauvinistic rhetoric/dreck.

Hogo's unabashed misogynistic message, while "comic," clearly proclaims both the culture's traditional subjugation of women and the arrogant disdain with which men like Hogo dismiss the stirrings of a nascent feminism. Emphasizing the violent usage of the term, Jane Mills notes in her etymological analysis that the word "cunt" has been "applied to people and things considered worse than excrement (shit-face is considered less abusive than cunt-face) or the penis which, as prick, was a term of endearment in the C16th and C17th."[78] In his Marxist analysis of pornography, Alan Soble similarly points out that the word "cunt," unlike the term "prick" which connotes a competitive, crafty and at times ruthlessly successful man in capitalist society, reflects a linguistic form of violent dismemberment perpetrated against women.[79] Hogo's reduction of women to "cunts" reflects "the deep fear and hatred of the female by the male in our culture"[80] and Jane's attraction to such a man would suggest that she, too, remains enmeshed in society's destructive, "pornographic" view of women.

Rejected by Hogo for Snow White, Jane, in keeping with her evil personality-type and fulfilling her fairy tale expectations, devises a plan to murder her competition by serving Snow White a poisoned vodka Gibson. Barthelme's postmodern version depicts the evil witch not as a vain stepmother but rather as a spurned lover who directs her avenging rage at the other woman who has stolen her man. Such a portrayal not only taps into a tradition in Western literature, both classical and popular, ranging from Euripedes' *Medea* to Morrison's *Sula*, in which women rejected by men try to harm other women; it also reflects a Madison Avenue advertising strategy, popular in the 1960's and 1970's, that pitted women against women in a struggle to win and keep the attention of men. Lucy Komisar provides a good review of the sexist messages implicit in American advertising of the 1960's, noting that women are depicted as engaged solely on "a quest for the Holy Male";[81] and as discussed in the film documentary, "Killing Us Softly: Advertising's Image of Women" (1979), a recurring image in ads ranging from cosmetics to cleansers portrays a woman's hostile competition with another woman to obtain recognition from a man.[82] Barthelme's Jane, although a postmodern character, still acts out the traditional divisiveness among women that is fostered by a literary tradition and pop media in a patriarchal culture.

While the malice directed against Snow White may reveal Jane's energy and clarity of purpose—thus setting her apart from Snow White, the seven dwarfs and Paul, all of whom seem to be floundering in a morass of doubt and indecision—her attempt to realize her iniquitous goals discloses both a comic ineptitude and a tragic vulnerability to male violence. Recalling Jane's comment in the cannibalistic fantasy of cooking Snow White, that "I am laughing because it is not me burning there," we begin to see how Barthelme has cleverly adapted the fairy tale version to reflect the culture's endorsement of women's betraying other women to eliminate competition for male approval. Yet, the fact remains that Jane, too, is to be "eliminated" in this fantasy and that her desire to be "one of the boys" and to enter the traditionally male domain of violent, expedient action against women is temporary and ultimately self-defeating. Like Snow White, who is to be "consumed" in the cannabilistic fantasy, Jane, too, will be "devoured" by the System. Furthermore, the fact that her vodka Gibson kills Paul instead of her "primary target" comically suggests that this contemporary woman, intent on maximizing her evil proclivities, cannot even do "her own thing" successfully. She is, in short, a stereotypical, bumbling female.

Jane, however, unlike the other characters in the tale, does seem, as Bruss argues, to display an awareness of the nature of language that enables her to assume an ironic distance from her own evil text.[83] In her "universe of discourse" letter to a Mr. Quistgaard, a name she arbitrarily picked out of the phone book, Jane (and presumably Barthelme) instructs us about the nature of human discourse and primarily the absence of an ontological primacy attending any one particular text:

> ...You and I, Mr. Quistgaard, are not in the same universe of discourse...Now it may have appeared to you, prior to your receipt of this letter, that the universe of discourse in which you existed, and puttered about, was in all ways, adequate and satisfactory. It may never have crossed your mind to think that other universes of discourse distinct from your own existed....You may have...regarded your own u. of d. as a plenum, filled to the brim with discourse...People like you often do...You are sitting there in your own house on Neat Street, with your fine dog...handsome wife and tall brown son...your gun-colored Plymouth Fury in the driveway...A comfortable American scene. But I, Jane...am in possession of your telephone number Mr. Quistgaard. Think what that means. It means that at any moment I can pierce your plenum with a single telephone call...You are correct, Mr. Quistgaard in seeing this as a threatening situation. (SW 44-45)

Barthelme, through Jane, argues in favor of the tentative and arbitrary nature of all human texts, denying an ontological primacy to any one universe of discourse and viewing language systems as rather humble, all-too-human attempts to organize the world into navigable patterns of experience. Barthelme here overtly embraces one of the fundamental tenets of postmodern language theory, namely, that cultural or linguistic discourses are, as Suleiman notes in her discussion of Lyotard's *The Postmodern*

Condition, "overlapping language games with shifting rules and players."[84] These competing universes of discourse, or, as Deborah Madsen terms them, these "provisional modes of truth,"[85] threaten to collide with each other in determining provisional forms of legitimation. Jane plays with the evil dimensions of her text by threatening a stranger with her capricious intrusion into his smug, unreflective middleclass existence, a world undoubtedly "stuffed with equanimity."

Far more conscious than Snow White of the imagination's creative playfulness in the construction of a "universe of discourse," Jane does possess an understanding of the nature of language that sets her apart from the linguistic ignorance of the other characters. Waugh observes that Jane's letter reveals Barthelme's jettisoning of the language of Romantic Correspondence and the old Idealist framework of a metaphysical, transcendent whole that would have served as a ground for "possible worlds" of consciousness; instead, "worlds" are now "universes of discourse" rather than states of consciousness which reflect not "transcendent unities" but perhaps nothing more than "exercises of power as rhetorical performances."[86] Waugh correctly concludes that Barthelme here projects a typically postmodern ambivalence: the recognition of alternative universes of discourse may "prove the possibility of a genuine recognition of otherness," but it may also "reflect a situation of competing language games where performance establishes validity and where the strongest win";[87] a closer examination of the passage suggests yet another layer of ambivalence. For, by casting Jane as the embodiment of a male-authored script of the stereotypical evil witch who at the same time articulates an acute awareness of the absence of any metaphysical validity for that script, Barthelme manages to create a paradoxical female voice, one that revels in a text of evil, witchy machinations, created by male oppressors, but which also intuits the possibility of escape from that script through the potential creation of other universes of discourse. However, while such a conscious relationship to language allows Jane to play with her own power and "freely cultivate the malice essential to her role,"[88] it does not, in Barthelme's version, free her from the text of female evil to which she has been confined by both pop culture and a literary tradition. Barthelme may have accorded Jane the power and insight to explore consciously the range of action inherent in her role, but he has not allowed this postmodern character, the strongest, most vital character in the story (except, perhaps, for Hogo), to discard the old text and create a new universe of discourse, one that emancipates her from the traditional stereotype of female evil. Jane remains the evil witch, a witch well-versed in contemporary linguistic theory, but still and inevitably a witch.

Despite their postmodern complexities, Barthelme's Snow White and Jane stay trapped in stereotypic female roles. Dimly aware of, but unexcited about, her imaginative possibilities, Snow White remains ensconced in her enclave of men, which eventually includes Hogo; her feminist "stirrings" result in no liberating change of lifestyle. Like the captured woman, Snow White will continue to live in the male-dominated household, articulating her discontent and sounding like the stereotypic nagging "bitch" who will soon be susceptible to Hogo's "tall brutality." Of all the women analyzed in this chapter, Jane initially appears to be the most articulate and powerful, exhibiting a vitality and intelligence that imbue her voice with "the crack of authority." However, Jane's energy is directed toward cultivating evil, the evil of the stereotypic witch, and not toward authorizing a new, innovative female text that would liberate her from traditional literary and societal gender roles. Barthelme's Snow White and Jane present the reader with a set of dismal alternatives for women in the contemporary world: either women quell the stirrings of discontent and continue to "fail to imagine anything better," or they enthusiastically explore the parameters of evil. Either alternative presupposes a resignation to, rather than an emancipation from, the externally-imposed patriarchal expectations of women, and creates an interesting ideological tension between Barthelme's innovative technical experimentation, on the one hand, and his reliance upon traditional, restrictive stereotypes, on the other. Given Barthelme's rather playful re-invention of literary forms and language formats, one might expect a concomitant re-envisioning of content and sex-roles. Yet, neither Snow White nor Jane can emerge from the "cultural sludge" to authorize a new universe of discourse.

Though far more articulate and certainly more conscious of her role in society than the enchanted princess, Jane is, in effect, poignantly connected to her and all of the other female characters discussed in this chapter. For, despite her sophisticated, deliberative analysis of her own text of evil, Jane remains as enslaved as the others to her assigned role. Although Barthelme seems sensitive at times to a woman's vulnerable position within male-authored texts, whether they be Freudian, Madison Avenue, fairy tale, marital or aesthetic texts, he does, in the works considered in this chapter, remain firmly rooted in negative, outmoded portrayals of women. Yet, that these portrayals "caricature" sex-stereotypes serves the crucial purpose of undermining the "naturalness" and unquestioned validity of such gender roles, revealing their performative rather than expressive dimensions. Whether intentionally or not, Barthelme seems to have taken a critical step in debunking conventional assumptions that femininity and masculinity are somehow inherently genetic predispositions. Parody, his literary vehicle, serves, as Judith Butler notes, "to expose the unnaturalness of gender roles."[89] Yet, paradoxically, his parodying of sex roles and subsequent failure to posit alternatives to gender stereotyping leave him, like his Snow White, enmeshed in old texts, "unable to imagine anything better." One wonders what might have happened in Barthelme's fractured version of *Snow White* if he had extended his experimental impulse to include a re-visioning of sex-roles. What kind of story would have followed if Barthelme had allowed Jane, the most articulate and energetic spokesperson for the author's postmodernist themes, to subvert the stereotype of the evil witch and to emerge as a benevolent force that would "save" Snow White by giving her a crash course in female autonomy? Could Jane not have imagined an alternative mode of being-in-the-world in which she bonds with Snow White to establish a feminist community or sisterhood? Could not Jane have been good, intelligent and strong? Conversely, can we not envision a strong, sensitive and kind male feminist in the text rather than the hackneyed misogynistic Hogo or the enervated Paul? Barthelme's traditional stereotypes not only run counter to the tenets of second-wave feminism, but they also are ideologically inconsistent with his experimental techniques. Even the elusive narrator, who lurks among the fragments and white spaces of *Snow White* as a presence that is other-than any one of the other characters, cannot muster the energy to envision textual alternatives. Barthelme is consistently critical in his writings of the cultural sludge and dreck that the media daily heap upon all of us, yet he seems to lack what Richard Poirier calls the energy and vitality of a "performing self" to emerge from the "cultural heap" and, for example, get past unquestioned gender stereotypes.[90] Barthelme is, in this respect, very much like Joan Didion whose enervation and reliance upon traditional images of women and men in her earlier writings seem somewhat incongruous with her brand of postmodern, experimental minimalism.

Dying Fathers and Emerging Daughters: Barthelme, Didion and *The Dead Father*

The depiction of woman as textual/sexual prisoner that pervades many of Donald Barthelme's texts also informs the thematic structure of Joan Didion's minimalist novels and journalistic chronicles. Less daring than Barthelme in her experimental techniques and leaning, perhaps, more toward a conventional realism at times, Didion nonetheless embraces the tenets of a postmodern minimalism, namely: a predilection for despair and disorder; a reliance upon an episodic format replete with fragments and white space so as to deal with parts in the absence of totalities; the use of those ominous textual silences that shout forth possibilities and require reader intervention to propel plot and flush out character motivation; and the jettisoning of traditional literary closure and linearity of temporal sequence. Larry McCaffery includes Joan Didion in his definitive compilation of postmodern writers, for she, like Barthelme, Pynchon and Morrison, displays a loss of faith in the philosophical underpinnings of traditional realistic fiction, a form "whose origins are intimately related to the assurances and optimism of empiricism and Western rationalism.[91] Focusing on the political and societal upheavals of the 1960's and 1970's, Didion employs structural innovations that reflect the jettisoning of those outworn ideologies that, as McCaffery notes, "misled us into the age of nuclear nightmare, into Vietnam, into ideological apocalypse, into political oppression, into an insane immoral sense of values that devalued human beings by glorifying abstractions and the inanimate."[92]

Furthermore, like Barthelme, Didion displays an ambiguity toward her female characters, especially in her earlier fiction when violence is perpetrated against women but seemingly with their complicity and acquiescence. Joanna Russ has even argued that Didion's novels have won wide acceptance precisely because Didion has created female characters who endorse society's "misogynistic view" that women are basically "non-agential": Didion's female protagonists are "passive, depressed heroines whose unhappiness is praised by the author as a sign of special, feminine sensitivity."[93] While it is true that Lily in *Run River*, Maria in *Play It As It Lays* and Charlotte in *A Book of Common Prayer* operate more or less according to a code of passive acceptance of their own exploitation by oppressive male figures, so that they come across as masochistic women who grasp onto suffering as the definitive mode of being in the world, Russ's claim that Didion relies solely upon an "acceptable female masochism"[94] is misleading and reductive; for Didion quite dramatically discloses the emotional and physical assaults against women in these earlier texts and succeeds in raising issues of concern to women living in a postmodern, patriarchal culture that range from nuclear annihilation to abortion and control of the female body and construction of a female identity; yet, the attendant ambiguity arises when she simultaneously undercuts the reader's sympathy for these characters by emphasizing their passivity and narcissism. It is not until *Democracy* (1984) that Didion creates a strong, assertive and heroic female character who emerges from the shards of contemporary existence and from the immobility of self-indulgence to reconstruct a self that can withstand the onslaught of potentially violent male characters. Published one year after *Salvador*—her journalistic recounting of her time spent in that war-torn country while witnessing the insidious role played by the U.S. in fomenting civil strife—*Democracy* implies, perhaps, that Didion has come to realize that the oppression of women in the domestic arena and the opportunistic intrusion into the affairs of foreign nations are inextricably linked substructures of patriarchal violence. One critic even suggests that the "war victims in [*Democracy*] are not American soldiers," but "the wives, daughters and lovers of the war profiteers."[95]

Just as critics have argued that *The Dead Father* represents Barthelme's pivotal work,[96] so too would I maintain that *Democracy* heralds a critical shift in Didion's perception of women in American culture. *The Dead Father* and *Democracy* raise similar structural and thematic issues that pertain to our analysis of women and violence in contemporary American fiction. Both texts: 1) aim to forge a new form of the novel, one whose structure will reflect a postmodern era that has lost faith in fairy tale endings and is no longer able to seek refuge and metaphysical solace in wished-for totalities, a structure that captures the fragmentary, apocalyptic nature of a contemporary world whose ultimate emblem of patriarchal violence is the potential for nuclear destruction; 2) disclose the frightening extent to which a woman's body and self-image, that is, her identity, have been invaded, staked out and claimed as the territorial domain of male ownership so that the view of woman-as-pub(l)ic property can be subtly used to sanction male control of female selfhood and self-expression, ranging from the creative pen to the procreative womb; 3) envision the possibility of women's breaking free from the traditional confinements of male textual domination either through innovative, linguistic play and female discourse (Barthelme) or through reconstructing a broken self *via* the act of witnessing and constructing another woman's story (Didion). An analysis of both texts will reveal that Barthelme's re-envisioning of female textual liberation is fundamentally inimical to the formulation of a female identity while Didion's assuming the posture of witness/storymaker represents her attempt to reconstruct a formidable identity, through bonding with another woman, one that is capable of surviving male aggression.

The Dead Father

Labelled by one critic as a "central postmodern text,"[97] Barthelme's minimalist text tells the tale of a Dead Father, 3200 cubits long, who is being hauled across the countryside to his burial site by twenty-three people, two of whom are his son, Thomas, and his daughter, Julie. Refusing to go gentle into that good night, this patriarchal giant, who is dying rather than dead, complains relentlessly during the trip of the travails and awesome responsibilities of fatherhood that have plagued men throughout time. He is painfully aware of his imminent death and cognizant of the erosion of his power over his "children," that is, the younger generation; consequently, the Dead Father resorts to intermittent bursts of speechmaking and to gratuitous bursts of violence (e.g. he slays a group of artists and musicians and slaughters some dogs) in order to flex what remains of his atrophying patriarchal muscle before he is rather ignominiously dumped into a hole and buried.

The Dead Father has elicited a variety of interpretive reactions: one critic sees in its extirpation of character and painful self-consciousness the death of modernism,[98] while another views the gradual dismantling of this oppressive, authoritarian figure (the Dead Father loses body parts along the way), who is given to issuing ukases, as paralleling the gradual extinction of the Victorian novel in favor of a more experimental form of minimalism:

> As elements drop away, as the novel moves through enemy territory (readers? critics? reviewers?) it changes its form somewhat, becoming even more truncated, lacking in parts, shifting from narrative to sensation, as Barthelme's own tale does.[99]

However, as a collection of multiple voices and echoes from myth, legend, Victorian authoritarianism, modernist beliefs and painfully familiar utterances of typical fathers, *The Dead Father* also represents the ubiquity of patriarchal power which, despite its being challenged in the 1960's and 1970's by various forces including feminism, refuses to relinquish its control over its "children." Similar to the other Barthelme texts considered in this essay, misogynistic male characters here become the targets of parodic humor, their anti-woman stance so hyperbolic that one cannot help but chuckle at the comically ludicrous nature of their utterances. Again, however, such humor takes seriously (indulges? exploits?) the very reality it seeks to mock—male aggression, and conversely, mocks the very reality it attempts to take seriously—female subjugation. By incorporating America's systemic misogyny into the structure of parody without concomitantly re-envisioning alternative roles for women and men that would avert the stereotypic "male predator/female prey" dichotomy, Barthelme's texts further embrace an ambiguity with regard to the victimization of women.

However, unlike the other Barthelme texts considered in this essay, in which feminist claims are treated somewhat sardonically, *The Dead Father* presents a female voice that reveals the dangerous excesses of male aggression and the capricious will of male power. That this voice remains an elusive series of utterances unconnected to a substantial self or abiding female identity vitiates the impact of this female challenge to patriarchal power by confining it to an aesthetic rather than a political level. As Klinkowitz observes, "If feminism can be considered a postmodern development, then its announcement in the text makes the *aesthetic* conflict all the more explicit."[100] That is to say, despite the sympathetic portrayal of female oppression in the text, Julie's feminist response as presented by Barthelme is confined to the arena of linguistic experimentation and word play and thereby remains politically ineffective in the struggle for liberation.

Barthelme's use of disembodied voices rather than centralized subjects or "characters" suggests that he has subscribed in part to the post-structuralist deconstruction of the coherent, stable self and instead posited a gendered subject as a "relational identity constructed through discourse."[101] As Felski notes, this tenet of French post-structuralist theory has generated much debate and anxiety among some American feminist scholars, some of whom argue for the necessity of a "core self," a central identity, in order to effect legitimate political change.[102] The ensuing rift in American post-structuralist feminist theory has pitted critics like Peggy Kamuf and Mary Jacobus—who embrace the tenets of French post-structuralist thinkers like Irigaray and Cixous and locate gendered female identity within language itself as eruption within patriarchal discourse—against those who, like Gubar, Gilbert, Suleiman, Waugh, Flax and Felski, proclaim the importance of some form of collective identity, some unified voice or discursive space to undermine gender-based oppression.[103] It is precisely with regard to the notion of a female "self" or "identity" that Didion and Barthelme part company. Rather than reconstructing a formidable sense of self, as Didion does in *Democracy*, Barthelme's feminist, Julie, remains content with a paratactic playfulness that fails to carry any serious pragmatic import in the struggle to emerge from the textual/sexual oppression of the Dead Father. Let us consider this in more detail.

While fatherhood is indeed a relational concept dependent upon the co-term "child," *The Dead Father* has been seen primarily as a story about fathers and sons, despite the presence in the text of a daughter, Julie, and her friend, Emma. That the tale contains a "Manual for Sons" and that, of the twenty-three players, only two are female would seem to suggest the relative insignificance of women in the text, tempting the reader to perceive their import as marginal at best. Yet, a more careful scrutiny of the female characters reveals that the fundamental dimension of Western patriarchy—its pulsating desire to perpetuate itself and guarantee its own posterity by whatever means necessary—often results in acts of aggression, both subtle and flagrant, against women whose reproductive function is required to insure patrilineal succession, but whose emerging demands to be perceived as other than the bearers and nurturers of future oppressive fathers is deemed as threatening to the patriarchy. Consequently, the excesses of fatherhood—the silencing of critical voices, the demand for blind obedience, the predilection for violence, the reluctance to display physical affection, and the self-aggrandizing conquering of territories—are manifested quite clearly in the text's delineation of the father-daughter and brother-sister relationships. For throughout the text, males comically view Julie's body as their property, subject to their needs and whims, and her utterances as digressive and peripheral to patriarchal discourse.

Within the framework of parody, the Dead Father's world view emerges, in part, as an exaggerated version of male hatred for women and is undoubtedly aimed at illuminating the illogical and oppressive nature of patriarchal attitudes. Underlying the Dead Father's comic behavior, and a necessary condition for the evocation of his humor, resides the very real and often violent subjugation of women in postmodern society. From the perspective of the Dead Father, children are viewed as either male or "not male"—males wore their "cap and bells" and "if not [males] observed the principle of *jus primae noctis*,"[104] the fundamental principle in Western patriarchy that relegates women and their virginity to male ownership. Submitting to the incestuous demands of a powerful, acquisitive father (and a brother who is a future-father), Julie, as the offspring of a "daughter-father," is viewed by him as his property even "in a way his wife is not" (DF 133).

Julie's status as "other-than-male," as a negatively-gendered subject whose body remains fair game to both male caprice and design, partially accounts for her using her body to negotiate an exchange of goods and protection from men, as did Snow White. She gives her brother, Thomas, who is a paler version of their father, sexual access to her body, allowing him to grasp her breasts (DF 9) and her "magic button" (clitoris) in order to establish a defense against the onslaught of the more powerful Dead Father, the "is," despite the fact that Thomas, a self-proclaimed "student of decay" (DF 68), has a bit of Hogo in him and will eventually exchange Julie for a younger woman. Despite Bruss' claim that Thomas represents a "toned down," more humanistic version of the Dead Father who is averse to explicit acts of violence and oppressive discourse,[105] he remains enmeshed in the traditional culture's reduction of women to sexual objects. One wonders to whom Thomas' new-found "humanism" will extend.

Like Cecelia in "A City of Churches," who is perceived as "our car rental girl," Julie is seen as the property of collective male ownership, a piece of goods subject to the public domain. During one "humorous" episode on their trek across the countryside, Julie removes her blouse in exchange for a drink from a lascivious bartender who expresses anger because he really wanted to see her "button." Introducing a comic, contemporary version of the topless bar, Barthelme proceeds to describe a crowd gathering to laugh at and enjoy the public display of Julie's nudity. The crowd turns angry, however, when Thomas appears and lays claim to her by touching her stomach:

> Leave our stomach alone! [a] man shouted.
> *Your* stomach? Thomas asked pointedly...
> Hands were stretched out toward the stomach...
> Thomas began to write something with lipstick on the stomach...
> Oh you rascal! cried the crowd. Oh, you rogue!...
> Thomas held out the shirt to Julie.
> Our stomach! they said. He's taking it away! (DF 31)

Despite its minimalistic, comic format, this scene limns the complex, degrading role imposed upon women in contemporary culture. Barthelme's parody undoubtedly intends to illuminate the absurdity of many of our unquestioned assumptions and societal "truths" regarding male control of women's reproductive capacity and sexuality; that is, he is in fact mocking explicit expressions of misogyny exhibited by writers such as Henry Miller, who in *Sexus* can have his male narrator observe, in that rather intimate, conspiratorial second-person voice that addresses all male readers: "It's wonderful to fuck your own wife as if she were a dead horse...The body is hers but the cunt's yours."[106] We should also remember, however, the tragic underpinnings in contemporary culture of such parody, that is, the tenacious grasp that American culture has on its systematic degradation of females to male-owned pieces of sexual/reproductive property that continues to pose such an imminent threat to women. O.J. Simpson's very real and public humiliation of his ex-wife and spousal abuse victim, Nicole Brown, on the dance floor of a crowded Los Angeles disco—he grabbed her crotch and announced, "This is where babies come from and it belongs to me"— chillingly reverberates with echoes of Miller and Mailer, and reflects a culture that in 1995 has failed to stem the rising tide of violence against women.[107]

Though comprised of both men and women, the crowd represents the dominate male culture whose voice angrily proclaims the female body to be its property and subject to its will. If the humiliating exposure of Julie's body generates public amusement, then the private claim of one man to that body will arouse public anger. While Thomas removes Julie from the potentially dangerous public arena and covers her breasts, he also inscribes his own signature or patriarchal message on her stomach, as cows are branded with the initials of their owners. "Rescued" from the leering crowd (we know from "The Glass Mountain" how easily crowds can transform themselves into angry mobs), Julie submits to Thomas' private claim to her in order to defend herself against the more brutal, untamed "is," the misogynistic culture. That Julie seems willing to escape the gawking crowd by submitting to Thomas' claim to her reflects what Susan Brownmiller observed in her seminal discussion of the history of rape, "a female fear of an open season of rape, and not a natural inclination toward monogamy, motherhood or love."[108] Contemporary psychologists have documented "the powerful and ubiquitous effect that the fear of rape and of other violent acts has on women's lives, and that this fear often requires women "to seek protection from others (the majority of the time, male others)."[109] Far from being liberated from the societal reduction of women to a piece of property, Julie has been pulled into the private domain of patriarchal ownership.

The implied patriarchal message or signature inscribed on Julie's stomach, "our stomach," suggests that the female body, including the uterus, required for patrilineal succession, become subject to the prevailing cultural will, so that abortion decisions, for example, be made not by the individual woman but by the male representative, whether it be the "lover," the husband, the brother, the father or the organized crowd called Congress. Julie herself describes the process by which male discourse and gender identification are imposed immediately upon newborn babies to insure male dominance and female subordination. Alluding to and perhaps parodying the French post-structuralist theories of Cixous and Irigaray that posit the gendered subject as a relational identity arising through discourse, Barthelme describes the "genderfication" of the child. Emerging as a pre-gendered "it," the infant, "in a paroxysm of not understanding," succumbs to the authoritative teachings of the post-like (phallic) father whose power eclipses that of the mother, pejoratively described as being "more like grime," that is, an "overall presence distributed in discrete small black particles all over everything" (DF 77). Whether or not Barthelme embraces the feminine voice as a potentially subversive force pulsating within the confines of rationality and oppressive male discursive registers, that is, whether he hears the female voice as a "transgressive force" that, as Felski argues, is held by French feminist theorists to be capable of "disrupting the single fixed meanings of a repressive phallocentric discourse,"[110] remains to be seen. At this point in the text, the hegemony of the Father leaves Julie decrying the inherent oppression of women by the authoritative male voice. For such "genderfication," Julie argues, serves to perpetuate the dichotomy of "males" and "not-males" that underlies the reduction of women to interchangeable objects of male amusement:

>...[Men] want to be nuzzling new women when they are ninety [said Julie].
> What is wrong with that? asked the Dead Father. Seems perfectly reasonable to me.
> The women object, she said. Violently. (DF 78)

While Julie "violently" objects to the process by which women are subordinated in a male-empowered culture and reduced to the status of "not-men," she, like Snow White, remains ensconced in a circle of voyeuristic, predatory figures, each of whom stakes a claim to various parts of her body: the bartender demands to see her "button"; the crowd views her stomach as theirs; Thomas has access to her breasts and clitoris; and the Dead Father, "feeling left out" from all this sexual romp, manages to nibble on her toes. While clearly mocking the mentality of such male predators, Barthelme nevertheless runs the risk of indulging the very aggression he seeks to parody, perhaps encouraging us to laugh at the idiocy of men rather than to empathize with the plight of women. Constantly vulnerable to both public and private assaults against her person, Julie must navigate her way through potentially violent straits to avoid being completely submerged by more powerful figures.

While the image of the Dead Father's nibbling on Julie's toes conjures associations of a loving father showering affection on his baby girl, it also, given Julie's age, resonates with the more uncomfortable incestuous tone that characterizes Thomas' behavior. Such an image also alludes to the ultimate mythic figure of Western patriarchy, Cronus, the God of time, who, fearing the prophesied overthrow of his reign by a subversive offspring, cannibalized his own children. Barthelme's Dead Father, as the principle of Western patriarchal thought throughout time, in effect consumes his own children by demeaning his sons and reducing his daughters to such insignificant ciphers that fathers who produce only daughters "don't count as fathers" (DF 134).

Cronus' attempt to retain power and defy the prophecy were thwarted by a clever woman: Rhea, his wife, snatched Zeus away at birth and gave her husband a blanketed rock to swallow, thereby causing all the previously consumed children to be regurgitated and subsequently to overthrow their father. Perhaps the Dead Father's reluctance to submit to the rule of time and relinquish his power stems, in part, from his intuitive fear of a clever woman, a woman who, unlike Rhea, will not birth future sons to perpetuate the patriarchy but rather offer an alternative to male-dominated rule. For Julie clearly represents an emerging postmodern threat to the Dead Father. He resents both her unflattering depiction of him in her "father-as-mother-fucker" speech (DF 76-77) and the fact that women object violently to his reduction of them to sexual toys (DF 78).

Within this parody of male domination, Barthelme accords Julie's feminist claims and arguments a degree of seriousnesses that he denied to Snow White's plaints by: 1)intensifying the magnitude and scope of male oppression in the later novel—we have moved from the private home of seven kinky dwarfs to the arena of Western patriarchy; 2) and imbuing Julie with a consciousness of her subordination as a woman and an imagination to offer an alternative. However, in keeping with Barthelme's minimalist project to re-envision only structural aspects of traditional genres and to play more with literary format and language than with content, he presents female emancipation in the text as a form of linguistic experimentation that is intended to offer an alternative to the self-aggrandizing, often violent tenor of male "speechifying." Rather than re-collecting and reconstructing the various parts of Julie's self that have been negotiated away in her attempt to survive male aggressions, Barthelme remains content with composing new voices rather than erecting new identities. By reducing Julie's feminist anger to a new, but incoherent, female discourse, Barthelme flattens out her identity to a voice that breaks free from the traditional, linear speech patterns of the Dead Father, but which carries no pragmatic value or political import necessary for female liberation. Consider the following conversation between Julie and Emma that occurs after the showing of a "pornographic" movie when one of the male viewers attempts to molest Emma:

> Whose little girl are you?
> I get by, I get by.
> Time to go.
> Hoping this will reach you at a favorable moment.
> Bad things can happen to people.
> Is that a threat?...
> Other fish to fry.
> We guarantee every effort will be made.... (DF 23)

Running on for four pages, this particular type of disconnected discourse between Julie and Emma appears on three other occasions in the novel; in each instance, the exchange occurs immediately following an incident that underscores the subordination of women in Western culture (DF 59,85,147), so that one can infer that the female response in this text to patriarchal oppression is, in effect, a pseudo-dialogical duet between two women who, like Jane in *Snow White*, are aware of the essential arbitrariness of any "universe of discourse" (including the reigning discourse of the male hero).

By stringing together a disparate number of fragmented and unconnected clichés and stripping them of their traditional contexts, Julie and Emma mock the ontological primacy accorded the traditional linearity of phallic texts and emerge, as Bruss argues, as the characters in the novel "most likely to indulge freely in the creative acts of the imagination."[111] As Robert Con Davis notes, "Their oblique communication" of "free association" and "indirection" suggests an "a-linear model" that is "foreign to the rational economies associated with paternal authority."[112]

Julie and Emma's new discourse of verbal collage reflects Barthelme's experimental minimalism and perhaps his feminist rejection of patriarchal language structures. Yet, while a re-examination and possible refutation of prevailing language structures may be a necessary prelude to a more pragmatic alteration of female behavior, Barthelme's "new" female discourse remains so far removed from the political concerns of women that one doubts his seriousness here. Could Barthelme, in fact, be parodying French post-structuralist feminist theory here, and could he, in effect, be confirming the suspicions of those American feminist writers who have voiced a concern with the apparent political impotence of the deconstructionist shift to an erotics of the text wherein a "feminine" subversive force of multiplicity, fluidity and openness can challenge the hegemony of any unified, "masculine" system of meaning? If so, he has illuminated the problem confronting feminist theorists who distrust the aesthetics of postmodernism, particularly its rather facile dissolution of the concept of a unified self in favor of a subversive linguistic *jouissance*. Gilbert and Gubar find the disappearance of the subject to be a threat to political activism;[113] and Jane Flax argues that while postmodernists like Lyotard, Derrida and Fouçault have made important contributions to "deconstructing the (apparently) universalizing forms of the conceptions of the self" as oppressive "artifacts of [white, male] Western Culture," she is "deeply suspicious of the motives" of those who would ask women to support a decentering of the self precisely at the historical moment that women have "begun to re-member their selves and to claim an agential subjectivity available always before only to a few privileged white men."[114] Rita Felski, questioning whether feminism has an ally in *avant-garde* literary strategies that, by definition, "lay exclusive stress on the disruption of existing styles and conventions," notes:

> Certainly feminism contains within it a negative moment [Elaine Showalter's "feminist stage" in history] which seeks to expose the illusory nature of patriarchal discourse; it also, however, goes beyond a strategy of negation to the development of alternative critical and political positions [akin to Showalter's "female stage"]…a limitation of a [postmodernist] aesthetic form from a feminist standpoint is its frequent dismissal of the category of content as an illusion to be deconstructed by the progressive text…The [postmodernist] equation of stylistic innovation with political radicalism is called into question by a social movement such as feminism; the specific interests of women cannot be encompassed in terms of a notion of linguistic indeterminancy and free play.[115]

The ability of Emma and Julie to indulge in a paratactic playfulness and to erect innovative linguistic structures that sacrifice any semblance of accessible content may indeed serve to illuminate the arbitrary nature of phallic discourse, but it also fails to construct a credible, alternative female voice. Whether Barthelme is parodying the post-structuralist theories of Cixous and Irigaray, or whether he is attempting to construct a transgressive feminine voice through the playful discourse of Julie and Emma remains ambiguous. What is certain is that the dialogue between these two female "voices" does not forge what Waugh would call a "potent agential self" capable of fighting for political change.[116] Even a critic such as Jeanette

McVicker who claims to find in the four conversations between Julie and Emma a covert celebration of female marginality that is "grounded in multiplicity and difference" rather than the "logic of identity and unity,"[117] concedes the pragmatic impotence of such discourse and its fundamental failure to disrupt the prevailing patriarchal order.

Like Barthelme, Morrison will employ narrative disruptions, fragmented discourse and the minimalist's strategy of withholding information so that, as one critic notes, what remains unsaid "reverberates" with implications and is as equally important as what is stated and specified.[118] Like Barthelme, Morrison, too, will innovatively challenge the hegemony of traditional linear discourse; yet, Morrison will also provide an alternative strategy—an accessible, often female voice that will "sing" those truths specific not just to African-American experience but to everyday human experiences that have been silenced by traditional narrative. Julie and Emma's collage of non sequiturs, while effectively undermining the primacy of phallogocentric, linear discourse, does not, as McVicker notes, enable the women to arrive "at a point where they can act on their observations"; their "feminine discourse," which occurs only "when they are alone together,"[119] seems more of a strategic retreat from the everyday world, a withdrawal from the all-encompassing sweep of the Dead Father's perspective, than an attempt to provide an alternative mode of communication that can seriously challenge patriarchal rule. In contrast, the chorus of women's voices at the end of *Beloved* liberates Sethe from the cycle of racist violence within which she has been imprisoned her entire life.

The amorphic texture of Barthelme's female discourse in which fragments tumble out in no apparent order or sequence is in keeping with a tradition of male literary constructions of female thought processes that embrace the stereotypic reduction of a woman's body and mind to liquidity and formlessness; yet such discourse also seems to point in the direction of French theorist Luce Irigaray who has argued for a biologically-determined difference between female and male speech as part of her feminist agenda.[120] Arguing against Irigaray's thesis, Joanna Russ rejects the concept of *l'écriture féminine* and maintains that the idea that women have a unique "fluid" writing style that is more "spontaneous" than the linear, consciously crafted texts of men implies that "what has been written is not art because there is no conscious organization."[121] While the very qualities Irigaray ascribes to women's writing—inconsistency, fluidity and incoherence—are, as David Richter notes, the very traits that male critics have used to denigrate the female intellect,[122] they also, according to Irigaray, reflect the potentially subversive power of female sexuality to topple phallocentric discourse. Whether Barthelme is adopting what Mary Ellmann has labelled a "phallic criticism"[123] to mock female discourse or whether he is extolling Irigaray's vaginal/clitoral libidinal power of female speech remains unclear. Julie and Emma engage in a verbal exchange that fails to convey any accessible content that may offer an alternative to the destructive nature of phallic discourse within the text; such a strategy suggests that while Barthelme may be sensitive to legitimate feminist concerns in *The Dead Father*, he runs the risk of envisioning a liberating female response in terms of a restrictive linguistic stereotype of the babbling, non-sensical woman. Ironically, he may have ended up parodying the very alternative to male discourse that he set out to celebrate.

Chapter II
✺✺
Joan Didion

While Barthelme's "linguistic heroes"—Julie and Emma—of *The Dead Father* suggest a playful feminist alternative to the arbitrary textual domination of patriarchal discourse, Joan Didion's two central female characters in *Democracy*, the narrator and Inez Victor, forge a symbiotic relationship that permits each woman to construct an "identity" that aims to withstand the assaults leveled against women in contemporary culture. Didion's experimental minimalism, in conjunction with her re-examination of the concept of a stable self or identity, locates her, as Sharon Felton notes, squarely in "the category of postmodernist authors"[1]—the sparse, elliptical prose surrounded by white space that serves to illuminate the fragments of everyday life within a "mosaic of nothingness";[2] the "technique of self-conscious admission";[3] the jettisoning of the "insular, autonomous self" in favor of a relational self constituted not only by a connection to others but also in part by the very act of writing itself, that is, as a "central and centerless textual construct"[4]—all serve to add "layers of postmodern complexity and irony" to *Democracy*.[5] In one very critical respect, *Democracy* represents the latest stage in a process of "self-reconstruction" in the Didion canon, a process that began with the painful dissolution of stereotypically passive, static and ineffective ways of being-in-the-world for women, as depicted in the earlier novels *Run River* and *Play It As It Lays*, and that has culminated in the positing of a tentative identity or "core self" that is, as Flax notes, "always in the process of becoming,"[6] and that is capable of acting upon the world to initiate political change. Like many postmodernists, Didion eventually does seem to deconstruct the concept of a fixed, closed unitary self—an isolated ego—but unlike so many of her literary male counterparts, she does not "lament [the self's] demise"[7] nor flounder in an abyss of amorphous subjectivity; rather, in both *A Book of Common Prayer* and *Democracy*, Didion re-assembles a potent, agential self that, though tentative, can evolve relationally and enter the arena of social activism.

While not an explicitly feminist tract decrying the exploitation of women in contemporary America, *Democracy* underscores what feminist critics now argue is of pivotal necessity in the creation of an effective, political coalition, namely a communal space that will establish a relational identity among women so that, as Coppelia Kahn and Gayle Greene observe, a "way of saying 'I'" is "also a way of saying 'we.'"[8] Didion may not openly connect the "I" with the "We" of a feminist community or, as Felski calls it, a "discursive space,"[9] but she does in *Democracy* endorse a relational concept of self that derives its power from a communal context, a "we" of shared activism. That is to say, while Didion herself might be reluctant to categorize *Democracy* as a feminist novel, this text does implicitly affirm a tenet that is, as Zimmerman notes, "central to feminism," namely, "the definition of a communal, not just an individual, self."[10] In short, *Democracy* reflects the experimental techniques of a minimalist author who, in her own words, remains "committed mainly to the exploration of moral distinctions and ambiguities,"[11] but who has also ultimately created a female character who can emerge from beneath the heap of oppressive male expectations to thrive as an interdependent, loving, adult woman. Published in 1984, *Democracy* stands, as of this writing, as one of the later novels in the Didion canon, and while it does not overtly embrace any tenets of second-wave feminism, it does, when compared to her earlier works, reflect a more sensitive awareness of the powerful force of sex-stereotyping and the complexities inherent in overcoming the subordinate position of women in society. That Didion in *Democracy* creates two assertive women who engage in a parallel quest for self-discovery that includes the construction of an identity independent of male-imposed expectations, suggests, if not a feminist leaning, at least an acknowledgment that females need not remain entrapped within stereotypically passive roles, as they do in her first three novels.

Didion's earlier novels, *Run River*, *Play It As It Lays*, and *A Book of Common Prayer* portray women in roles that are, in varying degrees, consistent with the author's criticisms of the 1960's women's movement presented in her collection of essays entitled *The White Album*. In the essay "The Women's Movement," which Martha Duffy labelled an "harangue" in her 1979 review and one of the author's "rare lapses into callousness,"[12] Didion expresses her antipathy to organized feminism, rejecting what she perceived to be the movement's trivialization of political issues, its reductive interpretations of literature to feminist ideology, its denial of the uniqueness of female sexuality, and, finally, its depiction of women as victims:

> That many women are victims of condescension and exploitation and sex-role stereotyping was scarcely news, but neither was it news that other women are not: nobody forces women to buy the package. (WA 115-116)

Written originally for *The New York Times Book Review*, July 30, 1972, the article, as Katherine Henderson notes, "with its one-sided mixture of half-truth and wild generalization," represents a "disquieting exception" to Didion's ability to assess American culture objectively.[13]

Most troubling is Didion's position regarding female victimization, her contention that the exploitation of women can occur only with their permission, and her rather sarcastic trivialization of the plight of women in American culture:

> The ubiquitous construct was everyone's victim but her own. She was persecuted by her gynecologist, who made her beg in vain for contraceptives. She particularly needed contraceptives, because she was raped on every date, raped by her husband, and raped finally on the abortionist's table... She was so intimated by cosmetic advertising that she would sleep "huge portions" of her day in order to forestall wrinkling, and when awake she was enslaved by detergent commercials on television. She sent her child to a nursery school where little girls huddled in a "doll corner," and were forcibly restrained from playing with building blocks. Should she work she was paid "three to ten times less" than an (always) unqualified man holding the same job. (WA 115)

Didion's angry refusal to acknowledge the power of institutions such as medicine, advertising and employment to shape and perpetuate restrictive sex-role stereotypes is rather naive and alarming; it reveals, perhaps, the cavalier attitude of one who has been privileged enough to possess the financial resources to avoid blatantly exploitive situations, that is, to "get herself another gynecologist" (WA 115), another job, to find a nursery school where girls are encouraged to engage in more than the traditionally repetitive, non-cognitive tasks of changing dolls' diapers and washing dishes, and to live in an area where, to borrow one of Didion's own phrases from another collection of essays, "rape is [not] as common as bullshit."[14] It also reflects, perhaps, what Susan Griffin notes is that "odd dissociation that so many successful women have toward young women trying to escape the common female fate,"[15] and what Carolyn Heilbrun describes as "that distressing attitude of achieving women" that asserts, "I made it, why can't you?", a view expressed by successful women who fail to "sympathize with the struggles of less vigorous female selves":

> They refuse to understand the tokenism they represent, refuse to see that their simple presence, far from proving that anyone can make it, determines, under the present system, that no one else will.[16]

Didion's refusal in 1972 to recognize the forces of socialization in influencing male and female behavior accounts for her rather questionable premise that women are completely responsible for their own victimization, and its attendant corollary that to achieve equality or to avoid discrimination all a woman has to do is, to borrow an equally vacuous phrase from the Reagan anti-drug campaign, "Just say no" to the package. While such an assertion did, as Henderson notes, "generate fierce controversy" when Didion articulated it,[17] such a position illuminates not only the author's early inveterate belief in a kind of rugged, frontier individualism, but also a problematic ambiguity regarding the three female protagonists in her early novels. In a 1977 interview with Sara Davidson, Didion expressed her aversion to social action and revealed her optimistic bias toward a Western frontier individualism:

> I never had faith that the answers to human problems lay in anything that could be called political. I thought the answers, if there were answers, lay some place in man's soul. I have an aversion to social action because it usually meant social regulation...interference, rules, doing what other people wanted me to do. The ethic I was raised in was specifically a Western frontier ethic, that means being left alone and leaving others alone.[18]

Such a position implicitly entails a romantic individualism, a belief, typically American, in the Gatsby-like, deific power of the individual to re-create himself in his own image, to confront and overcome obstacles with his own ingenuity. It also entails a belief that the individual somehow floats above societal processes, remaining ultimately unscathed and essentially untouched by intrusive institutions and free from the drag of the past to re-invent the present. Such a view tacitly endorses the concept of the traditional isolated ego that serves as the pillar of what Jean François Lyotard calls those grand Western Narratives,[19] that is, a "self" that is held to exist prior to and outside socio-political contexts and that Didion begins to deconstruct in her later fiction.

Didion's impatience with women who view themselves as victims of external forces stems, in part, from her frontier ethic, and helps to explain the ambiguity of her early female protagonists, Lily (*Run River*), Maria (*Play It As It Lays*) and Charlotte (*A Book of Common Prayer*).[20] By presenting three women who bemoan their positions in male-dominated relationships but who seemingly choose to remain in such deleterious situations, Didion, in effect, both invites and undermines the reader's sympathy for her characters. Her exposition of their victimization is so poignant at times that the reader comes to view their passivity as a strategy for survival rather than an indulgent escape from other more rigorous alternatives. Yet, her early female protagonists also display such an appalling lack of imagination, understanding of the world, and self-reflection regarding their position as women that the reader begins to grow impatient with their whinings as we did with those of Snow White. This problematic ambiguity is a result of Didion's reluctance to acknowledge explicitly the very same forces of socialization that shape our choices which she implicitly invokes in her portraits of fictional women.

For the choice of victimization as a lifestyle, if one can call it a choice, reflects an emotional aberration that psychologists have partly attributed to women's subordinate position in a society that fosters female dependency, submissiveness and low self-esteem.[21] One begins to understand the vacuousness of a notion such as "choice" when applied to women's roles once one comes to appreciate the pervasivenss of gender socialization. Psychologists point out that the socio-cultural norms and role expectations that support female subordination and dependency are transmitted in the home, the work place, the peer group, the military and the media: "Those norms pervade our legal system, our literary works, and our everyday discourse."[22] Susan Griffin, noting the deleterious effects of male genderfication and the inextricable linking of "masculinity" and war, states:

> Masculinity and the requirements of gender have a way of surrounding a life. Family history, the tradition of class, military training are as if at the

edge of our invisible army that is sequestered in the background, blending in so well, it can hardly be seen. To become a man, according to society's idea of manhood, seems to be an act of nature.[23]

Both women and men are besieged by an army of societal rules that perpetuate male aggression and female victimization.

The "choice" of female victimization also suggests what feminist existential theory has explained to be the internalization of Otherness that women, as an oppressed group in a sexist culture, experience. As Simone de Beauvoir, among others, has pointed out, women, having been denied their transcendental status as Subject and having been defined solely as Other, come to identify themselves through the gaze of the dominant group, and seek approval as Object.[24] Impatient with Lily, Maria and Charlotte's passivity, the reader, in spite of Didion's avowed anti-feminist stance in her essays, can simultaneously sympathize with their plights. So, while Didion's early "heroines" seemingly "choose" to remain "perpetual adolescents" (WA 117), fleeing adult commitments, wallowing, at times, in their narcissism and self-indulgent pain, their stories evoke not only impatience but compassion, almost as if Didion-the-novelist is unknowingly questioning the validity of the premise, espoused by Didion-the-essayist, that no one forces a woman to buy the package.

However, unlike her predecessors, Inez Victor in *Democracy* eventually refuses to "buy the package." Even more significant than her rejection of and victory over predatory male figures in her life is that the long, arduous process by which Inez extricates herself from male-authored scripts and demands, and the psychological price she pays for having remained trapped within her role as the "candidate's wife" reveal a more sympathetic understanding on Didion's part of women's position in postmodern America. While not embracing an unqualified endorsement of feminist principles, *Democracy* does point to a more sensitive awareness of the complexities inherent in the struggle of women to achieve an identity and sense of self independent of their roles as wife and mother; it also represents a shift away from the naive, reductive views expressed in "The Women's Movement" and the narcissistic inertia of her earlier heroines. An analysis of the earlier texts with regard to the phenomenon of women and violence will provide a clearer understanding of the pivotal position of *Democracy* in the Didion canon.

The female protagonists in Didion's three early novels—*Run River*, *Play It As It Lays* and *A Book of Common Prayer*—are remarkably similar in their paradoxical ability to survive potentially self-destructive relationships by adopting the seemingly passive role of the female victim. While Charlotte of *A Book of Common Prayer* may indeed transcend at times her own personal affairs and enter the more global sphere of political strife, Lily and Maria remain, as Hanley observes, "neurotic, well-heeled West Coast women whose brushes with the nuclear peril or the wars around the world are rare, accidental and unexamined."[25] In a rather telling comment, Didion, responding to the accusation leveled at her by feminist critics that her female characters tend to be rather passive and aimless, states: "I think there is confusion between passive and successful. Passive simply means passive and active means active. Active doesn't imply success."[26] Lily, Maria and Charlotte all appear to be fragile characters, but each manages to survive the cruelties of more powerful men; despite the fact that each of these women perceives herself as "de afuera," as alienated from herself and her societal role as either mother or wife, or as caught within the web of unsatisfying marriages or love affairs, she embraces her despair, nurtures her pain and manipulates others to respond to her, to cater to her own victimization. As Samuel Coale notes with regard to these early heroines: "Victimization becomes a woman's vision and, curiously enough, self-protection."[27]

Ironically, then, it is precisely because of their stereotypic passivity that these women persist; they "choose" to coincide with an externally-imposed definition in order to survive. Didion's early heroines display what feminist Meredith Tax has described as a colonized mentality, for they are keenly aware that their survival depends upon their pleasing the male Other and they are "tuned into the nuances of social behavior so that they can please those whom it is essential to please";[28] they have, in other words, strategically "bought the package" and acquiesced to societal demands that they function within traditional sex-role expectations, but the price they pay is very high. Each manifests the classic symptoms of female depression (e.g. despair, low self-esteem) which psychologists have found to be linked to a woman's subordinate position in society.[29] Never attempting to extricate themselves from their desultory, dependent lifestyles, Lily, Maria and Charlotte flounder in a psychological morass of pain and self-pity that leaves them feeling numb and hopeless. While "active doesn't [always] imply success," neither does "passive" insure happiness or well-being, despite society's dictates regarding proper female behavior. Didion's early heroines survive but they do not thrive. Far from achieving any modicum of success, either professionally or personally, each, to a varying degree, remains emotionally stagnant and bereft of a future of promise.

Stagnant River Matrons: *Run River*

Lily, in *Run River*, represents very clearly the traditional American woman of the 1940's and 1950's who married young, had children, and sought to establish an identity in terms of the conventional model of housewife and mother. Taking place in the countryside above Sacramento, Lily Knight McClellan's story is a tale of "paradise lost,"[30] unfolding against the backdrop of a vanishing edenic West, a "traditional agrarian culture which is being destroyed by the solipsistic values of the postwar boom."[31] Lily and her husband, Everett, both the offspring of twelve generations of ranchers, now witness the modernization of the frontier, the destruction of open spaces in favor of industry and aerospace technology. It is within this framework of a deteriorating cultural *milieu* that Lily McClellan emerges as a victim not only of demanding men but of her own learned passivity and dependency.

Marrying Everett not out of love but rather societal expectation, Lily leaves the protective home of her father to enter the security of an adult relationship. However, Lily herself is quite young, and when she has two children of her own and then is separated from Everett during the War, she begins to engage in a series of extramarital relationships that helps to contribute to the deterioration of the marriage. Impregnated by one of her lovers, Joe, Lily aborts the child in San Francisco. Aware of her infidelity, Everett, upon returning home, grows increasingly distant from and critical of his wife. Complicating their relationship is the character of Martha McClellan, Everett's sister, whose devotion to her brother is redolent with incestuous implications. She competes with Lily for her brother's attention, and when her opportunistic lover, Ryder Channing, marries another woman, Martha commits suicide. As the twenty-year period of the novel comes to a close, Lily, estranged from Everett, becomes amorously involved with Ryder, and it is the occasion of her *rendezvous* with him that serves to open the novel. Everett Knight shoots Ryder, and as he and Lily await the arrival of the police, the narrator recalls the past twenty-year period that has culminated in this act of violence. Beginning with the death of Ryder Channing, *Run River* ends with a second shot as Everett Knight takes his own life.

The least experimental of her works, *Run River* approaches the genre of conventional realism in its relative absence of white space and visual silences and, as Winchell notes, its preference for "straightforward exposition" over "arcane technical experiments."[32] Since much of the novel is told through Lily's omniscient third-person narration, we come to understand her thought processes and her reactions. While Didion's later novels will employ the silences and fragmentary exposition of a more experimental minimalism that obliquely convey the female protagonist's confrontation with the void at the center of her role as a woman in conventional society, *Run River* directly presents a woman who, as one critic notes, "functions minimally, but has lost her direction, identity and will."[33]

Didion goes to great narrative lengths to provide the reader with the necessary background to understand the origins of Lily's conventional lifestyle. Lily Knight was sold the package of traditional sex-stereotypes at an early age by a father, Walter Knight, a strong-willed, aristocratic rancher, who assumed the decision-making process in the family, relegated his wife, Edith, to the status of an accessory and expressed his love for Lily in a series of commonplaces—"Take care of yourself. Do you need any money. Write" (RR 31). It was also Walter Knight who, out of a self-proclaimed sense of *"noblesse oblige,"* hired a Mexican, whom he did not trust, to run the ranch while he spent every afternoon courting his paramour, Rita Blanchard, at the "white frame house on Thirty-eighth Street." When Lily, at age sixteen, suggests to her father that she is worried because she may not fit in with the family's long line of successful individuals who "wanted things and got them" (RR 32), Walter Knight responds paternalistically by saying, "I'll do the worrying." Lily remains her father's "princess" even after he loses the election for the California governorship, viewing him as the victim of a changing world who lost to a candidate who will usher California into the modern era of land reform and technology. That Lily's sense of self and of her identity remain so dependent upon her role as Walter Knight's "princess" and daughter is reflected in her response to his death in a car accident with Rita Blanchard, years later: "I am not myself if my father is dead" (RR 73).

As strong-willed and determined as her father is, Lily's mother remains somewhat of a cipher, content with occupying the shadowy background to an ambitious man and with watching the L.A. Dodgers play baseball on television. Reflecting the stereotypic demeanor expected of women of her generation, Edith Knight acts as hostess to numerous dinner parties, many of which include, among the guests, Rita Blanchard. Edith Knight participates in a marriage that is held together less by the passion of mutual fulfillment than by the weighty heritage of Old West propriety. Their perfunctory display of love, exhibited at every party, belies the lack of spontaneous, genuine affection between Edith and Walter, and captures the passive dependency of this river matron:

> There seemed a tacit promise between them, lasting the duration of each party: all they had ever seen or heard of affectionate behavior was brought to bear upon those evenings. One might have thought them victims to a twenty-year infatuation. As they said good night at the door, Edith Knight would stand in front of him and lean back on his chest, her face...radiant, her manner...languorous, her smallness, against Walter Knight's bulk, proof of her helplessness, her dependence, her very love. (RR 38)

Edith Knight's self-effacing role as the wife of an aristocratic rancher and Walter Knight's definition of his daughter as his "little princess" conjoined to produce a female child whose sense of identity and self-worth remain a function of her connection to a perceived stronger male figure.

Lily Knight's educational career at Berkeley was short-lived, for Lily had never been seriously encouraged to pursue intellectual goals or a profession. When she decided to drop out of school and marry Everett Knight, she was, in effect, following in the line of Knight and McClellan women who, having never been exposed to the possibilities of alternative roles for women, relinquished any bid for an autonomous identity and, instead, assumed the role of the "river matron" (RR 68). She was also succumbing to the societal pressure imposed upon young American women in the 1950's to sacrifice educational and career goals to more "feminine" pursuits, such as marriage and motherhood:

> Over and over women heard voices of tradition and of Freudian sophistication that they could desire no greater destiny than to glory in their own femininity. Experts told them how to catch a man and keep him, how to breastfeed children and handle their toilet-training...They were taught to pity the neurotic, unfeminine unhappy women who wanted to be poets or physicists or presidents. They learned that truly feminine women do not want careers, higher education, political rights—the independence that the old-fashioned feminists "fought for."[34]

Yet, haunting Lily's decision to "buy the package" is a gnawing doubt, not only concerning her feelings for Everett, but also regarding her role as wife, mother and hostess on the McClellan ranch. Trying to emulate the proper social custom of holding afternoon luncheons for the ladies from the adjacent ranches, Lily realizes, on one occasion, that despite the accolades heaped upon her for her hospitality, the afternoon get-together "had not quite worked":

It was nothing she had done or not done. It was simply that there existed between her and other women a vacuum in which overtures faded out, voices became inaudible, connections broke. (RR 73)

Her inability to connect with other women suggests not so much a self-imposed isolation from others as much as a lack of interest in the conventional "female" talk at such affairs, "the exchange of recipes," etc. (RR 77) and a failure to coincide fully with the feminine role she is playing. While Lily by no means consciously ponders her own displacement within the context of the performative nature of gender roles—Lily's failure to exercise any type of salient self-evaluation is one of her most annoying attributes—she does, through her *ennui* and her intuited discontent, tacitly sense the fictive dimension of the conventional stereotype of femininity. Lily is one of those women who, as Gilbert and Gubar note, "work at being female" but whose "strategies of impersonation" do not quite work, thus leaving them unfulfilled and alienated.[35]

Lily's role as mother is also alien to her, maternal affection apparently an emotion she has to strive for rather than something that comes naturally. Lily's detached concern for her two children, Julie and Knight, reveals a woman who is plagued by the sense that she is improvising as both mother and wife, lacking a knowledge that other women seemingly innately possess:

Mary Knight, her mother, the nuns in the corridor: they all seemed to know something she did not. Well she had at least given Everett what he wanted. Even Martha could scarcely have given him two children. But she could not escape the uneasy certainty that she had done so herself only by way of some intricate deception, that her entire life with Everett was an improvisation, dependent upon cues she might one day fail to hear, characterizations she might at any time forget. (RR 87)

The "improvisational" quality of Lily's life—her performing the role of Everett's wife and mother of their children—suggests again that Lily may be implicitly confirming what gender theorists like Judith Butler would later maintain, namely, that "gender is a kind of persistent impersonation that passes as the real," and that "being female constitutes more of a cultural performance than a natural fact."[36] Lily's failure to connect with other women of her generation who, as Friedan argues, were undoubtedly feeling the same sense of displacement and lack of "feminine fulfillment in their lives,"[37] may reflect the self-indulgent inertia of a pampered middleclass woman, but it may also point to the critical absence of what Felski calls a "feminist public sphere" in the 1950's, that is, a "discursive space" within which women could connect with each other as members of a gender-oppressed group.[38]

Far from remaining a "fascinating blank" who was "spawned in a closed Edenic valley world,"[39] Lily Knight emerges as a woman who painfully senses her displacement in a world in which females are raised to be ornamental, dependent creatures. Lily is deprived of the connection of the "I" to the "We," a liberating space that would open up the possibility of shared experiences and potential political action.[40] Hemmed in by learned gender roles and plagued by a failure to coincide with societal expectations, Lily exists in a claustrophobic space not even her own, perceiving herself to be an intruder in her husband's house and, therefore, remaining "upstairs as much as possible, nervous whenever she went downstairs that she was intruding upon the family she continued to think of as the McClellans" (RR 69). "Marriage," sociologist Anne Campbell tells us, "is bad for women's mental health," for data show that "married women have higher rates of neuroses and stress-related complaints than either married men or single women"; and it is the "claustrophobia of the nuclear family"[41] that Lily, in part, suffers from in her life with Everett. Reminiscent of the images of stale air and confinement that punctuate Sylvia Plath's *The Bell Jar*, Lily's stirrings of discontentment, although less focused than those of Plath's narrator, perhaps find adequate expression in Plath's poem "A Birthday Present":

> If you only knew how the veils were killing my days.
> To you they are only transparencies, clear air.
> But my god, the clouds are like cotton
> Armies of them. They are carbon monoxide.
> Sweetly, sweetly I breathe in,
> Filling my veins with invisibles, with the million
> Probable motes that tick the years off my life...[42]

That Lily is suffocating in such an existence, that, as the narrator tells us, "she had not been able to breathe for months" (RR 128), and yet remains ensconced in a life style dependent upon male approval are factors that reveal a woman who is painfully aware of her own insignificance, but who lacks the energy and will to extricate herself from an unfulfilling, yet familiar pattern of female behavior.

Despite her profound unhappiness, Lily seemingly "chooses" to perpetuate the male-defined pattern of behavior, inculcated in her as a child, of identifying herself in terms of a male figure—as her father's "princess," as Everett's wife and mother of his children, as Joe's lover, and as Ryder Channing's lover. The reader's impatience with Lily stems not so much from her having "bought the package," for many women of her generation were lured with false promises of self-fulfillment into the same societal trap of dependency and self-abnegation. Rather, our sympathy for her as an "entrapped" woman in a male-dominated world begins to abate once we realize that her anger, her doubts and her basic disgust with her own life fail to generate any modicum of psychological growth or any attempt on her part to envision alternatives. We can pity her psychological bondage to feminine stereotypes, but we decry the appalling lack of imagination and apparent inertia of this "well-heeled West Coast woman." Didion has created a character who, as part of an economically privileged class, remains free from "scut work" and yet fails to use her leisure time to ameliorate her situation. Lily is a character who, like Snow White, lacks courage and imagination, a character who senses her own victimization by men but fails to, or does not care to, raise the visceral awareness of her situation to a level of conscious acknowledgment. Her expressions of anger are sporadic and do not constitute progressions in a process of emotional growth. For example, Lily, in an outburst of rage, rejects Joe when he begins to play with the idea of marrying her, despite the fact that both he and Lily know that he will never divorce his wife. Asking him what he would give if she left Everett, Joe responds:

> "What do you mean, What would I give?"
> "Would you cut off your right arm?"
> "Yes. I'd cut off my right arm. What's the matter with you?"
> "That's right. You'd cut off your right arm." Lily paused. "*You all would.* Listen. You get out now but listen to me first: you think you've got some *claim on me*? You think it was some special thing that made any difference to me? Listen to me. Nothing we did matters to me." (RR 217 emphases mine)

Despite her cynical acknowledgment of the promised sacrifices that the men in her life profess they will make for her, Lily continues to place herself in a position of vulnerability to them, in a position that results, at times, in her being violently claimed by a male figure.

Informing Lily and Everett's marriage is a hostility that manifests itself in long periods of non-communication, bursts of anger and a blending of violence and love-making that reveal Lily's acceptance of a dimension of brutality in all male-female relationships. The year 1952, following Martha's death and Lily's abortion, is described as "the year they seldom talked" (RR 218), and when they did talk, their only subject of conversation was Lily's abortion, each using it "as the heaviest weapon in both their arsenals, the massive retaliation each withheld until all else had been exhausted" (RR 219). Described in martial terms, their marital spats erupt in outbursts of mutual antagonism in which acts of male-initiated violence are followed by moments of tenderness. Whereas Barthelme's minimalistic omissions and ominous silences comically yet frighteningly portray the vulnerability of the woman in "The Captured Woman," Didion's narrative fullness and fleshing out of Lily's tenacious hold on a child-like dependency partially undercut the reader's sympathy for her plight. Note the following scene between Everett and Lily at the end of one of their disputes:

> She could not sleep, she said, in the same room with him. She had managed to sleep, he said, in the same room with plenty of other people, hadn't she? No, she had not. And what did it matter if she had. When had he ever cared. He had slapped her then as she twisted away, and he took her in her arms and it was all right again for a while. *It's going to be all right baby*, he said...and she said over and over *Please Christ Everett keep us*. (RR 226)

The reader knows Lily too well at this point and has witnessed her rather passive acceptance of her role in an unfulfilling marriage. Acquiescing to Everett's infantilization of her, Lily, in effect, has remained emotionally stagnant, having gone from being her father's "princess" to Everett's "baby," a dependent creature who needs to be rescued.[43]

It is precisely the image of female dependency and its frequent corollary, female victimization, that informs one of the most revealing episodes in the novel, Lily's encounter with a man on her flight home from Italy. A variation on novelist Erica Jong's "the zipless fuck"—the no-strings-attached, quick sexual encounter with a stranger—this particular incident discloses Lily's complete lack of maturation in developing an autonomous sense of self that can muster the courage to repel what it intuitively finds onerous but what society has deemed to be appropriate male behavior toward women. Seated next to an intoxicated, salacious man who evidently finds her to be worthy of his predatory attention—"You're skinny but you're good-looking," he tells her (RR 228)—Lily, although uncomfortable by his presence, "smiled that way at men she did not know, unable to think of anything else to do and wanting them to want her, recognize her as the princess in the tower" (RR

228). Looking for acceptance as the dependent woman but uneasy with her companion, Lily reacts ambivalently, listening to the man's "loving, brutally obscene monologue" as it accompanies the "moan of the engine, the slight vibration of the cold window next to her cheek," as she repeatedly tells him, "Be quiet," "I don't want it," and "Don't talk that way" (RR 229). Filtered through Lily's consciousness, the third-person omniscient narration leaves the reader convinced of both Lily's attraction to him—when he fell asleep "she rather missed the sound of his voice," and her obvious "distaste" (RR 229-230).

By commingling love and brutality in this episode, Didion makes it difficult to empathize with Lily's susceptibility to a predatory male figure. Feminists such as Sandra Bartky who have focused on the internalization of male predatory attitudes by women that results in women's viewing themselves as sexual objects, would undoubtedly label this episode as an example of a "ritual of subjugation";[44] while we can sympathize with Lily's desire to please the oppressive Other, that is, to acquiesce to and participate in a societally-sanctioned, ritualized assault upon her own person, we simultaneously grow impatient with her passivity. For much of the episode is couched in the violent language of rape: his monologue is "brutally obscene"; "Did she know what he wanted to do *to her*"; "Did she know what he was going to do *to her*?" (emphases mine). However, from Lily's perspective, the obscene mutterings are also "loving" and, one might argue, appealing enough for her to retain her seat. Clearly, Didion has conveyed to the reader that Lily's "no" means, if not a "yes," at least a definite "maybe." In doing so, the author has reinforced the conventional myth, debunked by Brownmiller,[45] that women, even when they have the opportunity to avoid or defuse potentially dangerous situations, welcome submission to male brutality. As we shall see, Pynchon plays with this idea of inverse logic—when "no" means "yes"—in the sexual/aggressive dynamics between men and women, but he does so against the more universal schema of the limitations inherent in binary thinking. No such epistemological questions are at issue here for Didion. Intent upon driving home the total passivity and complete absence of self-awareness of the heroine, the author has Lily conclude, when queried by Everett—that she "had of course" moved her seat, hadn't she—that "she could not see then why she had not" (RR 230).

Lily Knight McClellan remains a stagnant, childishly dependent woman in her relationships with men, unhappy yet never willing to "move her seat," and thus the reader grows impatient with her complaints, her dalliances in dead-end relationships, and her seemingly self-indulgent inertia. That she manages to survive while those around her falter—her father dies, Everett kills Ryder and himself, and Joe goes limping back to his wife—ironically suggests that she is stronger than the men who she feels are controlling her, a fact that again serves to diminish the reader's sympathy for her as a "victim." While Lily, in part, suffers from what Betty Friedan called "the problem that has no name," that is, the inescapable sense of discontent that accompanies one's blind acceptance of the feminine mystique and one's "adjustment to the feminine role,"[46] her lack of introspection with respect to her position as a woman and her failure to move beyond a self-destructive dependency leave the reader sympathetic to and frustrated with her passivity.

Didion, in effect, has created a paradoxical female character, one who pulls the reader in opposing directions. The author's retrospective, narrative fullness, by disclosing a child who was raised to be a river matron and encouraged to pursue no other alternative than the traditional role of wife and mother, seems aimed at eliciting sympathy for Lily's confinement to an unfulfilling sex-stereotype; on the other hand, Lily's negative traits—her infidelities, her absence of adult responsibilities, and her childish dependency and narcissism—remind us of the "perpetual adolescents" that Didion-the-essayist had attacked in *The White Album*. Perhaps the ambiguity inherent in Lily's characterization reflects Didion's own unexplored lack of confidence in her rather untenable premise that women, to avoid male exploitation, simply need not "buy the package." Again, Didion-the-essayist seems to be somewhat at odds with Didion-the-novelist.

Female Bondage: *Play It As It Lays*

Like Lily, who unquestioningly takes all of her cues for proper female behavior from a society that entraps women in restrictive stereotypes, Maria Wyeth, in *Play It As It Lays*, succumbs to the dictates of importuning male figures, some of whom are unabashedly exploitive in their treatment of her. As one critic notes, "Maria *accepts* a life with men in which she is a *victim* of their need and indifference."[47] As in Lily's case, Maria's acceptance of her own victimization may, in effect, indicate a survivalist's strategy of masochistic passivity, but her concomitant absence of independent thinking and her failure to engage in a reflective analysis that would enable her to extricate herself from learned patterns of self-destructive behavior will, at times, strain the reader's capacity to sympathize with her plight.

As a female who is surrounded by opportunistic men who are, as Mickelson observes, "moral bankrupts,"[48] Maria, like Lily, reflects a literary archetype, popular in American literature, of the oppressed woman entrapped within a triad of exploitive males.[49] Like Lily, who felt unfulfilled by three men—Everett, Joe and Ryder, Maria bounces from Ivan to Carter to Les, futilely searching for an elusive sense of stability in the hedonistic cultural milieu of Hollywood that notoriously reduces women to their sexual marketability. Told in eighty-four brief chapters of 214 pages, *Play It As It Lays* employs a fragmented narrative method that is more experimental and minimalistic in its technique than *Run River*. The abundant white spaces, the staccato-like fragments of the shifting, first-person perspectives of Maria, Helene and Carter, interspersed by a limited third person narration, employ, as Wilde observes, a "vocabulary of disorder," a "syntax of parataxis" and "the expectation of irresolution" that also characterize Barthelme's texts and qualify Maria as a "connoisseur of chaos."[50] Not only the novel's *images* and Maria's first-person narrative revelations but also the minimalistic visual silences—the ever-increasing white space—serve to limn the female protagonist's growing alienation from herself and others, again emphasizing the price a woman pays for "buying the package" of female dependency.

Play It As It Lays was published two years after the appearance of *Slouching Towards Bethlehem*, Didion's compilation of her journalistic, minimalistic essays that not only presents a kaleidescopic view of the sociopolitical "wreckage" of 1960's America but also emerges as a "spiritual biography"[51] of a writer in crisis, a writer who, alluding to Yeats' "The Second Coming," senses that the cultural disintegration engulfing her is an objective correlative of her own internal dissolution of self. Referring to the title piece, in which she presents the entropic wasteland of America through the concrete images of the Haight-Ashbury district of San Francisco, Didion remarks:

> It was the first time that I had dealt directly and flatly with the evidence of atomization, the proof that things fall apart: I went to San Francisco because I had not been able to work for some months, had been paralyzed by the conviction that writing was an irrelevant act, that the world as I had understood it no longer existed. If I was able to work again at all, it would be necessary for me to come to terms with disorder. (STB xi-xii)

Just as Pynchon invokes part of the second law of thermodynamics, the principle of entropy, both as thematic content and as structural device in his novels, so too does Didion translate her sensitivity to both the external cultural disintegration and her private psychological malaise into a pervasive metaphor of the writer struggling to impose order upon chaos, to retrieve meaning from absurdity. If, as Evan Carton argues, "the drama of America—at least as America has been constructed in our literary and political rhetoric—has always been the drama of the self,"[52] then Didion's sense that "the center cannot hold" applies not only to the cultural matrix but to the self, to her *self*. It is precisely this destabilization of an identity, and her attempt to re-collect the fragments and to reconstruct some form of self, that become the pivotal enterprise in much of her writing from this point forward. The proliferation of white space and the kaleidoscope of fragmented images that inform *Slouching Towards Bethlehem* are strategies of a minimalism that will reappear in *Play It As It Lays*. For Didion, minimalism becomes a technique by which she will try to re-assemble a self, to put the "pieces" back together again; this "self" will eventually resemble neither the purely isolated, unitary ego of her former frontier individualism nor the purely decentered textual construct of poststructuralist theory. For Didion, subjectivity will emerge as a hybrid of a textual *persona and* a "core self" that is always in the process of becoming and that is, as Jane Flax argues, formed by important social relations, including the mother-child connection, the sexual division of labor,[53] and, I would add, gender stereotyping. *Play It As It Lays* and *A Book of Common Prayer* are stages along the way in Didion's formulation of a "self," and it is not until *Democracy* that such a concept emerges most fully in the characters of Didion-the-author and Inez Victor.

The very opening chapter of *Play It As It Lays* underscores the emotional vulnerability and fragility of Maria Wyeth, who, confined to a mental institution, provides the background necessary to understand the forces that have contributed to the gradual disintegration of her personality. Taking place primarily in Hollywood, the rest of the novel provides episodic and fragmented glimpses of the people and events that have preceded her mental breakdown: her failure to work as an actress for more than a year; her failed marriage to Carter, a movie director who starred his wife in a movie, "Angel Beach," in which she is gang-banged by a motorcycle gang and which he is not above sharing with his male friends in private showings; her demeaning and humiliating affair with Ivan Costello, a sadistic exploiter of women, and her fling with Johnny Waters, a self-centered, insensitive actor; her inability to "rescue" her brain-damaged daughter, Kate, from the institution to which she is confined; her guilt-ridden decision to abort a child, not certain of the father's identity—either Carter or Les, one of her more caring lovers, fathered the child; and her witnessing the suicide of her gay friend and wife-beater, BZ, who, "unable to play" the game anymore in an absurd world where nothingness abounds, swallows thirty capsules of Seconal.

While Henderson is correct to a certain extent in arguing that Maria is "both a victim of [Hollywood society's] values and a cause of her own undoing,"[54] again explaining the reader's mixture of sympathy for and condemnation of Maria's situation, the protagonist's *choices* and *decisions* themselves have been shaped by a socialization process that fosters low self-esteem and often self-denigration in women. To label her simply a "narcissistic personality" whose victimization is due not to society but to herself[55] is to fail to illuminate the sexist, political dimension of the text. To analyze her breakdown solely in terms of the isolated "causes" enumerated above without considering the more pervasive and abiding condition, namely, her position as "Other," that is, as a woman in a male-empowered environment, is to ignore the complexities inherent in her situation. David Geherin has argued against the reductive nature of viewing Maria's condition solely from a medical point of view:

> Viewed from a medical point of view, she might well be classified as a near schizoid personality whose experiences have perpetrated a severe emotional crisis resulting in a loss of an integrated personality. In a more profound sense, however, her sickness is neither emotional or psychological: it is ontological. She is suffering not from a nervous breakdown, but from the breakdown of a world around her which threatens to engulf her whole being with nothingness.[56]

There is, as Geherin goes on to prove, much evidence in the text to support his thesis that Maria, like the existential heroes of Camus and Sartre, suffers from the paralyzing shock of an encounter with the void. However, while her crisis does manifest an ontological insecurity in the face of nothingness, it is her *political* position in society—that is, her relative lack of self-empowerment in a male-dominated culture, that constitutes her overwhelming sense of vulnerability.

Maria's sickness is neither emotional nor psychological: it is political. The novel's opening narrative, delivered by Maria from the mental institution, connects Maria to a past and future of wounded or damaged women in the text, who, in one form or another, have been the objects of male neglect or exploitation. In Chapter 27, which deals with one of Maria's return trips to her home in Silver Wells, Nevada, we discover that her mother, Francine, who is noted for her culinary talents, is suffering from depression and that none of the men takes her malady seriously. Her father's business partner, Benny, tells Maria:

"Your mom's O.K, don't worry about your mom...Believe me it's nothing."
"What's nothing? What's the matter with her?"
"Nothing in God's earth, Maria...You might say she's a little depressed, naturally your father doesn't want to talk about it." (PIAIL 85)

Complimenting Francine on her meal, Benny and Harry Wyeth seriously suggest that she market her culinary expertise by opening a string of fast food franchises: "I'm talking about a quantity operation. Franchises, you rent out your name and your receipt," advises Benny. Ignoring Francine's expressed aversion to their scheme to co-opt her cooking talents, and unconcerned with Francine's depression or with Maria's desire not to return to Hollywood, Harry, who "did not look at his wife or daughter," continues to cajole Maria to go back to where he thinks she can make money, that is, where "she can win at the table," and to berate his wife for not pursuing his idea of a commercial enterprise: "'She can't win if she's not at the table, Francine.' Harry Wyeth threw down his napkin and stood up. 'You wouldn't understand that'" (PIAIL 86-87). As Cynthia Griffin Wolff observes regarding this telling scene: "The dinner table does a slow fade into a crap table" as "the mother's moral and emotional concerns must yield to the father's monied dreams."[57] While Francine's subsequent suicide cannot be clearly attributed solely to such neglect and lack of emotional support, her close association with two opportunistic businessmen, one of whom is her husband, leaves her vulnerable to depression.

Like *Democracy*, *Play It As It Lays* depicts three generations of emotionally "lost" females, a matrilineal legacy of wounded women who have been separated from each other by the men in their lives. Referring to Didion's psychological breakdown in the late 1960's, Sandra Hinchman notes that Maria Wyeth is living solely in the narrative present of the asylum and that Maria, like Didion for a time, "perceives no coherent narrative connecting the component scenes of one's life," so that the "bonds between past, present and future start to corrode."[58] Recent feminist analyses of the mother-daughter bond may help to illuminate the fragmented, temporal experience of Maria Wyeth. In her seminal work, *The Mother-Daughter Plot*, Marianne Hirsch argues that the inability of female characters to assemble meaningful narrative patterns, a characteristic of some postmodern texts, may reflect a disruption in the mother-daughter connection often brought about by the patriarchal institution of motherhood. Hirsch maintains that mothers are inscribed within a "heterosexuality of discourse" that requires daughters (and sons) to objectify their mothers and to break free from them so that they may move on to produce men and other potential mothers of men.[59] That is to say, traditional narrative discourse is oedipal in that "sexual difference is constituted as difference between male subjectivity and female objectification."[60] Daughters, therefore, participate within this discursive register to objectify, silence and distance themselves from their mothers so that they too will be objectified and silenced as mothers in the future. Turning to *Play It As It Lays*, *A Book of Common Prayer* and *Democracy*, we find that patriarchal institutions that objectify and silence women do indeed play pivotal roles in disrupting the bonds between mothers and daughters. If the development of a core self for women is dependent upon "the construction of identity in relationships,"[61] it is not surprising to encounter the fragmented narrative of Maria Wyeth who is confined to living in the present in a mental institution, separated from her mother and daughter.

As the opening image of Maria in a mental institution harkens back to her emotionally damaged mother, so too does it look ahead to the plight of her wounded daughter, Kate, who is permanently hospitalized. There are hints in the text that Kate, the ultimate symbol of the helpless female dependent upon male institutional care, suffers from neglect: "The last time [Maria] went to the hospital Kate's hair was tangled…they never brushed Kate's hair" (PIAIL 43); the female nurse in charge of Kate appears as an ominous figure, a stereotype of the masculinized, unfeeling pill-pusher and controller that was immortalized by Ken Kesey's Nurse Ratched in *One Flew Over the Cuckoo's Nest*: "the nurse had short hair and a faint moustache…and Maria did not like her" (PIAIL 71). Consigned to the hospital by Carter, a father who never even visits her, Kate unknowingly retains a tenuous connection to the outside world with a mother who, herself, is now confined to an institution that seems intent upon inscribing her experience within what Derrida has labelled a "phallogocentric" tradition; all female discourse is appropriated into a male-dominated, male-engendered and male-centered language of rigid, hierarchical binary oppositions that, as French feminist Hélène Cixous argues, elevate the phallus to the status of the self-evident ground of all knowledge and concomitantly subordinate women to the realm of marginality and silence.[62] Translating "phallogocentric" as "cocksure," critic Terry Eagleton observes: "It is this cocksureness by which those who wield sexual and social power maintain their grip."[63] Having reached back to a mother for affection and understanding, and now living only to rescue her daughter from the institution, Maria constitutes the connective link in what Henderson calls a "chain of love" in the novel,[64] a matrilineal chain that is systematically ignored not only by the psychiatrists in the hospital, who are concerned only with knowing whether or not "Maria projects a *cock* in this inkblot," but also by men in an exploitive and insensitive Hollywood industry that can inquire, after seeing Maria gang-raped in "Angel Beach":

> [H]ow did Maria feel about the gangbang, the twelve *cocks*, did she get the sense that they're doing it not to her but to each other, does that interest her...? (PIAIL 110; emphasis mine)

Maria is trapped within a patriarchal world view that mistakenly presupposes a female desire for aggressive, potentially brutal male behavior, a reductive world view of powerful "cocks" and subservient "cunts."

Maria's reduction to a "cunt," a sexist synecdoche, informs many of her relationships with men in the novel. On one occasion, she sleeps with an actor, Johnny Waters, whom she does not know and who uses her solely as a means to initiate a drug-heightened sexual pleasure. The following exchange captures her enforced passivity and sexual submissiveness and anticipates the more fully developed "pornographic" episodes in *Gravity's Rainbow*:

> ...the moment before he came he reached under the pillow and pulled out an amayl nitrite popper and broke it under his nose, breathed in rapidly, and closed his eyes.
> "Don't move," he said. "*I said don't move.*"
> *Maria did not move.*
> "Terrific"...
> "Wake me up in three hours," he said. "With your tongue." (PIAIL 152, emphases mine)

When Maria awakes and borrows his car to go home, he has her arrested for auto theft. Once he discovers that she is the wife of a director and that he may be blackballed in the industry, he rescinds the charges, telling her: "Just hold on, *cunt...You never told me who you were*" (PIAIL 156). Still a "cunt," Maria evidently rises in stature by being recognized as Carter Lang's wife, that is, by being associated with a powerful "cock" in the movie industry.

While her relationship with Carter is far more complex than her transient affairs, there is also here a pervasive sense of entrapment, of subtle exploitation and a feeling that Maria is being remade or recreated to fulfill a Hollywood image of women as the passive, sexualized creature, the "cunt." Just as the actor "directed" her to heighten his sexual pleasure, with little regard for her feelings, so too does Carter, in a very commercially exploitive manner, direct his wife in pornographic films that titillate male fantasies of sexualized aggression, films that emphasize both her passivity and her vulnerability.[65] Carter directed Maria in two movies, one entitled "Maria" that was never distributed:

> The picture showed Maria doing a fashion sitting, Maria asleep on a couch at a party, Maria on the telephone...Maria cleaning some marijuana, Maria crying in the IRT. At the end she was thrown into a negative and looked dead. (PIAIL 19)

Maria herself did not like the movie because "the girl on the screen...had no knack for anything" (PIAIL 20). While the first movie emphasizes her "negative" passivity, "Angel Beach" underscores her sexual vulnerability to male brutality and grossed in one year "just under eight million dollars" (PIAIL 18). Maria's role as sexual victim in "Angel Beach" is emblematic of her role as Johnnie Waters' submissive lover and later as Carter Lang's abused wife. Her acquiescence, her apparent acceptance of such a "pornographic" script, both in front of the camera and in her own personal life, suggests that she too has internalized society's objectification of women, what Adrienne Rich calls the "pernicious message relayed by pornography," namely that:

> [W]omen are natural sexual prey to men and love it; that sexuality and violence are congruent; and that for women sex is essentially masochistic, humiliation pleasurable, physical abuse erotic.[66]

Didion complicates the moral issues surrounding the cinematic exploitation of women by having Maria profess an enjoyment for "Angel Beach," a film that ends with a "shot of Maria strolling across campus," because "the girl on the screen seemed to have a definite knack for controlling her own destiny" (PIAIL 18-19). Given the violent central episode of the film, such a comment strains our credulity, but since Didion provides only a fragmented, minimal view of the film's content, it is difficult to judge the appropriateness of Maria's statement. Yet, one cannot help feeling disconcerted when hearing the young woman in the film, who has just been gang-raped, say, "I look at you and I know *that...what happened* just didn't mean anything" (PIAIL 18). Confined to a male-authored script, the character speaks words that reflect, perhaps, the insensitivity of a culture that has always trivialized rape and implicitly sanctioned male abuse against women. As psychologists note, "The basic heterosexual script in our culture reflects an androcentric heterosexuality that eroticizes sexual inequality and supports male dominance as normal and natural."[67] Furthermore, while Maria's enjoyment of the film may indicate her internalization of herself as "Other" in a sexist society, it may also point to a common response of women who have been victimized by men. One of the most common and immediate reactions of women to male sexual assault is apathy about life,[68] a psychological numbness that casts a neutral grey shield over the events and people in one's life. Rape therapists have detailed the shock that victims experience and the suspension of normal coping mechanisms that in the initial stage following a rape can allow the victim to distance herself from the horror of having been violated;[69] part of Maria's "enjoyment" of the film seems to stem from her sense that the "*girl on the screen was [not] herself*" (PIAIL 18; emphases mine), a very typical strategic defense mechanism by which a rape victim, either actual or "scripted," can magically retreat from herself into the temporary haven of denial. Such a response, however, may also signify, as Donovan notes, the fundamentally schizophrenic reaction of women that is emblematic of their status in a patriarchal society;[70] that is to say, the male authors have realistically incorporated into their script a common female response to rape by which, as Meredith Tax argues, the victim, a "colonized" member of society, "heals" the wound of her own oppression by shutting it out and claiming, "It's only my body they have abused, it doesn't affect my mind, the real me."[71]

Carter "uses" Maria in his movies to perpetuate a female stereotype of woman as sexual prey. While there are indications in the novel that their relationship was at one time a relatively caring one, their individual infidelities and their inability to communicate, the strain of Kate's condition and Maria's progressive loss of a sense of self erode their marriage so that they come to be antagonists in a perpetual combat. It is during these combative exchanges that Maria feels "trapped" in a meaningless, unfulfilling relationship (PIAIL 31); it is during these combative episodes that Carter would threaten to hit her (PIAIL 175) and "would knock her away" and "paralyze" her with his intense anger, inviting her to "go in that bathroom and take every pill in it"; it is during these combative episodes that Carter, like Johnny Waters, would call her "cunt" and issue a mandate: "Well go to sleep, cunt. Go to sleep. Die. Fucking vegetable" (PIAIL 184); and it is Carter who, angry at Maria's pregnancy, threatens to take Kate if she does not get an abortion:

> "Get a pencil,"he ordered...He was going to give her the telephone number of the only man in Los Angeles who did clean work...
> "I'm not sure I want to do that," she said carefully.
> "All right, don't do it. Go ahead and have this kid." He paused, confident in his hand. She waited for him to play it through. "And I'll take Kate." (PIAIL 54)

Even after Maria agrees to meet his demand to have the abortion, Carter refuses to rescind his threat to take Kate, the only person whom Maria loves: "I'm not promising anything," he said (PIAIL 55). The chapter ends with this ominous tone, leaving Maria to face the silence as we, the readers, confront the haunting white space of the empty page.

While there is no conclusive textual evidence to suggest that Maria would have decided to have this child on her own, her expressed, initial uncertainty about having an abortion raises the possibility, a possibility that Carter threateningly dispels. Carter's demand for an abortion underscores Maria's subordinate position and is consistent with the novel's subtextual acknowledgment of the vulnerability of a woman's body and spirit to male control. Although dismissed by Maria as just a "New York story," the Ceci Delano experience that constitutes Chapter 43 is emblematic of the text's implicit thematic concern with male domination of women's bodies. Unable to secure a legal abortion in New York at the time, Ceci called upon a friend in the D.A.'s office for help:

> "*Quid pro quo*," he had said, and late the same day that Ceci Delano testified to a blue ribbon jury that she had been approached by a party-girl operation, she was admitted to Doctor's Hospital for a legal D&C, arranged for and paid for by the D.A.'s office. (PIAIL 116)

A woman's uterus is indeed a negotiable item in the affairs of city government, just as it is in the dealings of Carter Lang. Both incidents capture the cultural attitude, parodied in *The Dead Father*, that perceives women's reproductive organs as "territory" to be conquered and claimed by more powerful men; such an attitude, as Gilbert and Gubar note, was expressed quite explicitly in 1845 by the American gynecologist Marion Sims who, having inserted a speculum into a human vagina, remarked: "I saw everything as no man had ever seen before...I felt like an explorer...who views a new and important territory."[72] As Gilbert and Gubar go on to observe, "Sims imagined himself as a colonizing and conquering hero...depicting himself as 'Columbus,' the vagina as his 'New World.'"[73]

Reflecting the imperialist attitude of Marion Sims, Carter Lang, like Ivan Costello—one of Maria's lovers who also threatens to prevent her from having a child (PIAIL 141), has claimed Maria's uterus and reproductive process as his own territory, subject to his rule. Just as he created and controlled the image of Maria on film, so too does he seek to co-opt her procreative freedom. In this light, Maria's abortion seems to be more of a male-dictated, ritual sacrifice than an act of free will.

Coerced into having an abortion, Maria again places herself in the position of being treated by cold, insensitive men who are intent upon "directing" her and "silencing" her, and who offer her no emotional support. When Maria arrives at the rendezvous point for her illegal abortion, she is met by a driver who is interested only in discussing the comparative gas mileage of an Eldorado and a Camaro (PIAIL 78). The doctor who performs the abortion rather mechanically and under less than optimum sanitary conditions is intent upon keeping her quiet:

"Hear that scraping, Maria?...That should be the sound of music to you...don't scream Maria, there are people next door...I said don't make any noise, Maria...six weeks from now you'll have a normal period, not this month, this month you just had it, it's in that pail. (PIAIL 82)

The doctor's rather insensitive remark to a woman whose ambivalence about the abortion was never openly explored either by her or anyone else, drives home the horror of the situation. Those critics who look to this incident as a litmus test for determining Didion's stand on abortion miss the pivotal issue here. Whether or not the mechanized procedure and subsequent guilt suffered by Maria reflect an anti-abortion stance on the part of the author is less significant than the fact that Maria was coerced by a more powerful male figure into subjecting her body to an illegal and relatively dangerous procedure in order to terminate a potential life. Even pro-choice advocates, who view abortion as a legitimate right for women, would decry this type of coercion precisely because it denies women the freedom to control their own bodies.

The cinematic rape scene, the abortion, and Maria's reductive status as a "cunt" in the Hollywood milieu are minimalistic images that accumulate to convey her vulnerable position in the novel. Separated from her daughter and her mother, alienated from her own body and deprived of any sense of a core self, Maria flounders in a morass of disconnected images that provides her with no temporal continuity, no sense of what Flax calls a "going-on-being," or a "basic cohesion within herself that makes the fragmentation of experiences something other than a terrifying slide into psychosis."[74]

The matrilineal triad of Maria, her mother and her daughter, Kate, does not exhaust the litany of abused women in this text. For Helene, BZ's wife, wears the evidence of her husband's sadistic love "games." Typical of many wives who have assimilated the cultural myth that they are somehow responsible for their husbands' often violent behavior toward them,[75] Helene recoils in shame from sharing her pain with Maria. Her face bruised and swollen from their drunken romp the night before, Helene tearfully tells Maria, "I don't want to talk about it" (PIAIL 162). When BZ arrives, he responds to his wife's depression by first telling her, "If you can't deal with the morning, get out of the game. You've been around a long time, you know what it is, it's play or pay" (PIAIL 163), and then by hitting her in the face in front of Maria. As a frustrated homosexual, who perhaps engages in sadistic love games to inflict pain upon his wife because she is not a man, BZ is reminiscent of Harry in Hubert Selby's *Last Exit to Brooklyn* (1957), a more expansive, experimental novel that contains one of the most graphic images of blatant misogyny in postmodern American fiction, the gang-rape and mutilation of Tra-la-la. Like BZ, Harry manifests a thinly-disguised misogyny that erupts in a litany of abusive epithets—on more than one occasion he calls his wife a "ballbreakin' cunt" and "no good sonofabitch," and in acts of physical abuse.[76] While Selby's graphic portrayals of male violence against women are similar to Pynchon's in evoking their own unique form of revulsion and disgust from the reader, Didion's withholding of details requires the reader to fill in the silences and white spaces with her own discomforting images.

Perhaps the novel's most frightening minimalistic image of potential male aggression that requires reader participation occurs in a parking lot. Maria, having taken to the freeways in a futile attempt to escape despair, emerges from a phone booth to face a group of bikers who have unsuccessfully tried to break into her car. Facing a situation eerily similar to her role in "Angel Beach," Maria approaches them as they stand in a semi-circle around her car. As she walks toward them "with extreme deliberation" and stares directly at each of them, "she admired the way that she and they together were evolving a choreography, hearing the same beat," their "complicity" so "total" that "one of them leaned across the hood and raised a hand in recognition of what had passed between them" (PIAIL 130). Whether Maria's behavior was courageous or foolhardy remains debatable;

what is clear, however, is that she had a distinct sense of working *with* rather than *against* predatory men, camouflaging her own vulnerability with an aesthetic veil; that is to say, she experienced the situation "abstractly" or cinematically, as a scene, distancing herself from her own potential victimization in much the same way as she did when viewing "Angel Beach." As we shall see, the choreographing of male aggression against women receives explicit treatment by more expansive novelists such as Pynchon and Morrison, but Didion's minimalistic technique conveys the horror more through omission and implication, inviting the reader to fill in the meaning:

> Later those few minutes in the plaza in Oxnard would come back to Maria and she would replay them, change the scenario. It ended that way badly, or well, depending on what you wanted. (PIAIL 130)

Didion has presented us with a woman exploited by others for their commercial success and sexual gratification, who has paid dearly for remaining in what seems to be a voluntary position of subordination. Like Lily, she seemingly acts with a certain degree of complicity to guarantee her own victimization. Bouncing from one unfulfilling relationship to another, bemoaning her sense of despair and numbing her anxiety with drugs, Maria surrounds herself with men who attempt to co-opt her body and spirit, giving herself, as Kazin notes, "to Hollywood hoodlums" while taking no pleasure in her body;[77] she unhappily remains in an industry that accords her little if any control over her own cinematic image or her own identity, an industry that perpetuates a potentially dangerous female stereotype of passivity and sexual vulnerability. Furthermore, while she is not completely bereft of introspective awareness, having concluded at one point that "whatever arrangements were made, they worked less well for women" (PIAIL 46), she does not use this reflective awareness to extricate herself from oppressive situations or to muster the energy and courage to author her own arrangements, to write her own script.

While we are not given the same expansive exposition of a woman's childhood as in *Run River*, the minimalistic images and fragmentary slices of Maria's past obliquely serve to suggest an explanation for her passivity and inertia. Her father's advice to Maria as he encouraged her to go to New York to pursue acting lessons was to "play it as it lays," to confront life as if it were a crap game, to sit back and optimistically cast her fate to a better role of the dice. Such advice counsels an acceptance of the rules of the game and an adherence to traditional gender expectations, rather than an initiative to envision a new game and alternative roles for women, that is, a new mode of life wherein she as a woman could exercise more control over her own destiny by creating her own rules. Maria succumbs to the dictates of a male-empowered culture that reifies women, reducing them to their physical selves or bodies; attempting to conform to the male ideal of female beauty, women again, as Donovan states, face two schizophrenic alternatives: "Either we deny the artificial mask of beauty as unnatural and not our real selves,"[78] or, as Densmore notes, we step into the schizophrenic world of play-acting and narcissism "so that we end up as prisoners of the very object we created in the minds of others and in our own minds."[79] Maria, as we have seen, vascillates between both "choices," alternately opting to deny her body and, at other times, attempting to coincide with an externally-imposed definition of beauty. Ironically, Didion's early female protagonists' inability to envision themselves as autonomous beings contradicts her own aesthetic freedom as a writer who daringly breaks the rules of traditional narrative.

Maria also tells us that the other lesson she learned was "that overturning a rock was apt to reveal a rattlesnake." As Henderson notes, this latter bit of advice teaches fear and passivity, a reluctance to take risks and a contentment with superficiality,[80] perhaps with her "ace"—physical beauty. While not absolving Maria of the responsibility for her "choices," such advice does help to explain the self-destructive choices of a woman whose passive acceptance of her role in an industry and a culture that entrap women in restrictive stereotypes leaves her emotionally depleted and institutionalized. In a telling comment following her "decision" to acquiesce to Carter's demand for an abortion, Maria experiences "a remote sense that everything was happening exactly the way it was supposed to happen" (PIAIL 54), as if by relinquishing control of her body to the chance of the crap game—in this case, a game weighted by Carter's avenging rules, everything would work out for the best. What Maria is experiencing is a sense that everything is happening exactly the way she had been socialized into believing that it should happen by a father and culture that counsel female submissiveness. If life is indeed a crap game, dictated by chance, the dice are usually loaded against women.

Lily and Maria survive, though Maria's psychological damage affords her only a pyrrhic victory and evokes a greater degree of sympathy from the reader than does Lily's plight. While Didion is not writing a feminist tract, she manages, through her rather cutting, "surgical prose"[81] and poignant images, to elicit compassion for a woman who, as Wolff notes, has been subjected not only to the "cuttings" of the abortionist but also to the "cutting" of the film director who can create what he deems her image should be, regardless of her own desires and identity.[82] The overtly brutal acts of male aggression, which Maria has experienced, resonate with a degree of terror that is augmented by the author's minimalistic presentation, her deliberate "cutting" of the storyline into fragmented, truncated scenes interspersed with ominous silences, and her calculated omissions and oblique suggestions of violence that are, for the most part, missing from *Run River*. Her minimalistic narrative technique, reminiscent of Eliot's "heap of broken images" from *The Waste Land*,[82] captures not only the ontological void but also the disintegration of a personality whose philosophical encounter with nothingness, while not a uniquely female experience, is precipitated by her oppression as a woman.

Female Bonds: *A Book of Common Prayer*

Female susceptibility to a more insidious and pervasive form of male aggression is subtly alluded to by an image that receives oblique recognition in *Play It As It Lays*, namely the transformation of Silver Wells, Nevada, Maria's hometown and former mining center, into a nuclear test site. Given Didion's former conservative political bent (she supported Goldwater in 1964) and her nostalgia for a lost American frontier, such an image undoubtedly reflects her aversion to the encroachment of Eastern technology upon the West; however, the inclusion of a nuclear facility, the ultimate symbol of patriarchal violence, in a text in which women are subjected to male abuse, serves also to underscore the more universal threat against women living in a postmodern, military-industrial society. While not evoking as overtly apocalyptic an image as nuclear weaponry, *A Book of Common Prayer* (1977) does, for the first time in Didion's novels, situate a female protagonist in the politically volatile arena of a national revolution, thereby tacitly reinforcing the images and references to male violence perpetrated against women that punctuate the text. *A Book of Common Prayer* retains the minimalistic technique of rapid-fire, sparse scenes, producing what one critic called a "kaleidoscopic effect."[84] The jumbled plot elements unravel in a "spare, sardonic" and "elliptical" prose that Joyce Carol Oates has described as "an art of indirection and emotion withheld."[85] The brevity of the scenes, the shifting settings—Boca Grande, San Francisco and New Orleans, and the oblique treatment of a woman's vulnerability to forces over which she exerts little, if any, control, all combine to heighten the dizzying, emotional turmoil of Charlotte Douglas, caught up not only in the political instability of a fictional banana republic, but also in the seemingly imminent social dissolution of her own country, the United States in the 1960's.

The story of Charlotte Doulas is told through a narrator, Grace Strasser-Mendana, who, at the beginning of the novel, openly avows her mission to serve as Charlotte's witness, and who provides the reader with a very skeletal summary of her subject's life:

> Here is what happened: she left one man, she left a second man, she travelled again with the first, she let him die alone. She lost one child to "history" and another to "complications" (I offer in each the evaluation of others), she imagined herself capable of shedding the baggage and came to Boca Grande, a tourist. *Una turista.* So she said. In fact she came here less a tourist than a sojourner but she did not make that distinction.
> She made not enough distinctions.
> She dreamed her life.
> She died, hopeful. In summary. (BCP 3)

The opening passage is significant in that it captures, through its repetitive use of the word "she," the often liturgical nature of the prose, as if this witness were participating in some religious ritual, chanting a hymn to a somewhat mysterious being. Critics have been quick to point out that the very title refers to the Anglican official prayer book and that perhaps its use is ironic in that a spiritual connection to a traditional deity is conspicuously absent in this postmodern, secular setting.

The title might also suggest the ironic bonding of two women in a religious rite from which women have been traditionally excluded. For Didion does experiment here, as she will again in *Democracy*, with a narrative technique that allows her not only to effect an aesthetic distance from a seemingly compliant female victim but also to bring together two women who, because of their gender, remain "*de afuera*" in their respective countries. By inscribing both the narrator and her subject within the text, Didion, as Patricia Merivale notes, utilizes both: 1) a "distinctively 'feminine' variant of the contemporary identity quest"—the narrator seeks to find herself through the act of writing about someone else; 2) and the "elegiac romance," that is, the "fictional autobiography which best disguises itself as the biography of a person now dead," a genre which, when employed here by Didion, for the first time posits female bonding as the central relationship.[86] While the text chronicles the life of Charlotte Douglas, it also illuminates both the narrator, Grace Mendana, and their relationship. That is to say, the novel is, as Coale points out, technically the story of Charlotte Douglas in much the same way that *Moby Dick* is the story of Captain Ahab, *The Great Gatsby* the tale of Jay Gatsby and *Absalom!Absalom!* the history of Thomas Sutpen.[87] Like Ahab, Gatsby and Sutpen, Charlotte Douglas remains an impenetrable figure; an aura of mystery attends each of these "subjects" due, in part, to the fact that their portraits are being assembled by narrators who themselves see the world and their subjects through their own interpretive lenses, often distorted by prejudices rooted in stereotypic assumptions, emotional needs and faulty conjecture. Grace, for example, reflecting the gender stereotypes of her culture that defines a woman in terms of her husband, observes at one point that Charlotte "talked as if she had no specific history of her own. No Leonard. No Warren" (BCP 41). Grace must attempt to construct an "identity" (both her own and Charlotte's) from her own limited, socialized perception and access to information, forging her own interpretive connections to create a montage of Charlotte out of: 1) bits of rumor and hearsay; 2) brief encounters with Charlotte that often yielded contradictory statements; 3) personal items said to be in Charlotte's possession at the time of her death; 4) and letters left by Charlotte after they had been rejected for publication by magazines back in the States.

As an anthropologist who initially set out to study her subject with the detached objectivity of the scientist, Grace undergoes her own internal transformation, sensing, but not consciously realizing, that gathered empirical data do not reveal the spiritual core of a human being but rather serve only to distract us from the inscrutable essence that constitutes each of us, a mystery that can be approached more successfully through love and compassion than through the scientific method. For over the course of her narrative quest to understand the enigmatic figure of Charlotte Douglas, Grace gradually relinquishes the posture of the detached, objective scientist; she moves, as Coale observes, from "measurement to mystery, from the testimony of an 'objective' logical spectator to the prophecy of an involved, mystified participant in Charlotte's story."[88] Her confident claim at the beginning of the novel to play "no motive role in the narrative" other than to study a woman's life of "delusion" (BCP 4) and to understand the meaning of Charlotte's existence, unravels into an epistemological uncertainty when, at the end of the text, she remarks that if this "story has been one of delusion," perhaps the "delusion was mine" (BCP 280).

Grace's connection with Charlotte evolves from that of an observer studying a subject to that of a friend forging the narrative of Charlotte's life with a degree of personal, emotional involvement. Expressing at one point a maternal affection for Charlotte, it is Grace who, as Henderson notes, not only assumes responsibility for Charlotte's body but also travels to Buffalo to inform Marin of her mother's death.[89] Such a bond provides a striking contrast to the male aggression whirling about these two women, aggression that manifests itself not only as the impending violence of political revolution but also as the hostility directed against Charlotte by Warren Bogart, Leonard Douglas, and the *macho*, Latin American men. Although Didion would undoubtedly recoil from being labelled a feminist novelist, she does, through the portrayal of the female bond between Charlotte and Grace, implicitly affirm a concept of self that presents an alternative to the objectifying and often oppressive male ego as represented by the men in the text. Patricia Waugh observes:

> [M]any twentieth century women writers (whether consciously feminist or not) have sough alternative conceptions of subjectivity, expressing a definition of self in relationship which does not make identity dependent axiomatically upon the maintenance of boundaries and distance, nor upon the subjugation of the other.[90]

Grace eventually erases the emotional boundaries and distance of the scientist in favor of the intimacy and love of the friend in her quest to assemble a portrait of Charlotte Douglas, and in doing so, constructs her own subjectivity in relationship to, rather than in an objectifying distance from, her subject. While Grace's inability to remain an objective observer leads her to confess her own epistemological limitations with a concluding remark—"I have not been the witness I wanted to be" (BCP 280), the humanistic concern she displays for Charlotte at her death conveys a moral responsibility for her subject that is both atypical of scientific detachment and thematically antithetical to the rather indiscriminate violence that surrounds her.

In an effort to "legitimize [her] voice" (BCP 14), Grace Strasser-Mendana provides the reader with what she considers to be relevant, autobiographical details. A Colorado native, Grace married into "one of the three or four solvent families in Boca Grande" (BCP 12) when she was in her thirties and gave up her career as an anthropologist. Her husband's death left her in "putative control of fifty-nine-point-eight percent of the arable land and the same percentage of the decision-making process" (BCP 12). As one critic notes, Grace's control of the country's purse strings affords her a degree of power that is atypical of Didion women.[91] However, Grace's "putative" power does not seem to entail the ability to stem the ceaseless outbreaks of political violence in Boca Grande as is evidenced not only by her failure to prevent the death of Charlotte Douglas, who is shot in the back by one of the guerrillas, but also by her uncertainty as to "which side killed her, who held the Estadio Nacional at the moment of her death" (BCP 276); and that while she maintains a degree of financial leverage over her *macho* in-laws, she remains, in their eyes, both a North American and a female, that is, a "norteamericana cunt" (BCP 207,208). Grace's alienation from the political subterfuge that propels the cyclical convulsions of war in Boca Grande renders her power somewhat vacuous.

Now dying of pancreatic cancer, Grace has returned to Boca Grande, a country on the verge of one if its many political upheavals, ostensibly because she likes the country's "harsh, still" and "flat" light, "dead white at noon" (BCP 13), a correlative, perhaps, of the dead, still center of this woman's soul as it contemplates its own mortality. On a less conscious level, she returns to Boca Grande to tell the story of Charlotte Douglas, a typical Didion female in many respects—an unreflective, seemingly passive victim who surrounds herself with abusive men and who, like Maria Wyeth, is trying to "rescue" a "lost" daughter, in this case, a Patty Hearst figure who is caught up in the revolutionary chaos back home. A country that brings into sharp relief the virtual impotence of women in the political machinations of more powerful men, Boca Grande, a "thinly disguised portrait of El Salvador in the mid-seventies,"[92] provides, like the United States, the appropriate setting to construct the story of Charlotte Douglas, a woman victimized by male aggression.

Through Grace-Strasser Mendana, we meet Charlotte Douglas, who, like Lily McClellan and Maria Wyeth, had been taught the frontier values and optimism of the American West. She had been "provided with clean sheets, orthodontia, lamb chops, living grandparents" as well as "casual timely information about menstruation and the care of flat silver" and "faith in the value of certain frontiers" and "the virtues of cleared, irrigated land," of "thrift, industry and the judicial system, of progress and education and the generally upward spiral of history" (BCP 56). She is, in Grace's early estimation, a "typical norteamericana," an assessment that reveals Grace's initial, rather condescending and detached appraisal of Charlotte as someone who is naive and subject to delusions of erotic female power that can be dangerous in so volatile a political climate as that of Boca Grande.[93] And as a "typical norteamericana," Charlotte has internalized her society's message regarding appropriate female and male behavior, so that, like Lily and Maria, she seems compelled to abdicate to exploitive, importuning men, relinquishing any control over her own life. As Maria vacillated between the oppressive and often sadistic treatment of Ivan Costello and Carter Lang, so too does Charlotte find herself not only playing a dangerous marital game with both her ex-husband, Warren Bogart, and her current husband, Leonard, but also courting the violent, flagrantly misogynistic men in Boca Grande.

Charlotte's relationship with Warren Bogart, and with all men in her life, can be understood, in part, by considering her reaction to a story told by Grace about the custom practiced by a village on the Orinoco in which "female children were ritually cut on the inner thigh by their first sexual partners, the point being to scar the female with the male totem" (BCP 83). Charlotte, Grace tells us, "saw nothing extraordinary in this, "claiming, 'I mean that's pretty much what happens everywhere, isn't it...Somebody cuts you? Where it doesn't show'" (BCP 83-84)? The image of being totemically inscribed with a patriarchal symbol as a sign of ownership links Charlotte with Julie of *The Dead Father*; the image of female "cuts" also thematically connects Charlotte to Maria Wyeth and underscores Charlotte's treatment at the hands of Warren Bogart, one of the most pugnacious,"cutting" and overtly abusive male characters created by Didion.

Having escaped perhaps the humiliation of marital violence herself, Grace tells us that she finds the sexual contract to be more "amusing" than did Charlotte. Again, Grace's reaction perhaps illuminates her own detached scientific posturing at this point in their relationship, for it belies a failure to empathize with Charlotte's experience, a refusal to discern and to feel the painful parallels between their two lives as vulnerable women; perhaps it also points to Didion's reluctance to let go completely of the notion of female complicity in one's own victimization. The implication that Charlotte's often immobilizing feeling that men traditionally claim their sexual partners as their territory is atypical of women is a bit naive and reveals Didion's continued ambivalence regarding female victimization. As Grace watches Charlotte walk between two men with whom Charlotte has slept, she observes:

> Her legs seemed to lock unnaturally into her pelvic bones. Her body went stiff as if convulsed by the question of who had access to it and who did not. Whenever I saw her with both Victor and Gerardo it struck me that her every movement was freighted with this question. Who had prior claim. Whose call on her was most insistent. (BCP 83)

While Grace (and perhaps Didion) can maintain an amused detachment from such a poignant image of a woman who viscerally reacts to her own vulnerability to male demands, Charlotte's discomfort reflects not only the reality of her past abuse at the hands of Warren Bogart and to some extent, Leonard Douglas, but also her culture's constant reminder that issues concerning her body are often subject to the caprice and design of more powerful men. While Didion may be *consciously* attempting to portray *an aberrant* female behavior here, Charlotte's reaction, given her past and the increasing rate of male violence against women in post World War II America,[94] is quite understandable and suggests, again, a certain tension or ambivalence in the text itself (and the author?) concerning the victimization of women.

Charlotte's relationship with Warren Bogart, a former college instructor and generally obnoxious social parasite, is, in many ways, a more realized, less "comic" version of the relationship exhibited by the captured woman and her captor in Barthelme's short story, "The Captured Woman"; that is to say, it is a hostile, tenuous union of a sadistic male and a seemingly masochistic female who, at times, have erected a façade of marital harmony to belie a more pervasive domestic discord. Belligerent in his dealings with all whom he meets, Warren reserves a special animosity for the women in his life, especially Charlotte, his ex-wife and mother of his daughter, Marin. We are told by Grace of an event one Easter Sunday during their marriage when Marin was a child. Upset over the deaths of her parents and her crumbling marriage, and having had too much to drink, Charlotte sleeps with her lawyer the night before Easter, only to awaken the next morning to the humiliating and taunting wrath of her husband:

> "Look at the slut on Easter morning."
> She had screamed.
> Marin had screamed.
> She had picked Marin and when Warren hit her again his hand glanced off Marin's temple.
> She had picked up the kitchen knife.
> She had thrown up. (BCP 136)

In an aborted attempt to defend herself, Charlotte, armed with a knife, seemingly internalizes her anger toward Warren by "using" her body to render herself weak and vulnerable—she throws up. That is to say, her response to his overpowering anger is an unreflective strategic retreat into the stereotypic passivity of her female role. Such a response, according to psychologists, is also very typical of women in abusive relationships, for as the victim "becomes more and more involved with internal defense mechanisms," as does Charlotte, "external activity may diminish, giving the appearance of extreme apathy."[95] Similar to the rhythm of "The Captured Woman," this violent episode is followed by a false display of domestic peace and a gentle gesture of the man towards his wife/victim: Warren, Charlotte and Marin celebrate Easter Sunday by dining at the Carlyle, appearing as the beautiful family" as "Warren gave her his coat" (BCP 136-37). As Mickelson notes, Charlotte edits her memory in this case to recall this event as a happy time,[96] a reaction that is, as psychologists point out, consistent with the thought processes of domestic abuse victims, who, far from exhibiting masochism in their "decision" to remain with an abusive spouse, are actually suffering from an intense passivity as a result of a "paralyzing terror."[97]

While not reducing the novel to a sociological tract on domestic abuse, one can, in an attempt to flush out characterization, fill in the white spaces and minimalistic silences with the growing body of knowledge about female victimization in postmodern America. Yet, what remains a mystery is Charlotte's decision to re-connect with Warren during her marriage to Leonard, to travel to New Orleans with Warren to visit a dying relative, Porter, who, she soon discovers, is not dying. Is there an implicit suggestion here, as there was in both *Run River* and *Play It As It Lays*, that women are attracted to male brutality, or does Charlotte's decision reflect her need for any form of family structure, no matter how injurious or dysfunctional? For it was with Warren that she mothered a child, and, perhaps, having "bought" the stereotype of woman-as-mother-and-wife, Charlotte views a negative, self-destructive family connection as better than none. The first option suggests that she is pathologically sexual in nature, masochistically inviting her own degradation by men, and the second option presupposes Charlotte's implicit acceptance of a societal reduction of women to self-sacrificing nurturers, destined to suffer. As Marilyn French notes, both views—that women are "by nature incarnations of sex" and that "woman's lot was suffering, one of the great privileges of the Christian life," still inform the fundamentally Protestant dimension of American culture that is intent upon negating any of the significant political gains made by second-wave American feminism and re-asserting unquestioned male hegemony both in the family and in the political arena.[98] When Charlotte discovers that Warren, like Grace, is dying of cancer, she remains with him despite his drunken, abusive treatment of her. His belligerent confrontation with her portends the negative tenor of their trip:

"I flew out here to see how you were."
Still Charlotte said nothing.
"I don't like your room, I don't like your house, I don't like your life..."
"Go away," Charlotte whispered...
"I want you to come to New Orleans with me..."
"I said I want you to come to New Orleans with me, are you deaf? Or just rude..." "If you won't do it for me you'll do it for Porter. Or you're a worse human being than even I think." (BCP 100)

When Charlotte initially refuses his demand, saying that she is meeting Leonard for lunch, Warren intensifies his sadistic assault, aiming at her point of maximum vulnerability, Marin:

"Don't let me keep you. Somebody who loves you is dying, *your* only child is lost, I'm asking you one last favor, and you've got a lunch date...You're never going to see Marin again, but you've got a lunch date? And maybe after your 'lunch date' you and your interesting husband can, what do you call it, 'get stoned'?"
"You fuck," Charlotte screamed.
Warren smiled.
Charlotte grabbed a pair of scissors and clutched them, point out... "You walk into the house four days ago, you haven't said Marin's name except to make fun of her. You try to use Marin on me, you don't give a fuck about—"
Warren still smiled...
Charlotte looked at her hand and opened it and the scissors fell to the floor. "About Marin," she said. (BCP 102-103; emphasis mine)

Like Carter, who threatened to take Kate if Maria refused to get an abortion, Warren coerces Charlotte into accompanying him on his trip by using Marin as a wedge. Referring to Marin as "your" child, not "our" child, Warren, in effect, disavows any paternal feelings for his daughter, using her, instead, as a target of his sadistic mockery and opportunistic manipulations. This scene bears a striking similarity to the previously discussed Easter Sunday episode, and Didion's brilliant use of connecting images—Charlotte's defensive grabbing of the scissors to repel the threat of physical attack, followed by her immediate retreat into passivity—underscores the repetitive, cyclical nature of the pattern of intimidation and abuse within which Charlotte remains trapped. Didion closes the scene with an image that captures Charlotte's withdrawal into a childlike submissiveness: "She stood like a child and let Warren put the coat on her shoulders" (BCP 102), again echoing the Easter Sunday episode in which Warren, in mock solicitude, gives Charlotte his coat.

Warren's sadistic demeanor toward Charlotte and his territorial claiming of her loyalty and her time help to explain Grace's observation concerning Charlotte's discomfort with men with whom she has slept, men who figuratively and sometimes literally cut women with their totemic symbols of ownership. Meeting Warren later in New Orleans, Grace begins to understand "what Warren Bogart could *do to* Charlotte Douglas," for "he had the look of a man who could drive a woman like Charlotte right off her head" (BCP 104; emphasis mine). While Grace (and, perhaps, Didion) invites us to view Charlotte's decision to remain with Warren in terms of a rather stereotypic, reductive explanation that women are concerned primarily with "sexual surrender and infant death," those twin "commonplaces of the female obsessional life" (BCP 53), the subtextual thread of misogyny, woven into the fabric of the minimalistic images and calculated omissions, pushes us in the direction of viewing female submission not as the common dream, but as the common nightmare of all women.

Remaining with Warren perhaps because she senses his "prior claim" to her (BCP 127), Charlotte leaves an ostensibly more stable relationship, her marriage to a liberal lawyer, Leonard Douglas. Leonard manifests a degree of humanity missing in Didion's early, fictional male characters and provides what one critic calls an Apollonian counterpart to the Dionysian abandon of Warren Bogart.[99] Not only does he tolerate Warren's anti-semitic slurs, but he also attends to the body after Warren's death; underlying his intermittent outbursts of angry frustration with what he perceives to be Charlotte's passive hostility and irresponsible decisions at times is a sincere concern for her well-being. Yet, he is a man who is always on the move, almost a caricature, as one critic observes, of a "certain, 'radical chic' sensibility," engaged in the obligatory self-scrutiny of psychoanalysis, smoking marijuana that he keeps in a silver music box that plays 'Puff the Magic Dragon' and creating a lifestyle rather than living a life.[100]

Furthermore, Leonard Douglas, anticipating the character of Jack Lovett in *Democracy*, is also an arms dealer, who surreptitiously arranges shipments of weapons to various third world countries. As Hanley argues, *A Book of Common Prayer* and *Salvador* reflect Didion's acknowledgment of the proximity of war to her domestic sphere: "That men we know are making the wars around us is a measure of how close, for [Didion], war has come to home."[101] Didion focuses her attention on small, more "intimate" and non-global conflicts—a "small war in a small country," Hanley notes, referring to Boca Grande/El Salvador, whereas Pynchon will traverse the panoramic landscape of World War II in *Gravity's Rainbow*. While their vastly different scopes may in part be dictated by their different technical approaches—the minimalistic format of Didion's vs. the mythic sweep of Pynchon's—one might also hypothesize that women and men experience war differently, the former viewing war more in terms of the devastation of individual relationships and the latter in terms of the impersonal clashing of anonymous masses of soldiers. For Didion cannot, as Hanley observes, "disentangle men at war from men in bed,"[102] as is evidenced by the blending of marital ties and martial intrigue in the character of Leonard Douglas. An irony lies in the possibility that Leonard Douglas, through his explicit endorsement of violence to achieve a political goal, may have supplied the very weapons that were used to foment the revolution in Boca Grande that led to the shooting death of his wife. Grace's limited access to information and her reliance upon hearsay render her belief in Leonard's lack of involvement somewhat suspect, especially since, as even she admits, "The *guerrilleros* appeared to have more of everything than anyone except Leonard Douglas had supposed they had" (BCP 272). The irony involved in suggesting that the long chain of events that culminated in Charlotte's death may have been set into motion by the man who once treated her fairly well perhaps escaped even the author, but again it serves to emphasize the subtextual vulnerability of women to male-initiated aggression, whether it be in the domestic arena or in the political sphere.

Charlotte's desire to have a baby with Leonard Douglas may reflect her need to forge another family unit or it may, as Leonard observes, just be a strategy to prove to herself that Warren doesn't own her anymore (BCP 86, 88), either alternative reflecting her continued dependency upon traditional gender expectations. Whatever the reason, the birth and death of their child subtly reveal Leonard's selfish desire to distance himself from the pain and anguish suffered by Charlotte who keeps the child with her for two weeks, watching her die:

> Leonard had not wanted her to see the baby but she had.
> Leonard had wanted her to leave the baby to die in the Ochsner Clinic but she would not. (BCP 152)

Charlotte names the child "Charlotte," while Leonard, having emotionally abandoned his daughter, calls her "it" (BCP 153); advising his wife to "forget it," "it's over" (BCP 157), the man who once treated Charlotte fairly well refuses to share her despondency and parental responsibility, leaving her to watch their child die in a Coca-Cola parking lot.

Abused by Warren and emotionally neglected by Leonard, Charlotte continues her pattern of female victimization by deciding to remain in Boca Grande at the inception of the revolution. If, as one critic argues, the author is trying to impart an heroic stature to her rather unheroic protagonist by having Charlotte stay and continue to give cholera injections at the clinic where she works,[103] Didion does succeed in creating a female character who at least has made a decision on her own without male interference. Unlike Lily and Maria, Charlotte does extricate herself from the narcissistic inertia of female dependency and the self-indulgent withdrawal into the solipsistic domain of the "I"; she evolves into a woman who freely decides to lend her body and spirit to the cause of alleviating pain in the local environs of Boca Grande. Again, while there seems to be no conscious agenda on the part of the author to present Charlotte Douglas as a fledgling feminist, the fact remains that Charlotte represents a significant step forward in the cast of Didion's female characters who succeed in establishing a positive relational identity, or sense of self, in terms of community that later feminist theorists, such as Flax, Greene, Kahn and Felski, argue forms the foundation of a feminist space.[104] That Charlotte's decision to assert her *self* will precipitate her death at the hands of American-funded *macho guerrilleros* ironically underscores the ubiquity of female vulnerability to patriarchal destruction.

For it is the Latin American male attitude toward American women that eventually costs Charlotte her life. Throughout the novel, Charlotte not only arouses the hostility of Warren and Leonard in America but also invites her own degradation by sleeping with Victor and Gerardo (Grace's son), two men who openly assert their disdain for American women (BCP 202,215). Like all of Didion's women, Charlotte displays an appalling lack of acquired knowledge concerning world affairs, the intellectual and academic development of this attractive woman not being an integral part of her family or culture's value system. Caught up in a maelstrom of revolutionary intrigue and jockeying for power that she does not comprehend, Charlotte seductively intrudes into a triangle of politically ambitious men—Victor, Gerardo and Antonio—all of whom view her with disdain and derision, referring to her as "the norteamericana cunt" (BCP 207, 208, 244, 258, 261, 277). Antonio resents not only the use of "her American vaccine" in the cholera epidemic but also her perceived sexual promiscuity (BCP 219), which, as an "unpredictable element," can fuel, Grace feels, an already volatile political situation. The circumstances surrounding Charlotte's death remain obscure, for Grace must rely upon the information given to her by her unreliable son—"I do not entirely trust Gerardo's version of it" (BCP 217); what is certain is that Charlotte died from a gunshot in the back which could have been fired by either side (BCP 276).

Both the omission of reliable information and the profusion of "unreliable" testimony regarding Charlotte's death require the reader to provide the connective explanations and to impose a degree of coherence upon the fragments of information presented. If, as Henderson suggests, Charlotte's affairs with Victor and Gerardo were the probable cause of her murder,[105] then Antonio, who succeeded in taking over Victor's office after the revolution, is perhaps responsible for her death. While the exact details and circumstances surrounding the murder of Charlotte Douglas remain a matter of conjecture in this minimalistic novel, the implications of her death clearly impart a message that transcends the limitations of any specific political locale, in that it reflects the unleashing of a male rage against women that even Grace senses is seething in those around her. Commenting on Antonio's deep-seated hostility toward Charlotte, Grace states: "She was a norteamericana, she was a woman, she was an unpredictable element. I suppose she was a version of me at whom he could vent his rage" (BCP 219-220). As a more "conscious," more reflective version of Charlotte, Grace understands herself to be an outsider, not just in Boca Grande, but during her whole life: "I am de afuera. I have been de afuera all my life" (BCP 52). As the less introspective and perhaps more naive version of Grace who is dying slowly of cancer, Charlotte succumbs to a violent death, a sacrificial victim of male intrigue and quests for power, and the "common target of sexual and international masculine enmities."[106]

Female sacrifice at the altar of patriarchal aggression is captured in two of the most compelling and lingering images in the novel, images that are woven into in a conversation between Grace and Leonard, who has come to Boca Grande to "rescue" his wife. Annoyed by Charlotte's involvement at the clinic and frustrated by her omission of details concerning a bombing there, Leonard complains that all Charlotte had told him about the incident is that it "went off while she was changing her fucking Tampax" (BCP 255). Grace supplies us with additional information, that Charlotte was so immersed in her work that she had forgotten to change her Tampax and had spotted "blood all over the clinic," and that a doctor who was operating on a woman at the time of the bombing "jumped and punctured" her uterus and that she is now dying of peritonitis (BCP 255). A war zone spotted with menstrual blood and a punctured uterus are sparse but effective images that not only commingle the seemingly incongruous elements of life and death but also resonate with overtones of female sacrifice and total loss of control in the masculine arena of war. Didion may be "witnessing the faces of men and women in the light of shell-fire"[107] rather than focusing directly on the war in Boca Grande; yet, the fragmented images of female death and mutilation obliquely suggest the broader context of carnage and devastation within which the particular horrors of this woman's surreal experience of war unfolds, a nightmarish experience poignantly captured in Susan Griffin's war rhetoric of female violation:

> "I wake from a dream. I am a city. My body, the streets, the building. A missile enters. The city is shattered. My clothes torn off and scattered, as in a rape." [108]

The appearance of such images of female victimization, in addition to the use of a narrator who distances us from Charlotte's seemingly compliant self-denigration at times, encourages a more sympathetic reaction to Charlotte's plight than to the situations faced by both Lily and Maria. Similar to both of her fictional predecessors, Charlotte remains trapped within a cycle of self-injurious relationships; yet, like Maria, she is capable of love, even if it is the painful love of a mother for a daughter who is "lost" to her. For Charlotte's very presence in Boca Grande is motivated by the rather unrealistic hope that Marin, on the run from the F.B.I. for participating in a revolutionary bombing of a bank in San Francisco, will meet her there.

Far from representing an articulate spokeswoman for social change, eighteen-year-old Marin, like many young people of that generation, spouts revolutionary rhetoric more as a form of rebellion against the values and expectations of middleclass America than as a conscious affirmation of Marxist-Leninist philosophy. She assumes, for example, that her mother did nothing in Boca Grande but play tennis; "Tennis," she tells Grace, "is just one more mode of teaching an elitist strategy" (BCP 266). Like her mother, Marin is caught up in events that she does not understand; she is a blind participant in a violent surge for liberation and social change in which she, as a woman, unknowingly remains oppressed by gender, chained to restrictive, traditional sex stereotypes.

Similar to the many female activists who, as Donovan notes, took part in the civil rights movement and the anti-Vietnam War campaigns and yet often incurred only contemptuous disdain from their male counterparts in the "New Left,"[109] Marin finds herself enslaved to a demeaning, conventional female role. Undoubtedly the victim of "the fear and hostility of her male comrades in the New Left who argued that gender issues were secondary and subordinate to the more basic modes of oppression based on class and race,"[110] Marin was ostensibly fighting for the emancipation of the oppressed classes while she ironically remains, as Mickelson notes, "the household drudge,"[111] left to clean up a dirty sink of dishes left by her comrades (BCP 267). Yet, it is this child, who claims to hate her mother, whose name is supposedly the last word Charlotte uttered. It is precisely Charlotte's capacity to sustain an unconditional love for Marin that also elicits sympathy from the reader.

Female Bonding: *Democracy*

Didion's minimalistic images of violence, her use of a self-conscious narrator and her creation of a female protagonist who is capable of love are factors that also inform her novel *Democracy*. While Inez Victor is, in many respects, reminiscent of Didion's earlier heroines, most notably Charlotte, she comes to display an autonomy of will and a clarity of purpose that eventually enable her to break free from the male-imposed textual role of the "candidate's wife." Unlike Barthelme, whose minimalist project aims at flattening out identities into a series of fragmented, elusive "voices," Didion, while similarly conscious of the failings of conventional narrative technique to render the postmodern world meaningful, struggles to forge a sense of self, that is, a provisional female identity, from the collage of images and broken dreams that constitute *Democracy*. Julie and Emma rebel against the arbitrary pronouncements of the Dead Father's sexist discourse by retreating into their own paratactic, playful dialogue; however, the narrator and Inez Victor remain in the traditional linguistic "game" but change the rules so as to: 1) construct a female identity that will enable Inez to escape the oppressive and self-effacing text of the "politician's wife," survive the death of her lover, Jack Lovett, and also thrive as an independent woman working in Kuala Lumpur to relocate Southeast Asian refugees at the close of the Vietnam War; 2) allow 'Joan Didion-the-narrator'—who, when confronted with a profusion of disparate sensory images, expresses early in the novel a lack of confidence "not only of personality but of narrative"[112]— to recover a conviction for the importance of the past and of memory that will enable her to retrieve not only a "self" for Inez but her own identity as a writer. Again, this "identity" will be synonymous with neither the traditional concept of the unitary ego of Enlightenment humanism nor the purely textual construct of the deconstructionist theorists; it will resemble rather a positional self always in the process of becoming, a "deep subjectivity" that is informed by critical social relations[113] and that is, according to Sally Robinson, more of a "doing" rather than a "being."[114] Didion's concept of the self in *Democracy* represents a compromise between humanism and deconstructionism in that it evolves into a positional and provisional identity constructed, as Waugh notes, in part by the subject's socio-political context.[115]

For at issue in this novel is the author's own crisis of confidence in her *self* as a postmodern writer. By overtly inscribing herself with the narrative as the persona 'Joan Didion,' the author, as Stout observes, strategically inserts her "struggle to understand her characters' story" as "part of the fiction";[116] and she also, like Barthelme and many other postmodernist writers, very self-consciously calls attention to the act of writing and to herself as the author. Most importantly, however, she raises the issue of identity. Introducing herself to the reader as "Joan Didion, the author" (D 16), she reveals that she began thinking about Inez Victor and Jack Lovett, her "subjects," at a point in her life when "I lacked certainty, lacked even the minimum level of *ego* which all writers recognize as essential to the writing of novels; lacked faith even in my own technique" (D 17;emphasis mine). While focusing upon the love affair between Inez and Jack and exposing the hypocrisy endemic to American political life—whether it be the left-wing posturing of Harry Victor or the militant C.I.A. subterfuge of Jack Lovett—*Democracy* also entails the process by which the "author" rescues herself from her own "identity crisis." By establishing a bond with Inez Victor by which she can serve as witness to Inez's capacity to love not only Jack but also her daughter Jessie and her sister Janet, the "author" can give testimony to a woman's continuing pattern of care and compassion and establish her own narrative identity, however tentative and self-conscious. As Henderson notes, "Didion the narrator discovers herself most fully by entering the life of Inez Victor, her double, her alter ego."[117]

Consequently, what is at stake for both Inez Victor and "Joan Didion the narrator" is some form of personal identity, a sense of psychological, emotional and physical continuity and integrity over time that is dependent upon one's maintaining a connection to others and to one's past through *memory*. In her collection of essays, *Slouching Towards Bethlehem*, Didion voices her dread concerning the disintegration of America in the 1960's, echoing Yeats' apocalyptic fear in "The Second Coming" that "the center is not holding." One of the underlying causes of the social atomization and widespread aimlessness of both adults and children was, she maintained, the failure to provide the individual with a connection to an historical and cultural past that fosters a sense of familial and personal identity, that in turn generates a sense of intrinsic self-worth (STB 84).

Didion's reliance upon traditional values as the glue "that held society together" (STB 84) reflects a conservative political bias that was under attack by the more radical activists of the '60's who, as was intimated in *A Book of Common Prayer*, seemed to be pressing for societal change in all areas except female liberation. Not surprisingly, Didion's explicit advocacy of traditional values (e.g. the binary opposition of male/female that delineates conventional gender roles) and historical continuity on the one hand, and her tacit condemnation of patriarchal violence (a result of the dichotomous hierarchy of male/female) which informs the subtext of her fiction, combine to generate an *aporia* in the text, that is, a tension and ambiguity inherent in her female protagonists. Even her own comments concerning the importance of memory for individual self-worth ironically undermine her once-conservative pose, expounded in her essays, by illuminating the critical causal connection, dealt with in *Democracy*, between the often culturally-sanctioned violence perpetrated against a woman and her failure to remember and retain an identity. While psychologists have emphasized the connection between memory and female identity—pointing out that both consciousness-raising groups and therapy show that "without access to many aspects of the self, memory in its fullness can't emerge"[118]—Didion, in her early essays, connects memory and identity but fails to link explicitly the subjugation of women and their expressed "loss" of selves or their emotional amnesia. In a key essay entitled "On Keeping a Notebook" (STB), Didion argues in favor of keeping a journal not in order to record accurately certain factual details, which, she admits, she usually misconstrues, but rather to remember an emotionally laden image, a tonal picture that captures what she *felt* at a specific time in her life (STB 134). The validity of objective facts is inconsequential—"perhaps it never did snow that August in Vermont"; what is of consequence is "that was how it *felt* to me." For "how it felt to me" becomes, for Didion, "how it felt to be me" (BCP 134-136), thus establishing an emotional connection to the past and generating a sense of personal continuity or identity. Marianne Hirsch points to a recurring motif informing some female postmodernist texts, namely, the desire to "come to terms with the past by integrating it with the present in order to assemble a "sense of self" and "meaningful narrative patterns."[119] While Hirsch focuses primarily upon the mother-daughter connection in the process of memory or "return," her observation that such a critical relationship unfolds within and is affected by its historical context serves to alert us to the fact that Didion's attempt to retrieve and assemble a self must be understood against the backdrop of the sexist politics of her time. Although Didion herself in *Slouching Towards Bethlehem* memorializes her own past in a rather apolitical, gender-neutral passage, that is, a passage devoid of references to her position as an American woman in the 1960's, her fiction conveys a subtextual sensitivity to the gender politics of her day.

The act of remembering constitutes much of *Democracy*, as it does the preceding novels. However, in this last novel, remembering takes on a redemptive quality; it becomes a moral act that rescues Inez Victor from the relative amnesia she suffers at the hands of exploitive men by helping her to construct an identity that will enable her to exist as an independent, loving adult woman who can engage herself in helping others. By recording Inez's memories, the narrator can both create her own narrative identity and aid Inez in remembering "what it felt like to be me," so that Inez can connect not only with her past but also consciously assume responsibility for her own future by rejecting the roles imposed upon her by others.

If, as Hanley argues, *A Book of Common Prayer* insulates women from war and the reader from the "realities of El Salvador," *Salvador* represents a "harsh awakening" and a stripping away of "consoling illusions."[120] For it is precisely Inez's memory that has been sacrificed in her reductive role as "the candidate's wife." As the narrator tells us, Inez, when asked by a reporter to identify the "major cost" of her public life, responds:

> "Memory, mainly," Inez said.
> "Memory," the woman from the Associated Press repeated.
> "Memory, yes. Is what I would call the major cost. Definitely…Something like shock treatment," she added.
> "You mean you've had shock treatment."
> "No, I mean I lose track. *As if* you'd had shock treatment.
> "I see. 'Lose track' of what exactly?"
> "Of what happened…"
> "I see. Yes. During the campaign."
> "Well, no. During your whole life." (D 51)

While the reporter fails to grasp the significance of the response, Didion, who is present at the interview, understands the dread of living a life that is, as Henderson notes, "jagged and discontinuous, its pressures leading one to drop a former self as one might drop cargo from a plane."[121] While Didion begins to piece together the jagged pieces of her subject's life, a process, as McCarthy notes, that is somewhat akin to assembling a jigsaw puzzle,[122] the picture that emerges is that of a woman who, having "bought the package" of female subservience and dependency upon patriarchal texts, has suffered a numbing loss of self. By comparing Inez's memory loss to that of someone who has undergone shock treatment—a "therapy" imposed significantly more frequently upon women than men in America—Didion employs a simile that evokes a violent image of enforced compliance to societal norms; such an image not only establishes her heroine's place in a long line of overtly subjugated American female characters, ranging from Gilman's narrator in *The Yellow Wallpaper* to Plath's Esther Greenwood in *The Bell Jar*, but also provides a thematic link to the violent eradication of the cultural memory and identity of the indigenous Indians of El Salvador, discussed by Didion in *Salvador* (1983).

Published one year prior to *Democracy*, *Salvador* presents what one critic calls an "exhaustive and picturesque catalogue of all the vices of Salvadoran society."[123] It depicts this Central American country as the quintessential "heart of darkness," ameliorated neither by the exported "apocalyptic obsession [with communism] of Reagan and others before him,"[124] nor by the more progressive notions of land reform and education. As a chronicle of her brief sojourn in El Salvador, the text, rooted firmly in the specificity of image, remains curiously apolitical, leading one critic to inquiry, "What is Joan Didion for? What is she against?"[125] Yet, if Didion stubbornly resists explicitly aligning herself to either traditional right wing or left wing agendas, her images certainly decry the disastrous effects of patriarchal aggression against weaker peoples.

Eerily reminiscent of the images depicting the unconscionable treatment of native Americans by the United States government is the compelling description of Didion's visit to a crafts fair in Nahuizalco, "sponsored by the Ministry of Education as part of the effort to encourage indigenous cultures,"[126] and perhaps, to feign compliance with human rights observance in order to receive U.S. aid. As Hanley argues, the U.S.-Salvador connection is a "game of smoke and mirrors," of shifting appearances, of corrupted language that shrouded U.S.-funded death squads and "disappearances."[127] Given the systematic annihilation of the Indian cultures by the Salvadoran militant regime during the *matanza*, the 1932 massacre of up to 30,000 peasants by the right-wing dictator, General Hernandez Martinez,[128] those few who have survived have wisely abandoned their local dress and language out of fear of reprisals from an equally barbaric regime. The display of indigenous cultures at the crafts fair captures the awkwardness of dying minority cultures which are hypocritically encouraged to celebrate their heritage but threatened with extermination if they attempt to resurrect their cultural identities and autonomy:

> [The dances] were Indian, but they were less remembered than recreated, and as such derived not from local culture but from a learned idea of local culture, an official imposition made particularly ugly by the cultural impotence of the participants. The women, awkward and uncomfortable in an approximation of native costume, moved with difficulty into the dusty street and performed a listless and unpracticed dance with baskets. (S 75)

Government-sanctioned violence has eliminated cultural memory and identity, for, as one critic notes, "these Indians have been methodically terrorized out of their identities."[129]

The images of a culture's memory and identity being obliterated by systematic patriarchal aggression find their individual counterparts in *Democracy* in the systemic, less conspicuously violent assault against a woman's sense of self in postmodern American society. If, as Didion argues in *Salvador*, "race remains the ineffable element at the heart of this particular darkness," many of the images still tend to feminize the terror, indicating again a female's particular vulnerability, despite her race, to male-organized hostility. Invoking again the powerful image of menstrual blood staining the ground of a war zone as she did in *A Book of Common Prayer*, Didion states:

> Here and there on the cheap linoleum inside the [Metropolitan] cathedral there was what seemed to be actual blood, dried in spots, the kind of spots dropped by a slow hemorrhage, or by a woman who does not know or does not care that she is menstruating. (S 79)

Immediately following this poignant image is a description of several women, dressed in black, in a state of shock and despair, all in mourning for those who have been "disappeared" by the (American-funded) death squads (S 80). Thrown into stark and terrifying relief in this "portrait of the macabre"[130] is the unspeakable horror of the ubiquitous atrocities against minority cultures and the weaker adult members of society, women. While Inez Victor "enjoys" the economic luxuries of an upper middleclass American life style, her female status in an inveterately sexist and violent culture renders her susceptible to a loss of memory incurred by those who have been socialized to relinquish an independent identity. If race remains "the ineffable element" in *Salvador*, perhaps gender persists as the critical subtextual element in *Democracy*.

Intent upon rescuing the memories of Inez Victor that have been lost in her subservient role as Harry Victor's wife, Joan Didion-the-narrator embarks upon a moral quest to redeem the integrity of her "subject" and to raise Inez to a level of conscious decision-making that will enable her to shed her dependent status and assume a responsibility for her future choices. The often liturgical nature of the prose—the intermittent "chanting" of the clause "Inez remembered," followed by a litany of sparse, cinematic images— ironically imparts a religious tone to this postmodern, secular novel, similar to that found in *A Book of Common Prayer* and links the narrator to Grace Strasser-Mendana. Inez's memory of a day with Harry and their two children is described as follows:

> [Inez] remembered rain streaming down the big window, rain blowing in the trees...she remembered Jessie crowing with delight...she remembered Harry unbuttoning Adlai's wet sweater. (D 59)

And again her memory of the political turmoil in Jakarta in 1969:

> [Inez] remembered mainly the cloud cover that hung low over the city... She remembered the rumors... Inez remembered Harry giving a press conference... Inez remembered Billy Dillon negotiating with the wire reporter.... (D 98-99)

The "sacred" effort to piece together the fragmented images of Inez's memory so as to reconstruct an identity yields not that clearly-defined portrait that would emerge when all of the jagged parts of a jigsaw puzzle are successfully locked into place; rather, what appears is a loosely assembled approximation of an identity or psychological portrait that would result if the pieces of the jigsaw puzzle just missed fitting together perfectly, and, instead, were surrounded by white space or visual silences. Such a metaphor of identity captures the provisional and tentative construction of a self that is always in the process of becoming, a process wherein one's subjectivity constantly slides in and out of various formations as one shifts in and out of interpersonal and socio-political contexts.[131]

What Didion seems to be pursuing here is a concept of identity that does not involve a static, permanent or "locked-in" self-coincidence but rather a flexible, tentative, more fluid sense of the possible multiplicity of "selves" that emerge in different situations.[132] Explicitly inviting the reader at one point to intervene and interpret the events, that is, to fill in the silences—"What does this suggest? You tell me" (D 188)—Didion-the-narrator acknowledges her authorial limitations while, at the same time, cleverly employing her minimalistic technique that strategically entails a withholding of information or, as Anderson notes, "a failure to signify," which of course itself "signifies" and thereby heightens the import of what takes place off the page.[133] As the jagged, ill-fitting pieces of this puzzle, the compelling images in *Democracy* provide enough subtextual hints to suggest to the reader that the interstitial white spaces, or the unwritten or withheld narrative, may be filled in with an understanding of Inez Victor's subordinate position as a woman in postmodern America.

Similar to Didion's other female protagonists, Inez Victor is an American woman who outwardly conforms to her societal roles as a wife and a mother but remains ultimately comfortable with neither. Born Inez Christian to Paul and Carol Christian and raised in Hawaii after WWII with her sister, Janet, Inez grew up economically privileged but emotionally deprived of parental love. Her father was rarely home and her mother, prior to leaving her children, "perfected a stubborn loneliness" as an outsider in the islands that resulted in her alienation from both her husband and her children (D 22). Like Lily in *Run River*, Inez's mother entered her husband's household, did not fit in, and, failing to embrace any alternatives outside the often claustrophobic role of femininity and dependency, succumbed to boredom and loneliness. On her seventeenth birthday, Inez meets Jack Lovett, a shadowy civilian version of Oliver North, who is undoubtedly a member of the C.I.A. in charge of "covert operations," a euphemism for the often illegal funding of right-wing military initiatives. After their brief affair, Jack leaves Hawaii and Inez eventually marries Harry Victor, a liberal, anti-Vietnam War politician who, under the clever machinations and glitzy image-making of his campaign manager, Billy Dillon, is elected to the U.S. Congress. As the parents of two children, both of whom are "lost" to them in their own unique fashion, Inez and Harry "play" at being the happily married couple to bolster his ratings in the polls. The only source of adult love for Inez is Jack Lovett, whom she continues to see intermittently for twenty years in various exotic locations.

These are some of the retrospective pieces of the puzzle that begin to cluster around a pivotal plot element—the 1975 murder of Janet Christian and her lover, a U.S. Senator of Japanese descent from Hawaii, by her father, Paul Christian. Opening in the spring of 1975, the novel juxtaposes an assemblage of destructive, fragmented images, from the evacuation of Saigon (1975) to the pre-dawn nuclear testing in the Pacific (1952–53). It is within this frame of impending chaos and disintegration that the novelist, confronting only "broken images and dreams" rather than "the stuff of traditional narrative," initially feels at a loss as to how and where to begin; yet, it is also within this montage of apocalyptic images that Inez Victor, with the aid of Joan Didion-the-narrator, will reconstruct a tentative identity that will enable Inez to abandon her dependency upon the exploitive men in her life—Harry Victor, Billy Dillon and even Jack Lovett. Pervading the entire novel, more through minimalistic omission than through conventional narrative inclusion, is the horrifying spectre of the Vietnam War. Didion, as Hanley notes, does not focus upon the "struggles, sacrifices and tragedy of the Vietnam soldier" so as to deflect our attention from the unconscionable position taken by America to inflict a war "for no good reason on the entire populations of three unoffending countries on the other side of the world";[134] rather, she zeroes in on "the politicians, businessmen and shady government officials" who managed to manipulate the policies of death and destruction for their own financial or political gain.[135]

Harry Victor and Billy Dillon together constitute a team that reflects the self-aggrandizing, opportunistic impulse that Inez seems to feel has informed the American political process. Ostensibly devoted to furthering liberal causes and stylish in their "anti-war" stance, Harry and Billy seem to be more interested in selling an image of the electable politician than in promoting democratic principles. Immersed in a kind of Orwellian double-speak or rhetoric designed to obfuscate rather than to clarify issues, Harry Victor, along with "the master of euphemism,"[136] Billy Dillon, choreographs all events in Inez's life with the sole aim of either enhancing, or minimizing any damage to, her husband's image.

Consequently, when Paul Christian kills his daughter, Inez' sister, and her lover, Wendell Omura, it is Billy Dillon who "directs" Inez to tone down her anger and disgust with her father who, she feels, is "crazy" and "needs to be put away":

> "That's definitely one approach, Inez… Forthright. Hard edge. No fuzzy stuff. But I think the note we want to hit today is a little further toward the more-in-sorrow end of the scale. Your father is a 'sick man.' He has 'an illness like any other.' He 'needs treatment.'
> "He needs to be put away."
> "That's what we're calling 'treatment' Inez. We're calling it 'treatment' when we talk to the homocide guys…" "You all right?"

"Yes."

"Then trot out the smile and move easily through the cabin, babe, OK?" (D 143-144)

Intent upon keeping Paul Christian out of prison in order to save Harry Victor the embarrassment of a criminal trial, Billy Dillon directs Inez to feign compassion and sorrow for her father, to "fuzz" the picture and soft-pedal her anger at a man who has wantonly murdered his own daughter. Riddled with euphemisms and clichés, Billy's "directive" seeks not only to sacrifice Inez's true feelings but also to disguise the heinous nature of this act of male violence against a woman and her lover. Furthermore, it is Billy who, in a gross abuse of power, proceeds to bribe a local defense lawyer and politician to insure that the case never comes to trial, an act that leads Inez to concur with Harry's assessment of Billy as "killer mick." Intended as an accolade by Harry, "killer mick" captures the thinly veiled substratum of aggression that constitutes the male-dominated political machine in which Inez remains enmeshed.

As a proponent of style over substance, Billy-the-public-image-maker strategically uses Inez to further Harry's political goals, reducing her to the ancillary role of the "candidate's wife." What is sacrificed in the process are Inez's autonomy and personal identity, her memory and her own sense of self-worth. Not only is Inez discouraged from pursuing her humanitarian impulse to work with refugees during Harry's bid for the Senate (because, according to Billy Dillon, "refugees were an often controversial and therefore inappropriate special interest" (D56)), but she is also forced to tolerate her husband's indiscreet marital infidelities as part of the package of a candidate's life: "Inez, I'm asking you nice, behave, girls like that come with the life," says Billy to Inez, regarding Harry's affairs with his campaign workers, Carrie Willis and Frances Landau (D 48).

A major part of Billy Dillon's responsibilities entails the orchestration and soft-pedaling of Inez Victor's emotions so as to create an image of the "candidate's wife" that is marketable to the public; as a fictional precursor of such first ladies as Jackie Kennedy and Barbara Bush, this image must embody the traditional stereotype of the subservient, obedient wife who, if not univocally concurring with her husband's political position and private (mis)behavior, remains publicly silent. Consequently, Inez displays a public persona that has muted her private self for so long (twenty years), that her "capacity for passive detachment" reflects not the boredom of an idle mind but rather, as Didion-the-narrator comes to realize, a strategy to survive a life "in which the major cost was memory" (D 70).

While Harry Victor, too, is in part a creation of Billy Dillon's deceptive marketing talents, his ambitious quest for power reflects a colonial impulse indicative of his privileged position as a "cock-sure," white male in American culture. More the politician than the statesman, Harry Victor immerses himself in the hypocritical, self-serving rhetoric of a bastardized liberalism that allows him to travel to Indonesia to confirm that country's compliance with human rights, to participate in a civil rights march in Mississippi, to join a sit-in at Harvard and the Pentagon in the '60's, and yet twist the law to his own advantage in the Paul Christian episode, openly cheat on his wife and more or less divorce himself from his own children, primarily his daughter, Jessie. Surrounding himself with self-effacing women who had, as Didion describes them, "the same way of deprecating their own claims to be heard" (D 104), Harry Victor manifests the "implacable ethnocentricity" (and egocentricity) of someone who sees the whole world as an extension of himself or of his policies (D 83).

Devoting himself to a life of artifice and "fuzzy" rhetoric, Harry distances himself from the gritty details and vicissitudes of family life. He is embarrassed more than concerned by his daughter's near suicidal "escape" into heroin and his son's reckless irresponsibility behind the wheel of a car that almost took the life of a young woman. A conversation between Inez and Harry captures not only their mutual hostility but also Harry's special disdain for his daughter:

> "I can't get through to her," Harry had said…"Adlai may be a fuck-up, But I can talk to Adlai. I talk to her, I'm talking to a UFO."
>
> "Adlai," Inez had said, "happens to believe that he can satisfy his American History requirement with a three-unit course called 'History of American Film.'"
>
> "Very good, Inez. Broad but good."
>
> "Broad but true…I asked Adlai to make a point of going to the hospital to see Cynthia. Here's what he said."
>
> "Cynthia who?" Harry said.
>
> "Cynthia who he almost killed in the accident. 'She's definitely on the agenda.' Is what he said."
>
> "At least he said something. All you'd get from her is the stare."
>
> "You always say *her*. Her name is Jessie."
>
> "I know her goddamn name." (D 62)

"Like father, like son"—Adlai's cold disregard for those whom he hurts and his escape into the vacuity of clichés forge a superficial bond with his father from which Jessie, like Inez, is excluded.

Reflecting a society that "exerts greater control over and expects more controlled behavior from our girls than our boys,"[137] Harry Victor adopts a "boys-will-be-boys" attitude toward Adlai's recklessness, an attitude that, as feminist Letty Cottin Pogrebin notes, proves increasingly more dangerous to women as young boys grow older and learn that the parameters of acceptable masculine expression often include increasingly egregious assaults against women;[138] he remains far more sympathetic toward his son who endangers the lives of others, in this case a young woman whose name and condition are of obviously little concern to either Harry or Adlai, than to his daughter who, like many females in this culture, internalizes her anger and harms herself.[139] The tacit message here is that women are expendable, often anonymous creatures in the affairs of men, not worthy of even being *named*.

Harry's refusal to refer to his daughter by name recalls both Carter Lang's neglect of Kate and Leonard Douglas' labelling of his dying infant daughter as "it"; such a practice suggests a depersonalization of girl children that is emblematic of the more pervasive patriarchal bias against women in American culture, a bias that is comically underscored in *The Dead Father* by negatively identifying females as "not male." While Adlai is being primed by his father to enter a corrupt political system of male power, Jessie, who sees through the façade of their rhetoric and rejects it, remains "*de afuera*" in her own family and her own country. Reluctantly having dinner with her brother and father, Jessie punctures the men's cliché-ridden, pretentious exchange concerning an article that Adlai is going to propose for *The New York Times*:

> "It's something we've been tossing back and forth at Cambridge."
> "Interesting," Harry Victor said. "Let me vet it. What do you think, Jess?"
> "I think he shouldn't say 'Cambridge,'" Jessie said.
> "Possibly you were nodding out when I went up there," Adlai said,"but Cambridge happens to be where I go to school."
> "Maybe so," Jessie said, "but you don't happen to go to Harvard."
> "OK, guys. You both fouled." Harry Victor turned to Adlai. "I could sound somebody out at the Times. If you're serious."
> "I'm serious. It's time. Bring my generation into the dialogue, if you see my point."
> "You asshole," Jessie said. (D 173)

Jessie impugns Harry's perfunctory gesture to include her in their conversation. Her spirited rejection of their "falsification" (D 172) and pretense makes her an appealing character whose self-injurious escape into drug dependency and eventually to South Vietnam poignantly reflect her own intuitive awareness of herself as alienated from the male-dominated power structure, a power structure within which she, like her mother and grandmother, have been traditionally silenced and marginalized. Jessie is the "inheritor of disorder" who "drifts through adolescence in a narcotic haze, without the slightest notion of a plan or goal for a life."[140] She is the latest casualty in a matrilineal triad of psychologically wounded women, each of whom has been alienated from the other by opportunistic and insensitive men.

Like Charlotte Douglas and similar to her own mother, Inez, Jessie senses her own displacement at home and naively seeks to establish roots in a politically volatile foreign country. Oblivious to the dangers of traveling to South Vietnam in the mid 1970's, Jessie, like most Didion women, manifests a dangerous ignorance of world affairs. Although more highly motivated and more intelligent than her brother (D 172), Jessie has fallen through the cracks of an educational system that, like her father, is intent upon passing on the mantle of power to its "sons."[141]

The hostility of a father towards a daughter, manifested by Harry toward Jessie, also informs the central episode of the novel, the event that brings Inez home to Honolulu and, as one critic rightly observes, "jolts" her into taking control of her life and refusing to conform to other people's expectations.[142] Paul Christian's murder of his daughter and Wendell Omura, carried out with cold deliberation and followed by no remorse, presents a chilling image of calculated male violence against a female family member, underscoring not only Janet Christian's vulnerability to her father's wrath but also Inez's alienation from him.

Re-inventing himself as a romantic outcast, an "impoverished noble," Paul Christian returned home from one of his many trips and assumed the posture of a poor, unwanted and unappreciated family member, reduced to eating "canned tuna" and living in a room at the Y. Enraged by a photograph of Janet presenting an award to Wendell Omura, a Nisei Senator, Paul Christian, out of an irrationally displaced show of loyalty to those Americans who were killed at Pearl Harbor ("lest we forget," he utters), violently sacrifices both his daughter and Omura: "I just want Janet to know," he had said, "that in my eyes she's hit rock bottom" (D 135). Upon confronting Inez at the police station following the shooting, Paul Christian protests his being handled like a common criminal and rebukes Inez for her angry silence:

> "Am I to interpret your silence as disapproval?"
> Inez said nothing.

"Now that I'm jailed like a common criminal you're going to administer the *coup de grace*? Step on me?" Paul Christian turned back to Billy Dillon. "Janet and I have always been close. Not this one."
There was a silence. (D 143)

Like her daughter who wears an angry stare when dealing with a father and brother from whom she is alienated, Inez responds to her father's taunting belligerence by saying nothing. Confronted with the convulsions of male hostility, Didion women are, as we have seen, often reduced to silence.

As the privileged son of a U.S. senator, Adlai Victor remains brazenly aloof from the destructive consequences of his behavior; he acts with impunity and bears no signs of remorse for causing an accident that permanently maimed a young woman, costing her her "left eye and the function of one kidney" (D 60). Symbolic of the American colonial presence in Hawaii and displaying an attitude of ethnic superiority, Paul Christian, Adlai's grandfather, proudly justifies killing his own daughter because of her liaison with a Japanese man, and, due to Billy's nefarious machinations, will not even have to face a retributive justice system. The chain of white male privilege in *Democracy* spans three generations and proves to be inimical to the safety of women.

The corresponding chain of matrilineal descent is occupied by victims of male neglect and a systemic discrimination against women, beginning with Carol Christian, "abandoned" by her husband's long, unnecessary absences from home and yet, like all Didion women, unprepared for any life style other than that of a wife and mother, and feeling uncomfortable even with that role. Resorting to alcohol to numb the profound loneliness stemming from her position as an outsider in the islands, Carol Christian anticipates her granddaughter's drug-enhanced retreat into self as a strategic coping mechanism. While Janet succumbs to a predatory father, it is Inez who finally manages to break away from those who wish to control her, to keep her entrapped in the self-destructive, secondary role of the "politician's wife."

Having returned home to Hawaii upon her sister's death, Inez, with the help of Didion-the-narrator, begins to piece together the remembered fragments of her life, to re-assemble a sense of self that eventually enables Inez to break her silence in the face of male intimidation and neglect; she musters the courage to express her anger and to make a decision regarding Jessie and herself that will sully her public image as "the candidate's wife." Frustrated by her husband's skepticism and failure to take any action to find their daughter in Saigon, Inez decides to leave Honolulu with Jack Lovett not only because his connections in the covert military community can retrieve Jessie but also because Inez loves him (D 181). Inez jettisons societal expectations and restrictive notions of propriety and acts to insure her own happiness and the safety of her daughter:

> "Oh shit, Inez," Jack Lovett said. "Harry Victor's wife."
> "Listen," Inez said. "It's too late for the correct thing. Forget the correct thing." (D 187)

That Inez's decision was a matter of careful deliberation rather than an impulsive gesture is suggested by the narrator who observes wryly that "Inez Victor's behavior the night she flew to Hong Kong may not have been so circumstantial after all. She had to have a passport with her, didn't she" (D 182). The implied deliberative nature of Inez's actions—the conscious decision to break free from externally-imposed notions of "correct" female behavior, the unwavering concern for a daughter at risk, a concern that she translates into *action*, her ability to *act* upon her love for Jack Lovett, and later her *active* commitment to help re-settle refugees from Southeast Asia—are factors that all reflect a woman who has relinquished the posture of "passive detachment," which is so typical of the Didion women considered in this study, in favor of a strategy of self-empowerment. In effect, Inez has converted her silence and seething discontentment into articulate action; by transforming her private anger into public expression, she has, as Hirsch explains in her analysis of maternal rage, "claim[ed] a place" and asserted "a right to expression and discourse, a right to intelligibility."[143] Having been reduced to silent objectivity by a culture that denies women a right to speak and to be heard, that is, a right to their own subjectivity, Inez breaks free from some of the restraints of her gender to establish her own voice, her own articulation of the "I" which, for her, is inextricably linked with the "we" of a shared community. Inez's communal connection begins with her association with the narrator and expands to the larger context of Kuala Lumpur, both experiences representing "victories"[144] for this woman who once bore her wrath and humiliation in silence.

In contrast to the self-serving rhetoric of abstraction spouted by Billy Dillon and Harry Victor, Inez adopts a moral code whose axioms are, as Didion states in *Salvador*, "firmly grounded in the specific," that is, in trying to help *individuals* improve their lot, whether it be a displaced daughter or displaced refugees or a displaced "self." Didion defends this kind of axiological system, pejoratively termed "wagon-train morality" by its detractors (STB 158), in her essay "On Morality," where she relates an incident in which a nurse's husband remained with the body of a young man who was killed in a car accident in the desert because it would have been, the nurse maintained, "immoral" to do otherwise:

> It was one instance in which I did not distrust the word, because she meant something quite specific. She meant that if a body is left alone for even a few minutes in the desert, the coyotes close in and eat the flesh...one of the promises we make to one another is that we will try to retrieve our casualties.... (STB 158)

Inez has set out to retrieve Jessie, a "casualty" of her failed marriage, because to do otherwise would be "immoral." Unlike Charlotte who passively waits for Marin to arrive in Boca Grande, Inez *acts* to rescue her daughter. Like the nuns whose lives are "grounded in the specific" in *Salvador* and who work amidst the diarrhea and dehydration of dying children to mitigate pain and suffering, Inez will work to aid displaced refugees in Kuala Lumpur. Inez, argues Michael Tager, is the only true democrat in the novel, because she tries to effect change at the local level.[145]

Given Didion's definition of morality, Inez is not the only ethical figure in the novel who tries to empower others and to improve the condition of individuals. The role of the narrator suggests a moral quest to help reassemble the fragmented pieces of an identity shattered by restrictive sex-role stereotypes and by neglectful and, at times, violent male behavior. Joseph Epstein argues that "it would have been better if Miss Didion had left out her character Joan Didion the novelist because it makes the narrative so difficult."[146] On the contrary, the role of Didion the narrator brilliantly parallels: 1)the moral commitment to "effect change at the local [aesthetic] level" and to retrieve some semblance of personal and narrative identities, themselves casualties of a postmodern nuclear age beleaguered by societal fragmentation, the threat of global annihilation and a preoccupation with the quick "sound bite," the "photo opportunity" and the fleeting image; 2)the ethical quest to retrieve and re-assemble the identity of Inez Victor, a female "casualty" of an oppressive patriarchal system. The unusual narrative device of "Joan Didion-the-narrator" also, as Stout observes, serves to lend an air of "verisimilitude" to the fictive world of the text that, in turn, "invites a sense of identification which generalizes the import of the story."[147] Consequently, the narrator serves as a bridge between the reader and Inez so that the female reader can identify with both women when they sense the gender restrictions imposed upon them by a sexist society.

The inclusion of Didion-the-narrator who, as a participant in the novel interposes herself between the reader and Inez Victor, also manages to tone down the heroine's earlier passivity, thus, as in *A Book of Common Prayer*, enhancing our sympathy for an entrapped female. More significantly, however, the device of Didion-the-narrator suggests to this reader that the re-assessment of Inez Victor's long compliance within an oppressive marriage perhaps points to Didion's increased understanding not only of the complexities inherent in a woman's desire to erect an independent identity in American culture but also the profound emotional price a woman pays for conforming to externally imposed gender expectations:

> [I once] thought of Inez Victor's capacity for passive detachment as an affectation born of boredom, the frivolous habit of an essentially idle mind. After the events which occurred in the spring and summer of 1975 I thought of it differently. I thought of it as the essential mechanism for living a life in which the major cost was memory. Drop fuel. Jettison cargo. Eject crew. (D 70)

Similar to her "subject" who gathers the courage and integrity of will to extricate herself from a self-destructive existence, Didion-the-narrator undergoes a pivotal change in her understanding of a woman's sacrificial role in a male-dominated relationship, and the difficulty of overcoming the inertia that settles in once she has bought the package of female subservience and dependency.

Unlike her predecessors—Lily, Maria and Charlotte—Inez emerges as an integrated, assertive woman, more conscious of her choices and ready to assume responsibility for those choices, whether or not they deviate from the traditional norms of correct female conduct. Having been spared, as a result of an innovative narrative device, any direct encounter with the often self-degrading whinings of an unhappy wife, and having witnessed, through the narrator, Inez's *moral* (according to Didion's definition) stance to "stay with the body" or "retrieve one's casualties," the reader feels comfortable in celebrating Inez as a hero. For it is Inez who remains with Janet as she slips from a coma into death; it is Inez who makes arrangements for returning the body of Jack Lovett after he dies in a swimming pool, and it is Inez who seeks to retrieve Jessie, her own marital "casualty." Finally, it is Inez who heroically devotes her life to caring for the *victims* of the Vietnam War, "casualties," in part, of an American foreign policy of imperialistic aggression.

As in *Salvador*, Didion's non-partisan stance in *Democracy* in effect champions neither political party at the expense of the other; nowhere does she overtly condemn hawkish intervention in Southeast Asia. One might even argue that her scathing portrait of Harry Victor, a liberal politician, is a not-so-subtle indictment of the 1960's left-wing anti-war activist, while her seemingly more positive depiction of Jack Lovett reflects her tacit endorsement of right-wing policies. However, while Didion refrains from explicitly leaning to the political left or right, she does in *Democracy* implicitly disclose an abuse of male power that transcends political partisanship and that reveals a predilection for violence and corruption as the integral mechanism of a political system that places the weaker members of society in danger. For while the liberal Harry Victor proves to be a self-serving, unprincipled opportunist, secret agent Jack Lovett sports his own unique brand of corruption, and is, in some respects, far more insidious and lethal in his dealings. That Inez "loves" him and rejects Harry for him may reflect her choosing the lesser of two evils rather than her having found an heroic male counterpart.

Far from representing the *parfit gentil knight* of her novel, as McCarthy argues,[148] Jack Lovett in fact manifests what Michael Tager describes as an "amoral detachment"[149] from the consequences of his active participation in the vast network of espionage and, what is euphemistically tagged, "covert operations." "War is," as Hanley notes, "Jack Lovett's business; he isn't for or against it; he's simply a pro."[150] Given the notoriously destructive nature of such operations and the arrogant disdain that he, as an "operative," displays toward congressional restrictions and the general public, in addition to the enormous, personal profits that he accumulates by dealing in black market weaponry, Jack Lovett's "detachment" seems more immoral than amoral. Jack Lovett may be the heroine's lover and the man who works to rescue Inez's daughter, but he remains a postmodern "soldier of fortune" who, like Harry Victor, retreats into the insular realm of abstraction, and views the world as a vast stage on which he, as director, manipulates the movements of other countries toward fulfilling both American foreign policy goals and his own personal financial objectives:

> All nations, to Jack Lovett, were "actors," specifically "state actors" ("non-state actors" were the real wild cards here, but in Jack Lovett's extensive experience the average non-state actor was less interested in laser mirrors than in M-16's...the everyday implements of short-view power, and when the inductive leap to the long view was made it would probably be straight weapons-grade uranium) and he viewed such actors abstractly, as friendly, committed or uncommitted, as assemblies of armaments on a large board.

Asia was ten thousand tanks here, three hundred Phantoms there. The heart of Africa was an enrichment facility. (D 37)

Jack Lovett's depersonalized, reductive world-view, wherein countries are perceived in terms of their "military capability" and destructive machinery, is, in effect, the kind of myopic perspective that primes humanity for aggression. By viewing countries as "assemblies of armaments" rather than vital habitats of individual people and thriving cultures, Jack Lovett bolsters the post-World War II American military complex that profits from the weapons business and maintains America's global influence. For a writer who declares morality to reside in the specific interactions of individuals helping one another, of working on the local level to ease pain and misery, such a description of Jack Lovett seems hardly complimentary.

Didion's concern with the specificity of images and the withholding of information, in addition to her conscious design to write a minimalistic novel and not a political tract results in the absence of the more explicit criticisms of the post-World War II military-industrial complex that appear in Pynchon's more expansive technique in *Gravity's Rainbow*. Yet, Didion's implicit critique of war profiteers, like Jack Lovett, anticipates Pynchon's indictment of American capitalism; Hanley's salient observation about *Democracy* could easily apply also to *Gravity's Rainbow*: "Capitalism is the ideology of war in America, war as business opportunity, a forum for the exchange of favors, a chance to put the right people together."[151] The oblique and passing references to Jack Lovett's nefarious activities and his reductive world-view suggest the author's disenchantment with a postmodern America and its powerholders who exercise their enormous influence for their own lucrative ends. A scaled down, non-comic version of Milo Minderbinder, Heller's successful entrepreneur in *Catch-22* who exploits the war to turn a very sizeable personal profit, Jack Lovett is not above using the Vietnam War itself as a specifically commercial enterprise to pull in some "covert" money to be hidden away in a Swiss bank account. As a matter of fact, for a man usually given to "abstraction," Jack Lovett becomes quite specific and "visceral"in this dimension of his work:

> [His] overriding concern during the months before Inez Victor re-entered the field of his direct vision…had been to insure the covert survival of certain business interests…For example…he watched the arrival and clearance from Saigon and immediate transshipment to Geneva via Vancouver of a certain amount of gold bullion crated and palleted as "household effects." (D159-160)

While overtly less harsh in her depiction of Jack Lovett than she is of Harry Victor, Didion seems to harbor some moral reservations about the man whom Inez loves.

For in addition to his duplicitous business dealings, Jack Lovett chillingly embodies a romanticization of the impulse for destruction that Pynchon will spin out more fully in the demonic character of Blicero in *Gravity's Rainbow*. Lovett personifies a culture pathologically in love with its own imminent demise. He discovers a transcendent beauty in the Pacific dawn during the testing of nuclear bombs: "Christ they were sweet," and "the sky was this pink no painter could approximate," he rhapsodizes to Inez at the opening of the novel. His remarks echo the rhetoric of the sublime and the poetry of apocalyptic ecstasy found in *The New York Times* description of a nuclear explosion at a 1951 Nevada test site:

> A white chimney of fire, a light with an intensity many times brighter than the noonday sun, golden, purple, violet, gray and blue, lighting every peak and crevasse of the mountain, the beauty great poets dream about followed by an awesome roar which warns of doomsday.[152]

Nostalgic for the aesthetic destruction of these Pacific locales and dismissing the testing islands as "just atolls, sand spits actually" (D 11), Jack Lovett considered the Aleutians as "just dog duty, ass end of the universe, they give the world an enema they stick it in Amchitka" (D 13). Even his memories of Inez emerge as coordinates positioned between the axes of nuclear bombing dates and locations:

> ...Those events in the Pacific, Jack Lovett said.
> Those shots around 1952, 1953...
> I remember I bought you some little souvenir from Manila." (D 12,13)

As a representative of patriarchal power in the postmodern world, Jack Lovett organizes his life around covert military-business transactions that include the clandestine sales of materials necessary for production of nuclear weapons to countries that align themselves with American economic interests and also with Jack Lovett's financial interests. Like Harry, Jack employs a euphemistic nomenclature to obfuscate his dealings: "guns and bullets" become "assets." These business transactions were in "the field of his direct vision" while Inez, for twenty years, remained primarily in his "peripheral vision, a fitful shadow" (D 160). Not completely free of the learned dependence upon a male figure, Inez manifests what Cixous describes as the plight of most women who have been so alienated from their bodies and sexuality in a patriarchal culture that they remain impotent as fighters in the struggle for their own liberation: such a woman "can't possibly be a good fighter; she is reduced to being the servant of the militant male, his shadow."[153] Like Harry, Jack is emblematic of the often destructive machinations of power that divest women of any substantive identity and relegate them to a shadowy periphery.

Inez remains one of Didion's most successful female characters, for she manages, partly through bonding with "Joan Didion-the-narrator," to extricate herself from socially sanctioned forms of female bondage and to articulate her own subjectivity through anger and community action in Kuala Lumpur. Both she and the narrator have assembled tentative identities or "core selves" that evolve within the arena of social interaction. The bonding of these two women serves to erect a protective, albeit fragile, barrier against the assaults of a militaristic culture that objectifies females and tries to deny them a voice; this female connection also suggests that Didion the author has broadened her scope and sensitivity to the plight of women in a sexist society. Although she may not be writing an openly didactic, feminist novel in which she focuses primarily and solely upon those issues confronting women in a patriarchal culture, Didion does effectively illuminate the subtle yet insidious strains of female subjugation in America: "Gender problems are implicated in Didion's broad social criticism, even when they are not specified."[154]

Democracy is a minimalistic novel whose ironic structure and textual ambiguities render any unified critical vision ultimately unstable. Joan Didion's most successful female character, Inez Victor, breaks free from Harry Victor and survives the death of Jack Lovett to continue to effect change at the local level in Kuala Lumpur, ironically retrieving the casualties of a war whose flames were fueled by the subterfuge and "covert actions" of men like Jack Lovett. Despite her courageous shedding of her "attitude of detached passivity" in favor of concrete action, despite her escaping the demeaning and self-destructive role of "the politician's wife," Inez continues to confront the horrifying consequences of male violence, organized as warfare. Overtly embracing neither conservative nor liberal ideologies, *Democracy* reveals an abiding vulnerability of women to patriarchal aggression in postmodern culture that transcends partisan leanings.

Chapter III
ಸು೧ಽ
Thomas Pynchon

The portrayals of women in the fiction of Donald Barthelme and Joan Didion reveal an ambiguity concerning the often violent degradation of females by abusive men that stems, in part, from the aesthetic strategies involved in their minimalistic formats: the calculated silences and omissions that serve to subvert traditional plot and character development; the inescapable "comic" quality that adheres to the fundamentally tragic episodes of female subjugation through Barthelme's parodic juxtaposition of incongruous scenarios; and the required intervention of the reader to fill in the compositional space left vacant by the authors with his/her own ideological assumptions concerning women's political status in postmodern America. In addition to the innovative technical dimension of these minimalistic texts, however, there seems to reside a more pervasive, thematic ambivalence concerning the plight of women in contemporary society: an abiding resistance to acknowledge the late 1960's women's movement as a valid attempt to redress gender-based inequities, as evidenced by Barthelme's satiric thrusts at feminist rhetoric in *Snow White* and Didion's early, explicit repudiation of the myth of the female victim; and a frequent reliance upon conventional stereotypes of women to populate their nonconventional, experimental fiction, whether it be the male-dependent female, the nymphomaniac, the passive, compliant victim who invites her own degradation, the evil witch or the carping bitch.

When turning to more expansive novelists such as Thomas Pynchon and Toni Morrison, novelists who not only invoke a mythic sweep in their experimental fiction but also fill in their broad canvases with more fully developed characters and plot details, we are able to extrapolate graphic episodes that provide more textual data concerning the psychology of violence and women in contemporary fiction than were available in the minimalistic tales of Barthelme and Didion. Yet, despite the relative profusion of information supplied in their texts, the innovative strategies employed by both Pynchon and Morrison carry with them their own interpretive challenges and obstacles for the reader. S. R. Suleiman notes that Pynchon's fiction "defies aggressively and provocatively the traditional criteria of narrative intelligibility and correlatively the reader's sense-making ability," and that instead of "logical and temporal development" and "consistency," Pynchon offers us "repetition and the juxtaposition of apparently random events," and "contradiction."[1] For example, in *V.* and *Gravity's Rainbow*, the reader, as a co-conspirator in the piecing together of discovered (fabricated?) clues that will reveal the existence of an insidious cabal (paranoid fantasy?), must tread cautiously and slowly through a fictional landscape of temporal and narrative disruptions, of identity confusions and seemingly endless heteroglossia, and of a surfeit of densely layered socio-cultural allusions, ranging from comic books and travel guides to Wittgenstein and Heisenberg, from burnt-out jazz musicians to Wagner and Rossini, from Venus the love goddess to the V-2 rockets that terrorized London in 1945. In Morrison's *Beloved* one must navigate through the often tumultuous seas of the juxtaposed time sequences of "re-memory" while remaining attentive to the voice of a supernatural "ghost" as she symbolically speaks for all the victims of slavery. The infusion of a surreal quality into seemingly realistic incidents that informs both Pynchon and Morrison's works poses an additional interpretive challenge, especially with regard to the episodes of violence and women that punctuate many of the texts. Yet, despite these innovations and the obstacles they present to the reader, both Pynchon and Morrison, through their expansive treatments of contemporary issues, provide yet another perspective on the phenomenology of violence and women in postmodern American fiction.

The previous chapters have alluded to a problem that attends the depiction of violence against women in art, namely, the uncomfortable commingling of exploitation, titillation and condemnation that informs many of the images, especially Barthelme's so-called "comic" images of female subjugation and Didion's version of the "zipless fuck" in *Run River*. Whether or not these images serve to stimulate (fe)male sexual fantasies, or whether they serve as aesthetic sublimations by which males can safely unleash their aggressions against an increasingly rebellious female population or by which women can magically regress to a fetal passivity, remain debatable but critical issues. With the more graphic depiction of sexualized violence against women in the texts of both Pynchon and Morrison, these issues come to the foreground and the controversy over pornography and art will again arise.

Furthermore, while the connection between women and violence in both Barthelme's and Didion's texts seems to be rather one-sided—male abuser vs. female victim (the bumbling, evil Jane notwithstanding)—the emergence of female characters who initiate acts of rage against men, women and children in the texts of Pynchon and Morrison presents us with another facet of the phenomenology of violence and women in American fiction. Do these women, like Damon Cross in Wright's *The Outsider* or Bigger Thomas in *Native Son*, succeed in establishing their own autonomy only through violence, forging a "femismo" or female counterpart to the "machismo" brutality of a Mailer protagonist? Is anger, especially maternal anger, an "instrument of cartography," as Marilyn Frye suggests, by which women who have been traditionally silenced and objectified articulate their subjectivity, and, as Hirsch adds, proclaim "a place and assert a right to expression and discourse"?[2] Do women in these texts break through the stereotypes of the evil witch to an innovative definition of female identity, one that challenges patriarchal restrictions? Legitimate expressions of female fury, virtually absent from Barthelme's stories, and the repressed anger, so typical of Didion's early female characters, explode into poignant acts of violence in Morrison's texts and take on a distorted, grotesque quality in Pynchon's tales. Female-initiated violence, as we shall discover, often acquires a sacrificial quality in Morrison's texts, becoming an action to which one resorts in order both to assert and articulate female subjectivity and to "save" the victim from a more horrific consequence; however, in Pynchon's texts, women adopt aggressive behavior as a means to secure a pathological role in an inherently pathological political system, a patriarchal dystopia over which they exert little, if any control, and which encourages human contact primarily through sado-masochistic relationships.

The encyclopedic nature of some of the works considered in this chapter compel our analyses to target specific episodes of violence and women rather than the texts in their entirety. Consequently, the following discussion should by no means be viewed as exhausting the allusive density and thematic richness of Pynchon's or Morrison's works; this caveat applies especially to a work like *Gravity's Rainbow* in which incidents explicitly involving women and violence are subsumed under a more over-arching concern with the military-industrial state, whose mythic stature is emblematized in the totemic figure of the Rocket. While the colonization and degradation of women may be symptomatic of the West's mad pursuit of its own technological demise, it is only one of the threads of insanity that Pynchon weaves into the intricately patterned fabric of the pathological State. Similarly, although an act of female infanticide constitutes the centripetal thematic force in *Beloved*, its significance transcends its own specificity, reaching beyond itself to stand as a commentary on the perverse but heroic and understandable "choice" of death over life within any oppressive master-slave state.

This chapter will isolate and discuss some of the episodes of women and violence that appear in two of the novels of Thomas Pynchon, *V.* and *Gravity's Rainbow*. In addition to the questions concerning pornography and art that arise in connection with his graphic depictions of female mutilation and dismemberment, informing many of these incidents are epistemological and metaphysical issues that Pynchon seems to view as symptomatic of a diseased society. Consequently, the following discussions, for example, will consider violence and women, specifically the rhetoric of rape, within the epistemological framework of binary thought processes and inverse logic; it will look at the relatively unmitigated fury unleashed against lesbianism within the metaphysical context of entropic, closed systems, for which Pynchon seems to maintain an especial scorn. Patricia Waugh argues that the postmodernist repudiation of totalities such as identity, transcendence and self-presence—all staples of the plots of nineteenth century realist fiction—generated a deep hostility and misogyny in writers who in the latter half of the twentieth century projected their nostalgia for such lost ideals onto the female.[3] While Pynchon, like many American male novelists from Fitzgerald and Miller to Mailer and Barthelme, seems quite comfortable in positing woman as a metaphor for many of the frustrations and ills that plague twentieth century America, his misogyny seems at times to seek a philosophical validation that, simultaneously, parodically subverts itself. Some of his more violent scenes display both a comic quality and a dimension of conscious self-deprecation. As Frederick J. Hoffman observes with regard to *V.*: "[*V.*] mocks the reasons why it mocks everything else so that we have dog biting man biting dog in a succession of etceteras whose only real conclusion" is the last page of the book.[4]

Consequently, we face an interpretive challenge similar to that encountered in our analysis of Barthelme's texts, namely, how to decode those images which, manifesting an inextricable linking of violence and parody, simultaneously exploit and mock misogynistic attitudes, and both celebrate and condemn sexually degrading fantasies of female bondage and mutilation. While Barthelme's minimalistic, parodic structure serves to obviate and defuse a potentially virulent sexism, Pynchon's infusion of a surreal, nightmarish quality into an expansive, detailed, recognizable landscape, frequently peopled with buffoonish characters engaged in comic antics, spawns images of female mutilation and femicide so grotesque in nature that they threaten to exceed the parameters of parody and become, instead, horrifying commentaries on the dehumanization of women in the military-industrial complex. Unlike Didion, who in *Democracy* focuses upon the love affair between Inez Victor and Jack Lovett and only subtextually explores the political status of a *woman* who falls in love with a privileged member of the military state, Pynchon, in *Gravity's Rainbow*, widens the literary lens to encompass the System itself, depicting women's roles within the military complex in gruesome detail.

Woman as Mystery: *V.*

Pynchon's first novel, like Hawthorne's *The Scarlet Letter*, teases the reader with a linguistic mystery that attaches itself to the enigmatic figure of a woman. As the signifier "A" persists in overflowing its original meaning—Adultery, and reverberates along a potentially endless chain of additional signifiers—Angel, Artist, Arthur, etc., all of which are indissolubly associated with the scorned and loved Hester Prynne, the sexual scapegoat and benevolent seamstress of her Puritan enclave, so too does the letter V in Pynchon's novel of that title, (and perhaps in *Gravity's Rainbow* and *Vineland* as well) also refuse to coincide with itself and come to rest as a stabilized signifier. As Tony Tanner has observed, in addition to the multiple incarnations of *V.* in her role as the "elusive female spy/anarchist" (Virginia, Victoria, Veronica, Vera,), the letter "V" acquires additional significance through the plethora of peripheral textual clues, including the jazz club called the V-Note, Veronica the sewer rat, Queen Victoria, Venezuela, Valetta, Vheissu, Venus and the German retaliation weapon, the *Vergeltungswaffe*.[5]

Unlike Hester Prynne, who exists within the fictional space of the novel as a concretized character localized within a specific spatio-temporal framework of a traditional narrative, V. remains a thematic, linguistic and structural mystery that defies resolution. Is she, as Alice Jardine argues, the "matrix" of a novel that questions the legitimacy of narrative structure, that is, "the locus of past, present and future" in a novel that is really "about interpretation, about the possibilities and impossibilities of 'making sense,' of 'making plots?'"[6] For, as Hutcheon notes, Pynchon's "historiographic metafiction" challenges those discourses operative in society and "yet use[s] them, even to milk them for all they are worth" so that the "terror of totalizing plotting is inscribed within texts characterized by nothing if not by overplotting."[7] Is V. a real historical woman or that dark, brooding, impersonal force that Hardy portrays in *The Dynasts*, propelling history along through an inscrutable series of violent fits and starts, revolutions and natural disasters? Or is she a projection of those conspiracy-obsessed paranoiacs who, needing to locate the insidious presence of a cabal in all events, feel quite comfortable in a patriarchal culture with projecting the fundamental sickness of our society, namely, our seemingly relentless slide away from our own humanness into the mortal stillness of the inanimate, onto the figure of a seductive woman? As Waugh notes, "One thinks of V. when one considers that traditional images of the castrating female, the unknown and therefore uncontrollable woman, are overlaid in a technological age with their representation as machines which have outstripped the controlled and rational dominance of the male."[8] Olderman asks, "Do symptoms of V. reveal a master cabal or universal paranoia or a world deluded by its need for mystery, to replace a lost mythology?"[9] Is she a postmodernized version of Hester Prynne, the receptacle of a Puritan culture's inveterate distrust of and disdain for female sexuality, only now raised to new metaphysical heights so that the vilification and scapegoating of women take on a philosophical rationale in a technological culture?

By focusing on episodes in the novel that contain images of women and violence, we will discover that V. will emerge as the emblem of man's metaphysical and epistemological frustrations in an increasingly materialistic culture. American literature often symbolically locates the Romantic quester's failure to find an objective correlative worthy of his idealism and hope in a female figure. In *The Great Gatsby*, the irresponsible and reckless Daisy, in part, personifies the materialistic culture's inability to provide a physical counterpart to Gatsby's transcendental ideal; in "The Glass Mountain," the princess stands for the lack of resonance of traditional aesthetic symbols in contemporary society; and in *V.* the elusive female figure will come to represent, in part, the failure of a culture not only to provide an appropriate correlate of the Romantic impulse but also to halt and reverse the culture's rapid descent into an identification with the inanimate. Images of inadequate women inform these texts, each of which vents male frustrations with the metaphysical, epistemological, aesthetic and cultural disruptions of twentieth century America.

As a metaphor for the culture's corruption, deceit and loss of spiritual transcendence, the inadequate or sexually lethal female, whether she symbolizes the vacuity of the American dream, the horrifying plunge into the inanimate or the comic emptiness of defunct artistic emblems, triggers a violent hostility against women that assumes a horrifying dimension in *V.* While the narrator's (Barthelme's?) aggression against the princess (women?) is partially deflated by the minimalistic structure and the comic thrust of "The Glass Mountain," Pynchon's violence towards women in *V.* becomes a virulent, erotic anger aimed, at times, at inflicting sexual mutilation upon his female characters. Here, Pynchon is part of a longstanding tradition in American literature, wherein female characters have been subjected to all kinds of sexualized disfigurement: Zenobia's breasts are "accidentally" torn apart when Hollingsworth pulls her from the river in Hawthorne's *Blithedale Romance*; there is the image of the ripped breast of Myrtle Wilson, who is "accidentally" run down by Daisy in *The Great Gatsby*; Temple Drake is raped by a corncob in Faulkner's *Sanctuary* and Joanna Burden is mutilated by Joe Christmas in *Light in August*; and Ambrose's mother's breasts are "comically" attacked by bees in Barth's *Lost in the Funhouse*. John Hawkes' texts abound with mutilated breast images: Henscher's mother in *The Lime Twig* dies in a fire, her "burning breasts" the dominant image; in *The Cannibal*, Stella's mother dies from a piece of shrapnel that pierces her breast; in *The Owl* the statue of the Madonna is knocked over by a kick to her breast; and in *The Blood Oranges*, Rosella's breasts become entangled in broken cobwebs during a symbolic rape scene. As mentioned in the previous chapter, one of the more explicit and troubling images of aggression in American literature involves the gang rape and sexual mutilation of Tra-la-la in Selby's *Last Exit to Brooklyn*, in which she not only has cigarettes extinguished on her breasts by her rapists, but also is vaginally assaulted with bottles and broomsticks. The images of Henry Miller's vaginal violations and those of Norman Mailer's rectal rapes also comprise part of the litany of male hostility toward women in American literature.

As we consider Pynchon within this literary landscape of female-directed aggression, the question that will arise entails the author's intent or purpose in presenting graphic portrayals of female mutilation and death. Do such images indulge and promote the culture's denigration of women and at the same time afford a socially "acceptable" expression of woman-hating?

Targeting writers prior to World War II, Katherine Rogers contends that since misogyny is not a morally defensible position, literature provides the writer with an acceptable way to unleash his anger, allowing him often to disguise his hatred of women in humor.[10] While this statement perhaps may apply to a writer such as Barthelme, Pynchon, along with Mailer, Hawkes, Selby and Barth, constructs such horrifyingly explicit images of male predatory brutality against women that one might conclude that a characteristic mark of much of the postmodernist American literary tradition, in addition to its structural innovations and the parodying of outmoded or, to use Barth's term, "exhausted" formal possibilities, is the *undisguised* depiction of misogyny. Whether Pynchon sanctions, celebrates and/or condemns such woman-hating through his images of aggression is one of the issues we will consider.

Metaphysics and Misogyny

V. chronicles the adventures of two seemingly antithetical male characters: Benny Profane, the "schlemihl" and paradigmatic "twentieth-century man" who, along with his dissolute buddies, "The Whole Sick Crew," remains content with "yo-yoing" or aimlessly wandering from one situation to another without any clear sense of direction, identity or purpose, oblivious of history; and Herbert Stencil who, in contrast, is obsessively immersed in history, seeking to resolve what may be the mystery behind the master cabal of the century, the meaning/identity of the elusive female, V., first mentioned in his late father's diary: "There is more behind and inside V than any of us has suspected. Not who, but what: what is she. God grant that I may never be called upon to write the answer."[11] Intent upon uncovering the connection between his late father and V., and the role she may have played in his father's death on the island of Malta, Stencil, as Jardine states, "sees and lives plots everywhere" so that he ends up not only "forcibly dislocating his personality" (he refers to himself in the third person), but also coercing the reader to participate in his preoccupation with conspiracies, "to follow these plots—even when 'Stencil' is absent—through a series of third person narratives."[12] Stencil's quest for V. and his obsession with the historical connections of events intermittently intersect with the aimless wanderings of Benny Profane and culminate in the two travelling to Malta together during the Suez crisis in 1956.

Despite their respective emphases concerning the exact identity of the mysterious V., critics, for the most part, agree as to her negative status in the novel, whether she be: the "Nothing at the heart of the dream" that, like the land of Vheissu, constantly changes her shapes and colors so as to create a dazzling and enchanting surface that only veils the void below;[13] or the "archetypal Terrible Mother," who, as the agency behind the ills of the age that has "sapped the vitality of modern men and made them a "Sick Crew," becomes the "compelling symbol of a culture that has destroyed itself with violence and drifted into dissolution and triviality";[14] or a "horrifying symbol of the inanimate" that is associated with disease and violence and reflects Pynchon's comic collapsing of Henry Adams' distinction between the Virgin and the Dynamo;[15] or, still yet, the "anti-goddess" who can provide the key to "the bewildering modern Wheel of Fortune."[16] According to Olderman, V. represents "a plunge toward annihilation brought on by our non-humanity,"[17] and to Wilde, V.'s "willing pursuit of the inanimate" makes her the "quintessential human of the twentieth century," the "incarnation of the entropic vision" that lures us to embrace nothingness.[18] Discerning a dimension of Roman Catholic eschatology at work in the novel, Golden argues that V., representing the future reign of nothingness which modern man desires as the end of history, symbolizes the apocalyptic leap into a "Third Kingdom" of chaos and multiplicity.[19] While W. T. Lhamon interprets the combination of apocalyptic and pentecostal images associated with V. as heralding a positive death and transfiguration of the world which Pynchon welcomes as a way to subvert myth and tradition,[20] it is, as we shall see, her plunge toward annihilation that symbolically dominates the novel. Even Alice Jardine, in her linguistic analysis of one of the various V-functions, Vheissu, concludes that the search for V. will lead you only "to interpretive Nothingness," for V. represents the "space of slippage, the spaces of non-resemblance, within the sign, among the signifier, signified and referent" that lurks in and among Stencil's and the reader's narrative strategies to "construct a plot, to chase through the novel for clues and meaning, only to get caught up in the circular interpretive machine of his or her own invention."[21]

From a metaphysical, epistemological, linguistic or political perspective, V., according to a majority of critics, emerges as a principle of chaos and disorder, the tantalizing, redoubtable power of annihilation that lures us to peek beneath the veil of the world's (or a plot's) dazzling surfaces to apprehend the Nothingness below. While Pynchon may bemoan the culture's collective slide into the dehumanized morass of the inanimate, his "feminization" of both the destructive principle and the process of that deterioration explains, in part, the relatively unmitigated assault against women in the text. Woman, for Pynchon, becomes, in part, the symbol of the Sartrean in-itself (one woman in *V.* is described as "warm and viscous-moving" (V. 137)), that is, the *en soi* or undifferentiated mass of contingent being that makes its appearance in a variety of particular feminine disguises (Vera, Veronica, Vheissu, Rachel, Esther, Fina, Lucille etc.), and that threatens to engulf us in an entropic decline. By refracting the concept of V. into a multiplicity of incarnations, Pynchon seems to approach a feminist strategy which, as discussed by Sally Robinson, calls for the "demystification" of the metaphysical and essentialist notion of Woman "and the concomitant positing of a plural and differentially marked category of women": by fracturing the unitary idea of Woman into women as a "multiple and internally contradictory category," theorists, Robinson argues, may now "challenge the artificial distinctions between Woman and Men."[22] While Pynchon does seem to toy with the idea of V. (Woman) as an elusive and perhaps non-existent Ideal of Western metaphysics throughout parts of the text, the final appearance and disassembling of her body parts on the island of Malta suggest that she ultimately resurfaces as the debased Ideal of a technological age, that is, as the concept of the artificial Woman of which all of her particular disguises (Vera, Victoria, etc.) are internally consistent incarnations. Pynchon can not, it seems, refrain from identifying Woman with matter and man's inability to transcend it: "The female now becomes the cause of the failure of masculine transcendence rather than the ideal object of the masculine quest for self."[23] For matter, as Scott Sanders observes, is, "as every Pynchon reader knows, governed by the laws of thermodynamics, which point toward annihilation."[24]

"The cultural associations of mind with masculinity and body with femininity are," as Butler argues, "well-documented within the field of philosophy and feminism"; and the metaphysical dualism so endemic to the Western philosophical tradition from Plato through Descartes, Husserl and Sartre, is part of the phallogocentrism that underscores the "political and psychic subordination" of women by men.[25] Marilyn French, Susan Griffin and others have offered feminist, historical accounts explaining the genesis of Western patriarchy in which woman, because of her reproductive functions, was initially associated with Nature and subject to man's desire to gain "power over" those forces needed to secure the survival of the community.[26] As Rosamarie Tong argues, "Power-over rapidly became, under patriarchy, a value cultivated simply for the experience of being the person in charge, the lawgiver, the 'boss.'"[27] In identifying women with materiality that must be conquered, Pynchon fits squarely into the entire

Platonic and Judeo-Christian tradition, which, as Jardine argues in her analysis of the writings of Jean-Joseph Goux, began "with Moses's anger at the worship of the golden calf, a female deity—*mater*—and the Jews' ensuing departure from Egypt with its female icons and hieroglyphic imagination." Through this symbolic negation of the Mother at the inception of Western patriarchal history, "'woman' has been but the passive matter to which 'Man' could give form through the ever-increasing spiral of abstract universals: God, Money, Phallus."[28] One could add that that ever-increasing spiral of abstract universals by which man has imposed form and order on the material world and symbolically "negated" the Mother has also entailed a very concrete intensification of violence and anger against women and the concomitant destruction of the feminized environment, trends toward dissolution and collapse which in *V.* are manifested in the culture's descent into the dehumanized world of the inanimate. Susan Griffin notes that the characteristic metaphysical dualism of the Western tradition that associates woman with matter (nature and eros) and man with spirit or mind (culture) is also the metaphysics of pornography wherein men, by conquering and humiliating women into submission, seek to unleash their hostility and revenge against the very force that threatens to engulf them in darkness and unfathomable mystery.[29]

The femininization of land masses, such as Vheissu and Malta, underscores the identification of the female with the contingent in-itself and accounts, in part, for the discourse of rape and violation that attends those episodes in the text: "Vheissu," states Hugh Godolphin, the "penetrator" of surfaces (*V.* 204) and explorer who is obsessed with unlocking metaphysical mysteries, "is like a woman" who, wearing the "skin of a tattooed savage" (*V.* 170), dazzles the eye with colorful façades only to hide the Nothingness below. Having discovered this mysterious land in Africa and, as one critic notes, having personified it as a "female Queequeg,"[30] Godolphin wants to penetrate it, to rape and flay the skin so as to see, touch and control its hidden secrets:

> [S]oon that skin, that gaudy godawful riot of pattern and color, would get between you and whatever it was in her that you thought you loved. And soon, in perhaps only a matter of days, it would get so bad that you would begin praying to whatever god you knew of to send some leprosy to her. To flay that tattooing to a heap of red, purple and green debris, leave the veins and ligaments raw and quivering and open at last to your eyes and your touch. (*V.* 171)

As a rather muted precursor of Rusty, Mailer's paradigmatic despoiler of Nature in *Why Are We in Vietnam?*, who applies the violent rhetoric of sexual assault against women to describe his "sodomizing" of the landscape, Godolphin couches his colonizing impulse in the metaphor of a love that disguises a destructive lust. His approach to Vheissu is sadistically sexual and reveals the frustrations of a lover who, growing impatient with his beloved's perceived façade, dreams of violently laying bare her mysteries. When his voyage to the South Pole, "one of the only two motionless places on this gyrating world" (*V.* 205), reveals the corpse of a spider monkey frozen beneath the skin of ice, Godolphin, like Roquentin in Sartre's *Nausea*, comes face to face with the essential meaninglessness of existence, the stark insignificance of the inanimate, the Nothingness at the heart of Vheissu and all material surfaces. He is very similar to Joe, the sarcastic misogynist in Miller's *Tropic of Cancer* who, lured by the alleged mystery of female sexuality lurking beneath women's clothes, probes and studies the "twat" of his "Georgia cunt" with a flashlight only to discover "just a crack between the legs...just a blank...nothing at all."[31] Susan Griffin, noting the analogous, patriarchal subordination of the female body and the natural environment, comments on the explorer—a Ponce de Leon like figure—who, looking for the fountain of youth, found only renewable nature and, in anger, claimed ownership and the right of posterity to despoil "her":

> Coming through finally to the end...he is disappointed. This land that he had devoted himself to has turned out to be a delusion. She is a house of mirrors...There is no fountain...But he will have something...he leaves a flag. The land will bear his name. After him will come other men...and they will change the face of this land.[32]

Disappointed by the vacuous mystery of the "feminine," both "explorers"—Joe and Ponce de Leon—vent their fury through a sexualized aggression; similarly, Godolphin would violate the land as he would a woman who has seductively dangled the hope of metaphysical solace before him only to bring him face to face with his own nothingness and the void at the heart of existence. As one of the avatars of V., Vheissu seems to elicit the sexualized violence of a man who discovers that his "beloved" is nothing but a "gaudy dream of annihilation" whose façade of thriving colors, fragrances and sounds belies a more primordial substratum of inanimate, meaningless existence.

Like Vheissu, Malta is also identified as female, having been feminized in the poetic writings of Fausto Maijstral's diary:

> Malta is a noun feminine and proper. Italians have indeed been attempting her defloration since the 8th of June. She lies on her back in the sea, sullen; an immemorial woman. Spread to the explosive orgasms of Mussolini bombs. (*V.* 318)

Perhaps representing a "parody exercise in the application of male weapons to female genitalia," as one critic argues,[33] the depiction of Malta, that "womb of rock," as a ravaged and violated woman also strengthens the metaphysical identification of woman with the inanimate, and accounts, in part, for the fury unleashed against women in the text. For it is on the island of Malta that the ultimate assault against V.—her disassembling—occurs. Having been incarnated as the "bad Priest," V is discovered beneath the ruins and debris by a group of children following a bombing raid. As the children begin to remove "his" clothing, they discover that the priest is really a woman who comes apart, piece by artificial piece (*V.* 342-343). While Pynchon may be tangentially interested in suggesting a typically postmodernist destabilization of dichotomous gender categories, his main concern is with parodying the basic mechanization of human existence in a technological age. Yet, because Pynchon has chosen a woman to characterize this "sinful" slide into nothingness (the Bad Priest's navel is a sapphire that, as Griffin notes, is a gem that in Western culture has come to "resemble the number eleven, which has transgressed ten, the number of commandments" and, therefore, "stands for sin"[34]), he does present a problem to the feminist reader: V is a woman and even "if she is constructed to expose the dehumanizing effects of an idealist philosophy, she also perpetuates them in her very form."[35]

Throughout *V.* women are continually identified with the undifferentiated mass of being and with particular things. There is "a lot of good stuff in Jersey," states Angel, one of Profane's buddies, during a discussion about states with the most available women (*V.* 42). The various incarnations of V., whom Stencil pursues, become increasingly reified and, as stated, culminate in the disassembling of her inanimate parts on the island of Malta. Even within the more prosaic world of Benny Profane, women either become, or try to "humanize," parts of the inanimate world. The foam-rubber breasts that supply the Whole Sick Crew with beer at Suck Hour, the erotic discourse between Rachel Owlglass and her MG, and the injection of synthetic materials into the facial structure of Esther Harvitz so that she can have a waspish nose, all suggest a culture that has not only given itself over to materialistic pursuits but, more profoundly, has, by denying its own humanity, obliterated the distinction between the human and the inanimate.

Reifying Rachel, Profane "sees" her as an object that speaks inanimate words:

> They talked in the car always, he trying to find the key to her ignition behind the hooded eyes, she sitting back on the right-hand steering wheel and talking, talking, nothing but MG-words, inanimate words he really couldn't talk back at. (*V.* 27)

That Profane's perception has some validity, that his inability to communicate with this "materialistic girl" is well-founded, becomes clear to us once we read that Rachel has, as one critic comically observes, literally become "autoerotic,"[36] having solidified her identification with the inanimate by eroticizing her MG:

> "You beautiful stud," [Profane] heard her say, "I love to touch you." Wha, he thought. "Do you know what I feel when we're out on the road? Alone, just us?" She was running the sponge caressingly over its front bumper. "Your funny responses, darling, that I know so well. The way your brakes pull a little to the left, the way you start to shudder around 5000rpm when you're excited..."It occurred to Profane that he might vomit...She had climbed in the car and now lay back in the driver's seat, her throat open to the summer constellations. He was about to approach her when he saw her left hand snake out all pale to fondle the gearshift...He didn't want to see any more. (*V.* 28-29)

A prescient and hopefully hyperbolic image of some of the contemporary auto ads that have dominated American advertising (e.g. Toyota's erotically-charged slogan, "I love what you do for me, Toyota!" comes to mind), Rachel-and-her-gear-shift undoubtedly parodies our culture's increasing identification with things; while this episode provides a humorous commentary on our growing tendency to relinquish and project our own humanity onto the inanimate, it also suggests that it is the woman, through her identification with the non-human, who feels most comfortable with society's drift toward cultural collapse and dissolution, again reinforcing the metaphysical connection between the female or "mater" and mater-ialism.

Rachel suffers not from the alienation that plagues Profane regarding the ontological gulf between man and nature, and far from harboring an angry desire to "piss at the sun," as does Profane, she feels quite at home amongst her commodities. As a matter of fact, Rachel manifests the very absence of alienation and *angst* that Herbert Marcuse describes in his analysis of advanced industrial civilization in *One Dimensional Man*:

[Industrialized society's] productivity and efficiency, its capacity to increase and spread comforts, to turn waste into need, and destruction into construction, the extent to which this civilization transforms the object world into an extension of man's mind and body makes the very notion of alienation questionable. The people recognize themselves in their commodities; they find their soul in their automobile, hi-fi set, split-level home, kitchen equipment.[37]

It is Profane who wants to vomit, who cannot communicate with Rachel's inanimate words, who senses the profound alienation of the human being living in a world of encroaching inanimateness, and who has "known for years" that "inanimate objects and he could not live in peace" (*V.* 37). Rachel, on the other hand, reflects the assimilation of the material world, the negation of the Mother, the merging of the animate and the inanimate. Having sexualized a commodity, she has effectively blurred the distinction between non-human and human and has magically bridged the ontological gulf.

Coupling Sartre's metaphysics with his own emphasis on our century's insane psycho/cultural desire to assimilate the characteristics of the inanimate, Pynchon seems to imply that violence directed against women reflects the individual's (a man's) last-ditch, frantic attempt both to conquer and to merge with the inanimate, that is, to "violate" (rape, murder, mutilate) and thereby control the symbol of the very force to which he has willingly abandoned his humanity. For, in effect, men in *V.* exhibit a profound ambivalence toward women, the symbolic in-itself, an "approach and avoid" posture that is metaphysically grounded in the human being's (in this case, man's) unrealizable desire to relinquish desire and need so as to achieve the self-coincidence of brute matter, while, at the same time, avoiding the annihilation of consciousness. Herbert Stencil's quest for V. reveals his desire, his humanness, the absence of completion and open-endedness, which, when completed or fulfilled, will threaten him again with that pull toward the pseudo-inanimate state of "half-consciousness: "He tried not to think, therefore, about any end to the search. Approach and avoid" (*V.* 55). And when Benny Profane considers "pissing on the sun to put it out for good," he, like most of the male characters in the novel, displays a metaphysical jealousy and hostility toward the inanimate's absence of need, or desire, that is, its absence of absence, or its fullness of being:

> By the time the sun was going down [Rachel Owlglass and Benny had] nearly finished the case between them. Profane was balefully drunk. He got out of the car, wandered off behind a tree and pointed west, with some

intention of pissing on the sun to put it out for good and all, this being somehow important to him. (Inanimate objects could do what they wanted. Not what they wanted because things do not want; only men. But things do what they do and that was why Profane was pissing at the sun. (*V.* 26)

The narrator's (author's?) parenthetical musings reveal not only an existential awareness of the ontological gap between human consciousness and the world but also the political exclusion of women from the domain of *angst*-ridden beings. "Only men," not women, in *V.* suffer the metaphysical stirrings of alienation, and while they (men) seem to be paradoxically in love with their own death, courting their immersion in the inanimate, their hatred for the in-itself, as self-coincident matter (*mater*), displaces itself in violent assaults against its symbolic manifestation—women.

When "No" Means "Yes": De-fusing the Rhetoric of Rape in Binary Thought Systems

"Why don't we send it through Central Park and see if anybody rapes it" (*V.* 143), suggests an unidentified voice during one of Benny Profane's bar-hopping, yo-yoing episodes. "Out prowling for cono" (*V.* 138) and having pursued a woman named Lucille and her friends into a rather conventional, refined social club, Benny Profane and his rowdy drinking buddies, Angel and Geronimo, find themselves surrounded by "fifteen or twenty curious-looking juvenile delinquents" dressed in "Ivy League suits" and "cocktail dresses." Disheveled, drunken and socially out of place, Benny and his buddies arouse the suspicions of the patrons who, fearing a bust by police, view Lucille, Benny and his buddies as possible undercover cops. In order to establish the identity and gender of the members of this rather dissolute looking group, the unidentified voice suggests that they "send it [Lucille, Benny?] through Central Park and see if anybody rapes it," the implication being that to be female and/or vulnerable is to be rapable. Lurking among the pages of the novel and emerging, now and then, from the dark corners of the narrative to engage in explicit acts of violent sexual assaults against women is a diabolical force that paradoxically perceives women as "rapable" creatures who, at the same time, invite and welcome their own degradation by predatory men.

That rather incorporeal, unidentified voice in the Mott Street Social Club becomes incarnated in a variety of punitive male characters who, harboring an "approach and avoid" attitude toward women, the symbolic in-itself, have also, as part of their descent into the inanimate, internalized the logic of computers, further justifying the release of aggressions and frustrations against vulnerable women who, according to the cybernetic logic of inversion, welcome their own humiliation and sexual denigration. For punctuating the text are gradations of sexual assault that range from "gang bangs" to mutilation and femicide, but informing all of these episodes is a cultural mentality that has always been inclined to read and hear female protests against sexual advances as disguised invitations, to interpret the initial "No" as meaning "Yes." In an early episode in the novel, Benny Profane has befriended Paola, the estranged and battered wife of Pappy Hod, one of the members of the Whole Sick Crew, and while she tries to communicate her need for him to be good to her, that is, to treat her better than did Pappy, Profane has difficulty understanding what she means:

> "What do you mean,"Profane said. "Be good to you."
> "What Pappy Hod wasn't," she said. He soon gave up trying decode her several hankerings. (*V.* 18)

His inability to decode her meaning suggests, as Tanner notes, the deterioration of language in the world of *V.* and the inability of people to establish any real contact.[38] Yet Profane's failure to communicate with Paola also points to an epistemological crisis in the affairs between men and women that informs the phenomenon of rape and sexual violence. For later in that same episode, Paola and Profane happen to wander into a "darkened room with a bed in it":

> "No," she said.
> "Meaning yes."
> Groan, went the bed. Before either of them knew it. (*V.* 19)

Almost minimalistic in structure and effect, this episode is sufficiently vague to raise questions about Paola's real intent so that the possibility of male force here remains unsubstantiated. For in a culture that both counsels female resistance to erotic advances and encourages male sexual aggression, Profane seems almost programmed to hear her "No" as "Yes" and she, perhaps actually wanting Profane, almost seems programmed to send a "No" that, in this case, could mean "Yes."

Yet, in a more protracted and developed dialogue between a male seducer and female participant, Pynchon clearly reveals a predilection toward the "victimless" woman. Having been "sexually turned on" by her plastic surgeon, Shale Schoenmaker, Esther, following her nose job, returns to his office to have the stitches removed. Arriving with the intent of seducing him, Esther displays a change of heart which Schoenmaker first re-shapes into ambivalence and then into willing submission. The dialogue reveals the sometimes subtle rhetoric of rape, and the complete mockery of female protest, and the inversion of resistance to signal compliance:

> In the back room":How do you feel."
> She laughed,too loud. "It hurts. But."
> "Yes,but. There are ways to forget the pain."
> She seemed unable to get rid of a silly, half-apologetic smile. It stretched her face, adding to the pain in her nose.
> "Do you know what we're going to do? *No, what I am going to do to you*? Of course.
> She *let* him undress her...
> "Oh.Oh God." An attack of conscience...
> "Stop. Stop the peep-show routine. You're not a virgin."
> Another self-deprecating laugh. "That's just it. Another boy. Gave it to me. Boy that I loved." (*V.* 109 emphases mine)

Despite her growing ambivalence, despite the clear indication that this will be an act that is done to her, denying her active participation and reducing her to the objectified status of victim, Pynchon implies that Esther's "No" really means "Yes":

> "Lie on the bed. That will be our operating table. You are to get an intermuscular injection."
> "No," she cried.
> "You have worked on so many ways of saying no. No meaning yes. That I don't like. Say it differently."
> "No," with a little moan.
> "Different. Again."
> "No," this time a smile, eyelids at half mast.
> "Again."
> "No."
> "You're getting better." Unknotting his tie, trousers in a puddle about his feet, Schoenmaker serenaded her. (*V.* 109-110)

Clearly, Pynchon has constructed the scene to suggest that women often employ a show of resistance as a coquettish strategy that can easily be disarmed by the persuasive but coercive plaints of men. Her "smile," anticipating the smile on the face of the gang-banged Fina, reveals the wantonness underlying her protestations, just as the "lacy undergarments and fetishes" seductively lurk beneath Esther's conventional attire (*V.* 109). Yet, what happens when the "No" really means "No" and accurately reflects the wishes and intent of the sender? Pynchon does not seem to allow for this possibility, and, despite his disdain for the ubiquity of mechanized, computer logic, seems to have succumbed to a misreading of women's protestations against sexual assault that reflects not only cybernetic inverse logic but also the deeply entrenched and traditional societal reduction of women to lascivious creatures. Pynchon seems to come perilously close to affirming the perceptions of the British judge who, in 1982, dismissed a woman's claim of rape by arguing that because the woman sustained no visible signs of brutality she must have consented, that her "no" was sufficiently vague so as to imply the possibility of consent: "Women who say no do not always mean no. It is not just a question of saying no. It is a question of how she says it, how she makes it clear."[39] The judge's perception, and perhaps Pynchon's, is shaped by a cultural myth about female sexuality, a misconception that serves to perpetuate rather than to curb violence against women. As one psychologist notes, "The linkage among all acts of violence is the commonality of the numerous myths attached to them."[40] One such myth is that of female masochism articulated in such statements as "It wasn't rape, only rough sex," "Women say no when they mean yes" and "Some women enjoy rape."[41] Despite recent empirical evidence suggesting that "women rarely say 'no' when they mean 'yes,'"[42] such myths continue to thrive in a misogynistic culture. The convenient inversion of the woman's "no" to "yes" embodies the prejudices of a patriarchal society that has confined women to restrictive stereotypes and that has acquired additional legitimacy in the computer age. With the advent of computer logic and the continual descent into the inanimate, which Pynchon decries throughout his texts, the assimilation of cybernetic thought-processes into the very mode of human perception further strengthens the societally-sanctioned misreading of the female negative response to sexual advances by inverting the "no" to mean only "yes."

In the binary system of computer logic and communications theory, the 1,0 dichotomy can be programmed *regularly* so that the input 1,0 will be read as 1,0 or *inversely* so that input 1,0 can be read as 0,1. While digital communication is so efficient in the transmission of messages, allowing only a minimum of leakage, its reliance upon an either/or mutual exclusivity has resulted in the omission of "excluded middles" (somewhere between "Yes" and "No" lies a "Maybe" or a "Not Just Yet") and the tendency to dismiss the epistemological validity of "revelations," that is, those moments that break through or co-exist outside the nexus of empirical causality, or those moments that occupy the indeterminate space between the 1's and the 0's, the "Yes's" and the "No's." As Jean-François Lyotard notes in his seminal discussion concerning the ubiquity of scientific discourse and the proliferation of information-processing machines:

> We can predict that anything in the constituted body of knowledge that is not translatable in this way will be abandoned and that the direction of new research will be dictated by the possibility of its eventual results being translatable into computer language...Along with the hegemony of computers comes a certain logic, and therefore a certain set of prescriptions determining which statements are accepted as "knowledge" statements.[43]

Throughout *V.* and *Gravity's Rainbow*, Pynchon continually bemoans the fact that we have indeed become like the digital computer, having incorporated the very logic of cybernetics into our brains so as to perceive the world in very neatly-ordered dichotomies of mutual oppositions. "The Man has a branch office in each of our brains," he tells us in *Gravity's Rainbow*,[44] for the ruling System of "either/or" cybernetics has been internalized by the constituents of a culture doomed to persist in its ceaseless slide into the inanimate. However, perhaps Pynchon himself has, in effect, oversimplified the language of erotic (mis)communication by excluding the possibilities of more protracted messages in the register of female sexual discourse; for psychologists have also found that women often say "no" as a "shorthand for more extended excuses like not feeling well, not being attracted to the person or not being ready."[45] Sexual scripts, psychologists now tell us, "must be studied with recognition of the power differential between men and women in a male-dominated society, and the constraints such a power differential places upon women's potential to be heard."[46] Yet, in a cybernetic, patriarchal culture, whatever phenomenon (e.g. female voice) does not conform or reduce itself to the epistemological paradigm of computer logic remains invisible, marginal and always irrelevant to the scientific world view. By portraying women as deliberate senders of inverse messages in sexually-charged situations, Pynchon has, in effect, virtually eliminated the concept of rape by insisting that all women basically want to be violated, that all female resistance ("No") really disguises assent ("Yes"). The irony of such a portrayal of women lies, of course, in the fact that Pynchon, himself, may have become entangled in the tentacles of the cybernetic monster, having fallen prey to that very same logic of binary opposition (the logic of inversion with regard to women and rape) that he condemns in his texts.

Throughout *V.* the culture's depiction of woman as the wanton whore who utters "no" but really means "yes" is personified in a variety of female characters who, when confronting their male aggressors, are also faced with the predatory mentality of the rapist that has acquired a "scientific" legitimacy through the inverse logic of the computer. As we have seen, when a woman says "no" in *V.* she always means "yes," but when she says "yes" she also always means "yes," so that the selective application of regular and inverse logic systems with regard to female sexual behavior perniciously serves to reinforce the inveterate prejudices and preconceptions of a culture that has already consigned women to the domain of active whore and virtually erased the concept of the female victim. When Lucille finally beckons to Profane to take her on the pool table (her reified vagina spread before him like the inanimate "corner pockets and "side pockets" (*V.* 143)), it never for a moment occurs to him to read her "Yes" inversely as a rejection of his advances; and when Fina, known as St. Fina, the "spiritual leader or Den Mother" of the Playboys, a youth gang (*V.* 137), tries to seduce Profane, he reads her "yes" as proof that she is at bottom a whore and a sinner, and that all her altruistic deeds for those "unfortunate delinquents down the street" belie a more fundamental salaciousness:

> [Profane] was sure any love between her and the Playboys was for the moment Christian, unworldly and proper. But how long was that going to go on? How long could Fina herself hold out? The minute her horny boys caught a glimpse of the saint, the black lace slip beneath the surplice, Fina could find herself on the receiving end of a gang-bang, *having in a way asked for it.* (*V.* 145, emphasis mine)

Pynchon has collapsed the traditional societal dichotomy that relegates women to the status of either Madonna or Whore by depicting all women, regardless of their surface demeanor, as basically wanton in nature, that is, by identifying women with carnality. When Fina finally does succumb to the horny gang-members following a rumble between the Playboys and the Bop Kings, she is found by her brother, Angel, lying, as Profane tells us, "on an old army cot, naked, hair in disarray, smiling" (*V.* 151). Of course, her *smile* suggests both her complicity and her enjoyment, so that Pynchon has effectively strengthened not only the selective epistemological inversion of compliance ("Yes") and resistance ("No") that virtually eliminates the concept of rape (all women ask for it), but also the metaphysical premise that identifies woman with the passive, inanimate in-itself: "Her eyes had become hollowed as Lucille's, that night on the pool table" (*V.* 151).

Grounded in metaphysical and epistemological assumptions, the paradoxical portrayal of woman as both active whore and passive matter that threatens and invites our submersion in the inanimate allows Pynchon to deny to most, if not all, of the women in *V.* the status of victim. All women in *V.* are ultimately responsible for the male-initiated abuse that they sustain. Consequently, when Angel discovers Fina "smiling" on the cot, he reacts punitively to her perceived complicity, beating her for "allowing" the gang members access to her body; and when Mafia Winsome, "authoress" of third-rate novels, that "like sanitary napkins had gathered in an immense and faithful sisterhood of consumers" (*V.* 125), is slapped around by her husband prior to sex, she too appears as having somehow invited her own humiliation:

> He entered the room as Mafia was bent, stripping off a knee sock. College girl attire, he thought. He slapped her hard on the nearest buttock; she straightened, turned, and he slapped her across the face. "Wha," she said.
> "Something new," said Winsome. "For variety's sake." One hand at her crotch, one twisted in her hair, he lifted her *like the victim she wasn't*, half carried, half-tossed her to the bed where she lay in a sprawl of white skin, black pubic hair and socks, all confused. He unzipped his fly.
> "Aren't you forgetting something," she said, *coy* and half *scared*, flipping her hair toward the dresser drawer.
> "No," said Winsome, "not that I can think of." (*V.* 221-222; emphases mine)

Her almost coquettish response to his aggression vitiates the otherwise rapacious tone of this passage and, like the smile on Fina's countenance, serves to challenge the reader's perception of her as victim.

Throughout the novel, the brutalization of women unfolds against the backdrop of an epistemological and metaphysical orientation (perversion) that includes not only the reduction of women to the Sartrean in-itself or, as Mary Allen notes, a ghastly symbol of the inanimate,[47] but also a mechanized or programmed misreading by men of female protests against sexual advances, an often politically motivated and deliberate inversion of the communication signals sent out by women to men. In what may very well be an allusion to the alleged erotically charged relationship between Lewis Carroll and Alice Liddell, Pynchon relates the tale of Maxwell Rowley-

Bugge, alias Ralph MacBurgess, the seducer of young girls and admirer of one of the early incarnations of V.—the young Victoria Wren—who is haunted by the memory of Alice, a ten-year-old girl who revealed his sexual abuse of her to the authorities and ruined his reputation:

> This particular girl, Alice, had shown at age ten the same half-way responses...of her predecessors. But they know, Max told himself: no matter how young, they know what it is, what they're doing...
> [Alice had] wanted it. Even afterward, dry-eyed among a protective cordon of hating faces, the eyes had said: I still want it. (*V.* 70)

Although a minor episode in the text, Max's violation of Alice and his rationalized misreading of her response to his abuse reinforce the pervasive reduction of women in the text to wanton creatures who, despite their protests, invite their own sexual pain and degradation. Invoking again the myth of female masochism, such a reductive view embraces the cultural propaganda of a misogynistic society that throughout history has compiled a litany of psychological "truths" about women: "that the infant girl wishes to be eaten, devoured by her father, that later she wishes to be beaten or whipped by him, that young girls dream of rape, that the grown woman wishes to be pierced, that women have a lust for pain."[48] Viewing Alice as an early incarnation of V., one critic even argues that ten-year-old Alice "apparently met [her seducer] half-way."[49] Even Benny Profane's pursuit of the alligators in the subterranean tunnels of New York City takes on an erotically violent tone as he begins to perceive them the way he does women: he, Angel and Geronimo track down alligators the way they search for "cono" and when Profane begins to "feminize" his prey, he also begins to apply the rhetoric of the "compliant victim" to his hunt:

> He thought back to the one he'd chased solo almost to the East River, through Fairing's Parish. It had lagged, let him catch up. *Had been looking for it*.... (*V.* 46; emphasis mine)

And then, after killing one that resisted, Profane mutters, "Baby, you didn't play it right. You don't fight back. That's not in the contract" (*V.* 147).[50]

Very rarely in *V.* do women try to repel the sexualized aggression of predatory men; far from displaying signs of resistance to male assault, Pynchon's women embrace their oppressors with a seemingly pathological enthusiasm that reinforces traditional metaphysical and societal notions of women as scattered, chaotic matter awaiting the often violent imposition of male form and definition. Three episodes in *V.* underscore female acquiescence to male-initiated sexualized brutality: Esther Harvitz' reconstructive surgery, the female labor camps on the islet of Lüderitzbucht and the sexual mutilation of V.'s lesbian lover, Mélanie l'Heuremaudit, a fifteen-year-old French ballet dancer.

Esther Harvitz' decision to undergo painful, elective surgery at the hands of Shale Schoenmaker (his very name suggesting that he is the "maker of beauty" with inanimate materials, a sculptor, a modern Pygmalion) implies the willingness of a woman to submit to the excruciating process of reconstruction in order to conform to an Anglican, male definition of female beauty.[51] Esther is, to use Mary Daly's clever inversion of Jerzy Kosinski's image of the "painted bird," a woman who has allowed herself to be "cosmeticized" with "patriarchal paint," that is to say, she is representative of most women who become "man-made women."[52] As a Jew who seeks male validation in the American marriage market, Esther reinforces not only Pynchon's bias against women as those who are obsessed with surface,[53] but also the often insidious domination of patriarchal assumptions over women's thought processes and self-image. Like the alligators that Profane pursues beneath the streets of New York City, destined to be transformed into the inert, marketable commodities of wallets, pocketbooks and shoes, Esther succumbs to the more subtle yet equally destructive force of Madison Avenue advertising that dictates an ideal of female beauty to which many women fall prey. Having internalized (and been victimized by) the male-authored aesthetic code of the perfect woman, Esther ironically seeks to reduce herself to a commodity in the marriage market.

Seeking to replace her semitic nose with one more Wasp-like, Esther submits to a surgical procedure which Pynchon graphically depicts in highly eroticized images that capture a blend of sexuality and violence. At the mercy of a trio of rather inept medical personnel and sadistic voyeurs—Schoenmaker, Irving and Trench, who, once they donned their surgical masks, "looked suddenly malevolent to Esther" (*V.* 104)—the patient, despite her quiet sobs and "obvious second thoughts," is strapped to the operating table and proceeds to undergo a series of invasive procedures that invokes not only the rhetoric of both female sexual mutilation and male sexual arousal, that is, of a gang-rape, but also, as one critic points out, the suggestion of concentration camp experiments.[54] For, at one point in the operation, having just disengaged Esther's original nose from its facial structure, Schoenmaker leans over this young Jewish woman and intones the ominous accent of the Nazi doctors: "See? It's all wobbly now. That's act two. Now ve shorten das septum, ja" (*V.* 107). A "concentration camp mentality" continues to inform this scene in their suggestion that she remain awake to observe her own "mutilation" and that the anesthesia may not be totally effective in assuaging her discomfort.

Irving, whose name suggests the masculinized nurse intent upon inflicting pain on her patients (the Nurse Ratched stereotype), and who has been assigned the role of anesthetist because, according to Schoenmaker, she "needs the practice," makes a number of injections around Esther's nose, and then is instructed to "switch to the big one," the two-inch needle:

> No one had told Esther that anything about the operation would hurt. But these injections hurt: nothing before in her experience had ever hurt quite so much. All she had free to move for the pain were her hips. Trench leered appreciatively as she squirmed, constrained, on the table...
>
> A series of internal injections to the septum...and the anesthesia was complete. The sexual metaphor in all this wasn't lost on Trench, who kept chanting, "Stick it in...pull it out...stick it in...ooh that was good...pull it out..."and tittering softly above Esther's eyes...
>
> "Maybe she wants to look," Trench said.
>
> "You want to look, Esther? "See what we're going to do to you?."
> (*V.* 104-105)

Just as Schoenmaker later disarms both Esther's resistance and ambivalence to his overt seduction, here he pacifies her pain and "second thoughts" by assuming the posture of a lover who has given her the gift of inanimateness by effectively denying her any degree of autonomy. Despite the implication that Esther has painfully submitted to a trio of "Nazi-like butchers," Pynchon cleverly undermines the validity of the concept of the female victim here not only through the "brutal playfulness" of the prose[55] but also by ascribing to the woman a compliance and celebration of her loss of self, as if her very fundamental nature as mass, *mater*-ial, has been released by the imposition of a male, sexual force for which she has harbored a secret longing:

> "Now," gently, like a lover, "I'm going to saw off your hump." Esther watched his eyes as best she could, looking for something human there. Never had she felt so helpless. Later she would say,"It was almost a mystic experience. What religion is it—one of the Eastern ones—where the highest condition we can attain is that of an object—a rock. It was like that; I felt myself drifting down, this delicious loss of Estherhood, becoming more and more a blob, with no worries, traumas, nothing: only Being.... (*V.* 107)

Again, women in *V.* feel most comfortable, almost religiously so in this case, with their slide into the non-human, and if that slide into the inanimate entails the absence of autonomy and resistance to male sexualized aggression, then the concept of rape not only proves to be epistemologically weakened in this text but also emerges as metaphysically unsound, given women's seemingly inherent affinity for passive, non-thinking matter. Esther seems to welcome Schoenmaker's painful injection of an inert substance into her face, just as Rachel "enjoyed" the gear shift and just as Mélanie, V.'s female lover, will later receive the allegedly welcomed and lethal "intermuscular injection" of a mechanical penis.

Esther, Mélanie, Rachel, and all of the other women within Profane's circle of acquaintances, manifest a pull toward the non-human which is mirrored, of course, in the pervasive but elusive figure of the Lady V. who, in her various incarnations, displays a progressive accumulation and eventual assimilation of inanimate accouterments and body parts, from her initial wearing of the five-figured comb of Venus when appearing as Victoria Wren, to the disassembling of her various mechanical limbs and fake navel in her final (dis)appearance as the Bad Priest on Malta. Whether V.'s gradual disintegration over the course of the novel serves as a "debased symbol of Western European cultural hegemony" as Roger Henkle argues,[56] or whether the "disassembling" of the "female into an aggregate of inanimate body parts" represents, as Gilbert and Gubar argue, an attempt to counter the "failure of masculine desire,"[57] it is quite clear that all women in the text reflect the dehumanizing pull toward the inanimate, an inclination that manifests not the feisty "approach and avoid" ambivalence of Profane and Stencil but rather the longing to return to their "natural" passivity of material being.

While the ambiguity surrounding Esther Harvitz' status as victim to male aggression derives in part from her having, on one level, consciously invited her own cosmetic "mutilation" at the hands of sadistic men—"Esther, after all," as one critic observes, "has asked for it"[58]—the episode detailing the rape and death of Sarah on the islet of Lüderitzbucht proves to be far more troubling in its portrayal of female compliance to male brutality. While the prose style of "playful brutality" that informs the Esther episode gives way, as one critic notes, to evocations of Melville and the Eliot of *The Waste Land* in the Sarah story,[59] the underlying cultural myth pervading all the episodes of male aggression against women, from the "comically brutal" nose job to the parodic rape and murder of Mélanie, is that all women are perversely "asking for it." In the Lüderitzbucht incident Pynchon choreographs the sadistic oppression of young Herero girls amidst the landscape of "natural concentration camps" (*V.* 267), creating an uncomfortable blending of perverse eroticism and female mutilation in his graphic images of femicide. In what turns out to be a macabre dress rehearsal for the subsequent, efficient and systematic annihilation of Jews during the Holocaust, the physical labor camp on the islet of Lüderitzbucht provides a glimpse of Von Trotha's genocidal campaign against the Hereros and Hottentots of Südwestafrika, the survivors of which reappear in *Gravity's Rainbow* as the Schwarzcommandos.

In re-telling the tale that was told to him, Stencil filters the Lüderitzbucht episode through the consciousness of one of the "civilian Schachtmeister," a German engineering student named Mondaugen who bemoans the fact that, under the von Trotha reign, he has been forced to give up the luxury of personal ownership and of viewing the Herero women as individual concubines; he sees them now only as an anonymous "collection" of replaceable laborers (a non-parodic counterpart of Hogo's portrayal of women as replaceable "cunts"), who inhabit a ghastly wasteland of rotting corpses, surrounded by a threatening sea. Subjected not only to the predatory forces of nature—"the brown hyena called the strand wolf prowled the beach singly or with companions in search of shellfish, dead gulls, anything flesh" (*V.* 268)—these young women also faced the inhumanity of the German colonial machine that preyed upon their powerlessness. In gruesome anticipation of Auschwitz and Buchenwald—"the fully rationalized institution of total domination under conditions of *population surplus*"[60]— these women, we are told, died at a rate of "twelve to fifteen" a day, only to be replaced by a seemingly inexhaustible supply of reserves (*V.* 268).

Within this horrifying, entropic landscape of dissolution and lust, the Herero women, like their future counterparts in the death camps of Europe, are systematically subjected to the process of sub-speciation, whereby they are divested of their humanity and reduced to beasts of burden, responsible for both the exhaustive and often deadly outdoor physical labor—"Women could be inspanned to the heavy-duty carts to pull loads of the silt dredged from the floor of the harbor; or to carry the rails for the road of iron being driven across the Namib toward Keetsmanshoop" (*V.* 269)—and the "domestic" chores which included traditional housework and not so traditional sexual duty. That these women were viewed as nothing more than dispensable beasts of labor becomes quite apparent when Mondaugen states that during one of his supervised treks he was forced to dispose of a woman who had fallen and broken her leg:

[I]t may have been because the fog and cold the previous week had been worse than usual, so that [the women's] sockets and joints may have become inflamed—that day his own neck ached and he had trouble turning to see what happened—but a sudden wail went up and he said that one of the women had stumbled and fallen and brought the whole line down...He went back to her, ascertained that the falling rail had broken her leg;dragged her out from under it without bothering to lift it,rolled her down the embankment and left her to die. (V. 269)

While Mondaugen's rather stolid description of the incident underscores the moral corruption of the death-camp mentality, his chilling coda captures what Pynchon recognizes as "the comfortable perversity of the heart" (*V.* 273): the disposal of the young woman "did him good, he thought; it took him temporarily away from nostalgia, which on the coast was a kind of despondency" (*V.* 270).

Within this surreal landscape of death and mutilation, "nigger women" come to occupy the nether world of the subhuman, just as the Jews were later to be reduced by the Nazi propaganda apparatus to the sub-human status of *Tiermenschen* or animal-people.[61] For when Mondaugen meets the Herero child Sarah, he finds "nothing about her at all of the animal he'd seen in other nigger women" (*V.* 271). In addition to their torturous field labor, the Herero women were forced into sexual bondage by a group of male oppressors given to pederasty, necrophilia and sado-masochism. Those in the military who occupied the highest rungs of power merited young boys to fulfill their sexual needs, but those less "fortunate" had to settle for Herero women who were often "masculinized" by their captors to simulate their more desirable male counterparts (their heads were shaved and they were kept naked except for shrunken army leggings (*V.* 270)). Often forced to lie still, "like corpses," many Herero women "were reprimanded with an elegant jeweled sjambok" if they showed any sexual response (*V.* 270). While Pynchon's main intent here seems not to explore the implications of gender ambiguity and construction but rather to underscore the "perversions" of the Nazi mentality, he perhaps unwittingly reveals the performative and cultural dimension of sex stereotypes by disclosing the forceful imposition of gender roles upon those enslaved by those in power. As one example of what Judith Butler labels the "existential dialectic of misogyny,"[62] the Nazi erasure of "femininity" here is not only emblematic of the silencing of the female voice in the military establishment but also symbolic of the often violent imposition of "masculine" form upon "feminine" matter.

When Mondaugen becomes obsessed with the Herero child named Sarah in the death-infested environment of Lüderitzbucht, he, in effect, violates the "coop"erative spirit of von Trotha's mandate against ownership of property: one may temporarily borrow a concubine from the general pool but one may not appropriate a woman for continual private use. While Barthelme parodies the concept of woman as belonging to the public domain in *The Dead Father*, Pynchon here presents us with a chillingly rational justification for outlawing exclusive ownership: surrounded by the stark, desolate forces of nature, men who shared the female slave labor could erect a sense of community against the onslaught of the Inanimate (*V.* 272); furthermore, the master should never become too enthralled with the slave, or else, as we saw in Barthelme's comic version, "The Captured Woman," he runs the risk of subverting the hierarchy of power, of becoming the slave himself, thus undermining his rationale of oppression. The machinery of the death camp can run smoothly only when the master maintains an air of impersonality toward the slave.

That Mondaugen harbors "unacceptable" feelings for Sarah should not be interpreted to mean that he has fallen in love with her. Far from exhibiting any genuine tenderness or concern for her well-being, he displays a desire to possess her as he would any other piece of attractive property, as a self-aggrandizing extension of his own power. For Sarah, like all of the other female slaves in the death camp, serves a specific function for her oppressor, and while her purpose may not be solely that of a sexual slave, she does undergo, nonetheless, an equally degrading and depersonalized reduction of her humanity that results in her meeting a fate no different from that suffered by all the other women who are literally worked to death. In effect, Sarah serves to bring Mondaugen's, and perhaps the narrator's, "discontent into focus; perhaps even became one reason finally why he quit it all and headed inland to try and regain a little of the luxury and abundance that had vanished with von Trotha" (*V.* 270). That is to say, her desirable presence and his lack of power to claim her as his exclusive possession trigger a nostalgic longing for the unquestioned male acquisition of unpaid domestic female labor (wives) in more traditional patriarchal arrangements: "Sarah might have cooked, cleaned, comforted, been the closest thing to a wife he's ever had" (*V.* 272). As Mary Allen points out, this foreign point of view about the status of wives illuminates American attitudes towards women as possessions legally gained through marriage. He wants Sarah because she serves wifely functions but because he cannot "legally" own her in von Trotha's system, he is at a loss as to how to control her: "The man's concept of the proper wife leaves him destitute in a situation where he may not use some kind of force or the more frequent American practice, bribery."[63]

Violating the mandates of the German regime, Mondaugen, upon first seeing her, issues a personal, coercive "invitation" to Sarah to visit him that night in his room: "He knew he didn't want to share this girl" (*V.* 271). When she ignores or refuses his directive, he retaliates the next morning by subjecting her to a sadistic flirtation with death:

> Next morning he caught her on the breakwater, made her kneel, placed his boot on her nape and pushed her head under the sea until his sense of timing told him to let her up for air. He noticed then how long and snakelike her thighs were;how clearly the musculature of her hips stood under the skin, skin with a certain glow, but finely striated because of her long fast in the brush. That day he'd sjambok her on any least pretense. (*V.* 271)

Aroused by her suffering, he anxiously awaits her to respond to his second "invitation" to visit his room that night. When she again defies him, he finds her the next morning, and while "two strong women" held her down against a rock, "he sjamboked her, then took her" (*V.* 272). Having twice resisted his sexual advances, Sarah is punished by rape.

Clearly Sarah emerges as the victim of male brutality. Having neither invited nor willingly acquiesced to her own humiliation, she remains deathlike, stolid and unaroused ("She lay in a cold rigor") during her sexual submission. Yet just when the reader feels comfortable experiencing an unqualified sympathy for this young female victim, Pynchon cleverly and perhaps with a degree of sadistic mockery, twists our compassion into knots with yet another surprising coda that seemingly subverts the initial sense of female victimization:

> And that night, long after he'd turned in, she came to his house and slid into the bed next to him. Woman's perversity! She was his. (*V.* 272)

How are we to interpret her "perverse" reaction? Has she, like the other women in the text, secretly welcomed and thereby invited her own degradation all along, strategically camouflaging her consent (her "Yes") with false acts of resistance (her "No")? Are her past shows of defiance retroactively negated by this bizarre acceptance of her own subjugation? Or does she, in this death-ridden environment, interpret his pursuit of her, despite its violent, degrading tenor, as a possible means of salvation? Still yet, does she view his increasingly violent responses to her resistance as heralding her own death if she does not finally submit to him?

While Mary Allen views this scene as a hyperbolic depiction of the American marriage arrangement, Sarah's "perversity," when considered in conjunction with the extremity of her situation, emerges as a revealing commentary not only on Western marriage customs but also on the more fundamental political status of women in a pathological, societal hierarchy of power that can systematize the sadistic submission of women to the often brutalizing force of male aggression. In such a dystopia, "perversity" easily slides into "normalcy." Reduced to a piece of his property and literally manacled to his bed in the daytime, Sarah perhaps "perversely chooses," rather than wholeheartedly welcomes, an existence as Mondaugen's "wife" rather than continuing to languish in agony as a laborer on the shore and as a piece of flesh in the "woman pool." As Julie prudently acquiesced to Tom's appropriation of her body as her "salvation" from the belligerent mob in *The Dead Father*, perhaps, too, does Sarah wisely opt to submit to one oppressor rather than to the German gang. For it is only when the other men discover Sarah in Mondaugen's room and decide to share her among the members of their platoon, that is, gang-rape her, that Sarah chooses suicide by running out to sea.

Whereas Barthelme parodies the reduction of women to male-owned property through his use of comic exaggeration and incongruous juxtapositions of events, Pynchon's narrator employs a sequence of images so grotesque, yet so frighteningly real to a postmodern consciousness imprinted with images of the Holocaust, that one cannot help but sense more than parody here. The most graphic depiction of femicide and mutilation appears in the ghastly description, created through the truly perverse vision of the Mondaugen's/Stencil's sadistic and misogynistic world-view, of the beach strewn with female corpses:

> The next day (Sarah's) body was washed up on the beach. She had perished in a sea they would perhaps never succeed in calming any part of. Jackals had eaten her breasts...the black corpse impaled on a thorn tree in a river swollen with sudden rain...

Within this same protracted sentence, fraught with gruesome pictures of death and disfigurement and with the narrator's recognition of his own "comfortable perversity of the heart," lurks the ultimately repulsive image of the ubiquity of terror and dehumanization that would be repeatedly flashed onto the screen of Western consciousness following the Holocaust, namely the unmarked, mass graves of unidentifiable, indistinguishable and non-human-looking corpses of victims:

> ...on that terrible coast, where the beach between Lüderitzbucht and the cemetery was actually littered each morning with a score of identical female corpses, an agglomeration no more substantial-looking than seaweed against an unhealthy yellow sand;...where, finally humanity was reduced, out of a necessity which in his loonier moments he could almost believe was only Deutsch-Südwestafrika's (actually he knew better)...

And the sentence finally comes to an end with a litany of images that underscores humanity's seemingly ineluctable slide into the granite stillness of the rock:

> ...a sun with no shape, a beach alien as the moon's antarctic, restless concubines in barbed wire, salt mists, alkaline earth...the inertia of rock...the unheard whimper of a dying woman; the frightening but necessary cry of the strand wolf in the fog." (*V.* 273-274)

Of all the episodes dealing with violence and women in *V.*, surely the Lüderitzbucht tale drives home the horrifying potential inherent in the traditional male colonizing mentality that appropriates women as an indigenous labor force to be harnessed for the realization of male-defined goals. Explicit in its depiction of female sexual bondage and mutilation (Sarah's breasts were eaten by jackals), the Lüderitzbucht episode, both in its non-parodic tone and its abundance of realistic images, strikes a recognizable chord in the soul of the postmodern reader; far from sounding "like the climax of a gothic playlet as parodied by the Monty Python comedy troupe," as Douglas Fowler argues,[64] this episode exceeds the parameters of parody to bring us face to face with our own history, with our own monstrous capacity to feel "perversely" comfortable in a pathological society.

It is clear that Pynchon in this episode impugns the treatment of Sarah, and that her ostensible submission to her oppressor following her rape *could be* an act of strategic self-survival; at the same time, however, Pynchon, having "stencilized" Mondaugen's yarn[65] and thereby, perhaps, distancing himself from the narrator's sensibility, remains sufficiently ambiguous concerning the sexual nature of women in the text as a whole so as to leave this reader unsure as to the young girl's motivation. Does Pynchon present Sarah as an exaggerated version of Esther, reduced to an identification with matter and eros, or "eroticized matter," so that she by nature welcomes the brutal imposition of male force; or does Pynchon view the very reduction of women to matter in Western thought as an implicit symptom of a pathological metaphysics invoked to justify the violent subordination of women, so that both Esther and Sarah, like all the other women in the text, come across as occupying different places on a continuum of female victimization? Again, one is reminded of Griffin's argument that the fundamental tenet of Western metaphysics—the dualism of mind and body, and its attendant corollary that aligns woman with matter (nature) and man with spirit (culture)—is not coincidentally also the "metaphysics of pornography."[66] The imposition of "masculine" form upon "feminine" matter, traditionally offered as the explanation for the advancements and accomplishments of a civilized culture, also informs the sub-cultural, pornographic depiction of women as mindless, eroticized creatures who welcome their own bondage to aggressive, sadistic men. Although Pynchon may not be exploiting the unabashedly brutal images of sexual rage that men often unleash against women in hard core pornography magazines (e.g., overt and graphic depictions of rape and dismemberment) to titillate male masturbatory fantasies, the image of Sarah's torn breasts, couched as it is within the repugnant setting of a concentration camp, perhaps encodes the author's own ambivalence toward the plight of women: the image and setting allow him both to condemn women's "inmate" status within traditional patriarchal arrangements and simultaneously to discharge his sexual aggression against women as the symbol of the inanimate. Griffin has clearly delineated the "metaphysics of pornography": has Pynchon, in his critique of our culture's descent into the inanimate, come to apprehend and also abhor the devastating effects of the "pornography of Western metaphysics?" Or does he remain unreflectively enmeshed in its very structure?

The ambiguity inherent in the treatment of Sarah in the Lüderitzbucht episode resides in Pynchon's position concerning the metaphysical identification of women with eroticized matter. Throughout *V.*, Pynchon has marshalled an army of images that reduces women to carnality and to material substances, from Rachel's fling with the gear-shift and Esther's "intermuscular injections" of inert material into her face, to Mélanie's "rape" by a mechanical phallus and V.'s ultimate "striptease" or dismantling of her prosthetic parts on the island of Malta. In each instance, a woman becomes rock-like, "welcoming" the insertion of brute matter into her being, thereby becoming less human, more humanoid. Esther's nose becomes a "rock" and V. unravels on the rock of Malta. The imagery surrounding Sarah is consistent with Pynchon's underlying identification of women with eroticized matter, for not only does Sarah spend her days carrying rocks from one part

Rocket—the "iron cock"—also becomes, as Tololyan notes, the postmodern counterpart to Achilles' shield, each a manifestation of the epic convention in Western literature centered upon the making of weaponry.[107] Yet, the making of weaponry and the initiation of wars have always been masculine activities so that the Rocket becomes the phallic text around which all citizens are organized or under which all citizens are subsumed in a hierarchy of importance, women and children occupying the lowest rungs of the ladder, the most dispensable creatures in the postmodern State and those most distant from the seats of power.

The gradual assemblage of the V-2 Rocket across the "Zone" of *Gravity's Rainbow* represents a "tragic" reversal of the "comic" process of disintegration of the authoritarian male icon of *The Dead Father*; or perhaps it augurs the rather ominous resurrection of the male principle devoid of any capacity for human understanding, having now been reincarnated as the penultimate, inanimate vehicle of destruction, the forerunner of nuclear weaponry. As we all sit under the parabolic path of the Rocket, eclipsed by its potential for destruction and its paradoxical power to organize our lives into patterns of behavior designed to promote our own demise, we, as readers of *Gravity's Rainbow*, begin to comprehend the fact that, as one critic observes, "the Rocket haunts the novel not just as a material power threatening global destruction but as an oppressive meaning system—a potent symbol of the primacy of technological rationalization in western culture."[108]

As the physical center of the text, the "Rocket Chapter," like the zenith in the parabolic arc of the V-2, represents a critical turn in direction, a discrete "instant" in the present that transforms the path of past ascent into the path of imminent descent, and it is at this point that Pynchon assembles past, present and future observations about rocket technology into a rather macabre mosaic of masculine oppression, ranging from sado-masochistic porno films to incest, child abandonment and incarceration, and ultimately to nuclear destruction. The following discussion will focus on the images of women and violence in the "Rocket Chapter" as they reverberate throughout the surrounding text and as they reflect not only the status of women in the postmodern State but also the attitudes of a writer who, having widened his scope to produce a rather scathing indictment of patriarchal technology, has somewhat extricated himself from many of the lairs of misogyny which had entrapped him in *V.*. One should keep in mind Rita Felski's argument against any necessary connection between literary experimentation and feminism when analyzing *Gravity's Rainbow*: it is not a feminist text simply because it "disrupts the strategies of symbolic discourse through which march toward the sacred/profane apocalypse,[70] while R. Golden argues that Mélanie's incestuous involvement with her father and *V.*'s lesbian fascination with Mélanie are all "part of a Baudelairian atmosphere of decadence" that finds its apotheosis in the lesbian incarnation of V., her most violently destructive manifestation in the text.[71] Alfred Kazin finds the final death scene to be a parody of the sexual act[72] and both Olderman and Tanner associate the lesbian experience with the "anti-life" images of the "wasteland."[73]

A closer analysis of the chapter reveals a complex blending of parody and personal vilification, a reliance upon clichéd female stereotypes, and an untempered misogyny that explodes in an act of rage against a woman who has had the temerity to reject one of the fundamental tenets of traditional patriarchal power—that women must remain dependent upon and vulnerable to male domination, whether it be economic, social or sexual domination. Woven into this intricate pattern of parody and personal indictment is the author's genuine philosophical disdain for closed, entropic systems of which lesbianism, in his view, is one example. Yet, just as Pynchon's views regarding rape and women's sexual submission indicate his perhaps unintentional complicity in an epistemological system that he otherwise repudiates, so too does his portrayal of V.'s lesbian affair reveal a traditional ontological bias against those women who seek to align themselves with non-traditional ways of being in the world.

Throughout his short stories and novels, Pynchon warns us of the imminent dangers of "closed systems," of our futile attempts to withdraw from the insanity of the modern world into the false security of self-constructed enclaves where repetition, habit and inertia breed a "death-in-life" sameness and boredom. In both "Entropy" and "Small Rain," Pynchon portrays characters who have failed to effect a successful retreat from the world. Nathan Levine, the army enlistee in "Small Rain" who had abdicated his capacity for autonomous thought and feeling to the stifling, conformist rigidity of the military "world" where "everybody is on the same frequency,"[74] is suddenly shocked out of his emotional numbness and apathy by a local hurricane that kills hundreds of people. When he is forced to retrieve the bodies from the water, he comes to *feel* the hideousness of death, the tragic horror of such devastation having penetrated "the closed circuit" of his once comfortable, military perspective. Levine's encounter with death transforms his perceptions, leaving him discontented with an existence in the cloistered world of the military and prompting him to imagine himself as a modern "Wandering Jew" who would meet other wandering

Jews and debate the "essential problems of identity" (SL 49). As Tanner notes, "It is as though the actual vision of—and contact with—death has brought him out of his anesthetized and paralyzed state."[75]

This rejection of closed systems, of closed circuits that promote conformity and sameness, that seal off individuals from the differentiation and variety of the outside world, also informs the short story "Entropy." On one floor of an apartment building, Callisto and his girlfriend Aubade live in a "closed system," an "hermetically sealed" jungle room, a "tiny enclave of regularity in the city's chaos" (SL 83). Having not left the room for seven years and having not allowed any of the "weather, national politics or civil disorder" to intrude upon them, Callisto and Aubade are, in effect, living a death-like existence. Even his attempt to save the life of a bird fails, for by creating an entropic enclave in which the temperature remains consistent and uniform, Callisto is unable to transfer heat from his hands to the dying bird. Their entropic existence is pitted against the wild party being held on the floor below by Meatball Mulligan and his friends, who, despite their gamboling and raucous music, represent a diversity and pull towards life that Pynchon seems to embrace. While Mulligan must attempt to prevent the partying and racket from deteriorating into "chaos" and "noise"—signs of encroaching entropy—he chooses to avoid retreating into his own closet as an escape from his friends and rather seeks to impose a degree of order upon their energy. In contrast to the "retreat and escape" mentality of Callisto and Aubade, Mulligan's approach is, as Tanner notes, "a gesture against chaos, a neg-entropic act."[76]

Pynchon's rejection of enclaves, of sealed-off retreats and escapes from the teeming diversity of life, of "closed circuits" that promote conformity and uniformity and that refuse the admission of "outside" information and differing perspectives, stems from his identifying sameness with entropic decline and death. Pynchon seems to have associated homosexuality with such closed systems, that is, with sameness and death, and consequently, he constructs the connection between Mélanie and V. as denoting the ultimate, entropic relationship, a relationship that "hides away" from the world outside, retreating to a "closet" of perversion that equates love with death. Employing a "closed circuit" or series of mirrors that stimulates sexual arousal without physical touch or friction or the exchange of heat, Mélanie and V. engage in a "symbiotic and mutual" voyeurism that, in effect, reduces each participant to a narcissistic reflection of herself in the other's eyes. Arranging the mirrors so as to multiply their reflections into a series of fragmented images—an "audience"—Mélanie and V. "pervert" their love not only by relating to dead images and surfaces but also by embracing parts or fragments of reflections for sexual arousal, so that each is, in effect, reducing the other to a "fetish." Throughout their affair, V. refers to Mélanie as her "fétiche," "something of a woman which gives pleasure but is not a woman. A shoe, a locket...You are not real but an object of pleasure" (*V.* 404). When she leaves with Mélanie on a train, V. observes: "Do you only lie passive then, like an object? Of course you do. It is what you are. Une fétiche" (*V.* 401).

While perhaps a parody of the Freudian reduction of homosexuality to narcissism, Pynchon's lesbian love scene also incorporates some of the homophobic myths and sexual strategies of a patriarchal culture that has always tried to control the potentially subversive power of female sexuality and to insure male hegemony. If Sally Robinson is correct in maintaining that male-dominated cultures reduce women to a "fetish object often to safeguard male subjectivity,"[77] then Pynchon, through his objectification of both Mélanie and V., may be parodying not only the male fetishization of Woman but also the entire idea of gender role playing whereby a woman (V.) plays at being a man who plays the "masculine" game of reducing "his" lover to an object in order to insure "his" subjectivity.

However, on another less parodic level, since both Mélanie and V. are fetishizing each other, Pynchon seems to be suggesting also that lesbian love, through its double objectification, comes closest to that state of inanimateness which he denounces throughout the novel. Instead of considering the possibility that lesbian love may offer an alternative to the male objectification of women, Pynchon embraces the typical "male pornographic gaze" and construction of lesbian love which, as Suleiman and others have pointed out, filters women's love for each other through the lens of male desire for and objectification of the female rather than through the "woman's desire for the other woman."[78] Pynchon decries the culture's slide into the inanimate but fails to consider the subversive potential of lesbianism to undermine the heterosexual paradigm of male subject/female object and to posit a non-hierarchical connection of double subjects, the "I/You" formation suggested by Luce Irigaray in the "Sex Which Is Not One." As Marianne Hirsch argues, Irigaray's dialogue between lovers or the monologue of the double subject I/You serves "to create a space outside patriarchal institutions"[79] that needs no subject/object division. Psychologists have even recently suggested that a study of lesbian relationships may help heterosexual women envision "possibilities for human interaction that are not encumbered by heterosexual gender role mandates, privileges and obligations."[80] Yet Pynchon, succumbing perhaps to an unacknowledged homophobia, fails or refuses to imagine the possibly redemptive dimension of a lesbian paradigm of double subjects (I/You) despite his ongoing indictment of a culture that is seemingly hell-bent on fetishizing itself out of existence.

Having fragmented and reified each other, Mélanie and V. participate in the entropic slide into inanimateness that, for Pynchon, always heralds death. As Deborah Madsen notes, "Mélanie and V. impersonate the inanimate and so serve the same ultimate design—the annexing of the human by the 'Kingdom of Death.'"[81] Their relationship is one more version of the tourist mentality that Pynchon excoriates in *V.* Content with surfaces, the "tourist" or "skin lover" sees the world through the reductive, superficial pictures (images) of the Baedeker manual and never comes to behold the cultural, emotional or spiritual life forces that constitute a place or people. Skin lovers, that is to say, apprehend two-dimensional images, "reflections" that fail to reveal a more profound dimension of human truth.

V.'s encounter with Mélanie occurs, we are told, while V. is travelling through Europe as a tourist, so that, in addition to reiterating the identification of women with the "eroticized inanimate"—here the sexual inanimateness of the fetish—the Mélanie episode also connotes the tourist's superficiality and lack of emotional involvement with the "other" that have been traditionally attributed to homosexual relationships. Subscribing to the stereotypic reduction of homosexuality to narcissism and autoerotic enclosure, Pynchon provides an additional metaphysical rationale for his disgust with homoeroticism, namely, its alleged entropic nature and affinity with anti-life forces, its supposed withdrawal from diversity and, perhaps, its biological inability to perpetuate life. *V.*'s love for Mélanie is not a human love but rather a tourist's infatuation with the superficial, lifeless image, the inanimate.

That Pynchon's depiction of homosexuality rests upon a clichéd reduction of same-gender relationships to sexual obsession and "kinky" bedroom antics reveals, again, a rather conventional, if not reactionary and myopic, perspective from an otherwise unconventional, innovative novelist. Not only does he fall prey to a heterosexist prejudice that remains blind to the millions of gay and lesbian people who have emerged from their closets of so-called narcissism to become actively engaged in the "real" world, who offer an element of diversity to the traditional heterosexual make-up of America, and who are involved in life-affirming forces of child-rearing and progressive politics; he even relies upon those hackneyed twin stereotypes of the "butch" and the "femme," that supposedly characterize all lesbian and gay relationships, to construct his portrayal of Mélanie:

> One day [Mélanie] arrived at Le Nerf accompanied by [V.] and wearing schoolboy's clothing: tight black trousers, a white shirt, a short black jacket. Moreover, her head—all her thick buttock-length hair—had been shorn. She was nearly bald; and but for the dancer's body no clothes could conceal, she might have been a young lad playing hooky. (*V.* 407)

If, as Marjorie Garber argues, the transvestite, by crossing over rigidly-defined social boundaries, emerges as "an index of category destabilization," that is, "both a signifier and that which signifies the undecidability of signification,"[82] then Mélanie's blatant display of her own gender/sexual ambiguity undermines the stability of the binary opposition male/female, and provides an alternative to the very form of hierarchical, either/or thought processes that Pynchon seems to assail. Furthermore, the enactment of the "butch-femme" dichotomy, while stereotypical, also serves to reveal the fictive dimension of heterosexual constructs. As Butler argues, "the replication of heterosexual constructs in non-heterosexual frames brings into relief the utterly constructed status of the so-called heterosexual original," revealing that "gay is to straight not as copy is to original, but, rather as copy is to copy."[83] Yet, rather than consider the possibility that "sexual identity, like nationality, is cultural and not genetic"[84] and thereby expand his parody to include the fluidity of so-called binary opposites such as male/female, masculine/feminine, straight/gay, Pynchon settles for the stereotypic, reductive depiction of the "butch" that he apparently believes to be paradigmatic of the "male" member in most lesbian relationships: Mélanie appears as the woman who perversely tries to deny her femininity and become a man. Ironically, Pynchon's seeming bias against female homosexuals and his succumbing to negative lesbian stereotypes have served to prevent his grasping the "power of the transvestite to unsettle assumptions, structures and hierarchies,"[85] that is, to open up an epistemology of "both/and" rather than "either/or."[86] Again, what Pynchon misses or fails to explore in *V.* is the revolutionary or disruptive potential of the lesbian impulse as a "challenging culture" that threatens the dominant culture and all of those binary oppositions which he denounces. Linda Hutcheon argues:

> There have been liberating effects of moving from the language of alienation (otherness) to that of decentering (difference) because the center used to function as a pivot between binary oppositions which always privileged one half: white/black, male/female, self/other, intellect/body, west/east.[87]

If we add the dualism "straight/gay" to the hierarchies of privilege, we begin to see that Pynchon's reductive treatment of the Mélanie-V. episode and his virulent dismissal of lesbianism in Chapter Fourteen prevent him from capitalizing on the subversive potential of lesbianism as a "challenging culture" that can destabilize old "either/or" oppositions and reveal the center as a construct, a fiction. Unfortunately, Pynchon's linking of homosexuality to a principle of entropy rests upon a series of stereotypic, reductive prejudices that may belie more of a homophobic bias rather than a sound metaphysical principle and that may blind him to the disruptive dimension of lesbianism as a challenging culture.

Within his treatment of homosexuality, Pynchon seems to reserve a special enmity for gay women or lesbians, a virulent hatred that reaches its climax in the death of Mélanie. As Mary Allen observes, "Pynchon never damns male homosexuality with any such violence—it is more foolish than awful, not hideously out of order as is V.'s affair with Mélanie."[88] Joseph Slade argues that Pynchon at times even seems to celebrate male homosexual love.[89] In *Gravity's Rainbow*, the rarefied, homoerotic connections among the men in the trenches during World War I take on an almost religious, ecstatic and redemptive dimension, whereby soldiers facing death could "find in the faces of other young men evidence of otherworldly visits, some poor hope that may have helped redeem even mud, shit, the decaying pieces of human meat" (GR 616).[90]

While Pynchon bemoans the deterioration of such epiphanic moments into the "idle and bitchy faggotry" of decadent World War II power brokers, who are committed to no transcendent ideal but rather to their own megalomaniacal lust, he still conveys a certain sympathy for their homoerotic passions. Even Blicero/Weissman, the mad leader of the German Rocket group and seducer of young boys and men, is allowed a degree of sympathy within the parameters of his romantic quest for death and the pursuit of his self-destruction, so that the thrusting of his Rocket and his defiance of gravity represent his incursion into another Kingdom, his bid at transcending the world that is succumbing to the impersonal manipulations of cartels and military-industrial complexes. Consequently, Blicero's sexual thrustings, his "coupling" with Gottfried, one of his young boys, takes on the religious and "transcendental" quality of forging a connection between two human beings in a world which increasingly discourages such intimate contact, so that "as man and woman, coupled, are shaken to the teeth at their approaches to the gates of life," Gottfried has "also felt more, worshipfully more past these arrangements for penetration" as he "approached the gates of that Other Kingdom" (GR 722). As Lawrence Wolfley notes, Pynchon conveys a sympathy for Blicero, who, exhausted with "this cycle of infection and death" (GR 724), struggles to break through to the Other Kingdom.[91]

Yet, when he deals with lesbianism, the author seems to strip this mode of homosexuality of any transcendent dimension or religious component, presenting it instead as one more version of the tourist mentality, content with surfaces and with the inanimate. Even when associated with the strong-willed, assertive female character Leni Pökler in *Gravity's Rainbow*, lesbianism is consigned to the realm of fantasy, to an infantile regression to a longed-for orgasmic, communal state of "coming together" that would subvert the oppressive Bürgerlichkeit and spawn a communist utopia (GR 156). Titillated by the prospect of "doing it not just with another woman but with a Jewess"—the ultimate "verboten" for this German woman—Leni incorporates into her fantasy the racial slurs and sub-speciation perpetrated by her teutonic heritage against Jews as she envisions "[t]heir animal darkness...sweating hindquarters, pushing aggressively toward her face" (GR 156). Leni's fantasy primarily symbolizes not the latent desire for a lesbian community of loving sisterhood but rather the excitingly dangerous but only imaginary transgression of the Aryan prescription for racial purity. Overtly heterosexual and perhaps unconsciously anti-semitic, Leni displays no waking political interest in attempting to effect a communist sisterhood; as she represents no threat to the patriarchal arrangements of power, whether they be capitalistic or communist, Pynchon, perhaps, feels no need to impugn her or to punish her for repudiating phallic rule.

Lesbianism in *V.*, however, is far more threatening. Presented as non-revelatory and anti-spiritual in nature, the relationship between Mélanie and V. becomes emblematic of the culture's descent into the inanimate that threatens to destroy humankind. While Pynchon often portrays the individual woman in *V.* as a "trap" who lures men into an identification with the non-human, two women engaged in a closed-circuit connection seem to present a double threat to humanity and consequently must be more violently and summarily dispatched. Heterosexual women, such as Rachel Owlglass and Esther Harvitz, are the targets of a more or less playful parody, but Mélanie incurs the unmitigated wrath of an author seemingly intent upon punishing women who, as Gubar and Gilbert argue, "have not been properly domesticated by the phallus."[92] While the climactic death scene cleverly conjoins the notion of the fetish with the metaphysical principle of entropy, it also limns the author's violent repudiation of lesbianism. As Tanner notes,

Pynchon's presentation of the Mélanie—V. relationship is "one of the two or three occasions when Pynchon uses 'we' or 'us' in the novel" (V. found love as a tourist, that is, "in her peregrinations through (let us be honest) a world if not created than at least described to its fullest by Karl Baedeker of Leipzig" (*V.* 408)), thereby suggesting "the presence of an authorial voice which we are bound—or invited—to agree with."[93] That is to say, the otherwise elusive author seems to surface here in a scene of unqualified violence against a woman who paradoxically both rejects the phallus and perhaps "invites" her own "phallic" punishment.

Having recreated the 1913 Paris premiere of Stravinsky's "Rites of Spring" which, due to its innovative "dissonance" caused a riot to erupt in the audience,[94] Pynchon cleverly choreographs Mélanie's mutilation against an entropic backdrop of noise and chaos. The "intermuscular injection" of a mechanical penis into Mélanie further underscores the assimilation by women in the text of the inanimate, and moreover, inverts the concept of the fetish, associated with the lesbian connection, to suggest again the welcoming of an inanimate "male" object to stimulate sexual arousal. Rachel's stickshift and Esther's needle evolve into a lethal instrument of phallic retribution.

In her role as Su Feng in "The Rape of the Chinese Virgins," Mélanie plays the role of a young woman who is tortured to death defending her purity against invading Mongolians. As the ballet progresses and the audience becomes more and more fragmented into warring factions (anti-Chinese vs. pro-Chinese, that is, anti-Stravinsky vs. pro-Stravinsky), reacting to the "dissonance" and "orchestral barbarity" of the music, noise and chaos overwhelm the theatre. When she appears on stage in the last portion of the ballet, entitled "Sacrifice of the Virgin," Mélanie is impaled at the crotch on the point of a pole that is slowly raised by male members of the dance company. Although she was to continue dancing when the pole was erect, her failure to wear the protective harness causes her movements to become so spastic and agonized that her mutilation and death seem to have been perfectly congruent with an orchestral dissonance and barbarity that sounded like "fragments of a bomb" (*V.* 414).

The explanation for Mélanie's failure to protect herself remains somewhat vague. There is the suggestion that V. accused the choreographer of premeditated murder (*V.* 414) or that Mélanie had "accidentally forgotten" to wear the device or, still again, that Mélanie committed suicide. The first possibility subtly anticipates the advent of contemporary, underground "snuff films" in which women, acting in pornographic movies, become the unwitting victims of their male producers and are actually mutilated and killed to intensify the masturbatory fantasies of the male viewers. The second suggestion drives home the continued association in the text between women and inanimate objects, for Mélanie was adorned with "so many combs, bracelets, sequins, she might have become confused in this fetish world and neglected to add to herself the one inanimate object that would have saved her" (*V.* 414). And finally, the possibility of suicide by phallic penetration not only suggests Mélanie's acquiescence to the patriarchal norm that places female sexuality back, as Mary Allen argues, in its "violent but heterosexual place";[95] it also, given the presence of a "voyeuristic" audience, imparts a narcissistic eroticism to her death that she had practiced in life with mirrors. While Pynchon leaves us guessing as to the real motive behind her death, he suggests to us that whatever the reason, lesbianism, as the paradigmatic expression of our entropic descent into the world of chaos and dissonance, has been appropriately dispatched. He also reveals, perhaps unwittingly, that "the heterosexualization of desire" which, as Butler maintains, "requires and institutes the production of discrete and asymmetrical oppositions between 'feminine' and 'masculine,'" will not allow certain kinds of identities to exist.[96] Whether Pynchon is parodying and/or endorsing the reductive cultural view of lesbianism remains ultimately open to interpretation; yet, his authorial use of "we" in this episode, coupled with his violent treatment of Mélanie, would suggest that Pynchon has allowed his own homophobia to prevent his seizing upon gender and sexual "outlaws" as signs of cracks in that supposed monolith of heterosexual desire that underlies so many of the binary oppositions that he denounces. Barthelme skewers Snow White on a barbecue spit during a dream-sequence in an obvious parody of male revenge fantasies against non-compliant women. In what turns out to be a "comparable vengeance dream,"[97] Pynchon, one could argue, transforms an actual historical event—the premiere of Stravinsky's "Rites of Spring"— into his own violently homophobic repudiation of women-identified women.

While the death of Mélanie "allows" V. to extricate herself from the "closet" of an entropic alliance and to realign herself to the "normal" heterosexual world ("V. ran off with one Sgherraccio" after Mélanie's death [*V.* 414]), it also, as Golden notes, symbolically serves to present the reader with an image of the ultimate "mechanical woman" when she is impaled upon one of the poles held by the male dancers.[98] Her violent, phallic demise captures, then, the punishment for both her affiliation with the inanimate and her rejection of male sexuality. While male aggression against all women in *V.* emerges as sexualized anger, its virulence is directly proportionate not only to the woman's degree of identification with the non-human but also to her rejection of male sexuality for definition, purpose and form.

Woman's Place In The Raketenstadt: *Gravity's Rainbow*

Any critical exegesis of Pynchon's *magnum opus* faces the intimidating challenge of entering an intricate maze of thematic and structural twists and turns and of clashing voices and dense allusions that reverberate along a variety of discursive registers, from comic books to theoretical physics. Unlike Theseus, who located and slew the Minotaur lurking within the center of the Cretan labyrinth, the critical reader of *Gravity's Rainbow* searches in vain for a textual center, an explanatory principle that will illuminate the often dark and nebulous pathways to plot, characterization and theme. As McCaffery notes, Pynchon's "attempts to deny his work a center that controls it lead to an ironic and yet familiar self-entrapment: they result in a work where a decentered and diffused control becomes the omnipresent issue."[99] Ariadne, of course, provided Theseus with the necessary plan and roll of thread by which he would be able to retrace his steps and find his way out of the maze; Pynchon, however, lures us into the intricate recesses of the post-industrial, techno-military complex and international cartels through discussions of rocket technology, benzene rings, Rilkean romanticism, pornographic films, World War II espionage and counter-espionage, sado-masochistic control and exploitation, Puritan cultural legacies and so on, with the hope of unraveling the meaning of the comic coincidence between an American lieutenant's (Tyrone Slothrop's) sexual encounters and the V-2 rocket strikes in London during the last nine months of the war.

Like Slothrop who engages on a quest to uncover the mysterious connection between his own sexual behavior and the technology of the Rocket, the reader warily enters the text only to find that this thread of potential meaning initially provided by Pynchon runs out, leaving us as lost and as scattered as Slothrop becomes in the "Zone," the war-torn, ravaged European landscape of unpredictability and danger. Like Slothrop who remains "uncapturable," the text resists being pinned down by any one system of meaning. Never do we discover the real connection between Slothrop and Laszlo Jamf, one of the early architects of the mysterious synthetic material, Imipolex-G, eventually used in the construction of the A-4 or V-2 rocket, nor are we provided with a satisfactory explanation as to why Slothrop's "erective capability" exactly anticipates, along the Poisson

Distribution curve, the pattern of V-2 strikes.

Just as Slothrop eventually loses interest and direction concerning his mysterious beginning, his explanatory principle, so too must the reader "let go" of the need for textual stability and give in instead to the disorienting yet revealing strategies of a novelist who seems hell-bent on subverting the very notions of order and centers, of identity, of beginnings, middles and ends. As one critic observes: *Gravity's Rainbow* "inscribes and then undercuts—in a typically postmodern way—the certainties of the ordering impulse of positivistic science as well as humanist history and literature, and it does so by over-totalization, by parodies of systematization."[100] If we are left alone in the "Zone" of a text that offers very few and at times too many clues or convoluted pathways, that celebrates paradox rather than consistency, that frequently jettisons the oppressive and reductive predictability of the logic of cause-and-effect and, as Joseph Slade argues, extols surprise and uncertainty,[101] then we face the interpretive challenge of constructing a locus of meaning, however tentative and "unstable," regarding the phenomenon of women and violence. The paucity of textual data in Barthleme and Didion has given way to a plethora of discrete, yet often seemingly disconnected or, at times, over-connected bits of information in Pynchon; consequently, the reader, abandoned by Pynchon and left groping in a textual labyrinth without a definitive thread of meaning to guide us to certainty and clarity, must, as we did when facing the minimalists, spin out our own strands of significance, while at the same time realizing that "to be certain about any clear message in *Gravity's Rainbow*...is in some sense to distort the text."[102] Even the paranoid compulsion to view everything as "plotted" or connected, manifested in such figures as the Pavlovian behaviorist Pointsman and the conspiracy-obsessed members of the White Visitation, leaves us facing no greater degree of interpretive certainty; for, like those in *Gravity's Rainbow* who indulge the "Puritan reflex of seeking other orders behind the visible" (GR 188), the critical reader, as Michael Berube points out, is never sure as to the locus of the Real Text: "Critical paranoia is simply interpretation without transcendental grounds."[103]

Acknowledging the absence of any totalizing interpretive principle or key in *Gravity's Rainbow*, and celebrating Pynchon's disdain for conventional literary staples such as temporal linearity, I have somewhat arbitrarily chosen the "middle" of the text with which to begin an analysis of Pynchon's images of women and violence. Superimposing the "rainbow-like" trajectory of Pynchon's rocket onto the text itself, with its ascent on the opening page—"A screaming comes across the sky" (GR 3), to its ominous fall to earth on the very last page—"the pointed tip of the Rocket, falling nearly a mile per second" (GR 760), one finds the apogee of the projectile and the "center" of the text to occur around episode 11 in Section 3, which, as Steven Weisenburger observes, is also the longest section of the book.[104] Significantly, this section, which I will for convenience call the "Rocket Chapter" (GR 397-433), details the interconnections among: the genesis and evolution of rocketry in the post-industrial State; the mad pursuit of global annihilation through our devotion to the Rocket; the sado-masochistic strategies devised by the high priests of Rocketry, the "Firm" or "Them"— those who sit, for example, on the Board of Directors of IG Farben or General Electric, who are dedicated to perpetuating their own power and to perfecting the Inanimate by controlling all citizens, both male and female; the clever co-opting by the State of any revolutionary factions or impulses; and ultimately, the very vulnerable position of the weakest members of the *Raketenstadt*, women and children. The "Rocket Chapter" is, in some ways, a microcosmic distillation of the entire text, for *Gravity's Rainbow*, as Madsen argues, not only "investigates the notion of World War II as a moment of crisis in the development of the ideological hegemony of the 'them,'" but also illuminates the "subliminal cultural strategies by which power is invested in the hands of the exploiters by the exploited themselves."[105]

While Pynchon may eschew a "transcendental ground" of signification, the Rocket, as the totemic figure of the military-industrial complex, takes on mythic proportions in the text, serving not only as the organizing principle of the post World War II State and international cartels but also as the symbol of the phallic victory over "lovable, but scatter-brained Mother Nature" (GR 324) and the complete dehumanization of postmodern existence. The inanimate "phallic" rocket is a fitting symbol of the mechanized sexuality and dehumanization of the personal which, for Pynchon, characterizes a postmodern American culture that worships technology and attempts to reify all that is human. One hears in *Gravity's Rainbow* echoes of the plaints of Allen Ginsberg in *Howl*, a poem which William Carlos Willams labels a "howl of defeat" in the face of the cultural wasteland of post World War II America:

> Moloch! Moloch! Robot apartments! invisible suburbs! skeleton treasures! blind capitals! demonic industries! spectral nations! invincible mad houses! granite cocks! monstrous bombs![106]

As a patriarchal icon of violence and potential global destruction, the of "the alkaline earth" to another, but she also suffers the sexualized anger of the narrator while being forced to bend "her back over a rock" (*V.* 272). While the motivation behind Sarah's submission to her oppressor remains ambiguous, Pynchon's imagery and seeming absence of ironic parody in this episode suggest an affirmation of the traditional metaphysical identification of woman and matter, an identification that entails a concomitant cultural myth that women "naturally" welcome the often brutal submission to male aggression.

If the imagery and tone informing the Sarah episode embrace the traditional association of women and materialism, the treatment of V.'s lesbian lover, Mélanie, strongly points to a strain of not-so-latent misogyny in the author's portrayal of women and violence. Again, however, Pynchon's rather virulent attitude toward this homosexual union is entangled in his rejection of closed, entropic systems; that is to say, his disgust with lesbianism is well-grounded in his metaphysics, or, conversely, perhaps, his metaphysics represents a philosophical rationale for his homophobia.[67]

The Mélanie episode of Chapter Fourteen presents us with yet another incarnation of the elusive Lady V., who now appears at the Christ-like age of 33 in Paris in 1913, while Europe ominously awaits the outbreak of World War I. She falls in love with Mélanie L'Heuremaudit, a fifteen-year-old French ballet dancer who has been sexually abused by her father and who is now being trained to play the role of Su Feng in "The Rape of the Chinese Virgins." After a brief "love affair" with V. that consists of a rather intricate arrangement of mirrors and voyeuristic arousals and very little, if any, physical contact between V. and Mélanie, Mélanie dies in a freak "accident" on stage during her premiere performance as Su Feng. Having "forgotten" to wear the "protective metal device, a species of chastity belt" (*V.* 414) that would have become attached to the point of a pole on which she was to dance her final scene, Mélanie is literally impaled to death on stage as the horrified audience looks on.

Not surprisingly, the (in)famous Chapter Fourteen, sardonically entitled "V. in love," has elicited numerous critical responses from Pynchon scholars. Feminists such as Mary Allen, Susan Gubar and Sandra Gilbert decry Pynchon's violent repudiation of what he, like Freud, perceives to be the ultimate expression of narcissism.[68] Intent upon elucidating the gothic dimension of the novel, Fowler interprets the death scene as a strange commingling of blasphemy, sex and death, Mélanie's having forgotten the one inanimate object that would have saved her.[69] Lhamon views their "surreal" love affair as the second stage (liberal love feast) of the pentecostal patriarchal culture is constituted";[109] conversely, however, the litany of gruesome crimes committed against women in the text does not automatically consign the novel to the category of anti-feminist propaganda. Contrary to the opinions put forth by critics who deem *Gravity's Rainbow* to be "a pretty blatantly sexist book,"[110] I agree in principle with Marjorie Kaufman's assessment that *Gravity's Rainbow* is not a "masculinist" text that promotes patriarchal values, and that Pynchon's portrayals of such sexist themes as male domination, enslavement and objectification of the body emerge as "symptoms of a pathological society, a loveless, diseased state of death-in-life";[111] yet, I also detect in *Gravity's Rainbow* an underlying ambivalence, though somewhat tempered since *V.*, on the author's part with regard to the victimization of women, an "approach and avoid" attitude toward female abuse that suggests that he may not be completely free of the very pathology he impugns. Such ambivalence parodies but, as Brian McHale notes, "does not resolve the narrative's ambiguous representation of pervasive structures of control,"[112] such as gender stereotyping and the subjugation of women. Yet having shifted his focus from what Stonehill labels "the vaginal V-1" to the "phallic V-2,"[113] and having accorded a more positive metaphysical dimension to Nature, Pynchon, in *Gravity's Rainbow*, targets primarily the male-dominated System as the recipient of his excoriating invective; it is a System which, as Madsen argues, manifests a "dangerous impulse towards conformity and propriety and an equally dangerous myopia towards poverty, violence, racism, sexism and the like,"[114] and in which most women, infected by the pathology of the State, perversely embrace their own subjugation.

The "Rocket Chapter" focuses primarily upon the character of Franz Pökler, a key figure in the early development of the V-2 in Germany. As an engineer working in the German Rocket program, Pökler, through his reminiscences and perhaps paranoid delusions, becomes Pynchon's emblem not only of the perverse rationalizations of the individual who unquestioningly sells his talents to the State, but also of the very society itself that constructs an intricate labyrinth between its own destructive technology and the well-being of its citizens. Madsen's observation that one of the marks of the postmodern culture is the "individual's manipulation by cultural institutions that work for the perpetuation of their own power through the masquerade of the 'common good,'"[115] applies to Pynchon's analysis of the military-industrial State in *Gravity's Rainbow* and in particular to Pökler's blind devotion to rocket technology. Having worked under the tutelage and supervision of the "high priest" of the German Rocket program, Weissmann/Blicero, Pökler provides a chilling insight into the teutonic lust for power that, in postmodern industrial society, either conscripts the weaker members of society into its service or, as Hawkes argues in *The Cannibal*, "consumes" them. Whether they are being stalked by predatory adults, to be flayed and quartered for the evening repast (*The Cannibal*), or being consigned to concentration camps, euphemistically tagged "re-education" camps, or, like the young Gottfried, strapped into the tail of Blicero's secret Rocket 00000 and launched into fiery oblivion, children in the military-industrial state become, to use one of Pynchon's most recurring allusions, vulnerable Hansels and Gretels, ominously awaiting their immolation in the oven of corporate greed. And like the children, women too succumb to the mandates of a masculinist culture, devising perverse strategies to survive, often falling prey to their own illusions of control and freedom. Significantly, the "Rocket Chapter" captures the plight of the weaker members of the *Raketenstadt*, the women and children.

"Sugar and Spice" and Every Conceivable Vice: Women and Little Girls of the *Raketenstadt*

Detailing the events in his life in July of 1945, the "Rocket Chapter" opens with Franz Pökler's reminiscence about a night, seven or so years earlier, when he and his wife, Leni, conceived their daughter, Ilse. Most prominent in his memory of that night are the images of female submission and compliance to male sexual abuse depicted in a porno movie ("Alpdrücken") he attended, featuring the porno star, Margherita Erdmann:

> ...yes, bitch—yes, little bitch—poor helpless *bitch* you're coming can't stop yourself now I'll whip you again whip till you bleed...Thus Pökler's whole front surface, eyes to knees: flooded with tonight's image of the delicious victim bound to her dungeon rack, filling the movie screen— close-ups of her twisting face, nipples under the silk gown amazingly erect, making lies of her announcements of pain—*bitch*! she loves it...and Leni no longer solemn wife, embittered source of strength, but Margherita Erdmann underneath him, on the bottom for a change, as Pökler drives in again, into her again, yes, bitch, yes...Only later did he try to pin down the time. Perverse curiosity. Two weeks since her last period. He had come out of the Ufa theatre on the Friedrichstrasse that night with an erection, thinking like everybody else only about getting home, fucking somebody, fucking her into some submission.... (GR 397)

Titillated by the images of a woman being beaten and sexually abused, Pökler emerges from the theatre with only one desire, to "fuck someone" into submission; that this someone happens to be his wife and that their coupling results in the birth of a child are two circumstances that accord a façade of civility to a fundamentally brutal, rapacious act. Pynchon, here, has brilliantly captured the deterioration of procreative love-making into a lust for power and domination in the postmodern military state. One might even argue that the causal connection that Pynchon seems to make between the graphic depiction of the images of female suffering on the screen and the danger awaiting so many women in the streets and in their homes parallels the causal argument that "men act out pornography" put forth by many anti-pornography feminists such as Susan Brownmiller, Andrea Dworkin, Catharine MacKinnon and Adrienne Rich.[116] Maintaining that pornography incites men to engage in the rape and torture of women, feminists point to the hardcore images of sexual degradation of women who supposedly invite and enjoy their own humiliation as misogynistic portrayals that reduce women to "objects of sexual appetite devoid of emotional content, without individual meaning or personality: essentially as a sexual commodity to be consumed by males."[117] Such images, anti-pornography critics argue, create an environment that gives "cultural permission for men to treat women as objects, not fellow human beings."[118]

Yet given the novel's underlying criticism of Pavlovian behavioristic thinking and its reductionist attempt to perceive all human behavior in terms of a physiological stimulus-response conditioning that can be controlled by activating "on" and "off" switches in the brain, how seriously can we take the author's seeming sensitivity to the feminist causal argument against pornography? While Franz Pökler's rapacious "response" to the cinematic "stimuli"—images of sexualized aggression—seems to confirm the anti-pornography feminists' causal argument that pornography is "implicated in the committing of violent crimes against women,"[119] Pynchon's pervasive disdain for behaviorists such as Pointsman and members of the experimental espionage force—The White Visitation—and their reliance upon binary thought processes, serve to render his stance somewhat ambiguous. Yet, whether or not Pynchon supports a strict cause-and-effect connection between pornography and male-initiated violence, the Franz Pökler episode clearly *implicates* the society's endorsement of negative female images in the systematic oppression and exploitation of women.

Perhaps it is precisely Pynchon's implied sympathy with the female victim here that accounts for the difference in effect between this episode and that depicting the mutilation of Mélanie in *V.* The Mélanie episode is presented to us by a narrative voice that is very close to that of the author's, but in the "Alpdrücken" scene, Pynchon steps back and presents us with images of female humiliation and torture not only through the eyes of a sadistic male patron but also through the cinematic gaze of an exploitive male porno director, Von Göll, who, we later find out, originally included in the movie a scene in which "jackal men come in to ravage and dismember" Erdmann's character (GR 461). While the gang rape and dismemberment scenes were cut before the film was released, the deleted footage "found its way into Goebbels' private collection" (GR 461). So, Pynchon not only narratively distances himself from the graphic depiction of female mutilation but also places such images within the larger political context of a pathological pursuit of male power and acquisitive domination: the porno films that Von Göll and Erdmann made were used to entertain the Nazi troops, to whip up their libidos into a frenzy of lustful destruction. Furthermore, while Berube is correct in arguing that the Erdmann episode is structured from the viewpoint of a director of a snuff film, it is not Pynchon, speaking as himself, who assumes this position, as Berube maintains,[120] but rather Von Göll who provides the directorial gaze.

Yet, one cannot also help but sense Pynchon's implicit exploitation of the male, pornographic gaze here, his indulging the very misogynistic fantasies he deems pathological simply by virtue of the scene's inclusion and its explicit details. For, although we are viewing the scene through the eyes of Pökler who in turn is witnessing the artistic creation of Von Göll, we detect, lurking in the background, behind all the deflective voices, a writer who, despite his shift toward a more compassionate understanding of the plight of women, remains caught up in his own Puritan culture's abhorrence of sexuality and its scapegoating of women. Yet, despite Pynchon's indirect indulgence in sadistic male fantasies, despite the virulent tone and reference to the familiar rationalization that the rape victim "loved it," he remains, at the same time, a critic of the abuses of power throughout *Gravity's Rainbow*; and here he depicts Erdmann as more or less a prisoner of the male-operated projector, just as all those oppressed members of the *Raketenstadt* remain entrapped under the rainbow of the male-operated projectile.

Furthermore, the reference to a woman's complicity in her own degradation, her uttering "no" but really meaning "yes," that remained so ambiguous and problematic in *V.*, emerges here more clearly as a strategy of male exploitive propaganda. Couched as it is within the context of hardcore pornography used to incite the troops, the seemingly contradictory image of Erdmann's "amazingly erect nipples making lies of her announcements of pain" unravels here as primarily cinematic "lies" contrived by the male gaze to justify female subjugation and to heighten male sexual arousal. "Sexual arousal as a result of viewing pornography is a characteristic [not only] of sexual offenders"[121] but also of men preparing for battle. The sexualized lust for destruction that informs much of the military mentality finds its stimuli in pornographic images of women. Speaking of Heinrich Himmler, Susan Griffin notes:

> Despite his high ideals regarding chastity he was drawn to torrid, even pornographic fiction, including *Ein Sadis Priesterrock* which he read quickly, noting in his journal that it was a book about the 'corruption of women and girls...in Paris.'[122]

Griffin also points out that the correlation between misogyny and warfare is not confined to the "satanic" Nazi personality of a Himmler but also characterizes postmodern American strategies of control:

> Pilots preparing to drop bombs in the Gulf War were actually watching pornographic films before they left in sorties. It has existed for a long time, an objectified relationship with women, as part of the training by which young men offer themselves to kill or be killed.[123]

The porno film which whips up Pökler's lust to "fuck" his wife into submission becomes, then, a cinematic emblem of the predominantly patriarchal "strategies of power, domination and control"[124] that pervade the pages of the text, strategies that Pynchon, for the most part, disdains.

Again, however, Pynchon's sensitivity to the fraudulent male claim that women, despite their protests, invite their own sexual humiliation, that their "No" always means "Yes," does not prevent him from exploiting the kind of grunt-funny male humor that purchases laughter at the expense of the so-called ambivalence of women's responses to male sexual aggression. Toward the end of novel, when the narrative is disintegrating into fragmented episodes that include glimpses of Slothrop's family history and the analyses of American slang and idiomatic expressions, a character named Säure, a "second story man," tells Slothrop a "joke" about a woman whose apartment he was about to burglarize. When caught in the act by his female victim, Säure threatens to blind her with acid if she screams for help. Despite his threat, the woman yells, but due to a "congenital" inability to pronounce umlauts, according to her predator, fails to convey the right message:

> [She] starts hollering for help to all the ladies of the same age in her building who feel that same motherly help-help-but-make-sure-there's-time-for-him-to-rape-me ambivalence about nubile cat burglars. What she means to scream is "Hübsch Räuber! Hübsch Räuber!" which means "Cute-looking Robber!"...but she can't pronounce the umlauts. So it comes out "Hubschrauber!"...which means "Helicopter".... (GR 683)

Since this incident occurred in 1920 before the invention of the helicopter, no one, Säure humorously points out, understood what she was shouting. Despite his presenting this comic tale through the voice of Säure, Pynchon, it seems, remains quite comfortable comically indulging the very phenomenon that informs the tragic dimension of Franz Pökler's vision of Erdmann's cinematic image. That the woman would indeed be screaming "Cute Robber!" comically suggests what is tragically presented in the Pökler incident and later confirmed in Erdmann's own desire to be whipped and beaten to achieve sexual arousal, namely, that women in Western technocracy have learned to affirm their own subordination. Yet this episode, like the Pökler incident, may also reveal that the State's most effective strategies to insure the domination and control of its women involve the perpetuation of degrading female images and stereotypes by which men are subtly taught to view women as masochistic creatures and by which women are taught to embrace and welcome their own victimization by sadistic men.

In *V.* Pynchon's metaphysical identification of women with brute matter or the Inanimate, and their seemingly "natural" proclivity to invite the imposition of male force, serve to undermine their status as political victims; however, in *Gravity's Rainbow*, Pynchon seems not only to shift his primary focus from the metaphysical to the political so that the distributions and abuses of power in the male-dominated State become the main target of his invective; he also seems to affirm a more primitivist concept of Nature as denoting a hylozoistic, mystical realm (GR 228) of vitality and life-affirming forces (GR 720) whose entropic tendencies may in fact be superseded by a more primordial cycle of eternal recurrence, symbolized in the Rocket Chapter by the "Great Serpent holding its own tail in its mouth, the dreaming Serpent which surrounds the World" and announces, "'The World is a closed thing, cyclical, resonant, eternally-returning'" (GR 412). Consequently, the female principle associated with Nature is far more positive in *Gravity's Rainbow* than it is in *V.*, and it is, Pynchon seems to suggest, only through the desacrilizing imposition of male force upon this female domain of mystical energies and vitality that the entire generative cycle of Nature has been violated.

Within the "Rocket Chapter," Pynchon, speaking in what surely must be his own critical voice, relates how the discovery of the benzene ring by the 19th century chemist Kekulé that "revolutionized chemistry and made the IG possible" (GR 410) was, in fact, a blatant example of the profit-driven rationality of Western science to transform and distort the realm of nature into the synthetic materials of the Rocket:

> Kekulé dreams the Great Serpent holding its own tail in its mouth, the dreaming Serpent which surrounds the World. But the meanness, the cynicism with which this dream is to be used. The Serpent…is to be delivered into a system whose only aim is to *violate* the Cycle. Taking and not giving back, demanding that "productivity" and "earnings" keep on increasing with time, the System removing from the rest of the World these vast quantities of energy to keep its own tiny desperate fraction showing a profit: and not only most of humanity—most of the World, animal, vegetable and mineral is laid to waste in the process. (GR 412)

Clearly Pynchon repudiates the de-animating thrust of Western rationality as it plunders the vital resources of "loveable" Mother Nature in its maniacal drive to exercise the legacy of the Protestant world view that levels fecundity to a two-dimensional plane of debits and credits. "Living inside the System," Pynchon tells us in the same passage, "is like riding across the country in a bus driven by a maniac bent on suicide." In effect, Pynchon decries the primarily male-driven process, epitomized in the construction of the phallic Rocket that looms above the natural landscape, by which Nature is perceived in Western technology as the enemy that must be conquered and reduced to a vast economic system of competitive markets. When Weissmann brought the young Herero Enzian to Europe from South West Africa to aid in the assembly of the rocket, he taught him that Western love had "to do with masculine technologies, with contracts, with winning and losing:

> Demanded in his own case that he enter the service of the Rocket…Beyond simple steel erection, The Rocket was an entire system *won*, away from the feminine darkness, held against the entropies of lovable but scatterbrained Mother Nature: that was the first thing he was obliged by Weissmann to learn, his first step toward citizenship in the Zone. He was led to believe that by understanding the Rocket, he would come to understand truly his manhood. (GR 324)

While it is primarily a masculine technological world view that persists in apprehending Nature as inanimate and lifeless, it resides within the intuitive powers of a woman in the text to perceive the world from a different angle, to penetrate the dead cultural accretions of profits and losses, of rocket fuel and benzene rings, and apprehend the living memory of the world as it existed before the Western male consciousness divided it up into dominions and conquerable territories. One of Pynchon's more positive female characters is Geli Tripping, a "witch" who uses her magical powers not only to transform the hatred of Tchitcherine, a Russian wandering in the Zone looking to kill his half-brother Enzian, into love, but also to intuit the vibrant throbbings of an animate Earth that "is too violently pitched alive in constant flow ever to be seen by men directly" and that has been systematically violated by those who take and do not give back:

> [Men] are meant only to look at it dead, in still strata transputrefied to oil or coal. Alive, it was a threat: it was Titans, was an overpeaking of life so clangorous and mad...[that] we, the crippled keepers were sent out to multiply, to have dominion, God's spoilers...*It is our mission to promote death.* (GR 720)

Geli's perception, as Madsen notes, "opens up the text of Creation," for her "pretextual alternative to 'their'discourse of rationality and determinism leads her to a 'Pan-theistic' vision of Earth's divine 'mind/body' motivated by love."[125] Yet despite Geli's supernatural powers and her appearance as a positive, "nurturing force,"[126] she, like all women in the text, fails to effect any radical change in the masculine, technological pursuit of power.

Symbolizing perhaps the once-potential anarchy of female witchery and subversion of patriarchal values, Geli remains, however, susceptible to the sexual lure of the Rocket, her primitivist vision having been effectively rendered obsolete by generations of Puritan "witch hunts," and her powers co-opted and trivialized by a corporate State dedicated to turning Nature into a locus of death-dealing profits. At one point during their brief sexual encounter, she informs Slothrop that she served as the model for the rocket insignia:

> Goosebumps crowd her bare little breasts. "I posed once for a rocket insignia. Perhaps you've seen it. A pretty young witch straddling an A4. Carrying her obsolete broom over her shoulder. I was voted the Sweetheart of 3/Art. Abt. (mot)485." (GR 293)

Geli's intimacy with Slothrop reveals a woman who indeed is sleeping with the enemy, for it is Slothrop's Puritan ancestors who initiated the violent eradication of witchcraft in America, targeting those women who, as Mary Daly argues, "were living outside the control of the patriarchal family, women who presented an option of 'eccentricity;'"[127] and it is Slothrop, himself, who has carried on their tradition of harnessing women and their powers to perpetuate misogynistic values. Geli's erotic image on the V-2 underscores the insidious power of the State to co-opt and assimilate for its own use any subversive faction that may threaten its existence; such an image may allude to the U.S.'s militaristic exploitation of female sexuality to promote its own nuclear weapons industry—the Rita Hayworth photo on the August 11, 1941 edition of *Life* that "decorated soldiers' footlockers, packs and tanks, was also pasted on the first nuclear weapon detonated over Bikini in 1946."[128] While Rita Hayworth, who professed to be against the war, "wept when the bomb bearing her image was detonated,"[129] Geli Tripping seems to acquiesce quietly to the State's appropriation and negation of her potentially subversive and "ex-centric" vision of creation. However, that Pynchon chose a female character to articulate his condemnation of the West's tradition of exploitation, a tradition spawned from the seeds of a patriarchal religion and perfected throughout history by the self-aggrandizing technologies of those profit-seekers whose "mission" is "to promote death" (GR 720), suggests a shift in sympathy toward the female principle that is absent in *V.*

Consequently, women who appear to invite their own humiliation by sadistic men emerge primarily as *political victims*, socialized by the forces of a pathological State over which they exert very little, if any, control, to embrace their own masochistic subordination. In *V.*, women, aligned with the inanimate in-itself, symbolize that alluring descent into entropic decline against which men also violently rail; however, in *Gravity's Rainbow*, the female's primordial connection to a vital Nature has been so perverted by a masculinist technology of greed and plunder that even individual women fail to perceive their own victimization.

Consequently, Margherita Erdmann's participation in the porno projects of Von Göll, her extolling him as a "genius" to Slothrop whom she meets in the Zone while she is searching for her lost child Bianca, and her request that Slothrop whip her into a sexual frenzy, must all be viewed against the more insidious strategies of a State that, again, maintains "a branch office in each of our heads." While her perverse attempts to break through the barriers of self and establish a community of pain within a spiritually-impoverished society may explain her sado-masochistic cinematic persona, she succeeds only in serving the iniquitous designs of a State intent upon spawning death, not love. As Joseph Slade argues: "The more a culture promotes sexual release through pornographic commercialization of sensuality the more sexuality loses its erotic power to subvert control."[130] Immediately preceding the "Rocket Chapter" and serving as a brilliant segue into Pökler's reminiscence about Margherita Erdmann's porno film appears an episode in which Erdmann interrupts the search for Bianca for a nostalgic return to the movie studio where she and her co-star, Max Schlepzig, made their "vaguely pornographic horror movies" (GR 393) for Von Göll in the 1920's and '30's. Having stumbled upon Slothrop, who just happens to be hiding out there under the alias "Max Schlepzig," Erdmann recalls her movie-making days with a pathological fondness for her own humiliation and objectification.

A more verbose version of that other porno star—Maria Wyeth from *Play It As It Lays*, Erdmann tells Slothrop, in so many words, that her cinematic persona was nothing more than that of a sexualized object, divested even of the "Dietrich-like" ability to control men: nicknamed the "Anti-Dietrich by "them," Erdmann clearly remembers her vulnerable passivity:

> "I watched all our films...some of them six or seven times. I never seemed to *move*. Not even my face. Ach, those long, long gauze close-ups...it could have been the same frame, over and over. Even running away—I always had to be chased, by monsters, madmen, criminals—still I was so...stolid, so...monumental. When I wasn't running I was usually strapped or chained to something. Come I'll show you." (GR 394)

Erdmann's remembrances of her own cinematic humiliations, her basic sense of succumbing to a dehumanized inertness even within the scenes of "movement," and her need to re-play that assault with Slothrop on the set all reveal a victimized woman inextricably caught up in a cycle of sado-masochism in which she has come to embrace her oppressor: "I knew he was a genius." Didion's absence of a larger political context within which her masochistic women, such as Maria Wyeth, compulsively play out their self-degrading fantasies, leaves the reader struggling to justify any compassionate response to their plights; however, Pynchon's more expansive focus on the political backdrop against which women and children are more or less compelled to adopt deleterious strategies of survival in a male-dominated State lends more sympathy to them as victims.

Like most of its citizens, Erdmann has been exposed to a rampant contagion, to a "virus of death," not only assimilating the State's hierarchical subordination of women into her own personal version of self-humiliation, but also transmitting the "disease" to her daughter, Bianca. One of the strains of this "virus of death" in *Gravity's Rainbow* seems to be the inculcation of the young with the virulent twin stereotypes of the aggressive, destructive male and the passive, compliant female. Pynchon would undoubtedly agree with Griffin's salient observation that "the requirements of gender are like the omnipresent yet partly hidden plans of a secret bureaucracy."[131] While "fathers are the carriers of the virus of death and sons are the infected" (GR 723), women and daughters remain the most vulnerable citizens in this patriarchal dystopia. Impregnated by one of the actors (probably Schlepzig, she tells us) who "rapes" her in the gang-bang scene in "Alpdrücken," Erdmann conceives Bianca in much the same manner as Leni conceives Ilse—during a violent sexual assault. That Erdmann is eventually reunited with her husband, Thanatz ("death"),[132] underscores her conjugal bonds to death, and the reduction of her body to a vessel of the State, capable of carrying within its womb the seeds of death that will germinate and produce future vulnerable children, that is, future Hansels and Gretels. Nicknamed "Greta" to suggest possibly her own vulnerability, Margherita Erd-mann (Earth-man) emerges not only as a symbol of a defiled Nature, but also as an emblem of the perversities and pathological behavior that such systematic contagion can generate: having become addicted to Oneirine, a product made by Jamf and IG Farben, Erdmann, in order to expunge her own imagined Jewish heritage upon her return to Germany from America before the war, engaged in a ritual slaughter of Jewish boys, stalking them as her sexual prey. Such expressions of female aggression, when considered within the larger context of the gender politics in *Gravity's Rainbow*, emerge as symptoms of the pervasive cultural disease transmitted by the carriers of "the virus of death." Erdmann's murderous rage against Jewish children reflects not only the rising tide of anti-semitism that would inundate Germany in the years to come, but also the psychological projection of her own self-loathing onto the "Other" and the violent "extermination" of those qualities of the self that have been deemed evil by the State. Having been taught to detest her own status as woman, her "femaleness," Erdmann, as we have seen, "willfully" submits to her own pornographic degradation, identifying with her aggressor, Von Göll. Internalizing the State's hatred of the Jews, she again comes to identify with a more pervasive, diffuse aggressor and becomes an instrument of a pernicious and lethal anti-semitism.

While Pynchon does not openly exonerate Erdmann or any of his female characters from responsibility for the atrocities perpetrated by the State, his focus on the male-organized system of power, the underlying culprit that is emblematized by the Rocket, allows him to impart to his women a degree of compassion that is missing in *V.* For if men are the carriers of the virus of death, then women are more or less the victims who are forced to perpetuate the death-infected species whose ultimate demise of course will occur *via* weapons technology. Just as Erdmann and all mothers living under the rainbow of the Rocket carry within their impregnated wombs the potential for further destruction, so too is Weissmann's Rocket equipped within its own "womb," the Schwarzgerät, that will be lined with Jamf's erotic material—the mysterious Imipolex G—and that will sacrifice the young Hansel-figure, Gottfried, to the culture's worship of Death.

"Puppy dog tails" and Rocket trails: Men and Little Boys of the *Raketenstadt*

Pynchon's insertion of a womb-like device into the phallic Rocket brilliantly symbolizes not so much the "androgynous nature" of the Rocket, as one critic maintains,[133] but rather the System's unlimited power to distort and pervert all facets of existence, its frightening ability to invade and co-opt the private sphere of sexuality and child-bearing, and to synthesize *synthetically* a weapon of destruction with the naturally life-affirming process of creation. Just as all images and tropes seem to gravitate toward the Rocket as the symbol of the military-industrial complex of cartels, so too does the Rocket mentality inform the conscious and unconscious activities of its citizens. Throughout the "Rocket Chapter" Pökler not only spends his every waking moment working to resolve the propulsion and trajectory problems involved in Rocket 00000 and perfecting the Schwarzgerät for Weissmann; he also dreams about the Rocket "with some frequency" (GR 399) and in sexual images, so that the steps for making the A-4 operational, to bring it to "its fullness" (GR 400), emerge as some form of autoerotic foreplay. The male lust for power over nature and others is consistently eroticized throughout the text so that the Rocket not only incorporates the phallic ideal but also serves as a trope for the sexual connections among some of the characters. Major Marvy, for example, one of the officers searching for Slothrop in the Zone, finds Manuela in a whorehouse and proceeds to ravage her "sweet and nigger submissiveness," heightening his pleasure with images that are "violent, less erotic than you think—more occupied with thrust, impact, penetration and such other military values" (GR 606).

Consequently, when Greta Erdmann asks Slothrop to whip her into submission, to re-enact the rape scene from "Alpdrücken," she does so as someone who has been conditioned to view her emotional/sexual "home" as one of masochistic compliance, to suffer the pain of submission to male force, and to acquiesce to the forced penetration of rape, that is, to the dictates of Von Göll, Schlepzig and any other spokesmen for the State who translates the ethos of the Rocket and its "victory over Mother Nature" into the violation of women. While Berube correctly points out that Erdmann is acting not as a "free agent inviting her own degradation but as a controlled subject looking for a nostalgic pain of a return home,"[134] the more fundamental issue here resides in Pynchon's criticism of the phallic world view that equates male sexuality with the intrusive resolution of nature's "mysteries." As Erdmann begins to seduce Slothrop into complying with her sado-masochistic desires, the narrator reflects rather sardonically upon the fetishist's worship of the eroticized inanimate, beginning with Margherita's "boned black rig she's wearing underneath" her skirt and culminating in the ultimate fetish, the Rocket:

> How the penises of Western men have leapt, for a century, to the sight of this singular point at the top of a lady's stocking, this transition from silk to bare skin and suspender! It's easy for non-fetishists to sneer about Pavlovian conditioning and let it go at that, but any underwear enthusiast worth his unwholesome giggle can tell you there's much more here—there is a cosmology: of nodes and cusps and points of osculation, mathematical kisses...consider cathedral spires, holy minarets...mountain peaks rising sharply to heaven...always holding potent mystery...In each case the change from point to no-point carries a luminosity and enigma at which something in us must leap and sing or withdraw in fright. Watching the A-4 pointed at the sky—just before the last firing switch closes...Do all these points imply, like the Rocket's, an annihilation? (GR 396)

Parodying our culture's erotic worship of the inanimate, Pynchon constructs an entire cosmology of the fetish and mockingly reveals the predilection of Western men to project their phallic world-view onto their surroundings, whether it be the potentially lethal razor blade, the rose thorns that prick us by surprise, or the mountain peaks or cathedrals that thrust themselves toward heaven. In each instant, the tip of the phallic projection contains a "potent mystery," for it is the interface between the known and the unknown, aroused by a desire to leap into whatever "unpleasant surprise" (GR 397) may await. If it is the thrill of "unpleasant surprises" lurking past the top of Greta's stockings that arouses Slothrop, causing his penis to leap and sing at the mysteries to be revealed by Greta's cries of pain and bruised breasts, then it is the ultimate thrill of possible annihilation, that "palpable mystery " (GR

402) residing in the tip of that synthetic erectile, the Rocket, that stands poised to violate the Earth. Paradoxically, the death-breeding State, in its worship of the inanimate, has both deified and reified the penis as the ultimate fetish.

As the organizing principle subsuming under its shadow people of all classes and backgrounds, the Rocket serves to unify a vast array of diverse characters, from "the Prussian aristocrat" and scientist, Werner von Braun, "down to the likes of Pökler, who would eat an apple in the street" (GR 402). As the symbol first of the "corporate Nazi crowd" and later the entire complex of the West's masculine technology organized into powerful economic cartels, the Rocket informs not only the dreams of those who work to perfect it but also the nightmares of those most vulnerable to its destruction, the women and the children of the *Raketenstadt*. Throughout *Gravity's Rainbow*, Pynchon poignantly portrays the horrors awaiting children who have been more or less abandoned by their parents, whether they be their natural, surrogate or national protectors, to a "forest" of corporate predators and adult manipulators whose primary mission is the acquisition of economic power and the perpetuation of the politics of pathology and death. These "Hansels and Gretels" appear as Gottfried (who is often "feminized" by Blicero to assume the female role in their homosexual union), Bianca, Ilse, Greta Erdmann and even Katje Borgesius, the double agent who, while working undercover for the White Visitation in Holland, is forced to play "Hansel" opposite Gottfried's "Gretel" in Blicero's sadistic "oven" games. Within the context of a substitution game that perhaps serves Pynchon's postmodernist strategy of destabilizing the concept of a fixed, static identity, all children in *Gravity's Rainbow* emerge as victims of sexual abuse, including Slothrop who, as an infant, was subjected to a form of molestation by Jamf that has resulted in the "comical" correlation between Slothrop's erections and the bomb sites. Gottfried, of course, soars to fiery oblivion in the tail section of Rocket 00000, a sacrificial victim of his mentor's Rilkean striving to transcend the "cycle of life and death." Bianca Erdmann, the ill-conceived child of her mother's "cinematic rape" by Schlepzig, falls prey to her mother's own sado-masochistic perversions.

Once she is found by Margherita and Slothrop, Bianca is subjected to a public "spanking" by her mother while they are travelling on the barge "Anubis." With Slothrop, Thanatz and the rest of the passengers looking on, Bianca's pain erotically arouses the crowd into a frenzied orgy that culminates in Slothrop's rather violent sexual union with this eleven-year-old child, and his eventual abandonment of her on the ship that results in her death. Having been evidently tutored quite well by her mother in the State's reduction of women to masochistic vehicles of male aggression, Bianca appears as the willing victim of Slothrop's advances:

> She moves toward him, smiling, pointing toes each step. "I watched you sleep. You're very pretty, you know. Mother also said you're cruel." (GR 469)

What follows is a rather graphic portrayal of their sexual encounter in which Pynchon, although perhaps indirectly indulging the distorted fantasies of every pedophile, at the same time captures the horror of this little girl's humiliation. The discordant images of her natural childlike beauty, juxtaposed against the artificial props of adult clothing and cosmetics, and her rather mechanical, erotic actions suggest a female victim who has been schooled by her elders in the art of self-degradation:

> ...there's one or two lavender bruises starting to show up on her bottom, which is perfectly shaped, smooth as cream. Small as she is, she's been further laced into a tiny black corset, which compresses her waist now to the diameter of a brandy bottle and pushes pre-subdeb breasts up into little white crescents...He starts taking giant, ass-enthusiast bites now, meantime reaching around to play with cuntlips and clit. Bianca's little feet shifting in a nervous dance...she has turned, and sinks to her knees to undo his pleated trousers...the little girl takes the head of Slothrops's cock into her rouged mouth...Knows exactly when to take her mouth away and stand up, high-heeled Parisian slippers planted to either side of him...then her face, round with baby-fat, enormous night-shadowed eyes comes swooping in as she kneels, guides his penis into her and settles slow, excruciating till he fills her, stuffs her full.... (GR 469)

Replete with images of an innocence that has been corrupted, the above passage implicates not only Greta, Thanatz and the State in the emotional abandonment of the child, but also Slothrop, who, having been infected with the virus of death in infancy, has, in effect, become as diseased as the others in his treatment of women and children.

To dismiss Pynchon as one of those postmodernist writers who simply presents the "penis as a pistol" or as an "instrument of rape and revenge" against women, or who fetishizes/objectifies the victim in order to insure male subjectivity,[135] is to ignore the complexities inherent in his vision of the military-industrial State. When placed in the political context of the entire novel, this image of male pedophilia/female masochism reveals the reductive objectification of both Slothrop and Bianca by a State which has conscripted all of its citizens to perpetuate its own "Bad Shit" (GR713) and which has, through subliminal strategies of control, manipulated eroticism and sexuality to further its own power. Slothrop, like all of the adults in the text, is both a victim and perhaps an unwitting agent of the State's "Bad Shit" that contaminates all of its citizens. For when we discover that Slothrop was himself a Hansel-figure, "abandoned" by his father to Jamf for sexual experiments that involved the synthetic Imipolex-G, all in exchange for a Harvard education, we realize that like everyone else in the *Raketentstadt*, Slothrop too falls under the arch of the State, his own sexuality having been co-opted by a "corporate intelligence." That Slothrop's erections are somehow connected to the destructive strikes of the V-2 underscores the unlimited power of the State to pervert the life-perpetuating dynamic of sexuality into the seeds of death. Carrying within himself the State's "Bad Shit," Slothrop—"taking giant, ass-enthusiast bites" out of Bianca—embodies the principles of male power that often sanction abandoning children in a forest of sexual and economic predators—angry, aggressive father figures who are, like Cronus, ready to consume their young. That Bianca seems willing to participate in her own molestation drives home the horrifying extent to which women and children have been conditioned to embrace their own subordination.

Like Pökler, Slothrop has internalized the State's degradation of women and children, abandoning Bianca in a "forest" of sexual predators as they sail toward Nordhausen, the site of the rocket's assembly, on the Anubis, Pynchon's version of Bosch's "Ship of Fools." The State's insidious power to infiltrate the psyches of its citizens and to transmit its misogynist messages so as to shape both the conscious perceptions and the unconscious dreams of its members appears again during Slothrop's liaison with Margherita as they wander through the Zone, scavenging for food and shelter. Comforted only by his sadistic whippings, Greta elicits Slothrop's contempt when she begins to voice her despair over her plight:

> "You have to eat."
> She moves her head aside, first one side, then the other.
> "Oh boy, what a sad story, listen cunt, you ain't the only one's ever suffered—you been out *there* lately?"
> "Of course. I keep forgetting how *you* must have suffered."
> "*Shit* you Germans are crazy, you *all* think the world's against you."

(GR445)

With thoughts about Margherita, the "German cunt" and porno star who was cinematically raped by jackal-headed men, Slothrop that night unconsciously constructs his own "porno" "poem" (GR 446) when he dreams about a middle-class woman who, beneath a veneer of social propriety and decorum, allows the sexual cries of her dog to arouse her into an erotic frenzy. Realizing that the sounds of ecstasy are really her own "interminable cry of dog-pleasure," she is driven to "go out and find other animal species to fuck":

> She sucks the penis of a multicolored mongrel...Out in a barren field near a barbed-wire fence...a tall horse compels her to kneel, passively, and kiss his hooves. Cats and minks, hyenas and rabbits, fuck her inside automobiles, lost at night in the forest.... (GR 447)

When she discovers that she is pregnant, the woman allows her husband to take her out on an American river where she is later found drowned. When a Neptune figure raises her bloated body to the surface, all the forms of life that filled her womb now stream out: "From out of her body streams a flood now of different creatures, octopuses, reindeer, kangaroos." Ultimately, the woman's body is abandoned in the river where "the creatures took their way" with it.

Pynchon goes to great lengths in this scene to emphasize the "poetic" and "cinematic" structure of this artistic creation of the unconscious, subdividing the dream into "Sections" and even scanning some of the lines, while at the same time offering cues as to color imagery as if it were to be filmed. While such heavy-handed intrusions from the authorial voice may, on one level, serve to impart a degree of parody to the episode, inasmuch as the opening images of female bestiality simulate a genre of hardcore pornography films, the more subtle allusions to a Gretel figure "lost at night in the forest" near "a barbed-wire fence" resonate with the more serious implications of female abandonment and incarceration. Again, Pynchon may, in part, be indulging the fantasies of the "snuff" film gazer, but his presentation of images of female abuse and mutilation within the larger political context of the abuses of patriarchal power prevents this episode, like the Pökler episode, from deteriorating into pure pornography. Slothrop's dream seems reminiscent of the Henry Miller of the *Tropic of Cancer* who viewed the vast, teeming array of existence as the uterine spillage from "the fucked out cunt of a whore."[136] That Pynchon incorporates into the dream images of female passivity, confinement and abandonment suggests a tempering of Miller's view and a sensitivity to the plight of the woman in the misogynistic State. Not only through direct mandate and socio-economic structures that restrict women from attaining positions of power but also through the more subtle processes of socialization that come to inform both the conscious and unconscious "artistic" representations of women, the State manages to confine women to the status of "inmate" behind the "barbed-wire fences" of a pathological world-order.

In the "Rocket Chapter," the "inmate" status of women within the *Raketenstadt* is poignantly embodied in the figure of Ilse, who, along with her pro-communist mother, has been interned in one of the State "re-education" camps, Dora, located next to Nordhausen. In order to insure Pökler's continued loyalty and concentration on the V-2, Weissmann allows Ilse to visit him once a year. During her first visit to Peenemünde, Ilse reveals the reality of the all-female concentration camp in which generations of women have been gathered together and sacrificed to the "needs" of those guardians of the Rocket State:

> [Dora] was chilly even in summer—surrounded by barbed wire and bright-hooded lights that burned all night long. There were no boys—only girls, mothers, old ladies living in barracks, stacked up in bunks, often two to a pallet. Leni was well. Sometimes a man in a black uniform came into the barracks and Mutti would go away with him, and stay away for several days. When she came back she didn't want to talk, or even to hug Ilse the way she usually did. Sometimes she cried.... (GR 408)

Reminiscent of the "woman pools" of Von Trotha's camp, Dora not only alludes to the sexual exploitation of the female inmates but also serves as an emblem of the "corporate intelligence" that forcibly relegates to the periphery all citizens not directly involved in the "worship" of technology. Rationalizing his abandonment of his "Gretel," Pökler wonders "if she really wasn't better off as a ward of the Reich":

> He'd heard there were camps, but saw nothing sinister in it: he took the Government at their word, "re-education." *I've made such a mess of everything...they have qualified people there...trained personnel...they know what a child needs.* (GR 410)

Conveniently, Pökler suppresses his own intuitive knowledge that people like Weissmann and the State cannot be trusted, and allows the recognition of his "ineptitude as a father" to prevent him from initially seeking Ilse's or Leni's release.

During the six years that Pökler worked for Weissmann as a plastics engineer, he was permitted to spend a summer furlough with Ilse or someone who, Pökler suspected, was impersonating his daughter and, perhaps, serving the State's conspiratorial designs; he began to entertain the suspicion that the State had sent Ilse to spy on him and not only monitor his fidelity to the Rocket program but also titillate his own incestuous desires by tantalizing him with an older, more seductive "child" each year (GR 418). The possibility of "multiple" Ilses may point to Pynchon's postmodernist subversion of the concept of a fixed and stable ego or identity, but it also serves to reveal the emotional abandonment of a child by her father. So removed from his paternal role as Ilse's natural guardian, Pökler, in sacrificing his child to a mad pursuit of the inanimate Rocket, has allowed the State to construct such an intricate labyrinth between his own natural love for Ilse and his distorted commitment to a weapon of destruction, that he really cannot accord her any temporal continuity or identity. Pökler has effected such an emotional distance from his own daughter that he does not even realize that his subsequent transfer to Nordhausen places him in a location contiguous to Dora. Pynchon, here, seems to echo, in a more expansive form, the comic revelations of Barthelme in *The Dead Father* who satirized a culture in which girl children are systematically reduced to the negatively-gendered status of "not male," depriving them of any substantial identity. While the incestuous activities of the Dead Father and Tom humorously disclose the subordination of women, the sexual power plays between parental figures and children in *Gravity's Rainbow* convey a darker, more insidious and pervasively pathological deterioration of love into lust. Their energies co-opted by a patriarchal state that is intent on insuring its own hegemony and continued existence, fathers like Pökler succumb to the lure of male power, of participating in the inner circles of a "corporate intelligence" while abandoning their children not only to their own perverted lust but to their reckless worship of a death-infested technology.

    That children indeed fall prey to the destructive energies of their "fathers" becomes quite evident in the "Rocket Chapter" not only through Pökler's incestuous fantasies about Ilse (GR 420-21), but also through the image of the *Zwölfkinder*, a Nazi Disneyworld where Franz takes Ilse on their summer vacations. Beneath a façade of "innocence," that is, of children's games, a zoo, fairytale characters and refreshments and ferris wheels, lurks the State's subtle presence, its machinations designed to inculcate the young with a corporate efficiency that dedicates itself not only to imitation and a defilement of Nature but also to a celebration of genocide. "In a corporate State," Pynchon informs us, "a place must be made for innocence, and its many uses" (GR 419). His description of *Zwölfkinder* reveals the fabricated, "synthetic" nature of such a place and the ultimate "use" that it serves in passing along to its citizens the gender stereotypes and national fervor that form the socio-political underpinnings of the State:

> Games, fairy-tales, legends from history, all the paraphernalia of make believe can be adapted and even embodied in a physical place, such as *Zwölfkinder*...If you were an adult you couldn't get inside the city limits without a child escort. There was a child mayor, a child city-council of twelve. Children picked up the papers, fruit peelings and bottles you left in the street...child police reprimanded you if you were caught alone, without your child accompanying. Whoever carried on the real business of the town—it could not have been children—they were well hidden. (GR 419)

In addition to providing the children with a little taste of corporate power and a hands-on lesson in "policing" others, this State-constructed fantasyland also celebrates the West's destructive domestication and reduction of the natural, untamed habitat into an artificial, controlled environment. The incarceration of animals in the *Tierpark* (zoo) and the illusory transformation of natural settings into prefabricated movie sets, replete with "wildlife" and "landscapes," underscores the State's desire to effect a comfortable distance between its citizens and "scatterbrained Mother Nature" so that the systematic destruction of the latter can proceed without interruption:

> Two or three boys hardly older than [Ilse] wandered through the imitation wilderness...Watching them made Pökler sweat. A few "sled dogs" lay suffering in the shade of the dirty papier-mache sastrugi, on plaster snow that had begun to crack. A hidden projector threw images of the aurora on a white scrim. Half a dozen stuffed penguins also dotted the landscape. (GR 419-420)

Paying homage to a "synthetic" natural world in a fantasy-setting trivializes the teeming diversity of life that inhabits the earth and, in effect, distances the young from the profit-driven strategies of Western "progress" that result in the extermination of 200 species a day.[137]

For Pynchon, *Zwölfkinder*, then, serves to imbue the young with the pernicious values of the State, from the destruction of the natural world to the "patriotic" domination of less "civilized" peoples. For "played" out in this fantasyland is the continual re-enactment by little German boys of Von Trotha's defeat of the Hereros. Within an artificial "patch of African desert," every two hours the "treacherous natives" attack von Trotha's brave men in blue, "all the parts played by exuberant boys." This particular "skit" proves "to be a great patriotic favorite with children of all ages" (GR 422), and serves somewhat the same function as do the "porno" films previously discussed, namely, to impart an official justification for repeated acts of male aggression. Pynchon's *Zwölfkinder* clearly serves to illuminate the process of genderfication in the militaristic State, that is, the process of socialization by which young boys are taught to be aggressive and destructive by a culture that, as Campbell points out, "rationalizes and even glorifies male violence." Boys learn to "fight to take possession of toys and territory, to compete and win socially, to be recognized as tough guys."[138] Like Susan Griffin in *A Chorus of Stones*, Pynchon seems to connect the "phallogocentric impulse to destruction" with the child-rearing practices of a patriarchal culture intent upon priming young boys for aggression and domination;[139] that Pynchon would align himself with some feminist theorists and endorse the mother-daughter connection as a possible avenue of escape from the seemingly suicidal route of patriarchal destruction is doubtful.[140] For the dark vision of *Gravity's Rainbow* seems to suggest that any potentially subversive movement, including that of a re-envisioning of childhood and child-rearing practices, seems doomed to "incorporation" by the State. Even this fabricated land of make-believe and childhood innocence remains ultimately vulnerable to the very phallic destruction it tacitly seeks to perpetuate. For, although the State has a vested interest in socializing the young, children, like women whose procreative powers are necessary to insure patrilineal succession, paradoxically emerge as sacrificial victims in the State's pursuit of the inanimate: for we are told that the distance between *Zwölfkinder* and Peenemünde just happens to be "280 kilometers, which was to be, coincidentally, the operational range of the A-4" (GR 419).

Not surprisingly, children, like women, become the most vulnerable "targets" in the *Raketenstadt*. They are, to borrow one of Ilse's phrases, "professional inmates" (GR 430) who must learn how to ingratiate themselves to the power-holders, that is, learn how "to get favors, who to steal from, how to inform" (GR 430), and whose "boots to kiss," a recurring image in the novel that conveys the fetishistic, sado-masochistic dimension of patriarchal power. As an official category of the State, "Childhood" reflects the workings of the "corporate intelligence" designed to mold the young through clearly-demarcated sex role divisions into compliant citizens. Similarly, "Motherhood," as another State-sanctioned concept, functions to socialize the adult female citizens to carry within their wombs the germinated "seeds of the death virus," that is, the "phallogocentric impulse to destruction,"[141] and engender future worshippers of the culture of death.

Leni Pökler, Franz's socialist wife and mother of Ilse, is, as Kaufman notes, a special Pynchon woman in that she knows how "they" work and does attempt to resist the State's strategies of domination and control.[142] Aware that her husband has become a tool of the State and that he has willingly lent his energies to the very System that will imprison her and her child, Leni leaves Franz, telling him, "They're using you to kill people. That's their only job and you're helping them" (GR 400). Her astrological leanings and her insistence that existence can be apprehended along an axis different from that of cause and effect provide an alternative, perhaps "female," vision, a striking contrast to the linear logic of causality represented by Franz, and align her with the more primordial vision expressed by Geli Tripping:

> [Franz] was the cause-and-effect man:he kept at her astrology without mercy, telling her what she was supposed to believe, then denying it. "Tides, radio interference, damned little else. There is no way for changes out there to produce changes here."
>
> "Not produce," she tried, "not cause. It all goes along together. Parallel, not series. Metaphor, Signs and symptoms. Mapping onto different coordinate systems, I don't know…"She didn't know, all she was trying to do was reach.
>
> But he said: "Try to design anything that way and have it work." (GR 159)

Like Geli, who resists the reduction of life to a plane of debits and credits, Leni recoils from the pragmatic epistemology of the State that reduces the tenets of truth and falsehood to that which "works" in the realm of cause and effect. As a member of the Firm, the "corporate Nazi crowd," Franz engages in scientific research on the V-2 that has harnessed the logic of causality to serve the logistics of mass destruction and death.

While Leni criticizes Franz' affiliation with the Rocket program as an overt example of the State's manipulation of its citizens to perpetuate its own legacy of death, she is equally critical of the role that women have been socialized into accepting, a role that assigns them to indoctrinate the young with the values of the State. "Motherhood," argues Leni, "is a civil-service category, Mothers work for *Them*. They're the policemen of the soul…" (GR 219). Pynchon here seems to counteract the post-World War II campaign against mothers launched by such vituperative texts as Philip

Wylie's *A Generation of Vipers* which vilified women as emotionally castrating their sons by means of an over-protective, feminizing "momism."[143] On the contrary, "motherhood," for Pynchon, is an institution of the State which serves the designs of the State; mothers in *Gravity's Rainbow* resemble those in Monique Wittig's *Virgile* (1985) in that they are presented as alienated victims of a patriarchy.[144] When her lover, Peter Sachsa, warns her that her incendiary activities could jeopardize her daughter's future, Leni responds by suggesting that the State, in fact, uses the propaganda of Motherhood to immobilize women, to keep them fettered in chains of maternal responsibility so that they will remain overtly apolitical:

> "That's what they—Peter can't you see, they *want* a great swollen tit with some atrophied excuse for a human, bleating around somewhere in its shadows. How can I be *human* for her? Not her *mother*. (GR 219)

Leni's argument here reflects the potentially subversive observations of an articulate, astute female who, in effect, summarizes the political inertia of women in traditional societies.

Pynchon seems to agree with Marianne Hirsch that motherhood is a political institution co-opted and sanctioned by the State to serve its own misogynistic ends, to assist in the process of "en-gendering," that is, in acculturating boys to assume the mantle of the "masculine, authorial subject" and girls to settle for the "feminine" objectified status of the breeders of male subjects.[145] Inscribed within a "heterosexuality of discourse," mothers perhaps inadvertently serve the insidious designs of a State that continues to objectify them and consign them to servitude. While Pynchon uses the character of Leni Pökler to interrogate and perhaps challenge the traditional concept of motherhood, deconstructing it to expose its dimension of male control, he does not go one step further to destabilize the "unquestioned" foundation of motherhood, namely female heterosexuality, which as Adrienne Rich and Judith Butler argue, is as much of a political construct as gender roles, motherhood, etc.[146] Motherhood posits female heterosexuality as axiomatic, an "enormous assumption to have glided so silently into the foundation of our thought."[147] Again, since it is Leni who "dreams" of a lesbian experience with a Jew, one might argue that Pynchon toys with the possibility of allowing this critic of motherhood also to question the axiom of heterosexuality. Yet, while "dreams" may indeed represent a revelatory and subversive vision, capable of disrupting the causal logic of patriarchal thought, such lesbian visions are ephemeral spasms of hope that remain not only closeted in the the region of the unconscious but also subject to the insidious influence of a totalitarian State itself: for, as discussed earlier, Leni's "unconscious" lesbian dream text is itself informed by the State's lethal anti-semitism.

Yet, Leni, in her analysis of motherhood, overtly expresses what Didion's Inez Victor only implicitly senses, for Leni's awareness of the State's dehumanizing reduction of women to breeders of future, compliant citizens and its relegation of women to the shadowy periphery of power enables her not only to offer some resistance against her own indoctrination by the State but also to humanize and sensitize Pölker to the plight of women and children, the "professional inmates" in the *Raketenstadt*. The last page of the "Rocket Chapter" relates the last day of Pökler's work at Nordhausen, as he entered Dora, armed with "the data" but not "the senses or heart" to look for Ilse. Yet, moved by the sight of an emaciated woman lying in the stench of "shit, sweat, sickness, mildew, piss," he removed his wedding band and placed it on her thin finger: "If she lived, the ring would be good for a few meals, or a blanket, or a night indoors, or a ride home…"(GR 433).

Pökler's act of humility may be attributed to Leni's humanizing influence; yet, against the backdrop of the novel's innumerable images of cruelty and devastation, it emerges as a rather paltry gesture; and while Leni's resistance to "Them" may be, as Kaufman argues, "heroic,"[148] her defiance, like Pökler's magnanimous gesture, remains but a flicker of compassion in the overwhelmingly dark wasteland of cruelty and exploitation. Not only does Leni eventually succumb to the powers of "them," again forced, perhaps, to adapt to her aggressors in order to survive, but also her subversive views of Motherhood are themselves eventually co-opted by the State to further its own designs. Leni, we discover, re-appears as Solange, a masseuse/prostitute, who will attempt to aid Slothrop in finding escape routes in the Zone, and while she dreams of Ilse as having eluded the forces of the State, her child must remain "underground," dependent upon the "strangers of the day, and hiding, out among the accidents of this drifting Humility, never quite to be extinguished, a few small chances for mercy…" (GR 610). Far from heralding a new world order of love and peace, Leni's dream at best projects intermittent and sporadic moments of compassion, fortuitous instances of empathy that stand out for their rarity, "a few small chances for mercy." Despite the comic underpinnings of the novel, Pynchon's vision remains quite tragic and brooding.

Unlike Margherita, Leni may have avoided infecting her child with the virus of death, since she refused to comply with the State's indoctrination process by which "mothers" police the souls of their offspring, molding their children into obedient citizens. Yet, if we were to look past *Gravity's Rainbow* into the future in search of Ilse or any other female offspring of intractable mothers, we might find them inhabiting Pynchon's next novel, *Vineland*. What we would discover is the State's insidious ability to co-opt the tenets of feminism as it has all other potentially subversive factions and assimilate them to expedite its own patriarchal agenda, suggesting, as Felski notes, that "advanced capitalism both engenders and controls subversive consequences of oppositional ideologies."[149] For, in *Vineland*, Brock Vond, the "fascist" agent in charge of conscripting spies and covert operators into the American government's dirty tricks campaign in the 1970's and 1980's, is envisioned by Frenesi, one of his less tractable operatives, as exploiting the very rhetoric of feminism to coerce her into obeying his demands. Invoking language and imagery almost identical to that employed by the revolutionary and passionate Leni Pökler, Bond would argue that Frenesi should resist the oppressive, traditional role of women and leave her child to go underground for the government because, "This is just how they [conventional citizens] want you, an animal, a bitch with swollen udders lying in the dirt, blank-faced, surrendered, reduced to this meat, these smells."[150] Far from expressing a genuine commitment to the emancipation of women in postmodern America, Brock, as an agent of the System, has appropriated the insurgent discourse of feminism, articulated so fervently by Leni, to further the "fascist" designs of the masculinist State, designs that include the manipulation of women to aid in the suppression of campus rebellions and to keep track of any potentially "dangerous" groups. What the protagonists and readers of *Vineland* experience is the "gradual discovery that even the forms of nonconformity and rebellion have already be taken into account and neutralized by the 'establishment.'"[151]

The incendiary efforts to "de-penis" the Man (GR 712) by the various counterforces in *Gravity's Rainbow* never come to fruition because, as Pynchon tells us, rebels, themselves subject to the indoctrination by the State, are as mesmerized by power, money and the advancement of the self as is anyone else, so that a collective assault against the firm, that is, an organized effort that requires the rejection of individual material gain in favor of a more equitable distribution of power remains virtually impossible. As long as we all remain "double-minded in the massive presence of money" and the accompanying "power over" others that such wealth engenders, as long as even the most potentially subversive individuals can continue to be tempted with the possibility of their own separate material aggrandizement, then, because the "Man has a branch office in each of our brains" and has manipulated us into believing his "Bad Shit," the System will prevail (GR 713). Pynchon argues that "we do know what's going on and we let it go on"; that is to say, we are all, in varying degrees, complicitous citizens who are responsible for the System. Yet, as we have seen, *Gravity's Rainbow* also suggests that the hierarchy of oppressive power is primarily a male-generated/dominated system that accords Western men a privileged status and that at times violently relegates women and children to vulnerable positions of dependency. Consequently, those who would be most tempted to abandon or repudiate any revolutionary commitment to change would be those most likely to become future members of the Firm. That women come to embrace the politics of their own oppression reflects not so much the very unrealistic hope of their becoming privileged members of the System as it does their adopting strategies of survival in a culture that denies female empowerment.

While *Gravity's Rainbow* is not an overtly feminist tract, it does, in general, indict a masculinist culture for promoting the principles of phallic violence against all of its citizens, especially women and children. The recurring image of the V-2 Rocket protruding from the landscape, an image of eroticized male aggression that haunts the text, finds its ominous inversion in the mushroom cloud hanging over Hiroshima following the dropping of the atomic bomb:

> In one of these streets in the morning fog, plastered over two slippery cobblestones, is a scrap of newspaper headline, with a wirephoto of a giant white cock, dangling in the sky straight downward out of a white pubic bush. The letters
> MB DRO
> ROSHI
> appear above with the logo of some occupation newspaper, a grinning glamour girl riding astraddle the cannon of a tank, steel penis with slotted serpent head.... (GR 693-94)

The "masculine technology" that assembled synthetic fragments to construct the V-2, that inanimate erectile protruding from the earth, has culminated in an apocalyptic leap into the mysteries of potential global annihilation, leaving as its signature a giant cock in the sky.

Chapter IV
ॐCR
Toni Morrison

At the very end of her novel *Jazz*, Toni Morrison, as the elusive narrative voice that "sings" the text, offers a seductive appeal to the reader-as-lover to participate in the "secret" and intimate act of co-creative love that will bring to life the complex and rather circuitously disclosed tale of Joe and Violet Trace and the young girl, Dorcas. Inviting the reader to celebrate this act of aesthetic co-creation by "making" and "remaking" the story, by playing the "notes" of the text, this mysterious voice seems to lament the fact that the writer, engaged in a very private enterprise, cannot "say out loud" to the reader what conventional lovers "have no need to say at all":

> That I have loved only you, surrendered my whole self reckless to you and nobody else. That I want you to love me back and show it to me. That I love the way you hold me, how close you let me be to you. I like your fingers on and on, lifting, turning. I have watched your face a long time now, and missed your eyes when you went away from me. Talking to you and hearing you answer—that's the kick.[1]

Offering itself up as the text itself, this mysterious voice intimately whispers to the reader what it "can't say aloud," namely, "Make me, remake me. You are free to do it and I am free to let you because look, look. Look where your hands are. Now" (J 229).

Morrison is appealing to Roland Barthes' concept of *jouissance*, which, as Suleiman notes, is "an erotic metaphor"[2] for the joyful, almost sexual bliss that connotes the reader's emotional involvement in and construction of the text.[3] Similar to the other authors in this study, Morrison, through her lyrically seductive entreaty to the reader as co-creator of the text, celebrates the autonomy of both the writer and the reader without invoking, as does John Barth, that troublesome dichotomy of masculine/writing/telling vs. feminine/reading/listening that, like all binary positions, accords a secondary, derivative status to the latter term. Throughout her texts, Morrison's fictional voices, at times, seem to transcend traditional gender demarcations (e.g. she deliberately obscures the gender identity of the mysterious voice in *Jazz*, implying at one point that like Eliot's Tiresias, the narrator is both male and female, rather than either male or female (J 63)), while at the same time presenting an alternative to the linear, rational narrative strategies often associated with phallic discourse. Critics such as Lorraine Liscio and Barbara Hill Rigney have argued for a uniquely "female" voice in Morrison, anchoring their claims in the theoretical assumptions of post-structuralist French feminists such as Cixous and Irigaray, whose emphases on the fluidity of language and the multiplicity of perspectives in a feminine style of writing allegedly find expression in Morrison's works;[4] whether "female" or, perhaps bi-gender in nature, Morrison's alternative discourse, presented most strikingly in passages in *Beloved*, represents, as does Barthelme's linguistic display between Emma and Julie in *The Dead Father*, a "deviation" from the traditional mode of narrative unfolding and seeks to lay bare hitherto unexplored realms of human experience.

Similar to the other authors in this study, Morrison challenges conventional modes of discourse, combining, at times, both the strategies of the minimalists who invoke those ominous silences and fragmented disclosures, and Pynchon's mythic sweep and profusion of information; both approaches demand reader intervention, whether it be filling in the compositional space of the "unsaid" in *Beloved* or *Jazz*, or sorting out the plethora of details needed to follow the intricate pathway in Milkman's search for his heritage in *Song of Solomon*. Morrison, herself, in an interview, has remarked directly on the necessity for reader participation in her works:

> My writing expects, demands participatory reading…It's not just about telling the story; it's about involving the reader…My language has to have holes and spaces so the reader can come into it. He or she can feel something visceral, see something striking. Then we (you, the reader, and I, the author) come together to make the book, to feel this experience.[5]

A more analytical, less impassioned plea than the closing lines of *Jazz*, Morrison's explanation of the critical role of the reader nevertheless emphasizes the emotional or "visceral" participation of the reader in the process of "making" the book.

By inviting the reader into the process of creating the book through a visceral cooperation with the author, Morrison, in effect, exposes the artificiality of all texts and undermines the traditional concept of the text as a totality of meaning that awaits the reader's discovery. Like the other authors of this study, Morrison implicitly endorses Barthes' idea, discussed in S/Z and "From Work to Text," of the reader as the co-producer of a multiplicity of texts rather than the consumer of a fixed work. Morrison relegates to secondary importance a more conventional approach to her texts that would concentrate on linear plot development, singularity of viewpoint, uninterrupted time sequences, resolution and closure, etc. To enter the text with one's "guts," that is, to "feel the experience," is to abandon the search for consistency, for the neat and tidy logic of cause and effect, and to embrace, instead, the often dizzying and contradictory perspectives of the heart.

Yet, Morrison employs her innovative technical strategies not only to call attention to the artifice of all fiction but also to confront the very real concerns of marginalized groups in American society. Her very conscious indulging of the metafictional impulses of postmodernist literary experimentation does not preclude her limning the exigent circumstances of racial/sexist bigotry confronting African-American women. Like many of her contemporary American feminist writers, Morrison, as a member of what Zimmerman calls an "undercapitalized cultural group," seems unable to afford the "apolitical luxury," enjoyed by many of her white male counterparts, of indulging solely in writing "self-reflexive fiction about the structure of fiction."[6] Firmly rooted in the exigencies of a slave past and a racist present in America, Morrison grounds her experimentation in realism, in the gritty and often biting images of racial and sexual oppression. Labelled "an experimental realist"[7] and a "magical realist"[8] by critics, Morrison employs postmodernist literary innovations to invoke and heighten both the sufferings and the triumphs of the African-American culture.

Morrison, for the most part, subverts the traditional narrative devices of uninterrupted temporal linearity, univocal voice and perspective, and the clear demarcations between dream and reality, in favor of a circular structure, a multiplicity of perspectives and, at times, a surreal ambiguity. The alluring invitation to the reader in *Jazz* to enter the fictional world of Harlem in the 1920's and, with the author, give birth to the text occurs at the "end" of the book so that the act of aesthetic creation, a "beginning," will start anew, thereby virtually erasing the linear distinction between "beginning, middle and end" in favor of a cyclical process of continual creativity. The murder of Dorcas by her lover, Joe Trace, is presented from a variety of narrative perspectives so that no one "voice" assumes an epistemological primacy as the Truth, but instead a multiplicity of "truths" emerges that resists conforming to any pattern of logical coherence. Similar to the scar on Sula's face which generates a variety of interpretations by the other characters as to its signification, Morrison's texts invite multiple perspectives. *Tar Baby*, *Beloved*, and *Sula* all display multiple narrators as well as "multiple centers" so that, as Rigney argues, events are gradually revealed in fragments and "related impressionistically," a technique that "subverts concepts of textual unity and defies totalized interpretation."[9]

Just as the innovative technical strategies employed by Barthelme, Didion and Pynchon have engendered some problematic issues concerning the images of women and violence in their respective texts, so too does Morrison's experimentation with mythic texture, language, structure and temporal sequence generate some disturbing portrayals of both female-initiated violence and female victimization. Like Pynchon in *Gravity's Rainbow*, Morrison unravels the complex interactions between women and men against an overtly political backdrop of white male supremacy, an oppressive system that for Morrison, as an African-American woman, poses a double threat to female integrity; however, unlike Pynchon, she does not infuse the tragic consequences of racist/sexist violence with a comic element and, consequently, as we shall see, most of the women in her texts who suffer the egregious assaults of men, such as Pecola Breedlove (*The Bluest Eye*) and Dorcas (*Jazz*), emerge as sympathetic victims who neither invite nor deserve their fates. Yet, by emphasizing the culturally racist framework within which such violence takes place, Morrison, in effect, "softens" her portrayal of the male aggressor by offering as an explanation for his behavior his oppressed status in society. Morrison here is completely in step with recent psychological research that links poverty and oppression to violence against women in the African-American community. One such study suggests that the increased risk of violence may be, in part, a "scapegoat effect, in which the black female becomes the repository of the anger and frustration of the black male" in American society.[10] While not completely exonerating either man for displacing his anger against the System onto the weaker members within his circle—Cholly for raping his daughter or Joe Trace for murdering his mistress—Morrison, through a cumulative series of poignant images of racist degradation that interweaves the past with the present, seems to invite the reader to fill in "the holes and spaces" of the narrative with compassion and forgiveness. Whether or not Morrison succeeds in winning the reader's forgiveness with respect to black male violence will be discussed in the following pages. Similarly, female-initiated acts of violence also unfold within the inescapable framework of a racist culture, so that both Eva's murder of her son, Plum Boy—a returning World War I veteran who, having fought for a country that continues to enslave him, seeks solace in the slow, numbing death of drug addiction—and Sethe's slaying of her baby daughter as the slave hunters approach their home, take on a sacrificial quality that more clearly elicits both our condemnation and our forgiveness.

Like Pynchon, Morrison often invokes a more primordial and vital mythic past, a time when people were on speaking terms with the gods and with nature, when the earth pulsated with life and vibrancy, to serve as an alternative vision to the spiritless stagnation at the center of postmodern, technological existence. Morrison offers her version of Geli Tripping in the "witch-like" character of Pilate in *Song of Solomon* who can "magically" change shapes, and whose absence of a navel (she "borned herself"[11]) and communication with the dead accord her a mythic stature: "Black people believe in magic," Morrison notes, for "it's part of our heritage."[12] Drawing upon both African folklore and Judaic-Christian myth, Morrison simultaneously evokes, at times, the rich associations of various cultures in the same image. As Jane Campbell observes, Milkman's great-grandfather Solomon bears a name that alludes both to the Hebraic "Shalom" meaning peace or prosperity and "those flying Africans" whose magical capacity for flight parallels Solomon's flight back to Africa.[13]

Like Pynchon, Morrison decries the perverted reduction of love by the West to the cold logic of "conquering and possessing" that establishes an adversarial relationship between the lover and the loved, between human and nature. "Love, in the Western notion," argues Morrison, "is full of possession, distortion and corruption. It's a slaughter without the blood."[14] Within such a schema, women, as we have seen in both Pynchon and Barthelme, are reified, reduced to the status of an object to be used by more powerful men. To combat the onslaught of a racist/sexist culture in which black women remain doubly susceptible to aggression, Morrison's female characters often seek to erect spiritual barriers by bonding with other women, again underscoring the interdependence of the "I" and the "we" of a shared female community, which, as feminist theorists have argued, begins to create a space of empowerment.[15] Female friendship in *Sula*, for example, emerges as a possible alternative to the traditional heterosexual and/or maternal modes of being for women, but, as Marianne Hirsch argues, not without some reservations.[16] Inverting the male triads of oppression that we found in Didion's novels, Morrison portrays the strength inherent in matriarchal arrangements that enable women to survive as colonized members in a hostile culture. Matrilineal triads inform *Sula* (Eva, Hannah, Sula), *Song of Solomon* (Pilate, Reba, Hagar), and *Beloved* (Baby Suggs, Sethe, Denver).[17] Existing as doubly marginalized people on the periphery of both the dominant white society and the acceptable black community, these women attempt to construct a haven that can withstand not only the continual threat of violence from the ruling culture but also the intrusions of black men who, at times, seem to share the dehumanizing, white male perspective that reduces women to pieces of property.

In *Song of Solomon*, Milkman's invasion of Pilate's home to steal her "gold" and his sexual use of Hagar as his private "honey pot" (SS 91) weaken their female refuge and reveal his perception of the three women as instrumental means to achieve male ends, and parallels his father's rather hostile treatment of the three women in his own house. While Eva-Hannah-Sula "peace"fully combine their "love of manliness"[18] with their independent female existence, celebrating sexuality as an experience to be shared rather than as a license to be enslaved, each woman is aware of the male gaze that reduces women to "pig meat" (S 52) and shies away from commitment. An almost mystical unity is achieved between Sula and her best friend Nel as they connect to form a childhood friendship that pulsates on a deeply sensual, non-verbal level of communication. Although the female bonding that occurs among Sethe, Denver and Beloved may indeed, as critic David Lawrence points out, be psychologically injurious and inimical to achieving an "individual identity,"[19] or create a "prison cell" for the "disturbed women,"[20] it does provide a safe setting within which Sethe will confront and partially exorcise the horrors of her "rememory," a setting that Paul D initially enters peacefully but later disrupts through jealousy and infidelity.

In Morrison's novels we find that women who bond together not only through their own speech but through a communal identity, and who resist succumbing to the West's notion of love and ownership and the destructive binary oppositions of Man/Culture vs. Woman/Nature, may erect a temporary barrier between themselves and their oppressors; these "ex-centric" communities or "challenging cultures" are, as Hutcheon explains in her analysis of *Song of Solomon*, "outside normal society (white or black), outside the town, and infinitely attractive because of [their] position."[21] Yet, they remain marginal and ultimately ineffective in combating their political subordination. Baby Suggs unifies her tiny community through the preaching of her Gospel of "Love Your Flesh," emphasizing laughter, dance and tears; yet her faith crumbles following Sethe's decision to murder her children as she withdraws into the reclusive contemplation of colors and awaits death.

The looming presence of Pynchon's phallic rocket has been replaced by Morrison with the insidious vestiges of a slave culture that seeks to impose upon its colonized African members the values of the West while simultaneously positing them as "Other." Those men who attempt to assimilate into the dominant culture, such as Macon Dead from *Song of Solomon*, are, like Enzian in *Gravity's Rainbow*, imbued with the West's destructive dominion over nature and women, and conspire, whether consciously or not, in relegating women to positions of silence or invisibility. Those women, such as Claudia and Geraldine (BE), Ruth Dead (SS), Helene Wright (S) and Jadine (TB),[22] who seek to suppress their African heritage lead "schizophrenic" lives, parading around as figures of autonomy and integrity within their own ghettoized community but continually subject to the more pervasive reality of their slave status once they step outside into the white world.

Nowhere is this tenuous existence more poignantly displayed than in *Sula* when Helene Wright, a woman who prides herself on being "respectable" and who would like to re-fashion her daughter's appearance to conform to the dictates of white male beauty (Helene wants to change Nel's nose and smooth her hair), is publicly humiliated by a white conductor as she mistakenly enters an all-white car on a train. Forfeiting what Morrison would call the "funk" or sexual vitality of a life that celebrates one's African heritage, one's body and one's mythic roots in favor of the routinized, mechanical life-in-death existence of a puritanical, white middleclass America, these women emerge as doubly displaced characters, being an integral part of neither a past that acknowledges their historical origins and provides a communal identity nor a present that posits them as colonized female subjects in a racist, sexist society. Succumbing to one of the dominant white myths that, Cornel West explains, depicts black women and men as "threatening creatures who have the potential for sexual power over whites,"[23] some of Morrison's more "respectable" women have internalized the white culture's hatred/fear of black sexuality in a futile attempt to gain acceptance. Such women have confined themselves to "white 'respectability' while they make their own sexuality a taboo subject."[24] Given their ambiguous position, it is not surprising to see them unfold as psychologically and sexually distorted, "grotesque" characters. In trying to assimilate to the white culture, Geraldine exchanges the passion and *élan* of "funk" for the frigidity and repression of bourgeois "respectability," perversely bestowing her affection on her cat rather than her husband and son; not surprisingly, we find her son growing into a boy who feels quite comfortable harassing girls such as Pecola and torturing animals. To achieve the sexual arousal denied to her by her husband, Ruth Dead, for example, not only sneaks off at night to rendezvous with her dead father (she lies down upon her his grave) but also erotically indulges herself by continuing to nurse Milkman until he is ten years old.

A woman like Sula, who refuses to submit to the mores of either the dominant white culture or the African community and who has not assimilated the concept of love-as-possession, is not only cast as a pariah by the townspeople of Bottom but also rejected by her best friend Nel for an act of "infidelity." Having been raised in a matriarchal household where "funk" reigned supreme, where sexual liaisons were joyful and often spontaneous expressions of physical and spiritual communication that entailed no permanent commitment or claims of ownership, Sula fails to understand not only the concept of infidelity but also Nel's acceptance of it. As one critic notes, Sula is an example of the "dangerously free people" that inhabit Morrison's fiction, possessing, as the author herself observes, "a nice wildness" that is often "misunderstood" and that consequently "has bad effects in society such as the one in which we live."[25]

Of the four authors considered in this study, it is Morrison, perhaps, who most clearly tries to break through traditional Western, female stereotypes to explore alternative modes of being in the world for women. The women who comprise Morrison's female enclaves—Sula, Hannah, Eva (S), Baby Suggs, Sethe, Denver (B)[26] or Pilate, Reba and Hagar (SS)—resist the artificial, reductive categories of "bitch vs. witch" or "Madonna vs. Whore" that inform so much of Western literature. Having rejected two fundamental tenets of modern Western thought, namely its repudiation of the human body and human sexuality, and its emphasis on property as an indicator of self-definition and worth, characters like Baby Suggs, Pilate and Sula, for example, celebrate "the body, laughter and tears" and, as Black women, directly understand the dangers awaiting those "weaker" members living in a society that elevates the concept of ownership to a theological ideal; such women do not easily conform to the stereotypes of the licentious woman or the acquisitive bitch.

Yet, these female enclaves exist within the larger framework of a sexist and racist culture that continually intrudes upon women's lives so that the images of women and violence emerge with a complexity somewhat different from that of the images studied in the works of the previous authors. While Morrison, for the most part, skirts the conventional stereotype of the female as compliant victim, her depictions of women and violence manifest certain troubling ambiguities. The following pages will investigate some of the images of women and violence that punctuate Morrison's texts and will attempt to disclose the complexity inherent in her depictions of incest, rape and infanticide.

Male-initiated Violence: *The Bluest Eye* and *Jazz*

In both her first novel, *The Bluest Eye*, and her later work, *Jazz*, Toni Morrison almost immediately confronts the reader with the unpleasant fact that a child or young woman has been the victim of male aggression. "Pecola," we are informed, "was having her father's baby" (BE 9), and Joe Trace had fallen for "an eighteen-year-old girl with one of those deepdown, spooky loves that made him so sad and happy, he shot her just to keep the feeling going" (J 3). Yet, the language and imagery in both passages serve to mute the horror inherent in the acts themselves so as to temper our awareness of the individual woman-as-victim and to court our forgiveness of the male-as-aggressor.

In *The Bluest Eye*, the narrator, Claudia, informs us that Pecola Breedlove, a young girl growing up in Ohio in the 1940's, is having her father's child. Her opening revelation of Pecola's situation does not employ the rhetoric of violence or rape but rather unfolds against an almost mythic backdrop that alludes to the temporary infertility of the natural world in the Fall of 1941, as America tottered on the edge of global warfare. Couched as it is within the analogous imagery of marigold seeds failing to take root and blossom, the act of incestuous rape and the subsequent death of the baby are divested of their aggressive, violative status and emerge, instead, as emblems of universal despair and arrested productivity:

> ...there were no marigolds in the fall of 1941. We thought, at the time, that it was because Pecola was having her father's baby that the marigolds did not grow....It never occurred to either of us [Claudia and her sister] that the earth itself might have been unyielding. We had dropped our seeds in our own little plot of black dirt just as Pecola's father had dropped his seeds in his own little plot of black dirt. Our innocence and faith were no more productive than his lust or despair. What is clear now is that of all

that hope, fear, lust, love and grief, nothing remains but Pecola and the unyielding earth. (BE 9)

Filtered through the consciousness of Pecola's friend, Claudia, the passage omits any reference to the blending of rage and tenderness that characterize the rape scene when it is portrayed more graphically toward the end of the novel. Cholly's action, according to Claudia, was an expression not of his pent-up fury or some deep, abiding hatred of women but rather an all-too-human (therefore, forgivable) embracing of sensuality to assuage the anguish of hopelessness. The rather matter-of-fact acknowledgment of Pecola's condition, while it reflects, perhaps, the denigrating self-image of the narrator, who, as a young black woman, has internalized the culture's reduction of black females to "little plots of black dirt," clearly soft-pedals the overtones of abuse inherent in the phenomenon of incest.

Despite Morrison's claim that it really "doesn't matter what happens" in the novel,[27] critics have been quick to point out that the rape of Pecola is one of the novel's main events.[28] By her rather stolid introduction of a such a critical plot element and the concomitant delaying of a more expansive, detailed description of the rape of Pecola one hundred pages later in this short novel, Morrison, in effect, creates the fictional space within which she will prepare the reader, through a series of poignant images, narrative interruptions and revelations of past events, to arrive at an understanding of the rape that will engender compassion for and forgiveness of a father who could subject his child to such an egregious assault.

Similarly, when turning to her later novel, *Jazz*, we find that the initial revelation of an act of male aggression unfolds within the imagery of a love that inhabits a mythic psychic sphere, "a deepdown, spooky" region which defies rational understanding, a profound love that captures the paradoxical commingling of sadness and bliss and prompts men to shoot their lovers so as to maintain the feeling. Related to us by the "mysterious" narrative voice, the opening section of the novel, like that of *The Bluest Eye*, inscribes the act of male aggression within a language of ambiguity, the "lust and despair" of Cholly Breedlove now giving way to the "sad and happy spooky love" of Joe Trace. The opening passage of *Jazz* also deflects the reader's preoccupation with Joe Trace's violent assault against Dorcas by introducing us to the character of Violet Trace, Joe's outraged and "unstable" wife who engages in a seemingly even more bizarre act of fury:

When the woman, her name is Violet, went to the funeral to see the girl and to cut her dead face they threw her to the floor and out of the church.

She ran, then, through all that snow, and when she got back to her apartment she took the birds from their cages and set them out the windows to freeze or fly, including the parrot that said, "I love you." (J 3)

The subsequent two or three pages focus upon Violet's futile act of rage rather than Joe's lethal jealousy, and we soon learn that while the murder of Dorcas does not even result in Joe's prosecution, since the prevalent feeling among the dead girl's family is that the police would not even care that much about meting out justice for the murder of a black girl, Violet's attack upon the dead girl has generated a great deal of interest among the black community: Violet becomes known as "Violent" and Joe continues to go door-to-door, selling his Cleopatra cosmetic line to willing customers. Again, Morrison will withhold any expansive exposition of the shooting until the virtual end of the novel, filtering the scene through the multiple perspectives of the mysterious narrator, Joe, Felice—Dorcas' friend—and the victim herself. In the intervening pages Morrison will provide us with the history and images of an oppressed black man in an attempt to mitigate our condemnation of his aggression against a young woman.

The Bluest Eye

In an interview in 1983, Toni Morrison commented on her strategy regarding her initial presentation of the rape of Pecola:

> I tell you at the beginning of *The Bluest Eye* on the very first page what happened, but now I want you to go with me and look at this, so when you get to the scene where the father rapes the daughter, which is as awful a thing, I suppose, as can be imagined, by the time you get there, it's almost irrelevant because I want you to *look* at him and see his love for his daughter and his powerlessness to help her pain. By that time his embrace, the rape, is all the gift he has left.[29]

Fraught with ambiguity as to the fundamental nature of the assault, the passage implies that the rape of this child by her father is both "as awful a thing as can be imagined" and a "gift" of love, an "embrace" that expresses both paternal affection and the powerlessness of racial poverty.

Furthermore, the actual rape scene, Morrison informs us, is constructed so as to direct our sympathetic gaze toward the aggressor and not the victim: we are encouraged to look at him and see his love for his daughter. An analysis of the scene reveals that Morrison, here using a third-person narrator who filters the incident through the consciousness of a man who has suffered the alienation and humiliation of living in a racist society, who has been denied a father's right to improve the lot of his family, has, indeed, attempted to impart a dimension of "gentleness" to an otherwise violent act of violation:

> The tenderness welled up in him, and he sank to his knees, his eyes on the foot of his daughter. Crawling on all fours toward her, he raised his hand and caught the foot in an upward stroke. Pecola lost her balance and was about to careen to the floor. Cholly raised his other hands to her hips to save her from falling. He put his head down and nibbled at the back of her leg. His mouth trembled at the firm sweetness of the flesh. He closed his eyes, letting his fingers dig into her waist. The rigidness of her shocked body, the silence of her stunned throat, was better than Pauline's easy laughter had been…Surrounding all of this lust was a border of politeness. He wanted to fuck her—tenderly. But the tenderness would not hold. The tightness of her vagina was more than he could bear. His soul seemed to slip down to his guts and fly out into her, and the gigantic thrust he made into her provoked the only sound she made—a hollow suck of air in the back of her throat. Like the rapid loss of air from a circus balloon. (BE 128)

Morrison succeeds in capturing, to a certain extent, the plight of the child in this scene and, unlike Barthelme, Didion and Pynchon, does not invoke the conventional and convenient stereotype of the woman-as-willing-victim who somehow invites her own degradation. Clearly deprived of any autonomy or avenue of escape and reduced to an objectified passivity, Pecola can only emit a noise that sounds like air rushing out of an inanimate balloon.

Yet, Morrison's infusion of a quality of "gentleness" and "politeness"— Cholly "saves" Pecola from falling to the floor in an almost paternal concern for her comfort—imparts an ambiguity to the scene that is further complicated by the narrative revelations concerning Cholly's state of mind immediately prior to the rape. For here we discover the evolution of emotion that Cholly undergoes as he contemplates the misery manifested in his daughter's posture of defeat and hopelessness as she stands at the sink. Experiencing first a revulsion and guilt for her helplessness as an "ugly" and poor black child whose physical and spiritual impoverishment he has been unable to alleviate, Cholly is moved to a furious hatred of his young daughter when he perceives himself as unworthy of her love, a hatred that makes him want "to break her neck" (BE 127). This visceral enmity gives way to a protective feeling of love when Pecola shifts her weight onto one foot so she can "scratch the back of her calf with her toe." Reminded of a similar gesture by Pauline, his wife, that once filled him with a "wondering softness" and a paternal sense of protectiveness devoid of lust (BE 128), Cholly initially approaches Pecola with the same tenderness that he had once manifested toward Pauline.

Viewed within the context of Cholly's mental and emotional state contained in the passage immediately prior to the rape, the initial image of the rape scene that depicts Cholly crawling to his daughter on all fours connotes both a father's playful tenderness and protective love for his child, and also the incipient predatory quality of a sexual attack. Morrison cleverly and perhaps, effectively, projects the ambiguous nature of this male act of aggression by inviting us to apprehend it not simply as an act of aggression but rather as an ambivalent expression of frustration and love. The ambiguity is heightened by the dreamlike atmosphere pervading the episode, an a-logical atmosphere in which contradictory emotions freely coalesce. Linking the rape to Cholly's loving reminiscence of Pauline, Morrison, as Linda Wagner points out, inscribes the rape scene within the rhetoric of a "dreamlike reverie to match the nostalgic account" of his earlier life.[30]

The Bluest Eye unfolds within the clashing and ironic juxtaposition of the mythic schema of the four seasons, on the one hand, and the white patriarchal text of the *Dick and Jane* reader on the other. Presented as it is within the sub-division of "Spring" and the "See Mother" and "See Father" categories of the elementary school primer, the rape episode captures the ironic disparity between Cholly and Pauline Breedlove's violation of their daughter's trust—his molestation and his wife's assignment of blame to the victim and subsequent eviction of Pecola from their home—and the ideal vision of the nuclear family presented in the *Dick and Jane* reader in which the home stands as a haven of protective love and security. Furthermore, as the season of fertility and the rejuvenation of life, Spring provides an ironic context for this devastating intrusion of an incestuous assault that not only spawns a dead baby but also "breeds" the final spiritual and psychological demise of Pecola. Having been ostracized by her family, the town, and eventually her friend Claudia, Pecola plunges deeper into madness and isolation, seeking refuge in the cloying hands of Soaphead Church, a child molester who has promised to provide her with the one gift that she feels will win her love: blue eyes. Far from "breeding love," Pecola's family and the society at large consign her to a life of pathological withdrawal.

The complex blending of violation and gentleness and the paradoxical commingling of love and brutality that inform the rape scene are intended to reflect, perhaps, the inevitable psychological distortions that can warp the lives of colonized members of a racist society. While profoundly aware of the abiding contradictions and ironies confronting those "victims" who must efface themselves to attain negative identities, Morrison still struggles to present a vision of hope, of the possibility for redemption. Doubly victimized by her poverty and perceived "ugliness," Pecola suffers the painful isolation from a white culture whose ideal of female beauty (blonde hair, blue eyes, tapered nose, etc.) eludes her, and the taunting scorn of the "respectable" black community that has left her behind in their pursuit of white acceptance. By placing Pecola at the center of the narrative and poignantly revealing her suffering, Morrison succeeds, as Barbara Christian explains, in "challenging the concept of physical beauty as monolithic, and as an ideal, not only as it relates to brown girls but to all women" and to "the social icons of beauty such as the Shirley Temple girl doll of her novel."[31] Succumbing to the prevailing notion of the beautiful and seeking only to make herself disappear, Pecola plunges into the pathological isolation of her own fantasies, convinced that she has been given the gift of the bluest eyes by the pederast, Soaphead Church.

Yet, Claudia, on the other hand, comes to apprehend her own abandonment of her friend as an attempt to assimilate into white society, to distance herself from the "shame" of a "nigger" who carried her father's child. Her sins, as Melissa Walker observes, "are those of omission, of acquiescing to the oppressor's values and reinforcing Pecola's self-hatred."[32] "We are wrong," Claudia finally realizes, to blame "the victim," and despite the fact that "it's too late" to redress the wrongs committed against Pecola, it may be possible to save the many Pecolas who inhabit other towns. A cautionary tale, the novel concludes on a note of guarded optimism: "It's too late. *At least* on the edge of my town, among the garbage and the sunflowers of my town, it's much, much, much too late" (BE 160; emphasis mine).

The desire to project this guarded optimism accounts, in part, for the ambiguous blending of gentleness and rage that inform the rape scene. As one critic notes, Morrison's "ironies are always gentle, meant to heal rather than to wound, to correct rather than to punish."[33] In addition to the "gentle" irony of constructing a rape scene in which Cholly Breedlove's paternal concern evolves into a sexual assault that breeds only death and madness, Morrison also connects this incident with a prior event in Cholly's life in which he is humiliated by white men. It is an incident that, Susan Willis argues, elucidates the "foundation of black male misogyny."[34] About to consummate their first sexual experience, Cholly and a young girl named Darlene are interrupted in the fields by a pair of white hunters who force Cholly to continue "performing" under the glare of their flashlight:

> "Hee hee hee heeeee." The snicker was a long asthmatic cough. The other raced the flashlight all over Cholly and Darlene.
> "Get on wid it, nigger," said the flashlight one.
> "Sir?" said Cholly, trying to find a buttonhole.
> "I said, get on wid it. An'make it good nigger, make it good." (BE 117)

As Cholly obeys the armed men, he experiences a sense of "violence born of helplessness" and displaces his hatred of the men onto the more vulnerable figure of Darlene, transforming the initially mutual pleasurable act of intercourse into an aggressive assault:

> Cholly, moving faster, looked at Darlene. He hated her. He almost wished he could do it -hard, long and painfully, he hated her so much. (BE 117)

Identifying the ray of white light as a "metonymn for the white hunters" who "screw" Cholly up for life," Susan Willis posits this episode as paradigmatic of the novel's definition of sexuality in terms of racial oppression.[35]

It is precisely this surging of "violence born of hatred" that is diverted away from the oppressor on to the weaker members of his family that, Morrison implies, underscores Cholly's rape of his daughter. In an interview, Morrison commented on the connection between the two incidents, noting her intention to undermine the appeal of male rape fantasies by "feminizing" the language:

> "It is interesting to me that where I thought I would have the most difficulty subverting the language to a feminine mode, I had the least: connecting Cholly's 'rape' by the white men to his own of his daughter. This most masculine act of aggression becomes feminized in my language, 'passive,' and I think, more accurately repellent when deprived of the male 'glamor of shame' rape is (or once was) routinely given."[36]

Pecola's rape must be understood, in part, then, as the grotesque but understandable expression of rage enacted by an emotionally disfigured "victim" of racial injustice against a weaker member of his own oppressed class. For the most part, critics indeed conclude that Cholly, like his wife, is himself a victim: the rape is a "physical manifestation of the social, psychological, and personal violence that, together with his wife, he has put upon Pecola."[37] By "feminizing" the language of Pecola's rape, which, for

Morrison evidently entails rendering Cholly more passive than aggressive, and by inscribing the scene within the "feminine" language of a dreamlike, gentle dissolution of temporal boundaries, she hopes to divest rape of its masculine appeal and as Rigney notes, subvert "the literary tradition of male rape fantasies."[38]

Morrison's ambivalent portrayal of the rape scene can be contrasted and compared to the equally problematic depictions of rape episodes in the fiction of black male writers, most notably Richard Wright and Ralph Ellison. In Wright's *Native Son*, the protagonist, Bigger Thomas, is on the run following the accidental murder of Mary, a young white woman. Knowing that he would eventually be falsely accused of raping Mary by a society that stills spins out myths about black male sexuality, Bigger confides in his girlfriend, Bessie, and then succumbs to the frustration and rage of the "innocent" condemned to "guilt" by raping and murdering Bessie for fear that she would reveal his secret. As Gilbert and Gubar note, "Bigger's femicides are extensively elaborated" in images that focus more upon the existential *angst* of the aggressor than on the victimization of the woman: each murder is filtered through the consciousness of the protagonist, a strategy that implies that the "anger of the black male artist often translates into an obsession not with the rape victim but with the existential desires of the would-be-rapist or the elemental dilemma of the framed-up rapist.[39] For, according to Bigger, "rape was not what one did to women. Rape was what one felt when one's back was against a wall and one had to strike out, whether one wanted to or not, to keep the pack from killing one." Despite Wright's use of the gender-neutral pronoun "one," it is clear that rape, for him, is a profound emotional state that taps into a *man's* ontological awareness of a sudden absence of choices when he is confronted by the predatory assaults of a racist majority: rape was what a man felt when he had been "stretched to the snapping point by a thousand white hands."[40] For this black male writer, rape is both a feeling and an act that, in effect, reduces the victim to a rather impersonal repository of the pent-up fury of the angry protagonist; far from gentle, rape, for Wright, manifests the aggressive expression of an "imperiously driven" male rage that pays no "heed" to the victim's protestations: "he rode roughshod over [Bessie's] whimpering protests, feeling acutely sorry for her as he galloped a frenzied horse down a steep hill in the face of a resisting wind."[41] Women, evidently for Wright, are the accidental victims of this involuntary male rage that periodically snaps under the pressure of racial oppression.

Like Wright, Morrison constructs the rape scene in order to focus upon the desperation and frustration of the aggressor. Like Bigger, Cholly emerges as a victim of white culture, suffering the humiliation of economic and spiritual impoverishment. But unlike Wright, Morrison does not couple the rape with murder nor does she invoke the rhetoric of untempered male rage. As previously noted, Morrison quite consciously sought to "feminize" the language in order to soften the scene: she would have us read Cholly's violation of his daughter as a "loving assault," a "gentle rape." Furthermore, Morrison's very sensitive portrayal of the psychological state of the rapist does not completely blind her to the plight of the victim. Wright's positioning of Bigger at the center of the narrative and his filtering of the rape through his protagonist's consciousness serve to augment the existential distress of the rapist while diminishing the pain of the victim. By according Pecola the central position in the narrative, Morrison, on the other hand, more effectively balances her empathy for the rapist's political oppression with her acknowledgment of the victim's physical degradation. While *Native Son* defiantly shouts forth the *angst*-ridden rage of the oppressed black male, *The Bluest Eye* whispers the sufferings of the traditionally silenced black female. As Barbara Christian explains: "Although Pecola Breedlove is a tragic victim, Morrison achieves a triumph in giving her, who has never had a voice, a story in her own right, in situating her who has been the margin of the margins, at the center of the narrative."[42] In what might be categorized as a clever, subversive feminist strategy, the narrative centering of a poor black girl who has been rejected by both white and "respectable" black communities opens up a dimension of empathy for the female vicitm that is absent in Wright's masculinized rhetoric of rage.

The "gentle rape" of *The Bluest Eye* also invites comparison to a tangential rape episode in Ellison's *Invisible Man*. Ellison softens Wright's hard and brutal images of masculine aggression and, like Morrison, employs the gentle rhetoric of a dreamlike reverie. *The Bluest Eye* and *Invisible Man* both deal with the incestuous rape of a daughter by her father and both episodes invoke images of romantic reminiscences so that the rape appears to be more or less a "gentle attack" by a man whose humiliations living in a racist culture spill over into a "loving" yet desperate expression of sexual violation. In *Invisible Man*, the unnamed young black male protagonist has been instructed to drive out into the countryside by Mr. Norton, one of the paternalistic, white benefactors and founding fathers of the Negro college which the protagonist attends. Having inadvertently strayed into a poor black area, Norton and the boy stop at a dilapidated log cabin inhabited by the Truebloods, a family that has garnered some local notoriety: Jim Trueblood has impregnated both his wife and his daughter. Both titillated and, of course, outwardly "indignant" about the situation, Norton lasciviously waits to hear the story of how a man could get away with sleeping with his own child. During the course of his conversation with Jim, it soon becomes apparent that Trueblood has been financially rewarded by the white community for sharing his tale of incest with all who would secretly seek to experience the vicarious gratification of the incestuous rape and at the same time publicly justify their own myths about untamed, licentious black sexuality.

Like Morrison, Ellison presents the rape tale against the backdrop of economic poverty and spiritual deprivation: the Truebloods are so poor that they must share a bed at night in order to keep warm. Cuddled up against his daughter, Matty Lou, Jim one night finds himself unable to sleep because he is worried about how he will find food to feed his family the following day. Listening to his daughter's sleepy moans and sensing that her burgeoning sexuality has already been shared with her boyfriend, Jim falls into a nostalgic reverie about his own edenic and erotic past when he courted a woman who reminds him now of his daughter:

> Then I got to thinkin' 'bout way back when I left the farm and went to live in Mobile and 'bout a gal I had me then. I was young then—like [my daughter's boyfriends]. Us lived in a two-story house 'longside the river, and at night in the summertime we used to lay in bed and talk, and after she'd gone off to sleep I'd be awake lookin' out at the lights comin' up from the water and listen' to the sounds of the boats movin' along.[43]

It is within the context of this nostalgic reverie that Jim drops off into a dream that brilliantly conveys the humiliation of racial bigotry, the thrill of violating the codes of the white oppressor and the "unwitting" assault against his own daughter. Encoded within the phallic and vaginal images of the dream text—female rooms, a striking grandfather clock, lighted candles, "soft stuff on the floor," female smells, opening doors and a white woman clad in a transparent nighgown—Jim's rape of his daughter begins to unfold beneath the veil of a dream about violating the rule of entering a white man's house by the front door to get "some fat meat."[44] Both hungry and fearful in the dream, Jim tries to extricate himself from the encroaching accoutrements of white luxury only to find himself entangled in the arms of the "forbidden" and frightened, screaming white woman. Jim awakens from his dream to find himself coupled with his daughter. Succumbing to their growing sexual arousal initiated evidently during the dream, Jim Trueblood and now his daughter do not want to interrupt the impending sexual climax, even when his wife, Kate, awakens to discover them.

Like Morrison, Ellison initially inscribes the rape within the gentle setting of a nostalgic reverie. Ellison, however, converts the dreamlike reverie into an unconscious dream text and further softens the horror of the rape by: 1) shielding the reader from a direct apprehension of the early stages of the rape; and 2) aiming Jim's unconscious sexual rage at the white woman of the dream text: if there is any rage here it is a rage "unknowingly" displaced onto his daughter. Both Jim and Cholly, with varying degrees of awareness, "scapegoat" their vulnerable daughters. However, while both Ellison and Morrison filter their respective rape episodes through the eyes of the "rapist," Morrison does not invoke that problematic concept of the complicity of the victim as does Ellison nor does she submerge her aggressor into the amoral realm of the unconscious as a possible means to mitigate his responsibility. Cholly Breedlove is not permitted to say as does Jim Trueblood:

> I tell myself, Maybe if you suffer for it, it will be best. Maybe you owe it to Kate to let her beat you. You ain't guilty, but she thinks you is.[45]

While not explicitly invoking the unconscious as a vehicle to abrogate culpability, Morrison does, like Ellison, ask us to consider the victimized status of the aggressor as a mitigating circumstance. More subtle than Ellison in conveying her ambivalence, Morrison, however, does not take refuge in the myth of the compliant or complicitous female victim but rather allows a gradual accumulation of images that limn the profoundity of Cholly's despair to nudge the reader in the direction of of exonerating Cholly.

Yet, Morrison's depiction of the rape scene raises some troubling issues. Unlike Pynchon, Didion, Ellison and Barthelme, Morrison avoids casting the female in the ambiguous role of "compliant victim," for clearly Pecola, like Celie in Alice Walker's *The Color Purple*, suffers the onslaught of her father as she has suffered the humiliations of those who have defined her as "ugly," of the those who have taunted her with racial epithets and physical harm, namely, as a "stunned" and "silenced" child who has been reduced to an object of derision and sexual gratification. On the other hand, Morrison's portrayal of Cholly as the "gentle aggressor" who has himself "suffered" a form of sexual humiliation at the hands of his white oppressors, who has endured parental rejection ("Abandoned in a junk heap by his mother, rejected for a crap game by his father" (BE 126)), abiding poverty and self-effacement, imparts to the rape scene a host of mitigating socio-political circumstances that seem to absolve the aggressor of full responsibility. Like Bigger Thomas and Jim Trueblood, Cholly Breedlove experiences what one psychologist calls a "geography of despair"—the sense of helplessness and unjust entrapment that spills over into rage against those who are closest and weakest.[46] By linking Cholly's "rape" by the white men to his own rape of his daughter, Morrison is, in effect, asking the reader to perceive Pecola's violation on two levels: literally, as the grotesque manifestation of a violent act of "love" by a victimized black father and symbolically as the systematic "rape" of all black women by the culture of the oppressor. Not only do the white men objectify Cholly within a context of sexualized aggression (thereby "raping" him, Morrison argues), but they also reduce him to a weapon of sexual assault against Darlene (thereby vicariously raping her); similarly, the systemic misogyny of the white culture, assimilated by Cholly as supposedly the only means to displace his anger and to achieve a modicum of identity by displaying "power over" someone, reduces his body to a weapon of sexual violation against Pecola.

Yet, within the confines of an oppressive society in which he is denied autonomy, Cholly, Morrison informs us, was also "dangerously free"; that is to say, he had experienced the liberation of feeling "free to feel whatever he felt—fear, guilt, shame, love, grief, pity. Free to be tender or violent, to whistle or weep" (BE 125). Based upon fulfilling his own impetuous desires that enabled him to act "on what he felt at the moment," Cholly's profound freedom entails the power to dominate women, to "take a woman's insults, for his body had already conquered hers," and the license to punctuate tenderness with physical abuse: he was "free even to knock her in the head, for he had already cradled that head in his arms" (BE 126). And while this freedom, which caters to his living within the almost solipsistic world of "his own perceptions and appetites" and which is, indeed, perhaps "dangerous" to women, proves somewhat inappropriate to his role as husband and father, it is the very code of behavior that he applies to the rape of his daughter.

Both "dangerously free" and an "objectified victim," Cholly emerges as an ambiguous presence that undermines the concept of the rapist as pure aggressor. Similar to another victim of parental abuse, Soaphead Church, whose sexual molestation of Pecola begins with a surge of understanding and love when she asks him to pray for her blue eyes, Cholly emerges as a pitiable character, a more fully-developed form of the "grotesque" that populates the short stories of Flannery O'Connor. That he is "reeling drunk" during the rape further emphasizes both the numbing despair and reckless abandon with which this "dangerously free" man approaches his daughter. Social critic Angela Davis and poet June Jordan correctly argue the necessity of situating the phenomenon of rape within its larger political context by disclosing the parallels between "sexual violence against individual women and neocolonial violence against peoples."[47] Yet, while we can sympathize with Cholly's oppressed status in a racist culture, we simultaneously also want to condemn the apparent ease with which he has stepped into the dominant society's misogynistic framework that sanctions, at times, the devastating release of male rage against women. It is here that Morrison falters somewhat, for in her attempt to temper the aggressive nature of the sexual violation, that is, to "soften" Cholly's image, the author has, in effect, written a "gentle rape" scene that uncomfortably blends predation and love, and strains the reader's credulity and compassion. Rape is not gentle; it is not a "gift" of distorted love but a clear assault upon a victim who has been reified by her attacker. Like his white male counterpart in the society at large, Cholly resorts to a form of "scapegoating" and seeks self-definition by achieving a "power over" someone weaker than he. Although politically enslaved, this "dangerously free" individual, like Sula and "Wild," remains free to envision other modes of self-definition that need not pose physical harm to women.

Furthermore, by characterizing Cholly's humiliation by the white hunters as a symbolic "rape," Morrison vitiates the physical and emotional devastation experienced by the victim of the actual assault, Pecola. Analogies whose validity rest upon parallels between sexual violation and other violent phenomena often ignore what Carol Adams refers to as "the absent referent," that point of intersection that seemingly connects discrete forms of violence:

> ...in descriptions of cultural violence women are...often the absent referent. Rape, in particular, carries such potent imagery that the term is transferred from the literal experience of women and applied metaphorically to other instances of violent devastation such as the "rape" of the earth in ecological writings of the early 1970's. The experience of women thus becomes a vehicle for describing other oppressions. Women, upon whose bodies actual rape is most often committed, become the absent referent when the language of sexual violence is used metaphorically. The terms recall women's experience but not women.[48]

While not as insulting and ridiculous as Ringo Starr's complaint that he felt "raped by beach-goers" who continually used his property as access to the water, Morrison's analogy "recalls women's experience but not women" and does not do justice to the unique physical and emotional pain suffered by victims of sexual assault. Cholly's humiliation at the hands of the white hunters, while leaving an indelible impression upon him that would distort his future perception and treatment of women, is qualitatively different from an actual rape. Although *The Bluest Eye* places Pecola at the center of the narrative and is punctuated with sporadic first-person fantasies about her own rape that reveal Pecola's traumatic loss of whatever vestiges of a self she had managed to salvage in her life up to that point, one wonders how Morrison would have constructed the actual rape scene if she had decided to filter it through the consciousness of the victim rather than that of the aggressor. By silencing Pecola during this critical episode, Morrison not only underscores the objectification of the rape victim but also avoids a direct elucidation of her anguish.

In tackling the complexities inherent in an act of male sexualized aggression, *The Bluest Eye* seeks both to condemn and to forgive Cholly's behavior by presenting him as both victim and perpetrator. Fraught with some troubling ambiguities concerning freedom and responsibility, love and hatred, Morrison seems to court our compassion for a black man who is both "dangerously free" and politically enchained. Perhaps her ambivalence toward Cholly reflects what one critic suggests, namely, a divided loyalty between her race and her sex.[49] Another critic also argues that while a case can be made for considering Morrison a black woman feminist postmodernist, the "question of priorities (race or gender?) remains."[50] More particularly, Morrison seems to be caught in the bind that a group of New York black feminists and lesbians would find themselves in at the end of the 1970's when they sought to explain why black women felt somewhat disenfranchised from the mainstream of the white feminist movement:

> We believe that sexual politics under patriarchy is as pervasive in Black women's lives as are the politics of class and race. We also find it difficult to separate race from class from sex oppression because in our lives they are most often experienced simultaneously...
>
> Although we are feminists and lesbians, we feel solidarity with progressive Black men and do not advocate the fractionalization that white women who are separatists demand. Our situation as Black people necessitates that we have solidarity around the fact of race...We struggle together with Black men against racism, while we also struggle with Black men about sexism.[51]

Sensitive to the vulnerability of all women to male aggression in a misogynistic culture, Morrison also seems intent upon humanizing the grotesque manifestation of a paternal love that has been distorted by racial oppression. Perhaps both *The Bluest Eye* and *Jazz* reflect her struggle to balance racial solidarity and a feminist sensitivity.

Jazz

Employing a more innovative technical strategy in *Jazz*, Morrison again invites the reader to sort out the seemingly impenetrable complexities of an ostensibly simple act of male rage against a young woman. Although the author continues to soften the act of aggression, both through imagery and the poignant exposition of past racial oppression, her inclusion of multiple perspectives of the shooting, including that of Dorcas, serves to humanize both the male aggressor and the female victim. Refracted through multiple consciousnesses, the shooting of Dorcas by Joe Trace presents the reader with the task of weighing responsibility and blame, of sorting out love and hatred, and, again, coming to understand the paradoxical emotion of gentle rage. In an interview with Tom LeClair in 1981, long before she wrote *Jazz*, Morrison observed that the sound of language is important to her and that often her words carry within them hidden meanings available only to those "who understand the context of the language: The analogy that occurs to me is jazz; it is open on the one hand and both complicated and inaccessible on the other."[52] Emblematic not only of the language but of the central violent episode of *Jazz*, the paradoxical quality of an "inaccessible openness" represents a challenge to the reader to plumb the depths of an ultimately inscrutable act of gentle rage that initially seems to be nothing more than the jealous outburst of a scorned lover.

Like *The Bluest Eye*, *Jazz* begins with the narrator's brief and rather matter-of-fact retrospective summary of events about an assault against a young woman by an older man, and delays further revelation of the psychological dynamics of the act until later in the novel. Opening in Harlem in the 1920's, the novel focuses upon the lives of Joe Trace, a door-to-door salesman of Cleopatra Cosmetics, his wife, Viole(n)t—a hairdresser who experiences multiple selves—and Dorcas, an eighteen-year-old raised by her Aunt Alice who had "worked hard to privatize her niece" (J 67) but has been unsuccessful in stifling the girl's burgeoning sexuality. After taking Dorcas as his lover for three months, fifty-year-old Joe Trace shoots her, and Violet, as the outraged wife, responds by visiting the funeral parlor where she attempts to slash the dead girl's face. While neither Joe nor Violet is prosecuted for his or her violent behavior, each suffers the pain of living with the memory of a dead girl whose absence becomes a haunting presence, directing them down circuitous avenues of pain, love, rage and, perhaps, a mutual forgiveness of each person's failure to understand the other's passions and longings.

Morrison alternates temporal sequences among the various layers of a past that includes: Joe and Violet's exodus from the cotton fields of Virginia to the City in 1900; the East St. Louis riots of 1917 that resulted in the deaths of 200 African-Americans and orphaned young Dorcas to her Aunt Alice; Violet's abandonment by her father and subsequent suicide of her mother that left her in the hands of her grandmother, True Belle, in Vesper County in 1888; and True Belle's connection to Vera Louise, a white woman who proudly bore the child of one of her black field hands and who, with True Belle, raised the child in Baltimore in the 1870's in what was "a renegade, almost suffragette thing to do" (J 139); and Joe Trace's emotional quest for maternal recognition that ironically links him with True Belle, for it is Golden Gray, Vera Louise's son, who in tracking down his black father, stumbles across Wild, a pregnant woman living in Nature, who gives birth to a child that may in fact be Joe Trace.

Pulsating throughout this song of temporal shifts and delayed revelations is a jazz-like rhythm that not only frees the language from the strictures of conventional construction but also becomes emblematic of the "dangerously free" meanderings of unchecked optimism, passion and rage that inform New York City in 1926, "when all the wars are over and there will never be another one":

> Daylight slants like a razor cutting the buildings in half. In the top half I see looking faces and it's not easy to tell which are people, which the work of stonemasons. Below is shadow where any blasé thing takes place: clarinets and lovemaking, fists and the voices of sorrowful women. A city like this makes me dream tall and feel in on things. Hep...Here comes the new. Look out. There goes the sad stuff. The bad stuff, The things-nobody-could-help stuff. (J 7)

It is within this setting of "sorrowful women" that the improvisational voice of the mysterious narrrator sings the tale of Joe, Violet and Dorcas; capturing the reckless abandon of a new-found freedom and the lyrical evocation of a slave-past, both embodied in the "race music," jazz (J 79), the narrative structure of *Jazz* can be compared to that of a jazz ensemble in which the various members at times during a performance turn over the lead to a solo voice, allowing each musician to experiment with tempo, modulation and dynamics and to plumb new depths of "deepdown, spooky" truths that must be heard by the soul. Although the dominant voice of the novel, the mysterious narrator relinquishes the microphone at times to other voices so that the various "truths" that unfold through the songs of Joe, Dorcas, Violet,

Felice, etc. present us with soothingly discordant insights into the realities of living the paradoxical existence of a free-slave in Harlem in the 1920's.

As the central episode of the novel, the shooting of Dorcas by Joe Trace, on the surface a simple act of jealousy, is, in fact, layered with accretions of social, psychological and mythic complexities that the reader must peel away and unravel in order to construct any locus of meaning concerning this act of male aggression against a young woman. Again, Morrison will invoke the injustices of a racist culture that not only subjugates African-Americans but also divorces them from an African heritage that acknowledges: magic; ancient tribal connections; the elemental consanguinity between the individual and the earth or that "pastoral kinship with nature" that spawns an "agrarian wisdom";[53] cyclical rather than linear time, which has been argued to be the essential difference between African and Western culture,[54] and which posits death not as an end but as a "changing of shape" and as a "passing on of the spirit;[55] "the role of the dead in the lives of the living";[56] and the spontaneous eruptions of "funk" or celebration of the flesh and the senses captured in the "dangerously free" rhythms of jazz. In his familial connection to Wild, Joe Trace, as his name suggests, embodies, perhaps, the absent presence of his "mother" or that vestige of African spirit that becomes distorted by the oppressive conditions of a slave culture. Like Cholly Breedlove, Joe Trace is "dangerously free" to fill up the emotional vacuum of parental love with an act of loving rage against his own "child," Dorcas.

In addition to evoking images of racist oppression, Morrison also tempers the reader's condemnation of Joe Trace by developing the unstable character of Violet who, living through multiple personalities, spins off into her own fantasy of motherhood; never wanting children when she and Joe were young lovers, Violet, at the age of fifty, finds herself longing for a child and musing about the three miscarriages she had suffered. Not only does she adopt in her own mind at times the "absent presence" of Dorcas as her child, but she also snatches a baby from its carriage one day while waiting for a hairdressing customer. As one critic notes, although Violet's plan was thwarted, "the longing remains, and the absence of a baby—or should I say the presence of an absent baby? forms the undertow of this book."[57] Although it does not mitigate Joe's murder of Dorcas, Violet's strange behavior, her "stumbling" into those "dark fissures" (J 22) or that "mental crack or two" (J 23) accords his taking of a mistress a degree of acceptability and understanding. Alienated from a wife who would rather talk to birds than to him, who impetuously "sits down" in the middle of the street and whose "renegade tongue" proves to be embarrassingly uncontrollable at times, Joe is first annoyed, then puzzled and finally depressed by Violet's silence and stillness at home (J 24).

Living as a colonized member in a racist society with a woman who has more or less abandoned him to dwell in her fantasy world of stillborn imaginings, Joe finds temporary solace in the arms of his young lover, Dorcas. Joe's alienation from his mother and what she mythically represents for him as an African-American man living in white America, in addition to his psychological estrangement from Violet, whose status as a African-American woman still enslaved in a racist and sexist culture leaves her seething with an ineffable rage that "seeps" through in strange behavior (J 16), are factors that contribute to his pursuit of a deep-down spooky love. Why he destroys the vehicle of that love in order "to keep the feeling going" remains on the surface an inscrutable mystery which can be approached only indirectly through the presentation of a multiplicity of possible "truths" provided for us by the limited perspectives of those involved.

Similar to her structuring of *The Bluest Eye*, Morrison's strategy in *Jazz* is to invite the reader into the critical past of the main characters, a past that always resonates with overtones of racial prejudice, and to connect that past to a present act of violence which, in both novels, is an act of male rage against a young woman. However, whereas *The Bluest Eye* is, as Melissa Walker observes, more or less a conventional narrative employing traditional flashbacks but remaining basically "straightforward and linear,"[58] *Jazz* expands Morrison's experimental impulse by offering the reader multiple interpretations of this male aggression, so that we must enter the text as the co-creators of meaning regarding the nature of responsibility and blame, love and hatred. *The Bluest Eye* relies primarily upon an objective third person narration interspersed with Claudia's "relatively impersonal, evaluative first-person"[59] voice and with the sparse but moving first-person and very personal reminiscence of Pauline and Pecola Breedlove. In *Jazz*, on the other hand, all voices are intensely personal, as if Morrison has at this point in her career come to embrace one of the tenets of postmodernism, namely, the relative nature of truth, and acknowledge the gnawing absence of any transcendental meaning. While we feel the main narrative voice nudging us toward compassion for and forgiveness of Joe Trace, it remains a profoundly personal and self-conscious voice that couches many of its statements in the tentative language of the hypothetical; the text itself, then, betrays an ambiguity that renders such exoneration problematic.

The Call of "Wild"

Re-"tracing" the path from Joe's murder of Dorcas to his almost "mythic" beginnings in the wild reveals a rather circuitous route by which a black man has suffered the gradual suppression of his more primordial African heritage that celebrates the human being's intimate association with the earth. The story of Joe's possible connection to Wild is presented to us by the mysterious narrator who imagines what may have occurred during Golden Gray's quest to discover and perhaps kill his father, "a black-skinned nigger" (J 143).

As a "yellow-curled" mulatto who appeared to be more white than black and who was groomed by Vera Louise and True Belle to fit into respectable middleclass Baltimore society, Golden Gray undoubtedly began his journey in a "two-seated phaeton" that carried a large trunk "filled with beautiful shirts, linen, and embroidered toilet articles" (J 143). Along the way to the little town of Vienna, he stumbles across a pregnant, "naked berry-black woman" who is covered with mud and leaves and who, upon seeing him, becomes startled, and, in attempting to flee, knocks her head against a tree and passes out. Initially repulsed and ready to abandon her to certain death, Golden Grey comes to realize that if he can feel affection for his horse which is also "black, naked and shiny wet," then perhaps he should overcome the nausea which she provokes in him and help her. His decision to place her in the back of the carriage stems not from a sense of genuine concern for her well-being but rather from the more ulterior selfish motive of later using this gesture of compassion as a means to offset the horror of patricide in the eyes of Vera Louise.

Having found the house and having deposited the "black liquid female" on the cot, Golden Gray, awaiting his father's arrival, begins to dissociate himself from Wild, from True Belle and from the image he envisions of his father, Henry LesTroy. He had always been convinced that there was only one kind of black—"True Belle's kind. Black and nothing. Like Henry Les Story. Like the filthy woman snoring on the cot. But there was another kind—like himself" (J 149). When Golden Gray finally does meet his father, a proud man who has shed his slave name and adopted the more mythic name of "Hunters Hunter," the clashing of this "city man's" (J 170) white respectability and pretentiousness with his father's black "close-to-the-earth" existence leaves Golden Gray rather disoriented by his father's pride and absence of humiliation. Offended by his son's arrogance and condescension, Hunters Hunter issues an ultimatum:

"Want to stay here? You welcome. Want to chastise me? Throw it out of your mind...You come in here, drink my liquor, rummage in my stuff and think you can cross-talk me just cause you call me Daddy? If she told you I was your daddy, then she told you more than she told me. Get a hold of yourself. A son ain't what a woman say. A son is what a man do. You want to act like you mine, then do it, else get the devil out my house!...Be what you want—white or black. Choose. But if you choose black, you got to act black, meaning draw up your manhood—quickly, and don't bring me no whiteboy sass." (J 172-173)

Golden Gray's initial reaction to his father's stinging reproof is to follow through with his contemplated patricide and "blow the man's head off. Tomorrow." That he does not must be attributed to Wild: "It must have been the girl who changed his mind" (J 173).

The pivotal element in the story of Golden Gray's quest to find his father is the discovery of the liquid black female whose presence forces Golden Gray to affirm the very heritage he has been repressing all of his life and that he would violently seek to extirpate through an act of patricide. Perhaps an embodiment of what Jungian analyst Clarissa Pinkola Estés has labelled the Wild Woman archetype, Wild may denote for Morrison "not the modern pejorative sense of the word, meaning out of control," but rather "its original sense which means to live a natural life, one in which the *criatura*, creature, has innate integrity and healthy boundaries."[60] Or, perhaps Wild points to what Julia Kristeva would call the "fantasy that is nurtured by the adult, man or woman, of a lost territory" that reflects not so much the "idealized archaic mother" but rather the "idealization of the relationship that binds us to her, the idealization of primary narcissism."[61] Experienced by the child during the pre-oedipal stage which Kristeva calls the semiotic, this primary "speechless" connection to the mother's body establishes the child primarily as a body that is "criss-crossed by a flow of pulsions or drives" which remain relatively unorganized until (s)he enters the symbolic Law of the father at which time the semiotic process is repressed. Pulsating within language, the symbolic order of the father, however, are vestiges of the semiotic which can erupt in the form of "contradiction, meaninglessness, disruption, silence and absence."[62]

Like the semiotic process which, for Kristeva, "encompasses both masculinity and femininity and which denotes a primal connection between boys and mothers as well as girls and mothers,"[63] the drive either to repress or celebrate the call of the Wild in *Jazz* manifests itself not only in the female characters of Violet and Dorcas but also in the central male figure of

Joe Trace: Violet's "strange" behaviors—her slipping into those mental cracks, her street sittings, her prolonged periods of silence all seeminly circumscribed by a profound hunger for "mother-love"—perhaps point to eruptions of the semiotic process into the repressive symbolic order of the Father; while Dorcas initially identifies with the symbolic order, the Law of the Father, by choosing to define herself first as Joe's mistress and then as the property of the young Acton, she does effect a figurative return to the maternal realm of the semiotic at the time of her death when the song of "Wild" ushers her "home" to a primal, albeit imaginary, unity with the mother; and as we shall see, Joe Trace engages in a life-long struggle to return home to the "powerful mythic space"[64] of the Wild, a "fantasmatic figure which looms as large for baby boys as for baby girls."[65]

In erecting a triad of "lost" characters comprised of a male and two females, Morrison cleverly avoids what Hutcheon calls "essentializing the ex-centric."[66] By including a male figure among those who manifest a living, semiotic connection to the mother and who are seeking a return home to the mythic space of the mother, Morrison, as she does in *Tar Baby*, circumvents positing the new female as "essence." That is to say, like Son in *Tar Baby*, Joe Trace serves to topple "that dangerous femininst centrism that would privilege an essentialized 'female'" and he does so by emerging, like Son, as a "creature of sexual not rational power, of fluid identity, of unclear origins."[67] While Hutcheon may be correct in her claim that Morrison very self-consciously avoids succumbing to a femininst centrism in *Tar Baby* by according a male figure a quality of subversive ex-centricity, I would argue that Morrison's purpose in positing Joe Trace as a wild, irrational power in *Jazz* serves not only the postmodernist strategy of subverting "centers" and essences and of undermining the concept of a static identity, but also the political agenda of portraying a violent black male in a more or less sympathetic light: if the repressive Law of the Father theoretically serves to distance us all from our idealized home with the mother, then the humiliating restrictions of racism can only exacerbate the frustration and impede the "return" of those forced to deal with the practical and everyday exigencies of political oppression.

One could also argue that not only does Joe Trace seek to return "home" to the "lost territory" of an idealized relationship with Wild but that the elusive Wild, herself, personifies the absence or idealization of this territory. Fluid, speechless, both present and absent, literally leaving a "trace" of herself behind, and in tune with the pre-lingual rhythms of nature, Wild could be seen as embodying the very semiotic process itself. Connected to the child's contact with the mother's body, the semiotic comes to represent that elusive imaginary home from which the child remains forever estranged.

Wild also comes to symbolize the unadulterated expression of the almost mystical unity between the human being and nature, that is, "funk" in its purest form. Described as the "black, liquid female," Wild becomes associated with the primeval ooze from which all life springs; and her "deer eyes" (J 153) suggest both her dehumanization by Golden Grey and her affinity with the creatures of the earth. Having assimilated the white culture's exploitation of nature for purposes of vanity rather than survival, Golden Gray boasts about having "gloves made from the hide of a very young cow" (J 154) while his symbolic mythic mother stands before him as a celebration of communion with, rather than dominion over, nature. Both a real woman and a mythically immanent presence that can inhabit cane fields, trees and caves, Wild is in harmony with the cyclical rhythms of nature: she, like cows, gives birth in August, and, like some species of birds, rejects her maternal instinct to care for her young when there is external interference during the birth process. Helpless in aiding the injured woman, Golden Gray looks on as his father and a friend act as midwives:

> This baby was not easy. It clung to the walls of that foamy cave, and the mother was of practically no help. When the baby finally emerged, the problem was clear immediately: the woman would not hold the baby or look at it. (J 170)

On a political level, Joe suffers the first estrangement from his mother because of the intrusion of Golden Grey, an envoy of white culture, into Wild's "home." Now, he is rejected by her once he is "touched" by others during birth.

Once it becomes inscribed within the local mores of a colonized culture that has itself been forced to repress its primal beginnings, Joe Trace's intuited connection to his earth-mother first generates a feeling of embarrassment—she has acquired the local reputation of being a crazy woman—then an obsession with finding her, and finally the pain of her rejection. Filled with both anger and love for Wild, Joe begins to speculate on "what it would take to kill Wild if [he and Victory] happened on her" (J 175). Hunters Hunter, however, tells them both:

> "I taught both you all never kill the tender and nothing female if you can help it. Didn't think I had to teach you about people. Now, learn this: she ain't prey. You got to know the difference." (J 175)

His father's exhortation does not deter Joe from attempting to "trace" her in the woods, to track her path by following the "scraps of song" that came from her throat (J 177). Unable to find her on his first excursion, Joe, we are told, returns "after the dispossession" to try again (J 177). Displaced again from his mother, this time by the intrusion of the white culture's violent acquisition of the land which entailed the razing of Hunters Hunter's home in Vienna, Joe now brings to his quest a bitter hatred for the mother who had rejected him and who even now refuses to bestow upon him any gesture of maternal recognition. Becoming more and more alienated from his mythic roots and more "housebroken," travelling from city to city to work for menial wages as a black farmhand, Joe Trace, forgetting Hunters Hunter's admiration of Wild, comes to see his mother as nothing more than a source of embarrassment, a pitiable creature who, "leaving traces of her sloven unhousebroken self all over the county, hadn't the intelligence even to be a witch: She was powerless, invisible, wastefully daft" (J 179).

Joe Trace's alienation from his birth mother leaves him filled with a longing that surpasses just maternal acknowledgment but comes to emblematize his political displacement from his mythic roots and perhaps his desire to re-enter the idealized "lost territory" of the semiotic process. While Joe's marriage to Violet and their subsequent exodus to Harlem provide him with a form of "civilized" stability, he harbors within himself a yearning to reconnect with (the) Wild. It is precisely with Dorcas, whose untamed sexuality matches the dangerous rhythms of jazz and echoes along the deepdown spooky regions of funk, that Joe tries to re-enter into a mystical union with his mother and his actual/mythical beginnings. Representing perhaps a "musical" eruption of the long-repressed semiotic contact with Wild, jazz, for Joe Trace, is heard as the song of his mother. It is, we are told by the mysterious narrator, precisely his mother about whom he is thinking when Joe "tracks" Dorcas down to shoot her:

> As he puts on his coat and cap he can practically feel Victory at his side when he sets out, armed, to find Dorcas. He isn't thinking of harming her, or, as Hunter had cautioned, killing something tender. She is female. And she is not prey. So he never thinks of that. He is hunting for her, though, and while hunting a gun is as natural a companion as Victory. (J 180)

While he remembers the cautionary words of Hunter, Joe nevertheless carries a gun and stalks Dorcas as female prey. Hoping she will not be with one of those younger vital boys, a "rooster," Joe convinces himself that when he finds Dorcas, she, like his mother, will "be alone. Hardheaded. *Wild*, even.

But alone" (J 182; emphasis mine). Having assimilated himself into the urban culture of steel structures where "daylight slants like a razor cutting the buildings in half" (J 7), Joe Trace nevertheless pursues the elusive (projected?) call of Wild through the urban jungle of New York City, intent upon regressing to that mystical union with his maternal and mythical origin, even if it entails destroying the physical embodiment of that origin, Dorcas.

If Dorcas does represent the "lost territory" of the idealized oneness with the mother and the emotional place where Joe can come to rest from his weary wanderings as a political exile in a racist society, then his affiliation with her exceeds the scope of being just a gesture of marital infidelity, and elicits our understanding. Both intensely sexual ("You would have thought I was twenty...satisfying my appetite for the first time under a walnut tree," Joe tells us (J 129)), and mystical, their "union" was for Joe both a temporary reprieve from a passionless marriage and a more primal desire to recover the idealized union with (the) Wild. Furthermore, his killing of Dorcas then emerges not only as the raging jealousy of a spurned lover but the violent attempt to eliminate another displacement from (the) Wild; having been rejected by Dorcas in favor of younger men, Joe tries magically to elevate to the realm of ideal permanence the feeling of oneness that comes from this deepdown spooky love. By eliminating Dorcas, the fickle embodiment of the mystical union, Joe tries "to keep the feeling going" (J 3).

Yet, our sympathy for Joe, a man perhaps driven by the mythic and psychological disruption of his connection to the maternal roots of his African heritage and compelled to walk the land as a political exile, is mixed with condemnation. For, like the culture at large, Joe feels "free" to consume or eliminate a woman to assuage his sense of displacement. Along with Dorcas' aunt Alice who considers "the *impunity* of the man who killed her niece just because he could" (J 73), the reader is continually reminded throughout the text of a unique form of enslavement faced by African-American women, an enslavement that supersedes racist prejudice and reflects an inveterate misogyny that has seeped through from the society at large to stain the fabric of a colonized culture. Toni Cade notes:

> There is nothing to indicate that the African woman, who ran the marketplace, who built dams, who engaged in international commerce and diplomacy, who sat on thrones, who donned armor to wage battle against the European invaders and the corrupt chieftains who engaged in the slave trade, who were consulted as equals in the affairs of state-there is nothing to indicate that they were turning their men into faggots, were victims of penis envy, or any such nonsense...There is evidence however, that the

European white was confused and alarmed by the egalitarian system of these societies, and did much to wreck it, creating wedges between the men and women.[68]

Rooted in the misogynistic attitudes of our white European forefathers, American society has continuously and effectively obliterated the egalitarian principles not only of those whom they had forcibly imported from Africa but also, as Cade notes, of the indigenous peoples whom they found living in harmony with the land of North America: the Sioux, Seminole and Iroquois nations. Joe Trace reflects the gradual assimilation of the colonizing culture's misogyny, a further indication of his displacement from his African heritage.

Both remembering and ignoring his father's exhortation to refrain from hurting women, Joe Trace has, like so many of his white male counterparts in contemporary America, indeed chosen to hunt his lover down with a gun, to avenge his rejection by violently eliminating the woman.[69] While Alice may in fact have overreacted in her attempt to protect Dorcas from the violence awaiting her as an African-American woman, her sensitivity to the plight of women living in what amounts to be a militarized zone whose ruling members feel free to stalk women as prey is very telling:

> Every week since Dorcas' death, during the whole of January and February, a paper laid bare the bones of some broken woman. Man kills wife. Eight accused of rape dismissed. Woman and girls victims of. Woman commits suicide…in jealous rage man. (J 74)

As a "chick" being pursued by both young "roosters" and an old "cock" like Joe (J 133), Dorcas manifests a domesticated connection to (the) Wild, not free to roam like the deer but entrapped within the male-defined parameters of predatory, sexual "meat" markets.

Furthermore, the alienation and displacement that plague Joe Trace and, undoubtedly all African-American men, also haunt their female counterparts who, however, having learned to turn their rage inward upon themselves, refrain for the most part from hurting others. As Anne Campbell has pointed out, men's anger tends to be uncomplicated by restraint and guilt while women's rage results in a tension between anger and control.[70] Taught by a sexist society to suppress expressions of rage, to flee from their own anger, women like Violet and the other hairdressers keep themselves occupied with trivial matters so as to avoid confronting their own seething unhappiness:

They fill their mind and hands with soap and repair and dicey confrontations because what is waiting for them in a suddenly idle moment is the seep of rage. Molten, Thick and slow-moving. (J 16)

As we discovered in our analysis of Joan Didion's' female characters, women tend to internalize their anger, at times even raising knives against abusive men but never following through; instead, like Charlotte Douglas, they redirect the rage inward and "safely" faint. Violet's rage erupts in a variety of ways, of course, the most virulent being her attempt to slash a dead girl's face. Again, however, this blatant display of female "violence," to disfigure the face of a corpse, is more symbolic than real, representing in part a "safe" and temporarily effective displacement of the real rage she has suppressed against Joe. Consequently, it is an expression both of violence against a dead girl and non-violence against Joe. That Violet's (non)violent action seems to generate more gossip and initial condemnation from the community than does Joe's murder of Dorcas underscores both the deeply-ingrained acceptance of male aggression against women as part of the *status quo* and the concomitant apprehension of female-initiated violence as peculiar and "unnatural."

Furthermore, Violet does not coincide with any of the traditional black female stereotypes so that her behavior not only generates discussion among her neighbors but also startles the reader. Violet subverts traditional narrative expectations because her act of mutilating a corpse does not conform to the cultural reduction of black women to the conventional stereotypes of "Jezebel (the seductive temptress), Sapphire (the evil, manipulative bitch) or Aunt Jemima (the sexless long-suffering nurturer"[71]). In addition, Violet's refusal to explain her action or to justify her demeanor serves not only to deny the reader the smug comfort of reducing her behavior to the linear logic of cause and effect but also to subvert the masculinist power structure of criminology, the traditional voice of authority. As Sally Robinson argues, "A Black woman who acts violently and does not offer to 'explain' her crime to authorities in effect undermines that authority."[72] Although Violet's aggressive behavior is more symbolic than practical, its subversive dimension succeeds, as Robinson would agree, in placing this Black woman "outside" culturally conditioned narrative expectations and in garnering the attention of the reader.[73]

While Violet's sense of psychological and mythic displacement leaves her roaming rootlessly around the solitary caverns of multiple selves, seeking perhaps "traces" of her heritage in the father who abandoned her, the mother who committed suicide by jumping down a well and her own miscarried, "almost" children, she directs her rage inward through those intermittent bouts of "abnormal" behavior that include periodic "street sittings," sleeping with dolls, conversational *nonsequiturs* and prolonged periods of silence. While all of these disruptions of the "normal" flow of rational discourse may indeed represent vestiges of the semiotic process that associates Violet with her mother, who died in that "deepdown spooky region" of the well, her behavior continues to be (mis)read by the community as odd, indicative, perhaps, of the menopausal distress of a childless woman (J 46).[74] The narrator even suggests that Violet is suffering from "mother-hunger," an ambiguous phrase, for it implies both a longing for her own mother (Violent was "*drowning*" in mother-hunger (J 108)) and a desire to be a mother. Doubly marginalized by both racism and sexism, Violet exists on the periphery of both society at large and her own community.

Like all of the women in the novel, Violet, for the most part, internalizes the rage spawned by such alienation and presents a striking contrast to the violent behavior of her husband. While the reader can perhaps join the narrator in forgiving a young man like Golden Grey "his self-deception" and "his worrying about his coat and not tending to the girl" (J 155), Joe Trace's murder of Dorcas, despite the mitigating circumstances of his birth and subsequent exile in a racist society, strains our unqualified compassion. Choosing to ignore the advice of his father to refrain from hurting women, Joe, unlike the women in the novel, directs his rage outward against a "tender" female.

The ambivalence conveyed through Morrison's evocation of Joe Trace's mythic and historic past is augmented by her technique of providing multiple accounts of Dorcas's death, accounts that not only accumulate relevant "facts" but also provide crucial insights into the psychological conditions of the participants involved in the shooting. Halfway through the novel, immediately following Joe's first-person account of his seven transformations, the reader is given Joe's perspective on the actual killing of Dorcas Manfred. Implying that it was Dorcas' vital sexuality that revealed to him the profound sense of loneliness he was living in his marriage to a woman who slept with dolls, Joe "blames" Dorcas as the "instigator" of his actions; she is the catalyst that awakens in him the instinctual desire to shed his skin for the final time and (re)enter the dark cave (womb) of a deepdown spooky love. In images that seek to abrogate any sense of autonomy or free will, Joe speaks to us as someone driven by impulses over which he can exert little, if any, control:

> How did I know what an eighteen-year-old girl might *instigate* in a grown man whose wife is sleeping with dolls? *Make me know* a loneliness I never could imagine in a forest of people for fifteen miles, or on a riverbank with nothing but live bait for company. *Convince me* I never knew the sweet side of anything until I tasted her honey. They say snakes go blind for a while before they shed their skin for the last time...*I wasn't looking for the trail. It was looking for me and when it started talking at first I couldn't hear it.* (J129-130; emphases mine)

Compelled by a force that pulls him toward the death scene, the echoes perhaps of his mother's scratchy song, Joe Trace roams the city jungle like an animal "blindly" sniffing his prey: "I tracked my mother in Virginia and [the trail] led me right to her, and I tracked Dorcas from borough to borough. I didn't even have to work at it. Didn't even have to think" (J 130). And when Joe distances himself from the shooting by projecting his own agency onto the gun—"I wanted to stay there. Right after the *gun went thuh!*" (J 130; emphasis mine)—we are moved to absolve him of total culpability since he seems to have been caught up in a whirl of passions and deep-seated longings over which he can exert little control. Finally, his desire "to catch her before she fell and hurt herself" accords this act of blind violence a degree of "gentleness" reminiscent of the ambivalent rape scene in *The Bluest Eye*. Joe Trace, like Cholly Breedlove, starts to take shape as the "gentle aggressor."

Yet, even Joe Trace undermines the sympathy he seeks to generate from the reader and ultimately presents himself as a man who is dangerously free to kill a young woman "just because he could." Celebrating his own free agency, his own premeditated decision to track her down, Joe addresses his absent lover and reveals his sense of conscious purpose:

> I *chose* you. Nobody gave you to me. Nobody said that's the one for you. I picked you out. Wrong time, yep, and doing wrong by my wife. But the picking out, the choosing. Don't ever think I fell for you, or fell over you. I didn't fall in love, I rose in it. I saw you and made up my mind. My mind. And I made up my mind to follow you too. (J 135)

Propelled through life as an exile in search of mythic and political roots, Joe Trace, according to his own first-person account, remains paradoxically free within his societal and emotional enslavement to choose to hunt a young woman down and harness, once and for all, that elusive force of the Wild. Like the men he observes exiting from the subway, each with a woman on his arm and each intent upon penetrating and subduing the formidable female power of the Wild that lies behind the women's red lips and silk stockings, Joe will violently "reach in, extend, get back behind that power, grab it and keep it still" (J 182).

Joe Trace's narrative of the shooting remains fragmented and incomplete and is interrupted frequently by the intrusive mysterious voice that, like a Greek Chorus, comments on his state of mind, informing us at one point that immediately prior to the shooting Joe was feeling "at peace" (J 184). Shifting from Joe's first-person perspective to the mysterious narrator and then on to the first-person narrative of the victim, Morrison creates a musical kaleidoscope of fragmented songs that seems to defy any stable pattern of logical coherence, an ensemble of solo voices that modulates among various key signatures of truths and explores the dangerously free linguistic rhythms of jazz. As the leader of this ensemble, the mysterious narrator zooms in on Dorcas as she sensually embraces her young partner, Acton, on the dance floor and informs the reader that Dorcas is "happier than she has ever been anytime" (J 188). Devoid of Joe's tender solicitude and a little "cruel" in his dealings with woman, this "savvy" young "rooster" "has never given her a present or even thought about it. Sometimes he is where he says he will be; sometimes not" (J 188). All the young women desire him and "Dorcas is lucky. Knows it. And is happy as she has ever been anytime" (J 188).

Employing still yet another voice and tonal shift, the controlling narrator now yields to the first-person musings of the victim who, despite her alleged happiness, senses the imminent predations of her spurned lover: "He is coming for me. I know he is because I know how flat his eyes went when I told him not to" (J 189). Caught up in the unpredictable and violent grabs for power that, according to the controlling narrator, constitute the dynamics of both love and war (J 191), Dorcas naively assumes that once Joe sees how she has emerged as a definitive personality under Acton's direction, he will leave her alone. Dorcas, perhaps ironically, has relinquished what little power she had, albeit a borrowed "phallic power" in her relationship with Joe, for the total submersion to Acton's ruthless will:

> "He is coming for me. And when he does he will see that I'm not his anymore. I'm Acton's and it's Acton I want to please. He expects it. With Joe I pleased myself because he encouraged me to. With Joe I worked the stick of the world, the power in my hand." (J 191)

Removed from the deepdown spooky force of the Wild which connotes a woman's ability to maintain an integrity within self-constructed boundaries,

Dorcas' relationship with Joe nevertheless enabled her to experience that vestige of a female mythic wholeness pulsating beneath the veneer of patriarchy; her "power" now resides in the paradoxical ability to deny herself autonomy, to cave in to societal pressure to define herself in terms of someone else's territory, to "be" Acton's woman.

In her concluding death solo, Dorcas provides the reader with a first-hand glimpse into the heart of a naive young woman who is struggling to carve out her territorial boundaries in a culture in which female life is male-dependent and dispensable, and who learns too late to hear the voice of her mythic mother, the call of Wild. Aware of Acton's callous and angry annoyance at her for being shot and bleeding all over him, Dorcas lets go of her worldly pretenses and slides into a mortal contemplation of a visual residue of the Wild, the luscious oranges spilling over a flat wooden bowl: "So clear the dark bowl the pile of oranges. Just oranges. Bright" (J 193). A more intense version of Baby Suggs and her immersion of self in the richness of colors, Dorcas comes to apprehend what Susan Willis refers to as one of the "eruptions of funk" in Morrison's novels, the sudden intrusion into the everyday practical world of another order of being, in this case the sensuality of color.[75] This visual component of funk, or the Wild, finds its auditory counterpart in the music of the jazz singer that Dorcas hears as she descends into unconsciousness, into that realm beneath the waking world in which she may come to re-collect her primal unity with her mythic mother: "Listen. I don't know who is that woman singing but I know the words by heart" (J 193). The scratchy song of (the) Wild that had called to Joe Trace through the cane fields and hills of Virginia and that has, for the most part, been silenced beneath the din of technological progress, now is clearly heard by Dorcas on her death bed as she recognizes the words *by and in her heart.*

Augmenting the reader's compassion for the victim through this first-person monologue, Morrison avoids depicting her as the dangerous slut who finally gets what she deserves. Still a little girl in many ways, Dorcas, like Pecola, plays a part in a violent scenario over which she has very little control. Yet, when we are later informed by her friend Felice, in still another perspective on the shooting, that Dorcas's wound was not initially a lethal one and that Dorcas's insistence that the police not be called contributed to her bleeding to death, we begin to understand the more "active" role she played in her own demise. According to Felice, "Dorcas let herself die." However, Felice too undercuts her own credibility when she informs us that despite Dorcas' protestations, Felice nevertheless did call the ambulance but because the call came from Harlem, the police didn't respond until morning. So, whether or not Dorcas bled to death because she "chose" to and/or because she was ultimately the victim of a racist/sexist culture remains ambiguous within Felice's narrative which in itself is just one of among four narrative voices that tease the reader with an absence of closure. Yet, Felice's revelations serve to temper our condemnation of Joe by suggesting that he may have not inflicted a necessarily mortal wound but rather initiated an act of violence that in conjunction with the racist inaction of the police contributed to Dorcas' death. Fragmented, biased and incomplete in their presentations of the shooting, each voice compellingly invites the reader to provide the "meaning" of the events and to arrive at some form of understanding, although perhaps an "unstable" one, of the paradox of gentle rage.

Compared to *The Bluest Eye*, *Jazz* complicates the process of the reader's making meaning through a more detailed evocation of a mythic past and a more innovative technical strategy of using multiple consciousnesses. Morrison seems to be pushing us toward a recognition of the instability inherent in any interpretation, since all approaches to the text, including that of the reader, is limited and fraught with biases and, hence, somewhat "unreliable." Intensely personal and self-consciously aware of its own limited knowledge, its own unreliability (J 137,160), the mysterious narrative voice becomes emblematic of the all-too-human process of constructing meaning from the residue of questionable facts, rumor and supposition. For Morrison, "truth" emerges as a hypothesis, a composite of the limited knowledge, conjecture, emotions and biases of the observer. While the "Truths" of Western thought—those traditional binary oppositions such as love/hatred, aggressor/victim and active/passive—threaten to collapse into an ambiguity that renders any permanent meaning ultimately unreliable, it is this particular reader's bias that posits Dorcas' fundamental vulnerability to male violence in American society as one of the more stable and sound explanatory principles of the meaning of the "central" event in *Jazz*.

Having incorporated and passed on to their children the white culture's denigration of female sexuality and its concomitant unleashing of hatred against women's bodies, many African-American women and men in Morrison's novels have unknowingly severed their connection to their primal Wild Mother and, in effect, become participants in the misogynistic police state of twentieth-century America. Alice Manfred recognizes the connection between the surrendering of female power and the resulting reduction of women to "prisoners of war" or, as Pynchon would describe them, "inmates." Like all women, Alice is a victim of the dominant society's ambivalence toward female sexuality, an ambivalence that reflects both a distrust of and a dependence upon the woman's procreative power that is necessary to perpetuate the patriarchy. Alienated from themselves by a society that both idealizes female beauty and impugns female sexuality, women have come to feel hatred for their own bodies and to surrender their autonomy and self-defining boundaries to the dictates of more powerful men. The "necessary evil" of female sexuality was the mixed message conveyed to Alice from her parents and in turn passed down from her to Dorcas as part of a process of socialization that engenders female self-hatred and male hostility:

> [Alice's parents] spoke to her firmly but carefully about her body: sitting nasty (legs open)...The moment she got breasts they were bound and resented, a resentment that increased to outright hatred of her pregnant possibilities and never stopped until she married Louis Manfred, when suddenly it was the opposite. Even before the wedding her parents were murmuring about grandchildren they could see and hold, while at the same time and in turn resenting the tips showing and growing under the chemises of Alice's younger sisters...Growing up under that heated control, Alice swore she wouldn't, but she did pass it on. She did pass it on to her baby sister's only child. (J76-77)

Alice Manfred's reflections reveal the cultural "imprisonment" of women, notably African-American women, in American society. Succumbing to the dictates of a subtle socialization process, Alice senses that by perpetuating male definitions of proper female behavior she has in effect contributed to the cuturally-created "war" between the sexes that reduces women to "prisoners of war" in a male-controlled police state: "War was what it was. Which is why she had chosen surrender and made Dorcas her own prisoner of war" (J 77). Like the "mothers" of *Gravity's Rainbow* who pass on the "virus of Death" to their children, Alice has attempted to inculcate in her "child" the values of a misogynistic culture as a means of survival.

Yet, Alice is also aware of black women who have not surrendered, of women all over the country who have armed themselves, who were fighting back against their oppressors. From the "negress" who sliced a Swedish tailor's face to the irate woman who stabbed the iceman in Springfield, black women were arming themselves in 1926: "Black women were dangerous and the less money they had the deadlier the weapon they chose" (J 77). While such gestures of female violence do not constitute a revolution, they are a source of "wonder" (J 77) to those who embrace the culture's dichotomy of aggressive male/compliant female, and they bespeak a disruption of the prevailing *status quo* that reveals women's capacity for violence. Tired of remaining passive in the pattern of male-abuse and female-victimization, of being "fondled in kitchens and the back of stores," of feeling the "fists" of policemen "in their faces," some women, Alice tells us, seek to break out of the cycle by unleashing their own rage against their oppressors (J 78). Again, if, as Marilyn Frye argues, we view female anger as an "instrument of cartography" by which we may chart the claims of subjectivity by those who have been traditionally objectified and silenced,[76] we may interpret these sporadic outbursts of aggression as the desperate cries for subjecthood, for autonomy and recognition. Like their black male counterparts—Bigger Thomas, Cholly Breedlove and Jim Trueblood—these women have been pushed up against the wall of a lethal racial bigotry and have, like Bigger, "snapped." Yet, unlike Bigger, Cholly and Jim, these women do not displace their rage onto the weaker members of their own community but rather direct their fury at the white oppressor. Of course, what Alice does not explicitly tell us, perhaps because it should be so obvious, is that such women who contravene the established mores of a sexist culture, who dare to violate the *status quo* and raise their supposedly compliant hand against their white, male subjugators, inevitably end up either incarcerated or dead.

Perhaps this is why such "violent" women do not seem to represent for Morrison an effective alternative to the prevailing victimization of women in American society. While understandable as an immediate mode of defense against specific acts of male aggression, violence in general for Morrison only begets more violence and in effect constitutes the victim's adoption of the degrading behavior of the oppressor, or as Alice Manfred calls American society—the Beast. To wreak violence upon others is to get caught up in the "Beast's desire for its own filth" (J 78). As we shall discover in our analysis of the images of violent women in both *Sula* and *Beloved*, Morrison seems to counsel more peaceful options that entail a woman's recovery of her societally repressed primal connection with the Wild, of her bonding with other women to celebrate the "funkiness" inherent in such female power and of her forging "experimental" lives that strive to avoid the sterility and enslavement of white middleclass existence.

When violence does erupt in Morrison's women, it results either in a grotesque form of self-mutilation or an impotent "stab" at some representative of the "Beast." Unlike some of those black women of 1926 who, according to Alice Manfred, directed their rage outward to their primary targets—abusive men—the women of *Sula* and *Beloved* often internalize their fury, harming themselves and their offspring. Furthermore, unlike Cholly's rape of Pecola and Joe's murder of Dorcas, female-initiated violence against children in both *Sula* and *Beloved* takes on either an "accidental" or sacrificial dimension that further complicates the reader's emotional response. Conveyed through images that bespeak the love and pain experienced by mothers who choose to end the lives of their own children rather than relinquish them to the death-infested torment of a slavish dependence upon drugs or the dehumanization of slavery itself, Morrison confronts the reader with the seemingly impossible task of deciphering issues of moral culpability and, again, juggling the feelings of condemnation and compassion.

Female-initiated Violence: *Sula* and *Beloved*

The act of female-initiated violence that occurs in *Sula* does not occupy the central narrative focus of the novel as does the infanticide that haunts every page of *Beloved*. Tangential to the main thrust of the novel, Eva's murder of her son Plum receives only passing mention by most critics who tend to focus on the "central" relationship in the book between Sula and Nel, a relationship that manifests a "deepdown spooky region" of female bonding that pulsates beneath the surface of rational, phallic discourse and connotes, if not a lesbian connection,[77] at least an alternative to the violent, sterile lives of the surrounding community. As the granddaughter of Eva, it is Sula who, with Nel, had come to realize early in life that because they were "neither white nor male," all "freedom and triumph was forbidden to them"; consequently, "they set about creating something else to be" (S 52). While the text more or less focuses upon the ebb and flow of this primary relationship between two females, it is Eva, the ruling matriarch of the family, who looms as an abiding influence in the lives of her progeny, and it is the death of Plum that captures the ambiguous nature of her character.

One could even argue that Eva's killing of her son is emblematic of the text's more central concerns: the gradual dismantling of the black community called Bottom by an encroaching and acquisitive white culture; the sacrificing of self that is often required of colonized members striving to survive in an oppressive society; the severing of bonds of instinctual love, be it the connection between a mother and son, or the "deepdown spooky" friendship between Sula and Nel and their temporary disruption of male discourse and male-dictated behavior by which they come to reconnect with the Wild, defining their own psycho-social boundaries, celebrating their own female interdependence and autonomy. While a relatively "minor" episode in the more or less straightforward, sequential narrative of *Sula*, a mother's "sacrificial" murder of her child becomes the "central" focus in the more innovative and technically experimental text of *Beloved*. Yet, this minor episode poignantly illuminates the paradoxical existence of black women who, like their black male counterparts, often forge experimental lives within a colonized community; both free and enslaved, women like Eva, Hannah and Sula, despite their celebration of "funk," cannot escape the ubiquitous presence of their white male oppressor. Whether it entails sending Eva's once-healthy son back to her from the War as a "damaged" drug addict, bringing the entire community of Bottom to its economic knees, or undermining the Africanist joy of "funk" with white middleclass respectability, the inescapable society at large continues to exploit those whom it has "freed."

Sula

Following a rather straightforward chronological order, *Sula* opens and closes with chapters entitled "1919" and "1965." While the intervening sections follow a sequential unfolding of events in the town of Bottom, the novel also displays a simple circularity of structure through its initial and final images: the opening retrospective gaze of the narrator reveals that the black community of Bottom, located at the top of a mountain, will now in 1965 become a white golf course to serve the residents of the town of Medallion, Ohio in the valley below; the concluding image of the novel depicts Nel's epiphanic moment, her sweet and painful realization that it is the loss of Sula, her childhood friend, that informs her profound sorrow:

> And the loss pressed down on her chest and came up into her throat. "We was girls together," she said as though explaining something. "O Lord, Sula," she cried, "girl, girl, girlgirl girl."
> It was a fine cry—loud and long—but it had no bottom and it had no top, just circles and circles of sorrow. (S 174)

Morrison connects the opening and closing images not only by alluding to a subversion of the linear concepts of "top" and "bottom" but also by underscoring the pervasive presence of "loss" that constitutes both the communal and individual lives of African-Americans. As Maureen T. Reddy observes, Sula begins and ends with images of death, the death of both a neighborhood and a friend.[78] More specifically, "if read as a historical novel," argue Gilbert and Gubar, *Sula* associates the war years with the destruction of women and their relationships:

> *Sula* begins with the portrait of Shadrack, a shell-shocked veteran of World War I and dates the rift in the friendship between Sula and Nel in 1939 and the death of Sula—whose last name is "Peace"—in 1940, one year before a large portion of the people of their town go down to death on the annual holiday Shadrack has set aside as "National Suicide Day."[79]

Framed by images of death, the text is replete with references to the seemingly inescapable violence that characterizes Western culture, from the repeated allusions to the global violence of world wars to the more concrete images of individual acts of aggression, ranging from Chicken Little's "accidental" death at the hands of the young girl Sula to the mass "suicide" of a group of residents from Bottom who die beneath the collapsing walls of a tunnel.

The images of death that frame the novel are emblematic of the grand "nigger joke" (S 4) played by white America against its black citizens: We will grant you "freedom" but not economic or social independence. Consequently, when a "good white farmer" promised to reward his slave with freedom and a piece of fertile "bottom" land in the valley in exchange for his completing "some very difficult chores," the slave was surprised to discover that the "bottom" land was in fact the "hilly land, where planting was backbreaking" (S 5). Told by the farmer that the land in the hills constitutes the "bottom of heaven" and therefore is "the best land there is," the slave happily agreed and the black community of Bottom was founded. As the narrator notes, "Freedom was easy—the farmer had no objection to that. But he didn't want to give up any land" (S 5).

Similarly, the final image of Nel's delayed encounter with her own grief over the death of Sula reflects not only the emotional barrier erected by a masculinist society that divides women but also the enforced economic dependence of women upon men in a patriarchal, capitalist structure. Both Nel and Sula always knew that traditional women "were not jealous of other women; that they were only afraid of losing their jobs" (S 119); that is to say, both women sensed that it is the fear of poverty that coerces women in a patriarchal culture to become possessive of their mates upon whom they must depend for economic security. Consequently, Nel's angry rejection of Sula for sleeping with her husband, Jude, reflects not so much Nel's deep-seated jealousy as it does her fear of poverty. Furthermore, it took Nel twenty-five years to mourn the death of her best friend and to embrace the love that she had suppressed in favor of a more conventional marriage, a marriage that left her abandoned by her husband and struggling to raise her children alone. The "joke" is on Nel, of course: for her desire to assimilate into white society and to conform to the standards of "respectability" passed down to her by her mother lead her not only to sacrifice the one genuine bond of love she had ever experienced but also to remain enslaved within the seemingly endless cycle of economic and spiritual poverty. Lured to pursue the American Dream, to sever her primal connection to a young woman with whom she could temporarily escape the patriarchal structure of a community intent upon mirroring white society, Nel ironically encounters the bleak reality awaiting many black women in contemporary America. In addition to becoming entangled in the net of a racist-induced poverty, Nel also suffers from her second-class status as a female. As Maxine Montgomery notes, "Marriage, family and the pursuit of middleclass standards of success all prove unfulfilling for Nel" primarily because these standards are grounded in the restrictive stereotype of women as "subservient, self-sacrificing beings."[80]

It is within this "circularized" linear structure where "top" and "bottom" subvert each other, where "absence" again becomes a haunting "presence" and where black females continue to eke out an existence as "free women" in a racist and sexist society, that the morally and psychologically enigmatic phenomenon of "infanticide" must be considered. To understand Eva's murder of her son, one must comprehend the rebellious and indefatigable personality of Eva herself, a woman who played her own painful "joke" on the System when she "accidentally" stepped in front of a train to collect the insurance money. Relegated to poverty and unable to care for her children, Eva resorts to self-mutilation in order to save her family. The loss of her leg and the subsequent financial settlement accord her a degree of financial independence that allows her to harbor homeless children.

A striking contrast to the more "respectable" residents of Bottom, Eva, like her daughter, Hannah, indulges her sensual appetites with an abandon that celebrates the joy of a non-violent, or "absence of bile" (S 42), association with men. Unlike their neighbors whose marriages have conformed to the stereotypic roles of male power and female subservience, Eva and Hannah's somewhat free-floating "love of maleness" does not completely compromise their autonomy or emotional independence. Although Eva "did not participate in the act of love, there was a good deal of teasing and pecking and laughter" that brought a "joy" to her face (S 41);

free to beat them in checkers and to disagree with their interpretation of news events, Eva exerts a subtle, non-threatening control over her men, a control that leaves them feeling that "somehow, in her presence, it was they who had won something" (S 41). Similarly, Hannah's "funky elegance," which prompted her to "fuck practically anything" (including her neighbors' husbands) without blindly trusting or committing herself to another person, accords her a degree of power over her own life that the other women of Bottom come to resent (S 44-45).

While both women pursue a somewhat nonconventional life style, their "love of maleness" leaves them vulnerable to a traditional dependence upon a patriarchal value system which discourages the bonding of women. Although the narrator, as Anne Mickelson notes, clearly endorses Hannah's generosity toward the men, preferring her funk to the sterility of the "good" women of Bottom,[81] the fact remains that it is precisely Hannah's inability to forge a connection with women that undermines her relationship with her own daughter, Sula. *Sula*, as Marianne Hirsch compellingly argues, can be read as a story about "missed communication" between mothers and daughters, from the matrilineal disruptions among Helene, her Creole mother and her daughter, Nel, to those of Sula, Hannah and Eva.[82] Whether it is repressing one's libidinal and emotional vitality to gain white respectability (Helene) or apparently flaunting one's eroticism and contravening traditional sexual mores (Hannah, Eva), these women remain primarily connected not to their daughters and granddaughters but to a masculinist culture that seeks to regulate female sexuality and to monitor relationships among women. As we shall see, the "experimental" life created by Sula is one that challenges patriarchal expectations of women and one that tries to combine her mother's and grandmother's appreciation of maleness with a recognition of her more fundamental femaleness. Whether or not Sula is successful in her attempt or that Morrison wholeheartedly endorses Sula's innovative "script" is debatable.

Eva's somewhat unconventional life style entails a willingness to employ violence in extreme situations. Contravening the traditional stereotype of the compliant, passive female, Eva not only harms herself but also is willing to end the life of her son in order to maintain a level of integrity for her family. Yet, while female-initiated violence ostensibly flouts a patriarchal value system that dictates female complacency and passive acceptance of society's inequities, the ultimate "joke" resides in discovering that sporadic outbursts of female aggression ultimately turn back upon the aggressor. Unable to attack that elusive monster—the System or the "Beast"—that interred her in a prison of poverty and servitude, Eva exacts a violence upon herself, temporarily beating the System financially by permanently losing a part of herself. Hirsch suggests that Eva, and later Sula, adopt male strategies of power-grabbing and in doing so reveal the male position as a "sham." Invoking Lacan's definition of femininity as a masquerade constructed in reference to male desire, Hirsch argues that by "flaunting her castration (her missing leg)," Eva "becomes the lack essential to the male posture" in order to gain a semblance of male power and thereby reveals how much of this power depends upon a masquerade.[83] That is to say, Eva's subversion of traditional gender roles—she "acts like a man" in resorting to violence—reveals that all power-roles are play-actings. While Morrison may be interested in disclosing the performative nature of gender stereotypes and the corollary that both men and women, in a fundamental way, "exert a power to disguise a powerlessness,"[84] Eva's *self*-mutilation also suggests that there remains a clear and undoubtedly societally-generated schism between women's and men's "acceptable" modes of power-grabbing. Bigger Thomas, Cholly Breedlove and Jim Trueblood direct their aggressions outwardly, displacing their anger at the "Beast" onto weaker, more vulnerable women; similar to most of the women discussed in this study, Eva has internalized her rage as a desperate gesture for survival. Her decision to sacrifice her leg in a train "accident" in order to save her family, while clever, courageous and understandable, reveals the successful yet self-damaging behavior of a woman pushed to extreme circumstances. Eva's act of self-mutilation is emblematic of the town's "decision" to yield to the pressures of white suburbanization, to take the "generous funds that have been allotted" to sacrifice Bottom and convert the area to a recreational retreat, a golf course that will undoubtedly be for "white members only." Unable to survive in a culture that has increasingly devoted itself to the acquisition of goods and property and in which they as Black Americans have been denied access to economic prosperity, both Eva and later the townspeople of Bottom have acquiesced to the lure of the "quick buck." Eva was willing to "dismantle" herself to insure her family's survival; so too does the neighborhood submit to its own demise in order to pursue the chimera of economic freedom in a racist culture.

On the surface Eva's murder of her son emerges as the sacrificial act of a woman who again "chooses" a course of action that contravenes conventional gender stereotypes but also destroys a part of herself. The death of Plum occurs somewhat early in the novel and is couched in images that again employ that uncomfortable blending of gentleness and despair that characterizes some of Morrison's other portrayals of violence. Like Shadrack who returns from the war, shell-shocked and compulsively driven to try to harness the phenomenon of death through his annual celebration of National Suicide Day, Plum comes home "blasted and permanently astonished by the events of 1917" (S 7). Abandoned by the very System that had conscripted him into the battle for "freedom," Plum is left to wander through his own dark labyrinth of drug-addiction, seeking solace not through a National Suicide Day but through his own agonizingly slow and self-induced demise: "It was Hannah who found the bent spoon black from steady cooking" (S 45), and it was Eva, his mother, who made the decision to finish what the American military had begun and end Plum's life.

Morrison allots four pages to the death of Plum and in surreal images that blend the love, discipline, frustration and pain of a parent who sees no other alternative available to her, tries to limn the horrors of a "sacrificial" act of "infanticide." Hobbling down the stairs on her crutches, Eva visits her son's room late one night where she finds him lost in a drug-induced sleep amidst the garbage and debris of half-eaten food, broken bottles and blood-tainted water. There she gathers him into her arms and allows her memory to recall his childhood laughter which has deteriorated now into the mindless "chuckles" of his hallucinatory imaginings. Cradling and rocking her "infantile" son, Eva appears as a contemporary, secularized Madonna thrust into the realities of a world intent upon the bloody sacrifice of its children. A variation of the Holy Mother as the source of spiritual nourishment and maternal care, Eva is also reminiscent of the first "earthly" mother Eve, who was sent out into the world to endure the mortality of her progeny; furthermore, as the archetypal "Great Mother" who not only gives life but takes life away,[85] Eva wields the deific power both of creation and of retributive and sacrificial death.

Morrison augments the sacrificial dimension of "infanticide" by filtering the episode through the surreal, synaesthetic images of Plum who experiences his own immolation as a release from his earth-bound anguish into the bright bliss of a baptismal rebirth:

> Plum on the rim of a warm light sleep was still chuckling. Mamma. She sure was somethin.' He felt twilight. Now there seemed to be some kind of wet light traveling over his legs and stomach with a deeply attractive smell. It wound itself—this wet light—all about him, smashing and running into his skin. He opened his eyes and saw what he imagined was the great wing of an eagle pouring a wet lightness over him. Some kind of baptism, some kind of blessing, he thought. Everything is going to be all right, it

said. Knowing that it was so he closed his eyes and sank back into the bright hole of sleep. (S 47)

As Plum lies in a fetal "snug delight," Eva ignites her kerosene-soaked child and then embarks upon "her painful journey back to the top of the house" (S 48). The matriarch of her tiny kingdom who decides the issues of life and death, and who wields the power of naming those who live in her household, Eva assumes a deific stature that accords her killing of Plum a sacrificial dimension. Critics have noted the imagery of rebirth that informs the death passage: the womb-like warm fire and secure bed from which Plum will rise like the eagle at twilight into the realm of an afterlife suggest the Africanist cyclical concept of time that "includes birth, life, death and rebirth."[86] Full of both anger and pity for a man who has regressed to an infantile dependence upon her and who, would, if he could, have tried "to get back up in [her] womb" (S 71), Eva exacts a godlike, punitive love that allowed him to "die like a man." Eva, later explaining the necessity of such drastic action, tells Hannah: "But I held him close first. Real close, Sweet Plum. My baby boy" (S 72).

Morrison's blending of anger and love, of gentleness and despair, in this female-initiated act of violence differs from the technique employed in the male acts of aggression discussed in the preceding pages. As we discovered, Morrison falters in her attempt to imbue Cholly's rape of his daughter with a positive "gift-like" quality, for his violation of Pecola is fundamentally an extension of her political violation by a society that subjugates her for being black, poor and female. While Cholly's "gift of love" succeeds only in accentuating Pecola's pain and humiliation, Eva's "sacrificial blessing" hastens Plum's inevitable death and terminates his suffering, releasing him to the joys of an afterlife. Pecola is "silenced" during the actual rape scene and the reader experiences the episode through the consciousness of the aggressor, a deliberate strategy employed by Morrison to shift the reader's attention to Cholly and away from the victim. However, the reader experiences Plum's imminent death through a drug-induced "religious" consciousness that conveys an element of joy, faith and trust, and that transforms the otherwise gruesome preparations into a ritualistic act of spiritual cleansing. Cleverly Morrison spares the reader any of the explicit details of the actual immolation, thereby muting our horror and sustaining our compassion for a mother who would courageously take the life of her son. Unlike Joe Trace, Eva "sacrifices" Plum not because she is attempting to retrieve some deepdown spooky connection to the Wild that compels her to kill in order to "keep the feeling going" but because she must alleviate the suffering of another human being. Filtered only through the consciousness of Plum, the pre-death scene leaves the reader with an impression of a mother's difficult sacrifice of her own child; while most recoil from the contemplation of such an act, Morrison has constructed the scene so as to elicit our compassion for Eva.

Yet Morrison also undermines the reader's compassion by presenting Eva at times in an ambiguous light, as someone who is both a caring mother and a punitive matriarch, who can speak in "two voices," and who must exercise a "control over," as much as a love for, the people in her domain. Like the slave masters at Sweet Home in *Beloved* who assert their control over their "chattel" by giving them all the same name—"Paul"—and eradicating each man's individuality, Eva names each of the young boys whom she has taken in "Dewey." She is willing to end the life of her most pampered, favorite child by fire, *and* she is willing to sacrifice her own life to extinguish the flames consuming Hannah, a daughter to whom she did not show much love. Enigmatic and complex, Eva manifests a degree of self-interest and self-preservation that contravenes society's image of the devout mother who should, of course, remain selfless. When explaining to Hannah her reasons for killing Plum, Eva discloses not only pity for her son but an abiding concern for her own well-being that seemingly detracts from her purely altruistic motives. The narrator tells us that "When Eva spoke at last it was with two voices":

> …he wanted to crawl back in my womb and well…I ain't got the room no more even if he could do it. There wasn't space for him in my womb. And he was crawlin' back. I had room enough in my heart, but not in my womb, not no more. I birthed him once. I couldn't do it again. He was growed, a big old thing. Godhavemercy, I couldn't birth him twice. I'd be laying here at night and he be downstairs in that room, but when I closed my eyes I'd see him…six feet tall smilin' and crawlin' up the stairs quietlike so I wouldn't hear and opening the door soft so I wouldn't hear and he'd be creepin' to the bed trying to spread my legs trying to get back up in my womb.... (S 71-72)

While this passage reveals Eva's concern for her own self-interest to be a motivating factor in the death of Plum, it does not eradicate the sacrificial dimension of the act but serves only to hold both contradictory elements in unresolvable tension in the text. Critics like Linda Wagner, Bernard Bell, and Anne Mickelson who argue that Eva's destruction of her son is either purely an "act of self-defense" against an "invader"[87] or solely an act of "maternal love"[88] fail to do justice to such an ambiguity and the attendant ambivalence it elicits from the reader who both sympathizes with Eva's compassion for her son and condemns her lethal self-interest. Hirsch more accurately suggests that Eva's double voice reflects her "double identity" and raises the issue of maternal anger as a means of mapping out a traditionally silenced female subjectivity. Embracing Kristeva's notion of the "maternal as the unspeakable," as the "locus of the semiotic," Hirsch interprets Eva's murder of Plum as a subversive articulation of maternal subjectivity.[89] The double-voice of maternal discourse, exemplified by Eva's objectified status as a mother who is expected to sacrifice her *self* to the needs and desires of the burgeoning subject or child, and her "subversive" and angry claims for her own *self*-preservation—her own status as subject—poignantly captures the tension or "self-division"[90] that perhaps characterizes maternal discourse and that reflects the paradoxical nature of this act of loving/angry "infanticide." When queried in an interview about the nature of Eva's killing of Plum, Morrison herself resisted any attempt to resolve the tension by simply evading the question. Asked directly if Plum's death was "an act of mother's love," the author responds:

> "Eva is a triumphant figure, one-legged or not. She is playing God. She maims people. But she says all of the important things."[91]

Morrison herself seems unwilling and perhaps incapable of solving the puzzle of Eva. Placed within the larger context of the political dynamics of the novel, Eva's selfish/selfless sacrifice of her son constitutes yet another example of the paradoxical pursuit of integrity through the "dismantling" of parts of the self or community that characterize the inhabitants of Bottom both individually and collectively. The "sacrificing" of a leg and then a son and finally an entire neighborhood to survive in an white-male dominated economic system are the ever-widening concentric "circles of sorrow" that engulf those who have been consigned to the margins of society.

While Eva and Hannah both lead somewhat atypical lives within the social structure of Bottom, it is Sula who presents a more rebellious and radical departure from the town's mores and who confronts the reader with an interesting variation on the theme of women-initiated violence. Like her mother and grandmother, she too appreciates "maleness," but unlike Eva and Hannah, Sula embraces an experimental "femaleness" in an attempt to extricate herself from the restrictions of "traditional womanhood as defined by maternity and enslavement to the family."[92] Her repudiation of the stereotypic female roles of wife and mother constitutes a threat not only to the white society at large but to the black community of Bottom that eventually casts her in the role of "witch" and town pariah. Upon returning to Bottom as an adult after a ten-year absence during which she attends college and has numerous affairs with both black and white men, Sula has the temerity to live among the residents of Bottom as a single, independent woman. She does not hesitate to renew her friendship with Nel and sleep with Nel's husband, Jude. It is the latter event, her brief sexual liaison with Jude and her consternation at the hurt and anger that such a betrayal engenders for Nel, that most clearly reveals the extent to which Sula has jettisoned the conventional tenets of male-female relationships. To understand the sincerity of Sula's surprise, one must consider the formative events of her childhood during which the seeds of her subsequent rebellion took root. For it is during her adolescent connection with Nel, a connection sealed by maternal rejection, violence and death, that Sula "decides" to escape the traditional adult life awaiting her in Bottom.

As the daughter of a mother whose love of maleness seemed to preclude an ability to demonstrate affection and love for women, Sula suffers the sting of Hannah's maternal rejection by bonding with her best friend, Nel. At the age of twelve, Sula overhears her mother speaking to one of the neighbors about children: "You love her, like I love Sula. I just don't like her. That's the difference" (S 80). Like her own mother, Eva, whose love of maleness predisposed her to her sons rather than to Hannah, Sula's mother, through her "transgressive maternal speech,"[93] displays an ambivalence toward her own female child that characterizes the contradictory attitudes towards women in a patriarchal culture. As critic Susan Willis observes:

> Ambivalence is the possibility of separating liking from loving. It is the way women experience contradiction in heterosexual relationships—precisely because they are male-determined in a society which valorizes maleness. And as children are for the most part born of heterosexual relationships, they are the living embodiments of the contradictions that have shaped their mother's life possibilities and sexuality.[94]

Hannah's ambivalence embodies not only the emotional contradiction plaguing women in a patriarchal society but also the attendant psychological fragmentation that impedes their "quest for wholeness"[95] or integrity. Often loved but not liked, women come to see themselves as disunified beings who in an extreme case like that of Violet Trace experience multiple selves or, like Eva, speak in two voices. While multiplicity, contradiction and marginality may indeed be characteristics of the potentially subversive power of the semiotic that is repressed by the symbolic Law of the Father, they also limn the political status of the "feminine" in a masculinist culture as that which has been fragmented and relegated to the periphery. It is precisely this fragmentation and contradiction that Sula and Nel try to circumvent through their "intense" (S 52) symbiotic friendship.

"Daughters of distant mothers and incomprehensible fathers" (S 52), Sula and Nel begin a relationship that will: 1) enable them to sustain the onslaught of threatening males; 2) carry them to the deepdown spooky region of a love that aspires to a mystical unity; and 3) reveal their capacity for a violent revenge against those forces which seek to rend them asunder. Confronted one day by the aggressive taunts of four poor white Irish boys who themselves had been the objects of derision and scorn by more respectable whites, Sula, with Nel standing by her side, manages to outwit the "predators" by wounding herself with a knife:

> Sula squatted down in the dirt road and put everything down on the ground: her lunchpail, her reader, her mittens, her slate. Holding the knife in her right hand, she pulled the slate toward her and pressed her left forefinger down hard on its edge...She slashed off only the tip of her finger. The four boys stared open-mouthed at the wound and the scrap of flesh, like a button mushroom, curling in the cherry blood that ran into the corners of the slate.
> Sula raised her eyes to them. Her voice was quiet."If I can do that to myself, what you suppose I'll do to you?" (S 54-55)

Very much the granddaughter of Eva, Sula paradoxically adopts the prevailing mode of male violence to mask her own vulnerability and to maintain her integrity by turning that violence upon herself in an act of self-mutilation. Again, however, while female-initiated violence in a patriarchal culture contravenes the conventional norms and may temporarily stun and "disarm" those who witness it, such actions constitute sporadic and ineffective defenses against a systemic and inveterate misogyny.

Sula and Nel's relationship provides them with only a temporary haven from the intrusive patriarchal order and introduces them to another realm of communication that transcends linear, verbal discourse. Immediately following Sula's overhearing of her mother's dislike for her, Sula flees with Nel to the river where the two girls experience an intensely sensual, non-verbal connection with both the natural world and each other:

> They ran in the sunlight, creating their own breeze, which pressed their dresses into their damp skin. Reaching a kind of square of four leaf-locked trees which promised cooling, they flung themselves into the four-cornered shade to taste their lip sweat and contemplate the wildness that had come upon them so suddenly. (S 57-58)

Of interest here is the allusion to that concept of the Wild that Morrison develops more fully in *Jazz*. "Fugitives" from a patriarchal society that mutes the female call of Wild, Nel and Sula are still young and "rebellious" enough to hear the "semiotic" call of their primal mythic mother, a voice that has been long silenced in their own biological mothers. As they lay in the grass, "their bodies stretched away from each other at a 180-degree angle," they begin to feel the "pleasant discomfort" of a pubescent sexuality. Replete with images that lend credibility to Barbara Smith's contention that Sula and Nel's relationship is "suffused with an erotic romanticism,"[96] the passage seems to point to the symbolic burying of the male sexual principle by two women who have temporarily merged into a mystical female unity, and achieved a playful "wholeness" and harmonious integrity denied them in the outside patriarchal world:

> Sula lifted her head and joined Nel in the grass play. In concert, without ever meeting each other's eyes, they stroked the blades up and down, up and down. Nel found a thick twig and with her thumbnail, pulled away its bark until it was stripped to a smooth, creamy innocence. Sula looked about and found one too. When both twigs were undressed Nel moved easily to the next stage and began tearing up rooted grass to make a bare spot of earth. (S 58)

Symbolically divested of the societal accretions that accord "maleness" power and associate "femaleness" with weakness, the phallic twig becomes for the two girls a tool which they can manipulate to unearth the vaginal cavern of their primal mother that connects them to the Wild:

> ...[Nel] poked her twig rhythmically and intensely into the earth, making a small neat hole that grew deeper and wider with the least manipulation of her twig. Sula copied her and soon each had a hole the size of a cup...Together they worked until the two holes were one and the same. (S 58)

Temporarily "lost" in their unconscious efforts to excavate their mythic beginning and achieve a permanent integrity in the male-dominated world,

Nel and Sula are painfully reminded of the futility of their efforts when, with the breaking of the twig, they are thrust back to an awareness of the defilement of this seemingly pristine setting. With "disgust" they both throw their twigs into the hole and gather up the surrounding debris and garbage, signatures of a culture that has defiled the Wild as it has women:

> Nel saw a bottle cap and tossed it in as well. Each then looked around for more debris to throw into the hole: paper, bits of glass, butts of cigarettes, until all the small defiling things they could find were collected there. Carefully they replaced the soil and covered the entire grave with uprooted grass. (S 58-59)

Both Sula and Nel symbolically strip male sexuality of its domination and temporarily become the "manipulators of the tool," not to control and subjugate others but to unearth the origins of their own femaleness. Like Dorcas, who with Joe "worked the stick of the world," Sula and Nel temporarily control their own destinies. That they remain ultimately frustrated in their attempt to connect with the Wild merely underscores the contradictory position in which they find themselves in a culture that loves but does not like them.

It is at the height of their "unspeakable restlessness and agitation" (S 59) that they encounter a representative of the male world, an "intruder" who perhaps elicits from both girls an unconscious desire for revenge against a system that will not let them achieve autonomy and wholeness. Sula's "accidental" killing of Chicken Little, the young boy whom she and Nel both taunt and help down from a tree immediately prior to his drowning, captures not only "the same ambivalence that Sula is made to feel about herself"[97] but also the sweet pain of revenge that she, like Cholly and Joe Trace, can experience by directing a hatred of the System against one of its more vulnerable members. Hirsch correctly maintains that Chicken's death is a "signal of Sula and Nel's rebellious, if as yet unconscious, refusal of adult heterosexuality and motherhood as they perceive it, as a clear refusal of the plot written for them."[98] The drowning of Chicken Little is both "accidental" and purposeful: what starts out as a playful romp with a four-year-old child—"Sula picked him up by his hands and swung him outward then around and around"—turns into a "passive" act of aggression—"When he slipped from her hands and sailed away out over the water they could still hear his bubbly laughter" (S 60-61). Neither girl attempts to save him, and while Sula does not actively "let go" of his hands, she creates the situation that results in his hands slipping away from hers.

Morrison has again portrayed that uncomfortable blending of love and hatred, of "frightened joy" and, in this case, of accident and intentionality, in an act of violence that captures both the victimization and free agency of the aggressor. Similar to Joe's killing of Dorcas in which the aggressor seeks to distance himself magically from the violence he perpetrates by projecting his own agency onto the weapon—"the gun went off"—the narrator in Sula muddles the issue of moral culpability by soft-pedaling the active role of the agent in Chicken Little's death—Sula did not let go of his hands; rather Chicken Little's hands slipped from hers. Furthermore, like Cholly's rape of Pecola, Sula's murder of Chicken Little starts out as a playful romp that deteriorates into a thinly-disguised act of aggression. Yet, unlike Cholly's rape of his daughter and Joe Trace's murder of Dorcas, Sula's killing of Chicken Little is far more "passive" and "accidental" in nature. She does not actively "track" him down as prey; and we, as readers, are denied immediate access to any of her possible internal musings that might reveal a premeditated contemplation of violence. Like Cholly, Sula is a "dangerously free" and impulsive character, given to acting on the whim of the moment; however, unlike Cholly, whose consciousness provides the perspective through which the rape is filtered and thus reveals his state of mind, Sula remains rather opaque to the reader during Chicken Little's death. Morrison's narrative strategy serves to heighten Sula's enigmatic nature. At the same time, however, the fact that Nel later recalls their "feeling good to see him fall" (S 170) points to a purposeful intent and suggests a temporarily self-satisfying yet ultimately ineffective gesture of revenge against the "Beast."

The ambiguous nature of Sula's character is again portrayed in an act of "violence by omission" in which she assumes a posture of total passivity and fails to act to help save Hannah from burning to death. Eva's belief that Sula was not paralyzed but rather interested in seeing her mother burn to death is confirmed later when Sula recalls the incident: "I stood there watching her burn and was thrilled. I wanted her to keep on jerking like that, to keep on dancing" (S 147). Sula enjoys the agonizingly slow death of her mother perhaps because she, at the age of twelve, is childishly exacting her own vicarious revenge against the person who could not like her, the woman who, as another representative of a culture that marginalizes the feminine and fragments female identity, deserves, in the eyes of a child, to die; yet, one wonders about the emotional/moral makeup of a child who could enjoy watching her mother burn to death.

Morrison's images of female-initiated violence are so fraught with ambiguity that one senses a discomfort on the part of the author with the very linking of women and aggression. Displaced or internalized, accidental or sacrificial, female-initiated violence for Morrison must wear a disguise that belies either an unacceptable self-interest or a dangerous rage against an indomitable "Beast." When Morrison depicts women who engage in "clean" acts of violence, that is, acts of aggression which are unambiguously aimed directly at the oppressor—the "negress" who sliced the Swede's face, the woman who stabbed the iceman—she does so only in passing, as if she herself can apprehend such female fury only out of the corner of her eye and must, like the ever-so-busy hairdressers in *Jazz*, repress the dangerous power of such unleashed rage.

"When creating Sula," Morrison states, "I had in mind a woman of force" who is "more powerful after she is dead than when she was alive."[99] While lauding such a "woman of force," Morrison also reveals certain moral reservations concerning Sula: she takes exception to Sula's "unbelievable" and cruel gesture of later confining Eva to an old folks' home (S 255) and notes Sula's basic lack of kindness.[100] Morrison's ambivalence toward Sula may point to what Hirsch identifies as an ambivalence toward women who "reject unconditionally the lives and stories of their mothers."[101] Although Sula is the character who most courageously sets out to break free from the gender expectations of her culture, she ultimately fails to write a "script" that will enable her to realize her professional aspiration of becoming an artist or to bond with Nel as an adult and to begin to erect that "feminist community" that they had unconsciously embraced as children that day by the river.

The ambivalence that Morrison displays towards Sula, both in her comments and in her portrayal, may also reflect the author's reluctance to endorse fully a woman who is both forceful and "violent," a woman who can trust her instincts but remain oblivious to the pain of others, a person who basically lacks the capacity to empathize. Having shared everything with Nel as a child, Sula "innocently" sleeps with Jude, assuming that he too would be communal property; yet, her failure to understand that Nel has succumbed to the societal pressures of marriage and motherhood and embraced a more traditional value system reveals a certain moral blindness and insensitivity to the feelings of her best friend. "I like people like Sula,"[102] Morrison states in an interview: perhaps Morrison's discomfort with violent women underscores the fundamental ambiguity that informs the character of Sula and reflects the author's inability to love the character she likes.

Beloved

Morrison's most poignant and perhaps controversial image of female-initiated violence occurs in the technically innovative novel *Beloved*. Like *Sula*, *Beloved* presents the reader with the horrifying act of maternal infanticide; yet, unlike the more conventional, linear narrative that discloses the killing of Plum Boy as one event among others within a sequential unfolding of events, the inversion and interweaving of past, present and future in *Beloved* accord the murder of *Beloved* a "central" position in the novel. Bonnie Winsbro observes: "The street number 124 suggests [that] the presence of Sethe's third child is most powerfully felt because of her glaring absence from the house on Bluestone Road."[103] Haunting every page of the text as an absent presence, as a force from the grave that comes to life in the present to compel those living to come to terms with their "rememory" of the past, Beloved intrudes into the house at #124 Bluestone outside Cincinnati in 1873 as a "trace" of both her mother's desperate love and a slave culture's inveterate hatred.

Invoking a more lyrical and at times daringly experimental language than that employed in her previous novels, Morrison, as she will in *Jazz*, requires the reader to enter the text as a co-creator of meaning, relinquishing now and then the security of conventional linguistic structures to embrace a non-linear and, according to some critics, a uniquely feminine mode of discourse. Citing the theories of Nancy Chodorow and Carol Gilligan, Barbara Schapiro has argued that "the fluidity of boundaries" between fantasy and reality, the "mutable, non-sequential time structure" and the "continuously altering narrative perspective" that characterize *Beloved* reflect a uniquely female mode of perception that is derived from the preservation of an original identity and pre-oedipal bondedness between self and mother.[104] Lorraine Liscio and Barbara Rigney have similarly argued that the language of *Beloved* invokes the fluidity, the *jouissance*, of female speech, what Cixous labels the "playfulness" of language and what Kristeva, refusing to collapse language into biology but rather positing a "feminine" mode of being and writing as available to both males and females,[105] refers to as the semiotic "non-sense of sense, laughter";[106] the novel recreates the mother and young child's "anarchic semiosis" through its "picking up and letting go" of incomplete fragments of individual stories in which "place and time collapse into each other."[107]

Morrison's attempt to inscribe the dynamics of the pre-oedipal bond between mother and daughter in a discursive mode that subverts the traditional logic of symbolic discourse is aimed not only at "disrupting the symbolic white schoolteacherly language that kills,"[108] itself a precursor of the racist and sexist rhetoric that would later inform such texts as the *Dick and Jane* reader"; it also seeks to give a voice to the often-silenced female slave's experiences. As Elizabeth House recognizes, "Morrison's Pulitzer Prize-winning fifth novel is about the atrocities slavery wrought both upon a *mother's* need to love and care for her children as well as a child's need for a family."[109] It is within a non-linear and at times fluid mode of discourse that Morrison seeks to resurrect the "underside" of historical events, the elusive emotional and psychic truths that are often crushed beneath the weighty preponderance of chronology, tractable data and hard facts in conventional histories. Similar to Joan Didion who attempts to *re*-construct an identity from the shards of memories of "what it felt like to be me," Morrison strives to *re*-collect the repressed, painful (re)memories that coalesce around an act of infanticide, and, in conjunction with the reader, enter what Liscio refers to as the otherwise "uninscribed life experiences" of female slaves.[110]

More specifically, *Beloved* veers from a "more conventional daughterly perspective to a maternal one."[111] Just as Eva's murder of her son may reflect the explosive assertion of a mother's claim to subjecthood that has so often been silenced in literature, so too may Sethe's decision to kill her children, when these children are seen as extensions of her *self*, emerge as a paradoxically destructive gesture of self-preservation and of self-determination that ironically challenges what Marianne Hirsch would call the "hierarchy of motherhood over selfhood."[112] Eva's murderous anger speaks in a double voice, both as the individual's response to preserve the integrity of the self that is being threatened by Plum's regressive, emotional return to the womb, and as the mother's desire to provide some closure to the terminal suffering of her child who has served the militaristic needs of the white oppressor and then been discarded onto the junk heap of drug addiction. As a text that, in part, explores the multiple voice of the maternal, *Beloved* more fully focuses upon Sethe's anger to reveal a mother's claim of subjecthood and, perhaps, to articulate more clearly the depths of Eva's inchoate rage against a racist culture that has traditionally denied mothers autonomy. Hirsch explains:

> Sethe's story—her life under slavery, the conception and care of her children in the most dire conditions, her escape and liberation and her desperately violent and loving act of infanticide—provides, in a sense, the background for the unspoken anger of Eva.[113]

While Morrison may invoke unconventional modes of disclosure, thereby revealing her awareness of postmodernist literary strategies, she never loses sight of the plight of the female slave as it unfolds within its historical context. Similar to the texts of Barthelme, Didion and Pynchon, *Beloved* and *Jazz*, while self-conscious artifacts that play with the possibilities of alternative speech, also point beyond themselves to the socio-political milieu from which they spring, a cultural milieu whose fundamental underpinning is an often "comic" but deleterious misogyny. Clearly unfolding within the framework of this country's slave past, *Beloved* is, as Deborah Horvitz notes, "so grounded in historical reality that it could be used to teach American history classes."[114] Consequently, critics like Liscio and Rigney correctly emphasize both the self-referential and the historical aspects of Morrison's *Beloved*, a text that pays homage to both the physical and the "psychic" deaths that are the legacy of slavery.[115]

The centripetal event of the novel—the murder of the two-year-old Beloved by her mother Sethe—is based upon one of those hard, indisputable facts in the "folk journey of Black America" that is chronicled in *The Black Book*, a project that Morrison edited for Random House.[116] Sethe's actual historical counterpart is a woman named Margaret Garner, who, like Sethe, murdered her child rather than see her returned to slavery. Morrison freely alters the "facts" of Margaret Garner's story, for unlike her historical predecessor, Sethe is neither tried for the murder of her child nor returned to her slave master.[117] Presented within the gradual unfolding of repressed "rememories," the murder of Beloved by her mother pays homage not only to the "underside" or untold emotional "truth" hidden in the factual account of Margaret Garner but also to the otherwise silenced "truths" of "the sixty million and more" lives lost to slavery to whom the book is dedicated.

The novel opens in 1873 in a little town outside of Cincinnati, Ohio. Living at House #124 are Sethe, her daughter Denver, and the angry ghost of her slain child whom Sethe had murdered some seventeen years earlier. Her mother-in-law dead and her two sons gone, Sethe has retreated into a numbing day-to-day existence, fleeing the painful memories of the past and avoiding the burdensome emptiness of the future. When Paul D escapes from the Sweet Home Plantation in Kentucky where Sethe and her husband, Halle, had been slaves some twenty years earlier, he exorcises the vengeful spirit from the house only to see it re-incarnated as a young, eighteen-year-old woman who has named herself Beloved. Moving into #124 with Sethe, Denver and Paul D, Beloved, through a series of probing questions and preternatural knowledge of the critical occurrences and objects in Sethe's life, re-awakens Sethe's repressed re-memories of her slave past and of the pivotal act of infanticide.

Beloved is a jealous and spiteful presence who demands the undivided attention and affection of her mother; consequently, she intrudes into the flourishing sexual relationship between Sethe and Paul D by not only literally seducing him and eventually driving him away, but also figuratively "seducing" her mother. An eighteen-year-old body inhabited by the spirit of a two-year-old murdered child, Beloved, at one point, attempts to monopolize her mother's affection through an infantile narcissism that manifests itself in a series of sensual kisses that, as critic David Lawrence points outs, forces Sethe up "against the wall of the incest taboo."[118] First enthralled by Beloved's tender kisses on her neck—Sethe did not know how "to stop and not love the look or feel of the lips that kept on kissing" (B 98)—Sethe is then repulsed by the implications of such sensuality and "said to her, stern and frowning, 'You too old for that'" (B 98).

Through a series of flashbacks and inverted temporal sequences in which the narrative moves at times seamlessly in and out of the various consciousnesses of Sethe, Beloved, Paul D, Denver, Baby Suggs, and an omniscient voice, the text gradually discloses the key details of Sethe's past, including the murder of her "crawling already? baby." The daughter of a nameless slave woman whose milk was used to nurse white children and who was later hanged, Sethe grows up at "Sweet Home" where she eventually "marries" Halle, one of the black farmhands who, along with Sixo, Paul F, Paul A and Paul D, plan an escape to freedom. Pregnant with Denver, Sethe manages to escape alone and arrives at Baby Suggs' house outside Cincinnati, where her other three children, Howard, Buglar and "crawling already? baby," have been hiding. When the slave hunters, led by Schoolteacher, the master of "Sweet Home," track Sethe down, she attempts to kill all of her children rather than return them to Kentucky, but succeeds only in slitting the throat of her two-year-old "crawling already? baby." Convinced that "something was wrong with this creature" who would murder its young, Schoolteacher decides to relinquish his claims to Sethe and the surviving three children. Sethe spends some time in jail and then returns to Baby Suggs who, having witnessed the slaughter of one of her grandchildren, retreats into an almost catatonic contemplation of colors until her death.

While this linear reconstruction of the story does not do justice to the convoluted and meandering revelations of the narrative itself, it does provide a skeletal outline of the critical "factual" details pertinent to the murder of Beloved by her mother. However, the emotional "truths" that constitute the underside of this act of infanticide can only be apprehended through an understanding of the key emotional experiences in Sethe's slave past, isolated but critical events that for her coalesce in the knowledge of the heart to reveal the unbearable horrors of bestial servitude awaiting her offspring. Unlike the other female victimized aggressors considered in this chapter, Sethe seems to face a moral dilemma that for the most part transcends her own immediate self-interest or self-gratification. She is not a punitive mother who, like Eva, recoils from the encumbrances of a dependent child, nor does she like Sula "accidentally" kill a young male child who intrudes upon a feminized edenic experience with another female.

"Sethe's flaw," one critic argues, is that "she loves her children too much," for "excessive mother love" can be both "empowering" and destructive."[119] Quite deliberate in her intent to kill her children rather than send them back to a life-in-death existence in slavery, Sethe becomes a "prototype of [Euripedes'] Medea"[120] who slays her two sons rather than send them off with Jason and his new wife where they will meet almost certain death once he has fathered another child of royal blood. Yet, Sethe's motives are even more pure than those of Medea, for the latter's commission of infanticide is partially motivated to inflict emotional pain upon Jason who at the time valued his progeny as his patrilineal successors.

Morrison has indeed presented the reader with a clear moral dilemma facing a mother: either quickly end the life of a two-year-old daughter or consign her to the seemingly interminable life-in-death humiliation of slavery. Her dilemma somewhat parallels Sophie's in Styron's Holocaust novel, *Sophie's Choice*, for in both instances a mother must face the agonizing choice between the life and death of her children. Sophie's choice, forced upon her by a sadistic doctor at Auschwitz, entails her choosing either her son or daughter for the gas chamber; her refusal to choose would result in the gassing of both children. Sethe, on the other hand, reacts less to an immediate threat of death but rather to the more prolonged process of schoolteacher's sadistic dehumanization awaiting her children, and generates her own decision to end their lives. Yet, like the images of violence considered in the texts of Pynchon, both situations limn the unique moral and psychological atrocities committed against women and children in patriarchal, militant states, atrocities that further generate many of the complications that inform the issues of maternal choices and responsibilities. *Medea*, *Sophie's Choice*, *Sula* and *Beloved* all tackle the overwhelming complexities of what Gilbert and Gubar would call "the moral responsibilities enmeshed in the metaphysics of maternity."[121] It is a metaphysics, however, always already inscribed within and subject to patriarchal disourse and control. Forever haunted by their dead children, both Sethe and Sophie pay dearly for their "choices," the latter by destroying herself through suicide and Sethe by almost "losing" herself to the devouring revenge of a destructive ghost.

Profoundly sensitive to the enormity of Sethe's "choice" and its resounding moral implications, Morrison approaches the novel's pivotal incident gradually and rather indirectly; she prepares the reader for the seemingly impossible task of tackling the moral question by interspersing the narrative with discrete but cumulative images of white male-initiated violence against Sethe that disclose the inescapable degradations of slavery and the unique horrors awaiting black women. Of the many revelations throughout the text, three are clearly emblematic of the racist misogyny inherent in the institution of slavery: the opening image of Sethe's sexual bartering of her body in exchange for the letters to be engraved on her dead child's tombstone; her rape by "nephew" and other slave bosses at Sweet Home; and Sethe's overhearing Schoolteacher's lesson on the duality of her animal-human nature. Each incident underscores her unique vulnerability to male-initiated violence within a culture that dehumanizes her for being both black and female.

Early in the novel, Morrison's omniscient narrator filters an incident through Sethe's perspective that poignantly reveals the "psychic death" through objectification that plagued Sethe's existence as a black woman. Unable to pay for a proper headstone for her "crawling already? baby," Sethe agreed to "ten minutes" of sex with the "engraver" who in turn chiseled out one word from the minister's eulogy—"beloved." According to the "chiseler," this act constituted a "gift" on his part—"You got ten minutes I'll do it for free" (B 5)—implying, of course that the body of a black woman was not even a worthy exchange for his ten-minute labor. Driven to humiliate herself before the white master so that she could memorialize her dead child and assuage those in the community who had condemned her, Sethe submits not only to the sexual degradation by the engraver but also to the voyeuristic sadism of his son:

> She thought [one word] would be enough, rutting among the headstones with the engraver, his young son looking on, the anger in his face so old; the appetite in it quite new. That should certainly be enough. Enough to answer one more preacher, one more abolitionist and a town full of disgust. (B 5)

Reminiscent of the image of the black woman Sarah in *V.* whose sexual objectification by the white *Schachtmeister* is underscored by her being pressed against the hard cold stone, Sethe's ten-minute debasement occurs against the "cool of unchiseled headstones...her knees wide open as any grave" (B 4-5). Like Sula and Dorcas, and even Julie, from Barthelme's *The Dead Father*, women have learned to mortify themselves in exchange for a temporary wielding of the "stick of power"; for Sethe, the literal power to name and inscribe her message resides in the hand of the white engraver, an emblematic image of the novel's pervading concern for the silencing of (black) female voices by a (white) male-dominated culture. Julie must relinquish control over her own body to Tom, who inscribes his mark of male ownership of her stomach, in exchange for safety from the sexually anarchic crowd; Sethe, as David Lawrence notes, must temporarily "kill off her own body to purchase the text that she thinks will bring her peace."[122] Ironically this incident occurs after her murder of Beloved, yet in this convoluted novel that emphasizes the circularity of experience and that subverts the linear unfolding of events, Sethe's sexual humiliation at the graveside serves to illuminate the chronologically earlier infanticide. Morrison has cleverly introduced the later graveside incident early in the novel, prior to the revelation of the infanticide, in order to underscore the atemporal nature of the mother-child bond. As Sethe reveals, the submission to the engraver's demands, though only ten minutes, was "longer than life" and occurred as another sacrificial act signifying the immeasurable depth of a mother's love for her child, a love that transcends the parameters of earthly time. While the graveside incident limns the male prerogative of inscription through the literal wielding of the instrument that has often been used to "chisel" women out of their power to write their own discourse, the rape of Sethe by white men at "Sweet Home" metaphorically captures the male silencing of the female voice.

During her stay at "Sweet Home," Sethe, pregnant with Denver, was sexually accosted by the nephews of Schoolteacher who not only perhaps raped her but sucked the milk from her breasts that she had been giving to her "crawling already? baby." When she informed on the boys, Schoolteacher had one of them whip her so that her wounds formed a "tree" of scars on her back. This incident is first revealed by Sethe to Paul D in the present time of the novel and points to her embarking upon the process of rememory by which she will eventually come to unearth the agony of a past so long repressed.

This pivotal experience in the life of a slave woman has been seized upon by critics who are quick to elucidate the symbolic significance of a mother's milk being taken from her by a rapacious group of white men. Barbara Rigney sees in this incident the symbolic violation of the "sacred state of motherhood" and the "African spiritual values which, for Morrison, that state represents";[123] Barbara Schapiro links the stolen milk to a severed matrilineal connection that spans three generations of slave women and that explains Sethe's absence of self-identity which derives from her being deprived as an infant of her own mother's milk: nursing milk is symbolic of the mother-child bond and if Sethe has "no nursing milk to call her own, she feels without a self to call her own."[124] Lorraine Liscio interprets Sethe's milk as reflecting a "subversive" mode of semiotic discourse meant to disrupt the "white schoolteacherly language that kills,"[125] a maternal mode of discourse that must be violently silenced by the prevailing symbolic law of the father.

While all of these interpretations serve to illuminate the unique susceptibility of black women to white male violence, none posits this violation as a contributing factor influencing Sethe's decision to silence her own children and sever the matrilineal thread. Just as the spilled menstrual blood in Didion's texts served as a trope for the violent eradication of the female powers of reproductivity, so too does the rapacious image of Sethe's milk being sucked from her breasts by "two boys with mossy teeth" (B 70) metaphorically drive home the vampiric consumption of women's procreative and nurturing force. Didion's menstrual blood is the "red ink" by which women inscribe their own message and which is often violently spilled by patriarchal aggression; Sethe's milk is the "white ink"[126] by which she can inscribe her own message, and it represents, perhaps, her unique power of pre-oedipal, semiotic bonding with the child, a bonding whose adherence to cyclical time and "disorder" is eventually repressed by the linear, goal-directed symbolic order.[127]

Just as the black ink she makes with her own hands is eventually used by the slavemasters to undermine her integrity and self-identity, so too is her milk stolen from her to erase the maternal signature. While Sethe attempts to explain this uniquely female form of degradation to Paul D, she keeps emphasizing not the beating or the rape but rather the theft of her milk, a point which, as Liscio notes,[128] escapes Paul D (B 34) who, filtering the experience through his own experience as a male slave, focuses on the beating:

> "They used cowhide on you!?
> "And they took my milk."

"They beat you and you was pregnant?"
"And they took my milk!" (B 17)

That this incident serves to influence Sethe's decision to reach first for her daughter in the sacrifice of her children is subtly suggested by Morrison through the death-scene image that mingles Sethe's nursing milk with the blood of her "crawling already? baby." Covered with the blood of her slain daughter, Sethe must still nurse her youngest child, Denver, who "takes her mother's milk right along with the blood of her sister" (B 152). The intermingling of maternal milk, a life-nourishing fluid, and the sacrificial blood of a child is an image that captures the paradox of Sethe's murderous love, and suggests, as Sethe herself points out, that she tried to send her children to a place where "they would be safe" (B 163), to "the other side" (B 200).

The image also serves to undermine any attempt to reach a simplistic resolution of the moral dilemma underlying Sethe's act. The patriarchal control of the institution of motherhood, comically alluded to in *The Dead Father* and more tragically delineated in both *Play It As It Lays* and *Gravity's Rainbow*, is thrust into stark relief in *Beloved*. Circumscribed within both a masculinist *and* racist culture, black motherhood is subject to the doubly egregious assaults of a sexist objectification and a racist sub-speciation. To divorce Sethe's act of infanticide from its socio-political context and facilely condemn her for transgressing an immutable moral dictate is to gloss over the resonant ambiguities of the text and its images. If Sethe is "guilty" of viewing her children as property over which she attemtps to exert control and to decide the issues of life and death, perhaps she, like Jim in *The Adventures of Huckleberry Finn* who comes to see himself as a piece of property with a certain monetary value, has internalized the culture's reduction of all slaves to property to be bought and sold. Always already inscribed within a patriarchal discourse that controls and objectifies women, the "lyrical images" of black motherhood in *Beloved* are, as Gilbert and Gubar explain, "contaminated by images that evoke the horrors of slavery."[129] To argue, as does Deborah Horvitz, that "either Sethe must be held accountable for Beloved's death or the institution of slavery alone killed the child,"[130] is to ignore the complexities inherent in such images. The image of Sethe's milk underscores her female power to create and nourish life; the blood of her child, however, points not just to her power to end life but also to the intrusive violence by white male slavemasters who seek to co-opt the procreative capacity of black women as they do domesticated animals so as to produce more chattel. Among those arriving at Baby Suggs' to retrieve Sethe and her children are the nephew who had stolen her milk (B 150) and the schoolteacher who, as we shall see, had stolen her humanity (B 163), both painful reminders to Sethe of the humiliation awaiting her daughters.

Morrison's images bespeak a "contamination" by the forces of a racist culture and underscore the ubiquity and insidiousness of the prevailing discourse, of what Sally Robinson has described as that "historical containment" that "imprisons black women in discourses of gender and race."[131] Yet, despite such contamination and historical confinement, black women can, as Robinson points out, cleverly articulate their subjectivity even within the restrictions of traditional narrative expectations. For, if the black woman is "the linchpin of a complex representational system where race and gender interlock to ensure the hegemony of the white man as subject of culture and power,"[132] then one effective strategy to insure the articulation of female subjectivity and to defy total female objectification entails "speaking" subversively even within the confines of the prevailing ideology. To disrupt narrative expectations, to present images of black women who subvert the traditional stereotypes, is to undermine the authority of conventional discourse. Just as Violet's refusal to explain her violent act to the authorities serves to undermine authority, Sethe's act of infanticide stuns Schoolteacher, and her refusal to explain her actions—the silence that she drapes over the murderous act like a shroud—emerges as an indecipherable enigma to her own community. As Winsbro correctly observes, Sethe never felt any compulsion to explain or justify her act of infanticide; she never sought understanding or approval from any perceived authority figure, whether it was the white "justice" system or her own black community.[133] Like Violet, Sethe, therefore, temporarily subverts "culturally regulated narrative possibilities"[134] and paradoxically, in her rage and subsequent silence, manages to speak to the reader.

What Sethe tells us is that we must not reduce her actions to a simplistic either/or explanation but rather approach an understanding of her act of infanticide cautiously with the heart as well as with logic. Free to allow her children to return to a life of dehumanizing servitude, Sethe *and* the institution of slavery are *both* responsible for the death of her child. Morrison, herself, resists any attempt to offer a facile resolution of the moral dilemma, suggesting that Sethe "did the right thing, but she didn't have the right to do it."[135] When Sethe does finally attempt to explain to Paul D the motivation for killing Beloved, we sense that he too does not plumb the emotional depths of her response but rather reduces it to a simplistic and logical distinction between animal and human behavior. Paul D rebukes her: "What you did was wrong, Sethe," and argues that because she is not an animal deprived of the capacity for reason, she could have figured out another way to solve the problem. Perhaps echoing the sentiments of many readers, Paul D's observations again are being filtered through the experiences of a black male slave who, while undergoing his own unique form of torture and degradation, was spared the humiliation of sexual assault and its attendant objectification. Unencumbered by a love for and the needs of dependent children, and "free" to take care of only himself, Paul D remains somewhat insensitive to the complexity of the situation that had confronted Sethe.

Paul D's observation that Sethe, possessing the capacity for reason, could have envisioned an alternative to the sacrificing of her children, connects to yet another crucial image in the ongoing process of Sethe's dehumanization as a black female slave. Again, as in *Sula*, a young girl overhears someone's hurtful comments about her, comments that serve to dissociate the child from herself, to undermine her integrity and her humanity. Sula suffered the painful recognition of a patriarchal culture's ambivalence toward women when she overheard her mother's claim that she could love but not like her daughter; Sethe, as a young girl living at "Sweet Home," overheard the racist/misogynistic message of white phallic discourse straight from the master's mouth. Schoolteacher, the master of "Sweet Home" who was intent upon exercising absolute rule over his slaves by showing them that "definitions belonged to the definers—not the defined" (B 190), one day was instructing his nephews as to the emotional and physical makeup of their slaves. Each boy was evidently given a particular slave to analyze, and by making a chart with the ink that Sethe herself had made, each "definer" proceeded to split the integrity of the "defined" by listing the animal characteristics on the right and the human characteristics on the left (B 193). When Sethe overhears one of the boys analyzing her characteristics and features, she is suddenly confronted with the culture's explicit expression of her own sub-speciation, of her bifurcation as a human-animal hybrid.

The irony of Sethe's being inscribed within a patriarchal discourse of white male domination with the ink produced by a black female slave has been noted by critics who connect the ink to Sethe's milk as a subversive mode of female language[136] or see it as a symbol of communication converted into ammunition to be used against the oppressed.[137] Again, however, this incident focuses upon a young woman who specifically hears herself being dissected by white men, and while the message is not one of total dehumanization but rather of ambivalence—she does, according to Schoolteacher, partake of some human features and characteristics—Sethe, like Sula, responds to the splitting of her personhood with shock. It is this shock of recognition that reverberates throughout her life as a constant reminder of what "white folks could do" and that serves to explain, not justify, Beloved's murder:

> ...anybody white could take your whole self for anything that came to mind. Not just work, kill or maim you, but dirty you. Dirty you so bad you couldn't like yourself anymore. Dirty you so bad you forgot who you were and couldn't think it up. And though she and others lived through and got over it, she could never let it happen to her own. The best thing she was was her children. Whites might dirty her all right, but not her best thing...And no one, nobody on this earth, would list her daughter's characteristics on the animal side of the paper. (B 251)

A more extreme version of Didion's later female protagonists who, suffering the less egregious violations of intrusive males, nevertheless bemoan an inability to remember who they are, Sethe decries the self-alienation and self-loathing that are the results of white male violence; she is not, however, totally devitalized by her victimization, for she has salvaged a moral center, albeit a controversial one, that enables her not only to rebuff Paul D's arguments and the town's condemnation but also to subject herself to Beloved's revenge as just punishment for "not having the right to do the right thing."

The ambiguity that attends Sethe's destructive love stems not from the imputation of selfish motives nor from any desire to sacrifice her children as a symbolic gesture of revenge against the System. Despite Stamp Paid's assessment that Sethe loved her children but was just trying "to outhurt the hurter" (B 234), the cumulative images of the text suggest that Sethe, in fact, was motivated primarily by her maternal need to keep her children safe from harm, and by a desperate need to assert her own subjectivity or selfhood to a racist society that had always silenced and objectified her. That perhaps she views her young children as extensions of her *self* serves to collapse, to some degree, the distinction and tension between traditional, maternal self-sacrifice and subversive maternal self-preservation that more clearly resonates in Eva's double voice. The ambiguity in Sethe's case rather turns on the issue of the willful taking of a human life that had not yet been plunged into despair or deprived of hope. One tries to understand the extremity of Sethe's situation, the drastic circumstances that could compel a mother to kill her baby; yet, the words of Paul D, his wish that she could have found an alternative, underscore the seemingly innate, human drive to preserve life, especially young life, at all costs. Morrison does not evade this issue but embraces it openly through the graphic depiction of Beloved's death. Filtered through Denver's perspective, the most detailed account of the murder captures the gruesome truth of infanticide, a truth from which the reader is supposed to recoil in horror:

> Sethe was trying to make up for the handsaw; *Beloved* was making her pay for it...she knew Sethe's greatest fear was the same one Denver had in the beginning—that Beloved might leave. That before Sethe could make her understand what it meant—what it took to drag the teeth of that saw under the little chin; to feel the baby blood pump like oil in her hands; to hold her face so her head would stay on; to squeeze her so she could absorb, still, the death spasms that shot through that adored body, plump and sweet with life—Beloved might leave. (B 251)

If Morrison were intent upon eliciting unqualified support from the reader for the moral rectitude of Sethe's act of infanticide, she would not have included such a graphic portrayal of Beloved's death. Instead, she captures the moral ambiguity of such an act in the very image of a mother's lethal love, an image that conveys both maternal affection and the inevitable destruction such love wrought upon a woman driven by forces outside of her control: while slitting her baby's throat with a handsaw, Sethe simultaneously holds her face so her head would stay on.

That Sethe dearly "pays" for her act also reveals the moral reservations of the author. Much of the text is devoted to the almost parasitic draining of Sethe's life force by a child who demands to know why she was murdered by her mother. Like the nephews who had stolen Sethe's milk, Beloved threatens to suck from her mother the paltry remains of emotional and physical nourishment that have kept Sethe alive for the eighteen years following the murder. Intent upon consuming Sethe and Denver, of annihilating their individuality, Beloved almost succeeds in incorporating her mother and sister into her own destructive death force. Morrison captures Beloved's usurpation of Sethe and Denver's identity:

> You are my face; I am you. Why do you leave me who am you?
> I will never leave you again
> Don't ever leave me again
> You will never leave me again

> You went in the water
> I drank your blood
> I brought your milk
>
> You forgot to smile
> I loved you
> You hurt me
> You came back to me
> You left me
>
> I waited for you
> You are mine
> You are mine
> You are mine
> (B 216-217)

What starts out to be a fragmented dialogue among the three women quickly deteriorates into the monopolizing demands of Beloved. As David Lawrence points out, "Their 'conversation' is a monologic discourse dictated by a fleshy ghost, a univocal tyranny silencing an attempt at dialogic communication."[138] Sethe, indeed, has paid dearly for her act, and is subject now to the predations not of a slave master but of an angry child.

Like the innovative dialogic duet between Julie and Emma in *The Dead Father*, Morrison's fragmented dialogue among Sethe, Beloved and Denver may offer an alternative mode of discourse that usurps traditional linear speech. Whereas Barthelme seeks to isolate and thereby parody hackneyed, vacuous phrases—the fillers and "dreck"—that have come to characterize traditional "fatherly" speech, Morrison seems intent upon disclosing the emotional underside of the ignominy and degradation of slavery, those "motherly" truths that have been carried and historically silenced in the hearts and memories of female slaves. Barthelme's alternative, parodic discourse between Julie and Emma seems so far removed from the political arena of the everyday concerns of women that we question his seriousness in presenting such speech as a viable instrument in the struggle for female emancipation. Similarly, while Morrison may be invoking a subversive mode of discourse that perhaps attempts to capture the pre-oedipal bond between mother and child, she also senses the limitations and dangers of a complete dissolution of self, a complete blurring of boundaries between two individuals, and advocates, instead, the need to erect a sense of self in relation to the community, so that the "I" remains connected to, rather than submerged by, the "we." For it is Denver who represents the healthy balance between identity and community. It is she who recoils from the consuming pathology of Beloved's narcissism and her mother's complicity; it is Denver who leaves the "womb" of 124 Bluestone to seek help for both her mother and herself; and it is Denver who serves as a catalyst for awakening the power of the community of women to rescue Sethe from a ravenous ghost and from her own guilt.

In contrast to the "sacrificial" violence perpetrated upon children by those who themselves have been violently oppressed, Morrison offers us the contrasting image of women peacefully bonding with other women to disarm the oppressor, to escape the cycle of violence-begetting-violence and to strive to exorcise the demons of a slave past. For it is the communal chain formed by the women of the town who, having forgiven Sethe her crime, arrive at House #124, at the behest of Denver, to save her mother from the vengeful spirit. In a surreal image that blurs the boundaries between fact and fantasy, thirty women "see" themselves as they once were as children sitting on the steps of Baby Suggs' house, enacting her gospel of love-thy-flesh, laughing and enjoying the sensual delights of food, drink and music. In a chorus of somewhat garbled voices that recalls, perhaps, the semiotic disorder of maternal discourse, the women fall to their knees and chant a prayer whose only audible syllables are "Yes, yes, yes, oh yes. Hear me. Hear me. Do it, Maker, do it" (B 258). Not only do these women manage to drive the spirit of Beloved from the house and thus free Sethe from the hauntings of a destructive love; they also succeed in terminating the seemingly endless cycle of violence that has plagued Sethe's existence. For when Edward Bodwin, the somewhat benevolent, original owner of #124 Bluestone, returns to his old home to reclaim some items from his childhood, Sethe mistakes him for the sadistic Schoolteacher. Thrown again into a murderous rage, Sethe is prevented from killing Bodwin by the assembly of sympathetic women. That Sethe has this time directed her violence outward toward the oppressor suggests perhaps a more morally comfortable though equally ineffective response to the imagined threat. By having Sethe almost murder the wrong man, however, Morrison again may be signalling the danger of assimilating the strategies of the Beast, of dirtying oneself with the filth of violence to combat a violent culture. The spiritual and emotional bonding of mothers, of women who have inscribed their life-affirming message with their red and white ink, offer, for Morrison, the best possibility of cleansing the Beast of its filth.

In *Beloved*, Morrison has presented an image of female-initiated violence that forces us to confront the often untidy complexity and basically unresolvable ambiguity inherent in moral issues. While all of her women who engage in aggressive modes of violence do so as primarily a reactive form of behavior to try to counteract the brutalizing effects of living in a racist/misogynistic culture, it is Sethe who most clearly, perhaps, demonstrates the purity of a mother's murderous love and the fundamentally inscrutable dynamics of maternal sacrifice.

Concluding Remarks

Syllables

Some words, full

of new meaning,
carry with them

the history of
what they once meant.

Others repeat their syllables
dry from age, marked

on parchment in
calligraphy...

These lead to the
art of whispering,

the secret made of skin.

In his poem entitled "Syllables," C.J. Morrissey bemoans the inadequacy of patriarchal language to effect an understanding among individuals, particularly women who have been traditionally relegated to the "art of whispering" by the prevailing male discourse. Subordinated by a culture that objectifies the female and that denies her the status as subject, a woman who remains confined to conventional speech finds herself repeating stale "syllables dry from age." Those women who break free to find an alternative mode of discourse re-connect with the primal pulsations of the body to articulate the "the secret made of skin."

This study has traversed part of the terrain of silenced women who are subjected to the egregious assaults of angry, articulate men in postmodern American fiction. Beginning with the mute and passive princess of Barthelme's "The Glass Mountain" and ending with the angry and aggressive slave mother of *Beloved*, the analyses of the images of women and violence in four experimental American authors have disclosed some of the troubling ambiguities attending the various depictions of both female degradation and female-initiated violence.

Many of the postmodern texts discussed in this study challenge and openly subvert the ontological primacy traditionally accorded the prevailing mode of phallic discourse. In addition to calling attention to themselves as "free-floating" artifacts stripped of any transcendental ground outside of their own creative impulses, and to offering alternative, destabilizing modes of speech that undermine the authority of conventional discourse, each text also emerges as more than just a self-contained play of signifiers. The texts of Barthelme, Didion, Pynchon and Morrison, while self-conscious artifacts, also point beyond themselves to the socio-political milieu from which they spring, a cultural environment whose underpinning is an often "comic" but deleterious misogyny. The texts considered in this study embody an ambiguity regarding the victimization of women. This ambiguity stems not only from the often conscious attempt of these writers to suspend the authority of all thought systems, including at times, that of feminism; it also reflects a postmodern American culture that refuses to take completely seriously the often violent oppression of women.

Notes

Introduction

1. Thomas Pynchon, *Slow Learner: Early Stories* (Boston: Little, Brown and Company, 1984), p. 11; all future references to this text will appear parenthetically within the body of the paper as SL.
2. Larry McCaffery, editor, *Postmodern Fiction: A Bio-Bibliographical Guide* (New York: Greenwood Press, 1986), pp. xiv-xv.
3. Susan R. Suleiman, *Subversive Intent: Gender, Politics and the Avant-Garde* (Cambridge, Mass.: Harvard University Press, 1990), pp. 35-36.
4. McCaffery, *Postmodern Fiction*, pp. xxv-xxvi.
5. McCaffery, *Postmodern Fiction*, p. xii.
6. Deborah L. Madsen, *The Postmodernist Allegories of Thomas Pynchon* (New York: St. Martin's Press, 1991), p. 120.
7. Rita Felski, *Beyond Feminist Aesthetics: Feminist Literature and Social Change* (Cambridge, Mass.: Harvard University Press, 1989).
8. Sandra Gilbert and Susan Gubar, *No Man's Land: The Place of the Woman Writer in the Twentieth Century, Volume 3: Letters from the Front* (New Haven: Yale University Press, 1994), p. xiv.
9. Felski, *Beyond Feminist Aesthetics*, p. l.
10. Jack Levin, "Hate Crimes Against Women" in *Bostonia*, January/February, 1991, p.66.
11. Karin L. Swisher and Carol Wekesser, editors, *Violence Against Women* (San Diego: Greenhaven Press, 1994), p. 18.
12. David Gelman, "The Rapist: An Overview" in *Violence Against Women*, p. 46.
13. Elizabeth M. Schneider, "Society's Belief in Family Privacy Contributes to Domestic Violence," in *Violence Against Women*, pp. 29, 30; Nancy Hutchings, "Sexism Promotes Violence Against Women," in *Violence Against Women*, p. 34.
14. *Violence Against Women*, p. 18.
15. *Violence Against Women*, p. 15.
16. Stephanie Rigor and Margo Gordon, "The Impact of Crime on Urban Women," in A.W. Burgess, editor, *Rape and Sexual Assault, Volume 2* (New York: Garland, 1988), pp. 139-156; M. P. Thompson and F. H. Norris, "Crime, Social Status, and Alienation," *American Journal of Community Psychology*, 1, 1992, pp. 97-119.

17. Mary P. Koss, Lisa A. Goodman, et.al., *No Safe Haven: Male Violence Against Women at Home, at Work, and in the Community* (Washington, D.C.: American Psychological Association, 1994), p. 27; Gelman. p. 43.
18. Gelman, p. 48.
19. *No Safe Haven*, p. 27.
20. Susan Rosenbaum, "Men's Group Studies Abuse," in *The East Hampton Star*, July 27, 1995, p. 8.
21. *No Safe Haven*, p. 6.
22. cf. Rigor and Gordon.
23. Marilyn French, *The War Against Women* (New York: Summit Books, 1992), p. 132.
24. S. E. Brown, "Police Responses to Wife Beating: Neglect of a Crime of Violence," in *Journal of Criminal Justice*, 12, 1984, pp. 277-288.
25. D. Kurz, "Responses to Battered Women: Resistance to Medicalization," in *Social Problems* 34, 1987, pp. 501-513.
26. Anne Campbell, *Men, Women and Aggression: From Rage in Marriage to Violence in the Streets—How Gender Affects the Way We Act* (New York: Basic Books, 1993), p. 149.
27. Susan Griffin, *A Chorus of Stones: The Private Life of War* (New York: Doubleday, 1992), p. 148.
28. Griffin, *A Chorus of Stones*, p. 121.
29. Randy Shilts, *Conduct Unbecoming: Gays and Lesbians in the U.S. Military* (New York: St. Martin's Press, 1993) p. 32.
30. *No Safe Haven*, p. 26.
31. Myra Sadker and David Sadker, *Failing at Fairness: How American Schools Cheat Girls* (New York: Charles Scribner's and Sons, 1994).
32. French, p. 164.
33. cf. *Take Back the Night: Women on Pornography*, edited by Laura Lederer (New York: William Morrow and Company, Inc., 1980) and *Violence Against Women*, Chapter 4.
34. Anne Campbell, p. 85.
35. Anne Campbell, p. 7.
36. Anne Campbell, p. 2.
37. *No Safe Haven*, p. 9 summarizing the findings of S. Bem's 1993 study *The Lenses of Gender: Transforming the Debate on Sexual Inequality* (New Haven: Yale University Press, 1993).
38. *No Safe Haven*, p. 9.
39. *No Safe Haven*, p. 36; cf. A. Browne, *When Battered Women Kill* (New York: MacMillan/Free Press, 1987).
40. *No Safe Haven*, p. 36; cf. L. Ross, "The Intuitive Psychoanalyst and His Shortcomings: Distortions in the Attribution Process," in *Advances in Experimental Social Psychology*, 35, L. Berkowitz, editor (New York: Academic Press, 1977).

41. Susan Faludi, *Backlash: The Undeclared War Against Women* (New York: Crown Publishers Inc., 1991).
42. Felski, *Beyond Feminist Aesthetics*, p. 7.
43. Linda Hutcheon, *A Poetics of Postmodernism: History, Theory, Fiction* (New York: Routledge, 1988), p. 189.
44. Gilbert and Gubar, *No Man's Land, Volume 3*, p. 337.
45. Carolyn Heilbrun, *Toward a Recognition of Androgyny* (New York: W.W. Norton & Company, 1982), pp. ix-x; cf, Gilbert and Gubar, *No Man's Land, Volume 3*, pp. 367-378; Toril Moi, *Sexual/Textual Politics: Feminist Literary Theory* (London: Routledge, 1985).
46. Bonnie Zimmerman, "Feminist Fiction and the Postmodern Challenge," in McCaffery, *Postmodern Fiction*, p. 176.
47. Sandra Gilbert and Susan Gubar, *No Man's Land: The Place of the Woman Writer in the Twentieth Century, Volume I, The War of the Words* (New Haven: Yale University press, 1988), pp. 47-50.
48. Moi, p. 106.
49. Gilbert and Gubar, *No Man's Land, Volume 3*, pp. xii-xv.
50. Christine Di Stefano, "Dilemmas of Difference: Feminism, Modernity, and Postmodernism," in *Feminism/Postmodernism*, edited by Linda J. Nicholson (New York: Routledge, 1990), p. 75
51. Patricia Waugh, *Feminine Fictions: Revisiting the Postmodern* (London: Routledge, 1989), p. 6.
52. Zimmerman, p. 176.
53. Frederick. R. Karl, *American Fictions: A Comprehensive History and Critical Evaluation* (New York: Harper & Row, 1983), p. 439.
54. Jane Flax, *Thinking Fragments: Psychoanalysis, Feminism and Postmodernism in the Contemporary West* (Berkeley: University of California Press, 1990), pp. 218-219.
55. Flax, p. 220.
56. *No Safe Haven*, p. 5.
57. Judith Butler, *Gender Trouble: Feminism and the Subversion of Identity* (New York: Routledge, 1990), Introduction.
58. Sally Robinson, *Engendering the Subject: Gender and Self-Representation in Contemporary Women's Fiction* (Albany: State University of New York, 1991), p. 9; Marjorie Garber, *Vested Interests: Cross Dressing and Cultural Anxiety* (New York: Harper Perennial, 1992).
59. Martine Rothblatt, The *Apartheid of Sex: A Manifesto on the Freedom of Gender* (New York: Crown Publishers, Inc., 1995), p. xiii.
60. Butler, p. 80.
61. Felski, *Beyond Feminist Aesthetics*, p. 40.
62. Gayle Greene and Coppelia Kahn, editors, *Changing Subiects: The Making of Feminist Literary Criticism* (London: Routledge, 1993), pp. 1, 13.
63. Marianne Hirsch, "Maternity and Rememory—Toni Morrison's *Beloved*," in

Representations of Motherhood, edited by Donna Bassin, Margaret Honey and Meryle Mahrer Kaplan (New Haven: Yale University Press, 1994), pp. 92-110.

Chapter One

1. Donald Barthelme, *City Life* (New York: Farrar, Straus & Giroux, 1970), p. 63. All future references to this text will be cited parenthetically within the body of the paper as CL.
2. Jerome Klinkowitz, *Donald Barthelme: An Exhibition* (Durham: Duke University Press, 1991), p. 8.
3. Larry McCaffery, *The Metafictional Muse: The Works of Robert Coover, Donald Barthelme and William Gass* (Pittsburgh: University of Pittsburgh Press, 1982), p. 108.
4. Alan Wilde, *Horizons of Assent: Modernism, Postmodernism and the Ironic Imagination* (Baltimore: The John Hopkins University Press, 1981), p. 176.
5. Wayne Stengel, *The Shape of Art in the Short Stories of Donald Barthelme* (Baton Rouge: Louisiana State University Press, 1985), p. 185.
6. Felski, *Beyond Feminist Aesthetics*, p. 7.
7. Hutcheon, p. 5.
8. McCaffery, *Postmodern Fiction* p. xvii.
9. Tom LeClair and Larry McCaffery, *Anything Can Happen: Interviews with Contemporary American Novelists* (Urbana: University of Illinois Press, 1985), p. 381.
10. William H. Peden, *The American Short Story: Continuity and Change, 1940-1975* (Boston: Houghton Mifflin Co., 1975), p. 179.
11. Charles Molesworth, *Donald Barthelme's Fiction: The Ironist Saved From Drowning* (Columbia: University of Missouri Press, 1982), p. 21.
12. Paul Bruss, *Victims: Textual Strategies in Recent American Fiction* (Lewisburg, Bucknell University Press, 1981), p. 110.
13. R. E. Johnson, Jr., "Bees Barking in the Night: The End and Beginning of Donald Barthelme's Narrative," *Boundary* 2 V (1976): p. 71.
14. Alan Wilde, *Middlegrounds: Studies in Contemporary American Fiction* (Philadelphia: University of Pennsylvania Press, 1987), pp. 34-35.
15. Wilde, *Middlegrounds*, p. 24.
16. Roland Barthes, *Writing Degree Zero*, translated by Annette Lavers and Colin Smith with preface by Susan Sontag (New York: Hill and Wang, 1967).
17. Wilde, *Middlegrounds*, p. 34.
18. Stengel, p. 185.
19. McCaffery, *The Metafictional Muse*, p. 130, emphasis mine.
20. Gilbert and Gubar, *No Man's Land Volume 1*, p. 41.
21. Gilbert and Gubar, *No Man's Land, Volume 1*, p. 47.
22. John Leland, "Remarks Re-marked: What Curios of Signs!" *Boundary* 2 V (Spring 1977): p. 795.

Notes

23. Patricia Waugh, *Practising Postmodernism, Reading Modernism* (London: Edward Arnold, 1992), p. 54.
24. Waugh, *Practising Postmodernism*, p. 54.
25. McCaffery, *Postmodern Fiction* p. xiii.
26. Carl Daryl Malmgren, *Fictional Space in the Modernist and Postmodernist American Novel* (Lewisburg: Bucknell University Press, 1985), pp. 48-49.
27. Waugh, *Practising Postmodernism*, p. 122.
28. Robinson, p. 17.
29. Felski, *Beyond Feminist Aesthetics*, pp. 1-4.
30. *No Safe Haven*, p. 5.
31. Butler, p. x.
32. Garber, *Vested Interests*, p. 3.
33. Flax, p. 39.
34. Tony Tanner, *City of Words: American Fiction 1950–1970* (New York: Harper & Row, 1971), pp. 404-405.
35. Peden, p. 179.; emphasis mine.
36. Waugh, *Practising Postmodernism*, p. 122.
37. Stengel, p. 170.
38. Carol J. Adams, *The Sexual Politics of Meat: A Feminist-Vegetarian Critical Theory* (New York: The Continuum Publishing Company, 1990), pp. 40-45. Maintaining that feminism must entail vegetarianism, Adams argues quite persuasively for the inextricable linkage in meat-eating, patriarchal culture between the subordination of women and the slaughter of animals.
39. Susan R. Suleiman, *Subversive Intent: Gender, Politics and the Avant-Garde* (Cambridge, Mass.: Harvard University Press, 1990), p. 36.
40. Gilbert and Gubar, *No Man's Land, Volume 1*, p. 43.
41. Donald Barthelme, *Sixty Stories* (New York: E. P. Dutton, Inc., 1982), p. 288. All future references to this text will be cited parenthetically within the body of the paper as SS.
42. Stengel, pp. 119-120.
43. Suleiman, p. 36.
44. Molesworth, p. 77.
45. Stengel, p. 22.
46. F. O. Matthiessen, *American Renaissance: Art in the Age of Emerson and Whitman* (New York: Oxford University Press, 1941), pp. 275-282.
47. Leland S. Person, *Aesthetic Headaches: Women and a Masculine Poetics in Poe, Melville and Hawthorne* (Athens: University of Georgia Press, 1988), p. 123.
48. Carroll Smith-Rosenberg, *Disorderly Conduct: Visions of Gender in Victorian America* (New York: Oxford University Press, 1985), p. 139.
49. H. R. Hays, *The Dangerous Sex: The Myth of Feminine Evil* (New York: G.P. Putnam, Sons, 1964), p. 86.
50. Carolyn G. Heilbrun, *Reinventing Womanhood* (New York W.W. Norton and Co.,Inc., 1979), p. 74.

51. Nathaniel Hawthorne, *The Scarlet Letter*, edited by Seymour L. Gross (New York: W.W. Norton and Co.,Inc., 1961), p. 118.
52. Anne Campbell, p. 37. Campbell goes on to observe that "the dramatic device of casting a woman as an aggressor—a twist that flies in the face of most children's experience of mothers and babysitters," tacitly insures conveying that woman in the role of villain (37).
53. Karl, p. 388.
54. Klinkowitz, pp. 7-8.
55. *Grimm's Fairy Tales* (London: Butler and Tanner, Ltd., n.d.), pp. 232-248.
56. Adrian Bailey, *Walt Disney's World of Fantasy* (New Jersey: Chartwell Books, Inc., 1984), p. 117.
57. Donald Barthelme, *Snow White* (New York: Atheneum, 1972), p. 22. All future references to this text will be cited parenthetically within the body of the paper as SW.
58. Gilbert and Gubar, *No Man's Land: Volume 3*, p. 336.
59. Gilbert and Gubar, *No Man's Land, Vol. 3*, p. 336.
60. Leland, p. 801.
61. Gilbert and Gubar, *No Man's Land, Vol. 3*. p. 336.
62. Waugh, *Practising Postmodernism*, p. 51.
63. Bruss, p. 139.
64. Gerald Graff, *Literature Against Itself: Literary Ideas in Modern Society* (Chicago: University of Chicago Press, 1979), p. 226.
65. Paul Maltby, *Dissident Postmodernists: Barthelme, Coover, Pynchon* (Philadelphia: University of Pennsylvania Press, 1991), p. 57.
66. Gilbert and Gubar, *No Man's Land, Vol. 1*, p. 37.
67. Adams, see endnote #38.
68. McCaffery, *Metafictional Muse*, p. 112.
69. Mary Gordon, *Good Boys and Dead Girls and Other Essays* (London: Penquin Books, Ltd., 1991) p. 13.
70. Bailey, p. 128.
71. Betty Flowers, "Barthelme's Snow White: The Reader-Patient Relationship," *Critique* 16, No.3 (1975): p. 35.
72. Bruno Bettelheim, *The Uses of Enchantment: The Meaning and Importance of Fairy Tales* (New York: Alfred N. Knopf, 1976), p. 214.
73. Bruss, p. 142.
74. Henry Miller, *Tropic of Cancer* (New York: Grove Press, 1961), p. 139; Henry Miller, *Tropic of Capricorn* (New York: Grove Press, 1961), pp. 176-177)
75. Gilbert and Gubar, *No Man's Land Volume 1*, p. 43.
76. Kate Millett, *Sexual Politics* (New York: Ballantine Books, 1969) p. 425.
77. Gilbert and Gubar, *No Man's Land, Volume 3*, p. 336
78. Jane Mills, *Womanwords: A Dictionary of Words about Women* (New York: The Free Press, 1992), p. 60.
79. Alan Soble, *Pornography: Marxism, Feminism and the Future of Sexuality* (New York: Yale University Press, 1986), pp. 56-58.

80. Mills, p. 60.
81. Lucy Komisar, "The Image of Women in Advertising" in *Woman in Sexist Society: Studies in Power and Powerlessness*, edited by Vivian Gornick and Barbara K. Moran (New York: Basic Books, Inc., 1971), p. 208.
82. *Killing Us Softly: Advertising's Image of Women*, film by Jean Kilbourne, Joseph Vitagliano and Patricia Stallone, Cambridge Documentary Films, 1979.
83. Bruss, p. 145.
84. Suleiman, p. 184.
85. Madsen, p. 120.
86. Waugh, *Practising Postmodernism*, pp. 56-57.
87. Waugh, *Practising Postmodernism*, p. 57.
88. Bruss, p. 145.
89. Butler, p. 146.
90. Richard P. Poirier, *The Performing Self: Composition and Decompositions in the Language of Contemporary Life* (New York: Oxford University Press, 1971), pp. 10-11.
91. McCaffery, *Postmodern Fiction*, p. xii.
92. McCaffery, *Postmodern Fiction*, p. xx.
93. Joanna Russ, *How to Suppress Women's Writing* (Austin: University of Texas Press, 1983) p. 29.
94. Russ, p. 30.
95. Lynne Hanley, *Writing War: Fiction, Gender and Memory* (Amherst: The University of Massachusetts Press, 1991), p. 113.
96. Klinkowitz, p. 5; Bruss, pp. 148-163.
97. McCaffery, *Postmodern Fiction*, p. xiii.
98. Klinkowitz, p. 13.
99. Karl, p. 386.
100. Klinkowitz, p. 13; emphasis mine.
101. Felski, *Beyond Feminist Aesthetics*, p. 23.
102. Felski, *Beyond Feminist Aesthetics*, p. 19.
103. Cf. Gilbert and Gubar, *No Man's Land, Volume 3* Introduction; Suleiman, p. 188; Felski, *Beyond Feminist Aesthetics*, p. 162; Waugh, *Feminine Fictions: Revisiting the Postmodern* (London: Routledge, 1989), p. 6; Waugh, Practising Postmodernism, pp. 124-125; Flax, *Thinking Fragments*, p. 219; in an article entitled "Postmodernism and Gender Relations in Feminist Theory," Flax argues that the emphasis placed on language by the French feminists tends to deflect attention away from "concrete social relations," such as the distribution of power, and results in the "obscuring of relations of domination," including gender arrangements, p. 47 in *Feminism/Postmodernism* edited by Linda J. Nicholson (New York: Routledge, 1990); Marianne Hirsch, in her deconstructionist reading of *Beloved*, nonetheless argues for the legitimacy of female subjectivity in *The Mother-Daughter Plot: Narrative, Psychoanalysis, Feminism* (Bloomington: Indiana University Press, 1989); Bonnie Zimmerman

in McCaffery's *Bio-Biliographical Guide*, p. 176; while Sally Robinson states that "subjectivity is an on-going process of engagement in social and discursive practices, not some immanent kernel of identity that is expressed through those engagements"(p. 11), she also suggests that women still need some category of woman if "feminism is to do its political work."(4) Also see Toril Moi's *Sexual/Textual Politics: Feminist Literary Theory* (London: Routledge, 1985), for a summary of this debate.

104. Donald Barthelme, *The Dead Father* (New York: Penguin Books, 1986), p. 17. All future references to this text will be cited parenthetically within the body of the paper as DF.
105. Bruss, p. 159.
106. Henry Miller, *Sexus: The Rosy Crucifixion I* (New York: Grove Press, Inc., 1965.), p. 83.
107. Cf. Introduction in *No Safe Haven* which chronicles the rise of such violence in American society; and pp. 15-16 in *Violence Against Women*.
108. Susan Brownmiller, *Against Our Will: Men, Women and Rape* (New York: Simon and Schuster, 1975), p. 16.
109. *No Safe Haven*, p. 6.
110. Felski, *Beyond Feminist Aesthetics*, p. 23.
111. Bruss, p. 149.
112. Robert Con Davis, "Post-Modern Paternity: Donald Barthelme's *The Dead Father*," *The Fictional Father: Lacanian Readings of the Text*, edited by Robert Con Davis (Amherst: University of Massachusetts Press, 1981), p. 174.
113. Gilbert and Gubar, *No Man's Land, Volume 3*, p. xii.
114. Flax, *Thinking Fragments*, pp. 218-220.
115. Rita Felski, "Feminism, Realism and the Avant-Garde," *Postmodern Conditions*, edited by Andrew Miller, Philip Thomson and Chris Worth (New York: Berg, 1990), p. 65; Elaine Showalter, *A Literature of Their Own: British Women Novelists from Bronte to Lessing* (Princeton: Princeton University Press, 1977), pp. 3-36.
116. Waugh, *Revisiting the Postmodern*, p. 6.
117. Jeanette McVicker, "Donald Barthelme's *The Dead Father*: 'Girls Talk' and The Displacement of the Logos," *Boundary* 2 (Winter, 1989): p. 380.
118. Barbara Hill Rigney, *The Voice of Toni Morrison* (Columbus: Ohio State University Press, 1991), p. 26.
119. McVicker, p. 387.
120. Luce Irigaray, "The Power of Discourse," *The Sex Which is Not One*, translated by Catherine Porter (Ithaca: Cornell University Press, 1985), p. 79.
121. Russ, p. 29.
122. David H. Richter, *The Critical Tradition: Classic Texts and Contemporary Trends*, edited by David H. Richter (New York: St. Martin's Press, 1989), p. 1072.
123. Mary Ellmann, *Thinking About Women* (New York: Harcourt, Brace & World, Inc., 1968), p. 74.

Chapter Two

1. Sharon Felton, editor, *The Critical Response to Joan Didion* (Westport, Conn.: Greenwood Press, 1994), Introduction, p. 1.
2. David Geherin, "Nothingness and Beyond: Joan Didion's *Play It As It Lays*," *Critique* #1, Vol.16 (1975), p. 76.
3. Felton, p. 7.
4. Evan Carton, "Joan Didion's Dreampolitics of the Self," in *The Critical Response to Joan Didion*, p. 37.
5. Felton, p. 7.
6. Flax, *Thinking Fragments*, p. 219.
7. Waugh, *Feminine Fictions: Revisiting the Postmodern*, p. 6.
8. Gayle Greene and Coppelia Kahn, editors, *Changing Subjects: The Making of Feminist Literary Criticism* (London: Routledge, 1993), Introduction, p. 1 and "Looking at History," by Gayle Greene, p. 21.
9. Felski, *Beyond Feminist Aesthetics*, p. 162.
10. Zimmerman, p. 178.
11. Joan Didion, *The White Album* (New York: Simon and Schuster, 1979), p. 113. All future references to this text will be cited parenthetically within the body of the paper as WA.
12. Martha Duffy, "Pictures from an Expedition," in The Critical Response to Joan Didion, pp. 128-129.
13. Katherine Henderson, *Joan Didion* (New York: Frederick Ungar Publishing Co., 1981), p. 129.
14. Joan Didion, *Slouching Towards Bethlehem* (New York: Simon and Schuster, 1968), p. 101. All future references to this text will be cited parenthetically within the body of the paper as STB.
15. Susan Griffin, *A Chorus of Stones*, p. 289.
16. Carolyn Heilbrun, *Reinventing Womanhood* (New York: W.W.Norton & Co., 1979), p. 42.
17. Henderson, *Joan Didion*, p. 129.
18. Sara Davidson, "A Visit with Joan Didion," *Joan Didion: Essays and Conversations*, edited by Ellen G. Friedman (Princeton: Ontario Review Press, 1984), pp. 14-15.
19. Jean-François Lyotard, *The Postmodern Condition: A Report on Knowledge*, translation from the French by Geoff Bennington and Brian Massumi (Minneapolis, University of Minnesota Press, 1984), pp. 37-41.
20. All future references to these texts will be cited parenthetically within the body of the paper as RR, PIAIL and BCP.
21. E.E. Levitt, B. Lubin and J.M. Brooks, *Depression: Concepts, Controversies and Some New Facts* (Hillsdale, N.J.: Laurence Erlbaum Associates, 1983), Janet W. Wetzel, *Clinical Handbook of Depression* (New York: Gardner Press, Inc., 1984). Both texts argue for a correlation between depression and socialization factors associated with the feminine stereotype.

22. *No Safe Haven*, p. 7.
23. Griffin, *A Chorus of Stones*, pp. 224-225.
24. Simone de Beauvoir, *The Second Sex*, translated and edited by H.M. Parshley (New York: Vintage Books, 1974), pp. xvi-xx.
25. Hanley, p. 78.
26. Davidson, p. 20.
27. Samuel Coale, "Didion's Disorders," *Critique* 25 (Spring 1984): pp. 160-170.
28. Meredith Tax, "Woman and Her Mind: The Story of an Everyday Life," *Notes from the Second Year: Radical Feminism*, edited by Shulamith Firestone and Anne Koedt (New York: Radical Feminism, 1970), p. 10.
29. Wetzel, Chapters One and Two; Juanita Williams, *Psychology of Women: Behavior in a Bisocial Context* (New York: W.W. Norton & Company, 1977), p. 337.
30. Michelle Loris, "Run River: A Western Story of Paradise Lost," in *The Critical Response to Joan Didion*, p. 20.
31. Mark Royden Winchell, *Joan Didion* (Boston: Twayne Publishers, 1980), p. 104.
32. Winchell, p. 102.
33. Karl, p. 398.
34. Betty Friedan, *The Feminine Mystique*—Twentieth Anniversary Edition (New York: Dell Publishing, 1983), pp. 15-16.
35. Gilbert and Gubar, *No Man's Land, Vol.3*, pp. xv-xvi.
36. Butler, p. x.
37. Friedan, pp. 20, 29.
38. Felski, *Beyond Feminist Aesthetics*, p. 162.
39. Coale, p. 163.
40. Greene, Kahn, Introduction, pp. 1,2; Greene, pp. 13, 21.
41. Anne Campbell, pp. 110, 113.
42. Sylvia Plath, "A Birthday Present," *The Collected Poems*, edited by Ted Hughes (New York: Harper & Row, 1981).
43. Lily's absence of positive action and her repeated withdrawal into a seemingly passive acceptance of male aggressiveness in her marriage and of her own chronic unhappiness may indeed point to a pervasive form of depression which, psychologists argue, is often accompanied by the phenomenon of "learned helplessness:" the depressed woman relinquishes any attempt to extricate herself from "an aversive situation" because she has lost the ability to predict the efficacy of her action (cf. *No Safe Haven* p. 84). Because Lily has failed to initiate any attempt to escape her own unhappiness our patience with her, unlike our compassion for her future counterparts in *A Book of Common Prayer* and *Democracy*, remains strained at best.
44. Sandra Lee Bartkey, "On Psychological Oppression," *Philosophy and Women*, edited by Sharon Bishop and Marjorie Weinzweig (Belmont, California: Wadsworth, 1979), p. 37.

45. Susan Brownmiller, *Against Our Will: Men, Women and Rape* (New York: Simon and Schuster, 1975), pp. 322-333.
46. Friedan, p. 21.
47. Josephine Hendin, *Vulnerable People: A View of American Fiction Since 1945* (New York: Oxford University Press, 1978), p. 184, emphasis mine.
48. Anne. Z. Mickelson, "Joan Didion: The Hurting Woman," *Reaching Out: Sensitivity and Order in Recent American Fiction by Women* (Metuchen: Scarecrow Press, 1979), p. 94.
49. cf. Mary Tyrone in O'Neill's *Long Day's Journey Into Night*, Edna Pontellier in Chopin's *The Awakening* and the narrator of Gilman's *The Yellow Wallpaper*; as we shall discover in Chapter Four, Morrison subverts the triad of male oppressors by positing a series of female triads that will strive to repel the onslaught of male aggression.
50. Alan Wilde, *Middle Grounds: Studies in Contemporary American Fiction* (Philadelphia: University of Pennsylvania Press, 1978), pp. 134-135.
51. Melvin Maddocks, Her Heart's with the Wagon Trains," in *The Critical Response to Joan Didion*, p. 34.
52. Carton, p. 36
53. Flax, *Thinking Fragments*, p. 210.
54. Henderson, *Joan Didion*, p. 31.
55. Rodney Simard, "The Dissociation of Self in Joan Didion's *Play It As It Lays*," in *The Critical Response to Joan Didion*, p. 68.
56. Geherin, p. 65.
57. Cynthia Griffin Wolff, "*Play It As It Lays*: Didion and the New American Heroine," *Joan Didion: Essays and Conversations*, edited by Ellen G. Friedman (Princeton: Ontario University press, 1984), p. 128.
58. Sandra K. Hinchman, "Making Sense and Telling Stories:Problems of Cognition and Narration in Joan Didion's *Play It As It Lays*," in *The Critical Response to Joan Didion*, pp. 86-87.
59. Marianne Hirsch, *The Mother-Daughter Plot: Narrative, Psychoanalysis, Feminism* (Bloomington: Indiana University Press, 1989), 139; cf. pp. 110-127 in Adrienne Rich's Of Woman Born: *Motherhood as Experience and Institution* wherein she depicts the "domestication of motherhood" as a patriarchal strategy employed to compensate for the male's initial understanding of himself as "son-of-the- mother" and later to insure the hegemony of his rule (New York: W W Norton & Company, 1995).
60. Robinson, p. 17.
61. Waugh, *Feminine Fictions:Revisiting the Postmodern*, p. 10.
62. Hélène Cixous, "The Laugh of the Medusa," translated by Keith Cohen and Paula Cohen, *The Critical Tradition*, edited by David H. Richter (New York: St. Martin's Press, 1989), pp. 1092-1093.
63. Terry Eagleton, *Literary Theory: An Introduction* (Minneapolis: University of Minnesota Press, 1983), p. 184.

64. Henderson, *Joan Didion*, p. 27.
65. While the debate between anti-pornography groups and first amendment absolutists rages, the corresponding increase in the production of cinematic images of female mutilation and the number of rapes and abuse cases in America continues to suggest, if not a simple causal connection, some kind of critical correlation between pornography and violence against women. (Cf. *Violence Against Women*; *Take Back the Night: Women on Pornography,* edited by Laura Lederer, New York :William Morrow and Company, 1980; for current rape statistics, see *No Safe Haven*, pp. 160-172). While Didion is not overtly advocating an anti-pornography platform in this novel, the character of Maria Wyeth is indeed the victim of men who have enjoyed viewing her being victimized on film.
66. Adrienne Rich, "Compulsory Heterosexuality and Lesbian Existence," pp. 177-205 in Powers of Desire: *The Politics of Sexuality*, edited by Ann Snitow, Christine Stansell and Sharon Thompson (New York: Monthly Review Press, 1983), p. 185.
67. *No Safe Haven*, p. 9.
68. *No Safe Haven*, p. 189.
69. Miriam F. Hirsch, *Women and Violence* (New York: Van Nostrand Reinhold Company, 1981) pp. 104-105.
70. Josephine Donovan, *Feminist Theory: The Intellectual Tradition of American Feminism* (New York: Frederick Ungar Publishing Company, 1985), p. 137.
71. Tax, p. 12. One could also argue that such a "schizophrenic" response to rape is theologically rooted in the Greco-Christian dichotomy of the spirit and the body; in his discussion concerning the rape of Lucretia who, according to Livy, committed suicide rather than bear the suspicions of her Roman countrymen as to her possible complicity, St.Augustine, in *The City of God*, argues that a woman can be raped "in body," but if her spirit is devoted to God she remains chaste. Consequently, continues Augustine, Lucretia's suicide was not a noble gesture but rather a cowardly act of shame, for if she had been devoted to a Christian God rather than to the ephemeral opinions of pagan mortals, she would have embraced her own chastity (*City of God*, Section 19). It is, I maintain, the West's dissolution of the wholeness or integrity of a person into the Cartesian duality of body and mind that accords a false legitimacy to such redundant constructions as "forcible rape" or "violent rape."
72. Sandra M. Gilbert and Susan Gubar, *No Man's Land: The Place of the Woman Writer in the Twentieth Century, Volume 2: Sex Changes* (New Haven: Yale University Press, 1989), p. 33., quoting from G. J.Barker-Benfield's *The Horrors of the Half-Known Life: Male Attitudes toward Women & Sexuality in Nineteenth Century America* (New York: Harper Colophon, 1976), p. 95.
73. Gilbert and Gubar, *No Man's Land, Vol. 2*, p. 33; cf. Cixous' observation in "The Laugh of the Medusa" that "what [men] have said so far [about their own sexuality], for the most part, stems from the opposition activity/passivity,

from the power relation between a fantasized obligatory virility meant to invade, colonize, and the consequential phantasm of woman as a 'dark continent' to penetrate and pacify'" (p. 1091); cf. also Carol Adams's citing of Barker-Benfield's anecdote about a 19th Century medical man who "came to the assistance of a man who wished to have sex with his wife. The physician arrived at the residence of the couple two or three times a week to 'etherize the poor wife.' The anasthetization of animals as a prelude to butchering reminds us of this complicity in marital rape," *The Sexual Politics of Meat: A Feminist-Vegetarian Critical Theory* (New York: The Continuum Publishing Company, 1990), p. 55.
74. Flax, Thinking Fragments, p. 219.
75. *No Safe Haven*, p. 7.
76. Hubert Selby, Jr., *Last Exit to Brooklyn* (New York: Grove Weidenfeld, 1964). p. 143.
77. Alfred Kazin, *Bright Book of Life: American Novelists and Storytellers from Hemingway to Mailer* (New York: Little, Brown & Co., 1973), p. 143.
78. Donovan, p. 138.
79. Dana Densmore, "On the Temptation to be a Beautiful Object," *Female Liberation: History and Current Politics*, edited by Roberta Salper (New York: Knopf, 1972), pp. 207-208.
80. Henderson. *Joan Didion*, p. 22.
81. John Leonard, *New York Times Book Review*, July 21, 1970, p. 33.
82. Wolff, p. 31.
83. Geherin, p. 75.
84. Karl, p. 40.
85. Joyce Carol Oates, "A Taut Novel of Disorder," *The New York Times Book Review*, April 3, 1977, pp. 34-35.
86. Merivale, p. 99.
87. Coale, p. 165. 88 Samuel Chase Coale, "Joan Didion: Witnessing the Abyss," in *The Critical Response to Joan Didion*, p. 118.
89. Henderson, *Joan Didion*, p. 8.
90. Waugh, *Feminine Fictions: Revisiting the Postmodern*, p. 22
91. Diane Johnson, "Joan Didion's *A Book of Common Prayer*," *New York Review of Books*, April 28, 1977, p. 6.
92. Hanley, p. 78.
93. Merivale, p. 100.
94. *No Safe Haven*, Sections I, II, III.
95. *No Safe Haven*, p. 62.
96. Mickelson, p. 106.
97. Miriam Hirsch, p. 179.
98. *French, The War Against Women*, pp. 50-65.
99. Coale, "Didion's Disorders," p. 161.
100. Winchell, p. 145.

101. Hanley, p. 79.
102. Hanley, p. 79.
103. Mickelson, p. 108.
104. Flax, *Thinking Fragments*, pp. 209-221; Kahn, pp. 1-2; Greene, pp. 4-27; Felski, *Beyond Feminist Aesthetics*, Ch. 5.
105. Henderson, *Joan Didion*, p. 69.
106. Hanley, p. 80.
107. Hanley, p. 86.
108. Griffin, *A Chorus of Stones*, p. 352.
109. Donovan, p. 141.
110. Nancy Fraser and Linda Nicholson, "Social Criticism without Philosophy: An Encounter between Feminism and Postmodernism," *Universal Abandon: The Politics of Postmodernism*, edited by Andrew Ross (Minneapolis: University of Minnesota Press, 1988), pp. 92-93.
111. Mickelson, p. 111.
112. Joan Didion, *Democracy* (New York: Simon and Schuster, Inc., 1984), p. 17. All future references to this text will be cited parenthetically within the body of the paper as D.
113. Flax, *Thinking Fragments*, p. 210.
114. Robinson, p. 11.
115. Waugh, *Feminine Fictions; Revisiting the Postmodern*, p. 12.
116. Janis P. Stout, "Joan Didion and the Presence of Absence," in *The Critical Response to Joan Didion*, p. 217.
117. Katherine Henderson, "The Bond Between Narrator and Heroine in Democracy," *American Women Writing Fiction: Memory, Identity, Family, Space*, edited by Mickey Pearlman (Lexington: University Press of Kentucky, 1989), p. 73.
118. Flax, *Thinking Fragments*, p. 221.
119. Marianne Hirsch, p. 139.
120. Hanley, pp. 87-88.
121. Henderson, "The Bond," p. 75.
122. Mary McCarthy, "Love and Death in the Pacific," *New York Times Book Review*, April 22, 1984, p. 18.
123. Mark Falcoff, "Two Weeks," *Commentary* Vol. 75 #5, May 1983, p. 66.
124. John Pilger, "Having Fun with Fear," *New Statesman* Vol. 105 #2720, May 6, 1983, p. 20.
125. Pilger, p. 20.
126. Joan Didion, *Salvador* (New York: Simon and Schuster Inc., 1983), p. 73. All future references to this text will be cited parenthetically within the body of the paper as S.
127. Hanley, p. 91.
128. America's Watch, *El Salvador's Decade of Terror: Human Rights Since the Assassination of Archbishop Romero* (New Haven: Yale University Press, 1991), pp. 3-7.

Notes

129. Frederick Kiley, "Beyond Words: Narrative Art in Joan Didion's Salvador," *Joan Didion: Essays and Conversations*, edited by Ellen G. Friedman (Princeton: Ontario Review Press, 1984), p. 186.
130. Pilger, p. 20.
131. Waugh, *Feminine Fictions; Revisiting the Postmodern*, p. 10.
132. Morrison more explicitly invokes the idea of a fluid, chameleon-like, female (non) identity in characters such as Pilate from *Song of Solomon* and the title character of *Beloved*.
133. Chris Anderson, *Style as Argument: Contemporary American Nonfiction* (Carbondale: Southern Illinois University Press, 1987), p. 154.
134. Hanley, p. 104.
135. Hanley, p. 107.
136. Michael Tager, "The Political Vision of Joan Didion's *Democracy*," *Critique* 31 (Spring 1990): p. 178.
137. Miriam Hirsch, p. 159.
138. Letty Cottin Pogrebin, "Boys Will Be Boys," *Ms. Magazine*, September 1989, p. 24.
139. Cf. Anne Campbell, pp. 40-44.
140. Stout, p. 223.
141. Myra and David Sadker's 1994 comprehensive study provides a summary of the inveterate sexist biases inherent in the American educational system in the 1950's and the 1960's in which girls were intellectually and emotionally short-changed by an institution that bred young white men to assume positions of leadership. Their findings with regard to present day educational practices and sex discrimination are rather dismal and discouraging, as girls still suffer often disabling gender biases in the American classroom (*Failing at Fairness: How American Schools Cheat Girls*, New York: Charles Scribner's and Sons: New York, 1994.)
142. Tager, p. 182.
143. Marianne Hirsch, pp. 169-170.
144. Stout, pp. 222-223.
145. Tager, p. 183.
146. Joseph Epstein, *Plausible Prejudices: Essays in American Writing* (New York: W.W. Norton & Company, 1985), p. 67.
147. Stout, p. 223.
148. McCarthy, p. 19.
149. Tager, p. 170.
150. Hanley, p. 109.
151. Hanley, p. 129.
152. Griffin, *A Chorus of Stones*, p. 31.
153. Cixous, p. 1094.
154. Stout, p. 224.

Chapter Three

1. Suleiman, pp. 36-38.
2. Marianne Hirsch, pp. 169-170.
3. Waugh, *Feminine Fictions: Revisiting the Postmodern*, p. 29.
4. Frederick Hoffman, "The Questing Comedian: Thomas Pynchon's *V.*," *Critique* 6 (1963-64): p. 177.
5. Tony Tanner, *City of Words: American Fiction 1950-1970* (New York: Harper & Row, 1971), p. 162.
6. Alice Jardine, *Gynesis: Configurations of Women and Modernity* (Ithaca: Cornell University Press, 1985), pp. 247-248.
7. Hutcheon, p. 133.
8. Waugh, *Practising Postmodernism, Reading Modernism*, p. 131.
9. Raymond Olderman, *Beyond the Wasteland: A Study of the American Novel in the 1960's* (New Haven: Yale University Press, 1972), p. 122.
10. Katherine M. Rogers, *The Troublesome Helpmate: A History of Misogyny in Literature* (Seattle: Washington Press, 1966), p. 265.
11. Thomas Pynchon, *V.* (New York: Harper & Row, 1963). p. 53. All future reference to this text will be cited parenthetically within the body of the paper as V.
12. Jardine, p. 247.
13. Tanner, *City of Words*, p. 170.
14. David Cowart, *The Art of Allusion* (Carbondale: Southern Illinois University Press, 1980), pp. 13-14.
15. Mary Allen, *The Necessary Blankness: Women in Major American Fiction of the Sixties* (Chicago: University of Illinois Press, 1976), pp. 37-38.
16. Alfred Kazin, *Bright Book of Life: American Novelists and Storytellers from Hemingway to Mailer* (Boston: Little, Brown and Company, 1971), p. 276.
17. Olderman. p. 136.
18. Alan Wilde, *Middlegrounds: Studies in Contemporary American Fiction* (Philadelphia: University of Pennsylvania Press, 1987), p. 79.
19. Robert E. Golden, "Mass, Man and Modernism: Violence in Pynchon's *V.*," *Critique* 44 (1972-73): p. 12.
20. W.T. Lhamon, "Pentecost, Promiscuity and Pynchon's V.: From the Scaffold to the Impulsive," *Twentieth Century American Literature* 21 (1975): p. 172.
21. Jardine, pp. 248-250.
22. Robinson, p. 3.
23. Waugh, *Feminine Fictions:Revisiting the Postmodern*, p. 27.
24. Scott Sanders, "Pynchon's Paranoid History," *Mindless Pleasures: Essays on Thomas Pynchon*, edited by George Levine and David Leverenz (Boston: Little, Brown and Company, 1976), p. 147.
25. Butler, p. 12.
26. Marilyn French, *Beyond Power: On Women, Men and Morals* (New York:

Summit Books, 1985, p. 69; Susan Griffin, Woman And Nature: The Roaring Inside Her (New York: Harper & Row, 1978), p. 1-46.
27. Rosemarie Tong, *Feminist Thought: A Comprehensive Introduction* (Boulder: Westview Press, 1989), p. 99. For the pivotal importance of the concept of "power over" in the socialization of women and men with regard to their experiences of aggression, see Anne Campbell's *Men, Women and Aggression*, (endnote #33, Chapter One), p. 7: "If, in men's accounts of aggression, we are told what it is like to take control, in women's accounts we hear about what it means to lose control...for women the aim is cataclysmic release of accumulated tension; for men, the reward is power over the person."
28. Jardine, pp. 32-33.
29. Susan Griffin, *Pornography and Silence* (New York: Harper & Row, 1981), pp. 10-20.
30. David Seed, *The Fictional Labyrinths of Thomas Pynchon* (Iowa City: University of Iowa Press, 1988), p. 93.
31. Miller, *Tropic of Cancer*, pp. 139-140.
32. Griffin, *Woman and Nature*, pp. 51-52.
33. Hoffman, p. 176.
34. Griffin, *Woman and Nature*, p. 5.
35. Waugh, *Practising Postmodernism, Reading Modernism*, p. 123.
36. Roger B. Henkle, "Pynchon's Tapestries on the Western Wall," *Pynchon: A Collection of Essays*, edited by Edward Mendelsohn (Englewood Cliffs: Prentice-Hall, Inc., 1978), p. 102.
37. Herbert Marcuse, *One Dimensional Man: Studies in the Ideology of Advanced Industrial Society* (Boston: Beacon Press, 1964), p. 9.
38. Tanner, *City of Words*, p. 160.
39. Joan Smith, *Misogynies: Reflections on Myths and Malice* (New York: Ballantine Books, 1992), p. 15.
40. *No Safe Haven*, p. 7.
41. *No Safe Haven*, pp. 8-9.
42. *No Safe Haven*, p. 13.
43. Lyotard, p. 4.
44. Thomas Pynchon, *Gravity's Rainbow* (New York: Viking Penquin. Inc., 1973), pp. 712-713; all future references to this text will be cited parenthetically within the body of the paper as GR.
45. *No Safe Haven*, p. 13.
46. *No Safe Haven*, p. 13.
47. Allen, p. 37.
48. Griffin, *Woman and Nature*, p. 45.
49. Cowart, p. 76.
50. In connection to Profane's linking of women and animals and his reduction of both to willing victims, see Carol Adams' *The Sexual Politics of Meat* (endnote #22, Chapter One), p. 55: "One of the mythologies of a rapist culture is that

women not only ask for rape, they also enjoy it; that they are continually seeking out the butcher's knife. Similarly, advertisements and popular culture tell us that animals like Charley the Tuna and Al Capp's Schmoo wish to be eaten. The implication is that women and animals willingly participate in the process that renders them absent."

51. Morrison too will prove sensitive to the deleterious effects on women of the white male's prescription for female beauty, but her depictions of the physical and emotional mutilation that women subject themselves to, in order to conform to this standard, are presented less sardonically than Pynchon's portrayals.
52. Mary Daly, *Gyn/Ecology: The Metaethics of Radical Feminism* (Boston: Beacon Press, 1978), pp. 333-334.
53. Allen, p. 43.
54. Hoffman, p. 176.
55. George Levine, "Risking the Moment: Anarchy and Possibility in Pynchon's Fiction," Mindful Pleasures: Essays on Thomas Pynchon, edited by George Levine and David Leverenz (Little, Brown and Company, 1976), p. 119.
56. Henkle, p. 101.
57. Gilbert and Gubar, *No Man's Land, Vol. 3*, p. 334.
58. Levine, p. 121.
59. John Dugdale, *Thomas Pynchon: Allusive Parables of Power* (New York: St. Martin's Press, 1990), p. 92.
60. Richard Rubenstein, *The Cunning of History: The Holocaust and the American Future* (New York: Harper Colophon Books, 1975), p. 41.
61. Rubenstein, p. 42.
62. Butler, p. 37.
63. Allen, p. 41.
64. Douglas Fowler, *A Readers' Guide to Gravity's Rainbow* (Ann Arbor, Michigan: Ardis, 1980), pp. 28-43.
65. Henkle, p. 211.
66. Griffin, *Pornography and Silence*, pp. 12-20.
67. Unlike Alan Wilde who views Pynchon to be generally homophobic, I, as argued in the following pages, find him to be more sensitive to gay males than to lesbians; see Wilde, *Middlegrounds*, pp. 86-89.
68. Allen, p. 44; Gilbert and Gubar, *No Man's Land Vol.1*, pp. 52-53.
69. Fowler, pp. 28-43.
70. Lhamon, pp. 170-176.
71. Golden, p. 11.
72. Kazin, p. 276.
73. Olderman, p. 133; Tony Tanner, *Thomas Pynchon* (London: Methuen, 1982), p. 45.
74. Thomas Pynchon, *Slow Learner: Early Stories* (Boston: Little, Brown and Company, 1984), p. 42; all future references to this text will appear parenthetically within the body of the paper as SL.

75. Tanner, *Thomas Pynchon*, p. 25.
76. Tanner, *Thomas Pynchon*, p. 35.
77. Robinson, p. 23.
78. Suleiman, p. 123.
79. Marianne Hirsch, p. 136.
80. *No Safe Haven*, p. 15.
81. Madsen, p. 49.
82. Garber, *Vested Interests*, pp. 36-37.
83. Butler, p. 31.
84. Rothblatt, *The Apartheid of Sex*, p. 22.
85. Garber, p. 37.
86. In an interview with "androgynous" pop singer k.d. lang, Leslie Bennetts notes that those engaged in gender-blending present a "deeply subversive presence: after you watch [lang] for a while you realize how warped your own stereotypes of femininity, gender and sexual preference are," in "k.d. lang Cuts it Close," *Vanity Fair*, August 1993, pp. 94-98, 142-146.
87. Hutcheon, p. 62.
88. Allen, p. 45.
89. Joseph W. Slade, "Religion, Psychology, Sex and Love in *Gravity's Rainbow*," *Approaches to Gravity's Rainbow*, edited by Charles Clerc (Columbus: Ohio State University Press, 1983), p. 194.
90. In connection with Pynchon's celebration of homoeroticism among men and his condemnation of "bitchy [female?] faggotry," see Editorial Comment, "A Democratic Army," *The New Yorker*, June 28, 1993, pp. 4-5: in the controversy over accepting gays in the American military, leaders will have to be sensitive to dealing with "old-fashioned, manly styles of bonding that seem to include an open contempt for homosexuality—along with, just to keep things humanly complicated, an unstated and intermittent subtext of homoeroticism."
91. Lawrence Wolfley, "Repression's Rainbow: The Presence of Norman O. Brown in Pynchon's Big Novel," *Critical Essays on Thomas Pynchon*, edited by Richard Pearce (Boston: G.K. Hall and Company, 1981), p. 105.
92. Gilbert and Gubar, *No Man's Land, Vol. 1*, pp. 52-53.
93. Tanner, Thomas Pynchon, p. 51.
94. Cowart, pp. 73-78.
95. Allen, p. 45.
96. Butler, p. 17.
97. Gilbert and Gubar, *No Man's Land, Vol. 1*, p. 52.
98. Golden, p. 9.
99. McCaffery, *Postmodern Fiction*, p. 489.
100. Hutcheon, pp. 57-58.
101. Slade, p. 153.
102. Brian Stonehill, *The Self-Conscious Novel: Artifice in Fiction from Joyce to Pynchon* (Philadelphia: University of Pennsylvania Press, 1988), p. 156.

103. Michael Berube, *Marginal Forces/Cultural Centers: Tolson, Pynchon and the Politics of The Canon* (Ithaca: Cornell University Press, 1992), p. 221.
104. Steven Weisenburger, *A Gravity's Rainbow Companion* (Athens, Georgia: University of Georgia Press, 1988), p. 194.
105. Madsen, p. 127.
106. Allen Ginsberg, *Howl and Other Poems* (San Francisco: City Lights Books, 1959), p. 22.
107. Khachig Tololyan, "War as Background in *Gravity's Rainbow*," *Approaches to Gravity's Rainbow*, edited by Charles Clerc (Columbus: Ohio State University Press, 1983), p. 52.
108. Paul Maltby, *Dissident Postmodernists: Barthelme, Coover and Pynchon* (Philadelphia: University of Pennsylvania Press, 1991), p. 161.
109. Felski, *Beyond Feminist Aesthetics*, p. 30.
110. Alec McHoul and David Wills, *Writing Pynchon: Strategies of Fictional Analysis* (Urbana: University of Illinois Press, 1990), p. 24.
111. Marjorie Kaufman, "Brunhilde and the Chemists: Women in *Gravity's Rainbow*," *Mindless Pleasures: Essays on Thomas Pynchon*, edited by George Levine and David Leverenz (Boston" Little, Brown and Company, 1976), p. 225.
112. Madsen quoting McHale, p. 115.
113. Stonehill, p. 148.
114. Madsen, p. 115.
115. Madsen, p. 116.
116. *Take Back the Night: Women on Pornography*, edited by Laura Lederer provides a good compilation of arguments erected by anti-pornography feminists.
117. Rich, "Compulsory Heterosexuality and Lesbian Existence," p. 185.
118. Cal Thomas, "Pornography Must Be Censored" in *Violence Against Women*, p. 125.
119. Helen E. Longino, "Pornography, Oppression and Freedom: A Closer Look," *Take Back the Night*, edited by Laura Lederer, p. 48.
120. Berube, p. 264.
121. *No Safe Haven*, p. 26.
122. Griffin, *A Chorus of Stones*, p. 137.
123. Griffin, *A Chorus of Stones*, p. 324.
124. Berube, p. 264.
125. Madsen, p. 105.
126. Kaufman, p. 202.
127. Daly, p. 186.
128. Griffin, *A Chorus of Stones*, p. 76.
129. Griffin, *A Chorus of Stones*, p. 96.
130. Slade, pp. 188-189.
131. Griffin, *A Chorus of Stones*, p. 60.
132. See Tong's discussion of feminist anti-pornographers and their distinction between "erotica" and "thanatica," the latter being designated as a destructive

form of sexually explicit speech that encourages men to treat women as objects, p. 111.
133. Kaufman, p. 200.
134. Berube, p. 253.
135. Gilbert and Gubar, *No Man's Land, Vol. 1.* pp. 46,48.
136. Miller, *Tropic of Cancer* p. 248.
137. Helen Caldicott, "If You Love This Planet: Dr. Helen Caldicott on Nuclear War," a video cassette (Los Angeles: Direct Cinema, 1982).
138. Anne Campbell, p. 19.
139. Griffin, *A Chorus of Stones*, pp. 147, 153.
140. Marianne Hirsch, *The Mother-Daughter Plot*, pp. 134- 135; Gilbert and Gubar, *No Man's Land, Vol. 3*, pp. 368- 369, 381.
141. Marianne Hirsch, pp. 134-135.
142. Kaufman, p. 217.
143. Gilbert and Gubar, *No Man's Land, Vol. 1*, p. 55.
144. Suleiman, p. 166.
145. Marianne Hirsch, pp. 134-135.
146. Rich, "Compulsory Heterosexuality and Lesbian Existence," p. 182; Butler, pp. x, xi, 17, 77-78.
147. Rich, "Compulsory Heterosexuality and Lesbian Existence," p. 182.
148. Kaufman, p. 219.
149. Felski, *Beyond Feminist Aesthetics*, p. 172.
150. Thomas Pynchon, *Vineland* (Boston: Little, Brown and Company, 1990), p. 287.
151. Madsen, p. 127.

Chapter Four

1. Toni Morrison, *Jazz* (New York: Alfred A. Knopf, Inc. 1992), p. 229; all future references to the text will be cited parenthetically within the body of the paper as J.
2. Suleiman, p. 38.
3. Roland Barthes, "From Work to Text," translated by Richard Howard, *Critical Tradition: Classic Texts and Contemporary Trends*, edited by David Richter (New York: St. Martin's Press, 1989), pp. 1006-1010.
4. Lorraine Liscio, "*Beloved's* Narrative: Writing Mother's Milk," *Tulsa Studies in Women's Literature*, Vol. II (Spring 1992): pp. 31-46; Barbara Hill Rigney, *The Voices of Toni Morrison* (Columbia: Ohio State University Press, 1991), Chapters One and Two.
5. Claudia Tate, editor, *Black Women Writers at Work* (New York: Continuum, 1983), p. 125.
6. Zimmerman, p. 176.
7. McCaffery, *Postmodern Fiction*, p. xxvii.

8. Zimmerman, p. 181.
9. Rigney, p. 32.
10. *No Safe Haven*, p. 54.
11. Toni Morrison, *Song of Solomon* (New York: Alfred A. Knopf, Inc., 1977), p. 246; all future references to the text will be cited parenthetically within the body of the paper as SS.
12. Mel Watkins, "Talk with Toni Morrison," *New York Times Book Review*, September 11, 1977, p. 50.
13. Jane Campbell, *Mythic Black Fiction: The Transformation of History* (Knoxville: The University of Tennessee Press, 1986), pp. 146-147.
14. Tate, p. 123.
15. Zimmerman, p. 178; Kahn and Greene, pp. 1,2,13,21.
16. Marianne Hirsch, p. 184.
17. Although Baby Suggs is Sethe's mother-in-law, her undisputed presence as the spiritual and physical head of the family and of the tiny community outside of Cincinnati establishes her role as matriarch.
18. Toni Morrison, *Sula* (New York: Alfred A. Knopf, Inc., 1973), p. 41; all future references to the text will be cited parenthetically within the body of the paper as S.
19. David Lawrence, "Fleshy Ghosts and Ghostly Flesh: The World and the Body in *Beloved*," *Studies in American Fiction* Vol.19 (Autumn 1991): p. 196.
20. Elizabeth B. House, "Toni Morrison's Ghost: The Beloved Who is Not Beloved," *Studies in American Fiction* Vol 18 (Spring 1990): p. 23.
21. Hutcheon, p. 63.
22. Toni Morrison, *The Bluest Eye* (New York: Simon & Schuster, Inc., 1970); *Tar Baby* (New York: Alfred A. Knopf Inc., 1981); all future references to these texts will be cited parenthetically within the body of the paper as BE and TB.
23. Cornel West, *Race Matters* (New York: Random House, 1994), p. 119.
24. West, p. 122.
25. Tate, p. 126.
26. Toni Morrison, *Beloved* (New York: Alfred A. Knopf, Inc., 1987); all future references to the text will be cited parenthetically within the body of the paper as B.
27. Tate, p. 125.
28. Melissa Walker, *Down from the Mountaintop: Black Women's Novels in the Wake of the Civil Rights Movement, 1966–1989* (New Haven: Yale University Press, 1991), p. 58.
29. Tate, p. 125.
30. Linda Wagner, "Toni Morrison: Master of Narrative," *Contemporary American Women Writers: Narrative Strategies*, edited by Catherine Rainwater and William J. Scheick (Lexington: University Press of Kentucky, 1985), p. 195.
31. Barbara Christian, "Being the Subject and the Object—Reading African-

American Women's Novels" in *Changing Subjects*, edited by Greene and Kahn, p. 198.
32. Walker, p. 53.
33. Rigney, p. 34.
34. Susan Willis, "Black Women Writers: Taking a Critical Perspective," *Making a Difference: Feminist Literary Criticism*, edited by Gayle Greene and Coppelia Kahn (London: Methuen, 1985), p. 230.
35. Willis, "Black Women Writers," p. 230.
36. Tate, p. 126.
37. Wilfred D. Samuels and Clenora Hudson-Weems, *Toni Morrison* (Boston: Twayne Publishers, 1990), p. 14.
38. Rigney, p. 32.
39. Gilbert and Gubar, *No Man's Land, Vol. 1*, p. 49; cf. Michele Wallace's interpretation of the use of the image of the Black Macho as a counterproductive strategy in the struggle for black liberation in Black Macho and the Myth of the Superwoman (New York: Routledge, Chapman and Hall, Inc., 1990), p. 73.
40. Richard Wright, *Native Son* (New York: Harper & Row, 1940) p. 263.
41. Wright, p. 268.
42. Christian, p. 198.
43. Ralph Ellison, *Invisible Man* (New York: Vintage Books, 1972) pp. 54-55.
44. Ellison, pp. 57-58.
45. Ellison, p. 62; emphasis mine.
46. *No Safe Haven*, p. 54.
47. Angela Y. Davis, *Women, Culture and Politics* (New York: Vintage Books, 1990), pp. 36-37; June Jordan, "Poem About My Rights," *Naming Our Destiny: New and Selected Poems* (New York: Thunder's Mouth Press, 1989), pp. 102-104.
48. Adams, pp. 42-43.
49. Karl, p. 443.
50. Suleiman, p. 248.
51. Combahee River Collective, "Black Feminist Statement," All the Women Are White, *All the Blacks Are Men, But Some of Us Are Brave*, edited by Gloria T. Hull, Patricia Bell Scott and Barbara Smith (Old Westbury: The Feminist Press, 1982), p. 15.
52. Tom LeClair and Larry McCaffery, editors, *Anything Can Happen: Interviews with Contemporary American Novelists* (Urbana: University of Illinois Press, 1983), p. 257.
53. Jane Campbell, p. 148.
54. Samuels and Hudson-Weems, p. 85.
55. Jane Campbell. p. 150.
56. Bernard W. Bell, *The Afro-American Novel and its Traditions* (Amherst: The University of Massachusetts Press, 1987), p. 6.

57. Edna O'Brien, "Jazz," *New York Times Book Review*, April 5, 1992, p. 29.
58. Walker, p. 60.
59. Walker, p. 61.
60. Clarissa Pinkola Estes, *Women Who Run With the Wolves: Myths and Stories of the Wild Woman Archetype* (New York, Ballantine Books, 1992), p. 8.
61. Julia Kristeva, "Stabat Mater," *The Kristeva Reader*, edited by Toril Moi, translated by Leon S. Roudiez (New York: Columbia University Press, 1986), p. 188; cf. "Revolution in Poetic Language," *The Kristeva Reader*, p. 90-136 for Kristeva's elucidation of her theory of the semiotic.
62. Kristeva, "Revolution in Poetic Language", pp. 91-92 in *The Kristeva Reader*; cf. Eagleton, p. 188.
63. Toril Moi, p. 165.
64. Marianne Hirsch, p. 133.
65. Toril Moi, p. 165.
66. Hutcheon, p. 68.
67. Hutcheon, p. 68.
68. Toni Cade, "On the Issues of Roles," *The Black Woman: An Anthology*, edited by Toni Cade (New York: Signet, 1970), pp. 103-104.
69. cf. *No Safe Haven* (pp. 72-73; 112) for statistics regarding partner homocides: "In the United States, women are more likely to be killed by their male partners than by all other categories of persons combined"(p. 73).
70. Anne Campbell, *Men, Women and Aggression*, p. 40.
71. West, p. 119; cf. Sally Robinson, p. 26.
72. Robinson, p. 26.
73. Robinson, p. 26.
74. Violet's failure to translate her ex-centricity into productive and self-enhancing behavior is emblematic, perhaps, of the ultimate futility of the semiotic to enact an effective subversion of the repressive symbolic Law of the Father. Indeed, one could read the "fates" of the three main characters, each attuned in some degree to the call of the Wild Mother, as indicative of Morrison's implicit rejection of Kristeva's confidence in the semiotic to challenge the "primacy of the Logos"(Marianne Hirsch, p. 132): Violet is relegated to the periphery of the "psychologically disturbed;" Dorcas dies at the hands of her lover; and Joe Trace destroys what he loves. While the intermittent semiotic interruptions in the symbolic order catch the reader's attention, they remain, as Judith Butler argues, "futile gestures, entertained only within the derealized aesthetic mode which can never be translated into other cultural practices."(Butler, 77-78).
75. Susan Willis, "Eruptions of Funk: Historicizing Toni Morrison," *Black Literature and Literary Theory*, edited by Henry Louis Gates, Jr. (New York: Routledge, 1990), p. 278.
76. Marilyn Frye, *The Politics of Reality: Essays in Feminist Theory* (Trumansburg, NY:The Crossing Press, 1983), p. 94.
77. Barbara Smith, "Toward a Black Feminist Criticism," *The New Feminist*

Criticism: Essays on Women, Literature and Theory (New York: Pantheon Books, 1985), pp. 168-185.
78. Maureen T. Reddy, "The Tripled Plot and Center of *Sula*," *Black American Literature Forum* Vol.22 (Spring 1988): p. 29.
79. Gilbert and Gubar, *No Man's Land, Vol.3*, pp. 259-260.
80. Maxine Montgomery, "A Pilgrimage to the Origins: The Apocalypse as Structure and Theme in Toni Morrison's *Sula*," *Black American Literature Forum*, Vol.23 (Spring 1989): p. 132.
81. Anne Z. Mickelson, *Reaching Out: Sensitivity and Order in Recent American Fiction by Women* (New Jersey: The Scarecrow Press, 1979), p. 172.
82. Marianne Hirsch, p. 180.
83. Marianne Hirsch, p. 181.
84. Marianne Hirsch, p. 182.
85. Samuels, Hudson-Weems, p. 39.
86. Samuels, Hudson-Weems, p. 40.
87. Wagner, p. 198.
88. Bell, p. 274; Mickelson, p. 130.
89. Marianne Hirsch, p. 171.
90. Marianne Hirsch, p. 181.
91. Bettye J. Parker, "Complexity: Toni Morrison's Women, An Interview Essay," *Sturdy Black Bridges: Visions of Black Women in Literature*, edited by Roseann P. Bell. Bettye J. Parker and Beverly Guy-Sheftall (New York: Anchor Press, 1979), p. 255.
92. Marianne Hirsch, p. 182.
93. Marianne Hirsch, p. 182.
94. Willis, "Black Women Writers," p. 231.
95. Montgomery, p. 132.
96. Smith, p. 176.
97. Willis, "Black Women Writers," p. 232.
98. Marianne Hirsch, p. 183.
99. Parker, *Sturdy Black Bridges*, p. 254.
100. Parker, *Sturdy Black Bridges*, p. 254.
101. Marianne Hirsch, p. 183.
102. Parker, *Sturdy Black Bridges*, p. 253.
103. Bonnie Winsbro, *Supernatural Forces: Belief, Difference, and Power in Contemporary Works by Ethnic Women* (Amherst: The University of Massachusetts Press, 1993), p. 202.
104. Barbara Schapiro, "Bonds of Love in Toni Morrison's *Beloved*," *Contemporary Literature*, Vol. 32 (Summer 1991): pp. 201-202.
105. Rosemarie Tong, *Feminist Thought: A Comprehensive Introduction* (Boulder: Westview Press, 1989), p. 229.
106. Rigney, p. 11.
107. Liscio, p. 37.

108. Liscio, p. 37.
109. House, p. 17; emphasis mine.
110. Liscio, p. 37.
111. Gilbert and Gubar, *No Man's Land, Volume 3*, pp. 379- 380.
112. Marianne Hirsch, pp. 7-8.
113. Marianne Hirsch, p. 197.
114. Deborah Horvitz, "Nameless Ghosts: Possession and Dispossession in *Beloved*," *Studies in American Fiction*, Vol.17 (Autumn 1989): p. 157.
115. Schapiro, p. 195.
116. Toni Morrison, editor, *The Black Book*, compiled by Middleton Harris, Introduction by Bill Cosby (New York: Random House, 1973).
117. Elizabeth Kastor, "Toni Morrison's Beloved Country," *The Washington Post*, October 5, 1987, B12.
118. Lawrence, p. 196.
119. Winsbro, p. 137.
120. Gilbert and Gubar, *No Man's Land, Volume 3*, p. 384.
121. Gilbert and Gubar, *No Man's Land, Volume 3*, p. 384.
122. Lawrence, p. 192.
123. Rigney, p. 68.
124. Schapiro, p. 198.
125. Liscio, p. 35.
126. Hélène Cixous, "The Laugh of the Medusa," translated by Keith Cohen and Paula Cohen, *Classic Texts and Critical Trends*, pp. 1090-1102.
127. Julia Kristeva, "Women's Time," translated by Alice Jardine and Harry Blake, *The Kristeva Reader*, pp. 187-213.
128. Liscio, p. 40.
129. Gilbert and Gubar, *No Man's Land, Volume 3*, p. 384.
130. Horvitz, p. 161.
131. Robinson, p. 26.
132. Robinson, p. 25.
133. Winsbro, p. 138.
134. Robinson, pp. 25-26.
135. Elaine Showalter, editor, *Modern American Women Writers* (New York: Charles Scribners and Sons, 1991), p. 332.
136. Liscio, p. 34.
137. Lawrence, p. 193.
138. Lawrence, p. 196.

Bibliography

Primary Sources

Barthelme, Donald. *City Life*. New York: Farrar, Strauss & Giroux, 1970.
———. *The Dead Father*. New York: Penguin Books, 1986.
———. *Sixty Stories*. New York: E.P. Dutton, Inc., 1982.
———. *Snow White*. New York: Atheneum, 1972.
Didion, Joan. *A Book of Common Prayer*. New York: Simon & Schuster, 1977.
———. *Democracy: A Novel*. New York: Simon & Schuster, 1984.
———. *Play It As It Lays*. New York: Simon & Schuster, 1970.
———. *Run River*. New York: Simon & Schuster, 1963.
———. *Salvador*. New York: Simon & Schuster, 1983.
———. *Slouching Towards Bethlehem*. New York: Simon & Schuster, 1968.
———. *The White Album*. New York: Simon & Schuster, 1979.
Morrison, Toni. *Beloved*. New York: Alfred A. Knopf, Inc., 1987.
———. *The Bluest Eye*. New York: Simon & Schuster. 1970.
———. *Jazz*. New York: Alfred A. Knopf, Inc., 1992.
———. *Song of Solomon*. New York: Alfred A. Knopf, Inc., 1977.
———. *Sula*. New York: Alfred A. Knopf, Inc., 1973.
———. *Tar Baby*. New York: Alfred A. Knopf, Inc., 1981.
Pynchon, Thomas. *Gravity's Rainbow*. New York: Viking Penguin, Inc., 1973.
———. *Slow Learner: Early Stories*. Boston: Little, Brown and Company, 1984.
———. *V.* New York: Harper & Row, 1963.
———. *Vineland*. Boston: Little, Brown and Company, 1990.

Secondary Sources

Adams, Carol J. *The Sexual Politics of Meat: A Feminist-Vegetarian Critical Theory*. New York: The Continuum Publishing Company, 1990.
Allen, Mary. *The Necessary Blankness: Women in Major American Fiction of the Sixties*. Chicago: University of Illinois Press, 1976.
America's Watch. *El Salvador's Decade of Terror: Human Rights Since the Assassination of Archbishop Romero*. New Haven: Yale University Press, 1991.
Anderson, Chris. *Style as Argument: Contemporary American Nonfiction*. Carbondale: Southern Illinois University Press, 1987.

Bailey, Adrian. *Walt Disney's World of Fantasy*. New Jersey: Chartwell Books, Inc., 1984.

Barker-Benfield, Graham J. *The Horrors of the Half-Known Life: Male Attitudes toward Women & Sexuality in Nineteenth Century America*. New York: Harper Colophon, 1976.

Barthes, Roland. *Writing Degree Zero*. Translated by Annette Lavers and Colin Smith and Preface by Susan Sontag. New York: Hill and Wang, 1967.

———. "From Work to Text." Translated by Richard Howard. *The Critical Tradition: Classic Texts and Contemporary Trends*. Edited by David H. Richter. New York: St. Martin's Press, 1989. pp. 1006-1010.

Bartky, Sandra Lee. "On Psychological Oppression." *Philosophy and Women*. Edited by Sharon Bishop and Marjorie Weinzweig. Belmont, California: Wadsworth, 1979.

De Beauvoir, Simone. *The Second Sex*. Translated and edited by H.M. Parshley. New York: Vintage Books, 1974.

Bell, Bernard W. *The Afro-American Novel and its Tradition*. Amherst: The University of Massachusetts Press, 1987.

Bem, S. *The Lenses of Gender: Transforming the Debate on Sexual Inequality*. New Haven: Yale University Press, 1993.

Bennetts, Leslie. "k.d.lang Cuts it Close." *Vanity Fair* August 1993: pp. 94-98, 142-146.

Berube, Michael. *Marginal Forces/Cultural Centers: Tolson, Pynchon and the Politics of the Canon*. Ithaca: Cornell University Press, 1992.

Bettelheim, Bruno. *The Uses of Enchantment: The Meaning and Importance of Fairy Tales*. New York: Alfred N. Knopf, 1976.

Brown, S.E. "Police Responses to Wife Beating: Neglect of a Crime of Violence," in *Journal of Criminal Justice*, 12. 1984, pp.277-288.

Browne, A. *When Battered Women Kill*. New York: MacMillan/Free Press, 1987.

Brownmiller, Susan. *Against Our Will: Men, Women and Rape*. New York: Simon & Schuster, 1975.

Bruss, Paul. *Victims: Textual Strategies in Recent American Fiction*. Lewisburg: Bucknell University Press, 1981.

Butler, Judith. *Gender Trouble: Feminism and the Subversion of Identity*. New York: Routledge, 1990.

Cade, Toni. "On the Issues of Roles." *The Black Woman: An Anthology*. Edited by Toni Cade. New York: Signet, 1970.

Caldicott, Dr. Helen. *If You Love This Planet: Dr. Helen Caldicott on Nuclear War*. Los Angeles: Direct Cinema, 1982.

Campbell, Anne. *Men, Women and Aggression*. New York: Basic Books, 1993.

Campbell, Jane. *Mythic Black Fiction: The Transformation of History*. Knoxville: The University of Tennessee Press, 1986.

Carton, Evan. "Joan Didion's Dreampolitics of the Self," in *The Critical Response to Joan Didion*, pp. 34-51.

Christian, Barbara. "Being the Subject and the Object—Reading African-American Women's Novels," in *Changing Subjects*, edited by Greene and Kahn, pp.195-200.

Cixous, Hélène. "The Laugh of the Medusa." Translated by Keith Cohen and Paula Cohen. *The Critical Tradition: Classic Texts and Contemporary Trends*. Edited by David H. Richter. pp. 1090-1102.

Coale, Samuel. "Didion's Disorders." *Critique* 25 (Spring 1984): pp. 160-170.

———. "Joan Didion: Witnessing the Abyss," in *The Critical Response to Joan Didion*, pp. 106-125.

Combahee River Collective. "Black Feminist Statement." *All The Women Are White, All The Blacks Are Men, But Some of Us Are Brave*. Edited by Gloria T. Hull, Patricia Bell Scott and Barbara Smith. Old Westbury: The Feminist Press, 1982.

Con Davis, Robert. "Post-Modern Paternity:Donald Bartheleme's *The Dead Father*" in *The Fictional Father: Lacanian Readings of the Text*, edited by Robert Con Davis. Amherst: University of Massachusetts Press, 1981.

Cowart, David. *The Art of Allusion*. Carbondale: Southern Illinois University Press, 1989.

Daly, Mary. *Gyn/Ecology: The Metaethics of Radical Feminism*. Boston: Beacon Press, 1978.

Davidson, Sara. "A Visit with Joan Didion." *Joan Didion: Essays and Conversations*. Edited by Ellen G. Friedman. Princeton: Ontario Review Press, 1984.

Davis. Angela Y. *Women, Culture and Politics*. New York: Vintage Books, 1990.

"A Democratic Army." Editorial Comment *The New Yorker*. 28 June 1993: pp. 4-5.

Densmore, Dana. "On the Temptation to be a Beautiful Object." *Female Liberation: History and Current Politics*. Edited by Roberta Salper. New York: Alfred A. Knopf, Inc., 1972.

DiStefano, Christine. "Dilemmas of Difference: Feminism, Modernity and Postmodernism," in *Feminism/Postmodernism*, edited by Linda J. Nicholson. New York: Routledge, 1990.

Donovan, Josephine. *Feminist Theory: The Intellectual Tradition of American Feminism*. New York: Frederick Ungar Publishing Company, 1985.

Duffy, Martha. "Pictures from an Expedition," in *The Critical Response to Joan Didion*, pp. 127-132.

Dugdale, John. *Thomas Pynchon: Allusive Parables of Power*. New York: St. Martin's Press, 1990.

Eagleton, Terry. *Literary Theory: An Introduction*. Minneapolis: University of Minnesota Press, 1983.

Ellison, Ralph. *Invisible Man*. New York: Vintage Books, 1972.

Ellmann, Mary. *Thinking About Women*. New York:Harcourt, Brace & World, Inc., 1968.

Epstein, Joseph. *Plausible Prejudices: Essays in American Writing*. New York: W.W. Norton & Company, 1985.

Estés, Clarissa Pinkola. *Women who Run with the Wolves: Myths and Stories of the Wild Woman Archetype*. New York: Ballantine Books, 1992.

Falcoff, Mark. "Two Weeks." Review of *Salvador* by Joan Didion. *Commentary* Vol.75, No.5 (May 1983): pp. 66, 68-70.

Faludi, Susan. *Backlash: The Undeclared War Against American Women*. New York: Crown Publishers, Inc., 1991.

Felski, Rita. *Beyond Feminist Aesthetics: Feminist Literature and Social Change*. Cambridge: Harvard University Press, 1989.

———. "Feminism, Realism and the Avant-Garde" in *Postmodern Conditions*, edited by Andrew Miller, Philip Thomson and Chris Worth. New York: Berg, 1990, pp.66-78.

Felton, Sharon, editor, *The Critical Response to Joan Didion*. Westport, Conn.: Greenwood Press, 1994.

Flax, Jane. "Postmodernism and Gender Relations in Feminist Theory," in *Feminism/Postmodernism*, edited by Linda J. Nicholson. New York: Routledge, 1990, pp.39-62.

———. *Thinking Fragments: Psychoanalysis, Feminism and Postmodernism in the Contemporary West*. Berkeley: University of California Press, 1990.

Flowers, Betty. "Barthelme's Snow White: The Reader-Patient Relationship," *Critique* 16, No.3 1975, pp. 30-40.

Fowler, Douglas. *A Reader's Guide to Gravity's Rainbow*. Ann Arbor: Ardis, 1980.

Fraser, Nancy and Linda Nicholson. "Social Criticism Without Philosophy: An Encounter between Feminism and Postmodernism," in *Universal Abandon: The Politics of Postmodernism*. Edited by Andrew Ross. Minneapolis: University of Minnesota Press, 1988.

French, Marilyn. *Beyond Power: On Women, Men and Morals*. New York: Summit Books, 1985.

———. *The War Against Women*. New York: Summit Books, 1992.

Friedan, Betty. *The Feminine Mystique—Twentieth Anniversary Edition*. New York: W.W. Norton & Company, 1983.

Frye, Marilyn. *The Politics of Reality: Essays in Feminist Theory*. Trumansburg, N.Y.:The Crossing Press, 1983.

Garber, Marjorie. *Vested Interests: Cross-Dressing and Cultural Anxiety*. New York: Harper Perennial, 1992.

Geherin, David. "Nothingness and Beyond: Joan Didion's *Play It As It Lays*." *Critique* 1 Vol.16 (1975): pp. 64-78.

Gelman, David. "The Rapist: An Overview," in *Violence Against Women*, pp.46-52.

Gilbert, Sandra M. and Susan Gubar. *No Man's Land: The Place of the Woman Writer in the Twentieth Century, Volume 1: The War of the Words*. New Haven: Yale University Press, 1988.

———. *No Man's Land: The Place of the Woman Writer in the Twentieth Century, Volume 2: Sex Changes*. New Haven: Yale University Press, 1989.

———. *No Man's Land: The Place of the Woman Writer in the Twentieth Century, Volume 3: Letters from the Front*. New Haven: Yale University Press, 1994.

Ginsberg, Allen. *Howl and Other Poems*. San Francisco: City Lights Books, 1959.

Golden, Robert E. "Mass, Man and Modernism: Violence in Pynchon's *V.*" *Critique* 44, #2 (1972-73): pp. 5-17.

Gordon, Mary. *Good Boys and Dead Girls and Other Essays*. London: Penquin Books, Ltd. 1991.

Graff, Gerald. *Literature Against Itself: Literary Ideas in Modern Society*. Chicago: University of Chicago Press, 1979.

Greene, Gayle and Coppelia Kahn, editors. *Changing Subjects: The Making of Feminist Literary Criticism*. London: Routledge, 1993.

Griffin, Susan. *A Chorus of Stones: The Private Life of War*. New York: Doubleday, 1992.

———. *Pornography and Silence*. New York: Harper & Row, 1981.

———. *Woman and Nature: The Roaring Inside Her*. New York: Harper & Row, 1978.

Grimm's *Fairytales*. London: Butler and Tanner, Ltd., n.d.

Hanley, Lynne. *Writing War: Fiction, Gender and Memory*. Amherst: University of Massachusetts Press, 1991.

Hawthorne, Nathaniel. *The Scarlet Letter*. Edited by Seymour L. Gross. New York: W.W. Norton & Company, Inc., 1961

Hays, H. R. *The Dangerous Sex: The Myth of Feminine Evil*. New York: G.P.Putnam, Sons, 1964.

Heilbrun, Carolyn G. *Reinventing Womanhood*. New York: W. W. Norton and Co., Inc., 1979.

———. *Toward a Recognition of Androgyny*. New York: W. W. Norton and Co., Inc., 1982.

Henderson, Katherine. *Joan Didion*. New York: Frederick Ungar Publishing Company, 1980.

———. "Joan Didion: The Bond Between Narrator and Heroine in Democracy." *American Women Writing Fiction: Memory, Identity, Family, Space*. Edited by Mickey Pearlman. Lexington: University Press of Kentucky, 1989.

Hendin, Josephine. *Vulnerable People: A View of American Fiction Since 1945*. New York: Oxford University Press, 1978.

Henkle, Roger B. "Pynchon's Tapestries on the Western Wall." *Pynchon: A Collection of Critical Essays*. Edited by Edward Mendelsohn. Englewood Cliffs: Prentice-Hall, Inc., 1978. pp. 97-111.

Hinchman, Sandra K. "Making Sense and Telling Stories: Problems of Cognition and Narration in Joan Didion's *Play It As It Lays*," in *The Critical Response to Joan Didion*, pp. 82-94.

Hirsch, Marianne. "Maternity and Rememory—Toni Morrison's *Beloved*," in *Representations of Motherhood*, edited by Donna Bassin, Margaret Honey and Meryle Mahrer Kaplan. New Haven: Yale University Press, 1994, pp.92-110.

———. *The Mother-Daughter Plot: Narrative, Psychoanalysis, Feminism*. Bloomington: Indiana University Press, 1989.

Hirsch, Miriam F. *Women and Violence.* New York: Van Nostrand Reinhold Company, 1981.

Hoffman, Frederick. "The Questing Comedian: Thomas Pynchon's *V..*" *Critique* 6 (1963-64): pp. 174-177.

Horvitz, Deborah. "Nameless Ghosts: Possession and Dispossession in Beloved." *Studies in American Fiction* Volume 17 (Autumn 1989): pp. 157-167.

House, Elizabeth B. "Toni Morrison's Ghost: The Beloved who is not Beloved." *Studies in American Fiction* Volume 18 (Spring 1990): pp. 17-26.

Hutcheon, Linda. *A Poetics of Postmodernism: History, Theory, Fiction.* New York: Routledge, 1988.

Hutchings, Nancy. "Sexism Promotes Violence Against Women," in *Violence Against Women*, pp.33-38.

Irigaray, Luce. "The Power of Discourse" in *The Sex Which Is Not One.* Translated by Catherine Porter. Ithaca: Cornell University Press, 1985.

Jardine, Alice. *Gynesis: Configurations of Women and Modernity.* Ithaca: Cornell University Press, 1985.

Johnson, Diane. Review of *A Book of Common Prayer* by Joan Didion. *The New York Review of Books* 28 April 1977: p. 6.

Johnson, R.E. Jr. "Bees Barking in the Night: The End and Beginning of Donald Barthelme's Narrative" in *Boundary* 2 V 1976, pp. 71-92.

Jordan, June. *Naming our Destiny: New and Selected Poems.* New York: Thunder's Mouth Press, 1989.

Karl, Frederick R. *American Fictions: 1940-1980: A Comprehensive History and Critical Evaluation.* New York: Harper & Row, 1983.

Kastor, Elizabeth. "Toni Morrison's Beloved Country." Review of *Beloved. The Washington Post* 5 October 1987: p. B12.

Kaufman, Marjorie. "Brunhilde and the Chemists: Women in *Gravity's Rainbow*." *Mindless Pleasures: Essays on Thomas Pynchon.* Edited by George Levine and David Leverenz. Boston: Little, Brown and Company, 1976.

Kazin, Alfred. *Bright Book of Life: American Novelists and Storytellers from Hemingway to Mailer.* New York: Little, Brown and Company, 1973.

Kilbourne, Jean. "Killing Us Softly: Advertising's Image of Women." Boston: Cambridge Documentary Films, 1979.

Kiley, Frederick. "Beyond Words: Narrative Art in Joan Didion's Salvador." *Joan Didion: Essays and Conversations.* Edited by Ellen G. Friedman. Princeton: Ontario Review Press, 1984.

Klinkowitz, Jerome. *Donald Barthelme: An Exhibition.* Durham: Duke University Press, 1991.

Komisar, Lucy. "The Image of Women in Advertising" in *Woman in a Sexist Society: Studies in Power and Powerlessness*, edited by Vivian Gornick and Barbara K. Moran. New York: Boston Books, Inc., 1971.

Koss, Mary P. and Lisa A Goodman, et.al. *No Safe Haven: Male Violence against Women at Home, at Work, and in the Community.* Washington, D.C.: American Psychological Association, 1994.

Kristeva, Julia. "Revolution in Poetic Language," in *The Kristeva Reader*, edited by Toril Moi, translated by Leon S. Roudiez (New York: Columbia University Press, 1986, pp.90-136.
———. "Stabat Mater," in *The Kristeva Reader*. pp.160-186.
———. "Women's Time." Translated by Alice Jardine and Harry Blake. *The Kristeva Reader*. Edited by Toril Moi. New York: Columbia University Press, 1986. pp. 187-213.
Kurz, D. "Responses to Battered Women: Resistance to Medicalization," in *Social Problems* 34, 1987, pp. 501-513.
Lawrence, David. "Fleshy Ghosts and Ghostly Flesh: The World and the Body in Beloved." *Studies in American Fiction* Volume 19 (Autumn 1991): pp. 189-201.
LeClair, Tom and Larry McCaffery, editors. *Anything Can Happen: Interviews with Contemporary American Novelists*. Urbana: University of Illinois, 1983.
Lederer, Laura. Editor. *Take Back the Night: Women on Pornography*. New York: William Morrow and Company, Inc., 1980.
Leland, John. "Remarks Re-marked: What Curios of Signs!" in *Boundary* 2V Spring 1977, pp. 796-811.
Leonard, John. Review. *Play It As It Lays*, Joan Didion. *The New York Times* 21 July 1970: p. 33.
Levin, Jack. "Hate Crimes Against Women," in *Bostonia*. January/February, 1991, p.60.
Levine, George. "Risking the Moment: Anarchy and Possibility in Pynchon's Fiction." *Mindless Pleasures: Essays on Thomas Pynchon*. Edited by George Levine and David Leverenz. Boston: Little, Brown and Company, 1976. pp. 113-136.
Levitt, E. E., B. Lubin and J. M. Brooks. *Depression: Concepts, Controversies and Some New Facts*. Hillsdale, New Jersey: Laurence Erlbaum Associates, 1983.
Lhamon, W. T. Jr. "Pentecost, Promiscuity and Pynchon's *V.*: From The Scaffold to the Impulsive." *Twentieth Century American Literature* 21 (1975): pp. 163-176.
Liscio, Lorraine. "Beloved's Narrative: Writing Mother's Milk." *Tulsa Studies in Women's Literature* Volume 11 (Spring 1992): pp. 31-46.
Longino, Helen. E. "Pornography, Oppression and Freedom: A Closer Look." *Take Back the Night: Women on Pornography*. Edited by Laura Lederer. New York: William Morrow and Company, Inc., 1980., pp. 40-54.
Loris, Michelle. "Run River: A Western Story of Paradise Lost," in *The Critical Response to Joan Didion*, pp. 20-31.
Lyotard, Jean-François. *The Postmodern Condition: A Report on Knowledge*. Translated by Geoff Bennington and Brian Massume. Foreward by Fredric Jameson. Minneapolis: University of Minnesota Press, 1984.
Maddocks, Melvin. "Her Heart's with the Wagon Trains," in *The Critical Response to Joan Didion*, pp. 33-34.
Madsen, Deborah L. *The Postmodernist Allegories of Thomas Pynchon*. New York: St. Martin's Press, 1991.

Malmgren, Carl Daryl. *Fictional Space in the Modernist and Postmodernist American Novel*. Lewisburg: Bucknell University Press, 1985.
Maltby, Paul. *Dissident Postmodernists: Barthelme, Coover, Pynchon*. Philadelphia: University of Pennsylvania Press, 1991.
Marcuse, Herbert. *One Dimensional Man: Studies in the Ideology of Advanced Industrial Society*. Boston: Beacon Press, 1964.
Matthiessen, F. O. *American Renaissance: Art in the Age of Emerson and Whitman*. New York: Oxford University Press, 1941.
McCaffery, Larry. *The Metafictional Muse: The Works of Robert Coover, Donald Barthelme and William Gass*. Pittsburgh: University of Pittsburgh Press, 1982.
——. editor. *Postmodern Fiction: A Bio-Bibliographical Guide*. New York: Greenwood Press, 1986.
McCarthy, Mary. "Love and Death in the Pacific." Review of *Democracy* by Joan Didion. *The New York Times Book Review* 22 April 1984: pp. 1, 18-19.
McHoul, Alec. and David Wills. *Writing Pynchon: Strategies of Fictional Analysis*. Urbana:University of Illinois Press, 1990.
McVicker, Jeanette. "Donald Barthelme's *The Dead Father*: 'Girls Talk' and The Displacement of the Logos", Boundary 2, Winter 1989, pp.363-390.
Mickelson, Anne. Z. *Reaching Out: Sensitivity and Order in Recent American Fiction by Women*. Metuchen: Scarecrow Press, 1979.
Miller, Henry. *Tropic of Cancer*. New York: Grove Press, 1961.
——. *Tropic of Capricorn*. New York: Grove Press, 1961.
——. *Sexus: The Rosy Crucifixion I*. New York: Grove Press, 1965.
Millett, Kate. *Sexual Politics*. New York: Ballantine Books, 1969
Mills, Jane. *Womanwords: A Dictionary of Words About Women*. New York: The Free Press, 1992.
Molesworth, Charles. *Donald Barthelme's Fiction: The Ironist Saved from Drowning*. Columbia: University of Missouri Press, 1982.
Moi, Toril. *Sexual/Textual Politics: Feminist Literary Theory*. London: Routledge, 1985.
Montgomery, Maxine Lavon. "A Pilgrimage to the Origins: The Apocalypse as Structure and Theme in Toni Morrison's *Sula*." *Black American Literature Forum* Volume 23 (Spring 1989): pp. 127-137.
Morrison, Toni. Editor. *The Black Book*. Compiled by Middleton Harris. Introduction by Bill Cosby. New York: Random House, 1974.
Nicholson, Linda J, editor. *Feminism/Postmodernism*. New York: Routledge, 1990.
Oates, Joyce Carol. "A Taut Novel of Disorder." Review of *A Book of Common Prayer* by Joan Didion. *The New York Times Book Review* 3 April 1977: pp. 1, 34-35.
O,Brien, Edna. "Jazz." Review of *Jazz* by Toni Morrison. *The New York Times Book Review* 5 April 1992: p. 29.
Olderman, Raymond. *Beyond the Wasteland: A Study of the American Novel in the 1960's*. New Haven: Yale University Press, 1972.

Parker, Bettye J. "Complexity: Toni Morrison's Women—An Interview-Essay." *Sturdy Black Bridges: Visions of Black Women in Literature*. Edited by Bettye J Parker, Roseann P. Bell and Beverly Guy-Sheftall. New York: Anchor Press, 1979. pp. 251-157.

Peden, William H. *The American Short Story: Continuity and Change, 1940-1975*. Boston: Houghton Mifflin Co., 1975.

Person, Leland S. *Aesthetic Headaches: Women and a Masculine Poetics in Poe, Melville and Hawthorne*. Athens: University of Georgia Press, 1988.

Pilger, John. "Having Fun with Fear." Review of *Salvador* by Joan Didion. *New Statesman* 6 May 1983, pp. 20-21.

Plath, Sylvia. *The Collected Poems*. Edited by Ted Hughes. New York: Harper & Row, 1981.

Pogrebin, Letty Cottin. "Boys Will Be Boys." *Ms. Magazine* September 1989: p.24.

Poirier, Richard. *The Performing Self: Compositions and Decompositions in the Language of Contemporary Life*. New York: Oxford University press, 1971.

Reddy, Maureen T. "The Tripled Plot and Center of *Sula*." *Black American Literature Forum* Volume 22 (Spring 1988): pp. 29-45.

Rich, Adrienne. "Compulsory Heterosexuality and Lesbian Existence," in *Powers of Desire: The Politics of Sexuality*, edited by Ann Snitow, Christine Stansell and Sharon Thompson. New York: Monthly Review Press, pp. 177-205.

—— *Of Woman Born: Motherhood as Experience and Institution*. New York: W.W. Norton & Company, 1995.

Richter, David. *The Critical Tradition: Classic Texts and Contemporary Trends*. New York: St. Martin's Press, 1989.

Rigney, Barbara Hill. *The Voices of Toni Morrison*. Columbus: Ohio State University Press, 1991.

Rigor, Stephanie and Margo Gordon, "The Impact of Crime on Urban Women," in *Rape and Sexual Assault, Volume 2*, edited by A.W.Burgess (New York: Garland, 1988), pp.139-156.

Robinson, Sally. *Engendering the Subject: Gender and Self-Representation in Contemporary Women's Fiction*. Albany: State University of New York, 1991.

Rogers, Katherine M. *The Troublesome Helpmate: A History of Misogyny in Literature*. Seattle: Washington University Press, 1966.

Rosenbaum, Susan. "Men's Group Studies Abuse," in *The East Hampton Star*, July 27, 1995, p.8.

Ross, L. "The Intuitive Psychoanalyst and His Shortcomings: Distortions in the Attribution Process," in *Advances in Experimental Social Psychology*, 35., edited by L. Berkowitz. New York: Academic Press, 1977, pp.485-494.

Rothblatt, Martine. *The Apartheid of Sex: A Manifesto on the Freedom of Gender*. New York: Crown Publishers, Inc., 1995.

Rubenstein, Richard L. *The Cunning of History : The Holocaust and the American Future*. New York: Harper Colophon Books, 1975.

Russ, Joanna. *How to Suppress Women's Writing*. Austin: University of Texas Press, 1983.

Sadker, Myra and David. *Failing at Fairness: How American Schools Cheat Girls.* New York: Charles Scribners and Sons, 1994.

Saint Augustine, *City of God.* Translated by Gerald G. Walsh, et.al. Garden City, N.Y.: Image Books, 1958.

Samuels, Wilfred D. and Clenora Hudson-Weems. *Toni Morrison.* Boston: Twayne Publishers, 1990.

Sanders, Scott. "Pynchon's Paranoid History." *Mindless Pleasures: Essays on Thomas Pynchon.* Edited by George Levine and David Leverenz. Boston: Little, Brown and Company, 1976. pp. 139-159.

Schapiro, Barbara. "Bonds of Love in Toni Morrison's *Beloved.*" *Contemporary Literature* Volume 32 (Summer 1991): pp. 194-210.

Schneider, Elizabeth M. "Society's Belief in Family Privacy Contributes to Domestic Violence," *Violence Against Women*, pp. 26-32.

Seed, David. *The Fictional Labyrinths of Thomas Pynchon.* Iowa City: University of Iowa Press, 1988.

Selby, Hubert Jr. *Last Exit to Brooklyn.* New York: Grove Weidenfeld, 1964.

Shilts, Randy. *Conduct Unbecoming: Gays and Lesbians in the U.S. Military.* New York: St. Martin's Press, 1993.

Showalter, Elaine. *A Literature of Their Own: British Women Novelists from Bronte to Lessing.* Princeton: Princeton University Press, 1977.

———. Consulting Editor. *Modern American Women Writers.* New York: Charles Scribner's Sons, 1991. pp. 317-338.

Simard, Rodney. "The Dissociation of Self in Joan Didion's *Play It As It Lays*," in The Critical Response to Joan Didion, pp. 68-82.

Slade, Joseph W. "Religion, Psychology, Sex and Love in *Gravity's Rainbow.*" Edited by Clarles Clerc. Columbus: Ohio State University Press, 1983. pp. 153-198.

Smith, Barbara. "Towards A Black Feminist Criticism." *The New Feminist Criticism: Essays on Women, Literature and Theory.* Edited by Elaine Showalter. New York: Pantheon Books, 1985. pp. 168-185.

Smith, Joan. *Misogynies: Reflections on Myths and Malice.* New York: Ballantine Books, 1992.

Smith-Rosenberg, Carroll. *Disorderly Conduct: Visions of Gender in Victorian America.* New York: Oxford University Press, 1985.

Soble, Alan. *Pornography: Marxism, Feminism and the Future of Sexuality.* New Haven: Yale University Press, 1989.

Stengel, Wayne B. *The Shape of Art in the Short Stories of Donald Barthelme.* Baton Rouge: Louisiana State University Press, 1985.

Stonehill, Brian. *The Self-Conscious Novel: Artifice in Fiction from Joyce to Fiction.* Philadelphia: University of Pennsylvania Press, 1988.

Stout, Janis P. "Joan Didion and the Presence of Absence," in *The Critical Response to Joan Didion*, pp. 210-227.

Suleiman, Susan R. *Subversive Intent: Gender, Politics and the Avant-Garde.* Cambridge: Harvard University Press, 1990.

Swisher, Karin L. and Carol Wekesser, editors. *Violence Against Women*. San Diego: Greenhaven Press, 1994.
Tager, Michael. "The Political Vision of Joan Didion's *Democracy*." *Critique* 31 (Spring 1990): pp. 173-184.
Tanner, Tony. *City of Words: American Fiction 1950-1970*. New York: Harper & Row, 1971.
———. *Thomas Pynchon*. London: Methuen, 1982.
Tate, Claudia. Editor. *Black Women Writers at Work*. New York: Continuum, 1983.
Tax, Meredith. "Woman and Her Mind: The Story of an Everyday Life." *Notes form the Second Year: Radical Feminism*. Edited by Shulamith Firestone, 1970.
Thomas, Cal. "Pornography Must Be Censored," in *Violence Against Women*, pp.124-126.
Thompson, M. P. and F. H.Norris. "Crime, Social Status, and Alienation," in *American Journal of Community Psychology*, I, 1992, pp.97-119.
Tololyan, Khachig. "War as Background in *Gravity's Rainbow*." *Approaches to Gravity's Rainbow*. Edited by Charles Clerc. Columbus: Ohio State University Press, 1983. pp. 31-67.
Tong, Rosemarie. *Feminist Thought: A Comprehensive Introduction*. Boulder: Westview Press, 1989.
Wagner, Linda W. "Toni Morrison: Mastery of Narrative." *Contemporary American Women Writers: Narrative Strategies*. Edited by Catherine Rainwater and William J. Scheick. Lexington: University Press of Kentucky, 1985. pp. 191-205.
Walker, Melissa. *Down from the Mountaintop: Black Women's Novels in the Wake of the Civil Rights Movement 1966-1989*. New Haven: Yale University Press, 1991.
Wallace, Michele. *Black Macho and the Myth of the Superwoman*. New York: Routledge, Chapman and Hall, Inc. 1990.
Watkins, Mel. "Talk with Toni Morrison." *The New York Times Book Review* 11 September 1977: p. 5.
Waugh, Patricia. *Feminine Fictions: Revisiting the Postmodern*. London: Routledge, 1989.
———. *Practising Postmodernism, Reading Modernism*. London: Edward Arnold, 1992.
Weisenburger, Steven. *A Gravity's Rainbow Companion*. Athens, Georgia: University of Georgia Press, 1988.
West, Cornel. *Race Matters*. New York: Random House, 1994.
Wetzel, Janet W. *Clinical Handbook of Depression*. New York: Gardner Press, Inc., 1984.
Wilde, Alan. *Horizons of Assent: Modernism, Postmodernism, and the Ironic Imagination*. Baltimore: The Johns Hopkins University Press, 1981.
———. *Middlegrounds: Studies in Contemporary American Fiction*. Philadelphia: University of Pennsylvania Press, 1987.

Williams, Juanita. *Psychology of Women: Behavior in a Biosocial Context*. New York: W.W. Norton and Company, 1977.

Willis, Susan. "Black Women Writers: Taking a Critical Perspective." *Making A Difference: Feminist Literary Criticism*. Edited by Gayle Greene and Coppelia Kahn. London: Methuen, 1985. pp. 211-237.

——. "Eruptions of Funk: Historisizing Toni Morrison." *Black Literature and Literary Theory*. Edited by Henry Louis Gates, Jr. New York: Routledge, 1990.

Winchell, Mark Royden. *Joan Didion*. Boston: Twayne Publishers, 1980.

Winsbro, Bonnie. *Supernatural Forces: Belief, Difference and Power in Contemporary Works by Ethnic Women*. Amherst: The University of Massachusetts Press, 1993.

Wolff, Cynthia Griffin. "*Play It As It Lays*: Didion and the New American Heroine." *Joan Didion: Essays and Conversations*. Edited by Ellen G. Friedman. Princeton: Ontario Review Press, 1984.

Wolfley, Lawrence. "Repression's Rainbow: The Presence of Norman O, Brown in Pynchon's Big Novel." *Critical Essays on Thomas Pynchon*. Edited by Richard Pearce. Boston: G.K. Hall and Company, 1981. PP. 99-123.

Wright, Richard. *Native Son*. New York: Harper & Row, 1940.

Zimmerman, Bonnie. "Feminist Fiction and the Postmodern Challenge," in *McCaffery's Postmodern Fiction: A Bio-Bibliographical Guide*. New York: Greenwood Press, 1986, pp. 175-188.

Index

Absalom! Absalom! 82
Adams, Henry 123
Adventures of Huckleberry Finn, The 254
Awakening, The 275n49

Barth, John xxii, xxiii, 122, 190
Barthelme, Donald
    "Captured Woman, The" xxi, 14, 15, 17, 18, 22, 64, 86, 87, 143
    "City of Churches, A" 18, 19, 20, 21, 42
    Dead Father, The xvi, 26, 27, 7, 36-49, 75, 85, 105, 143, 145, 161, 180, 190, 252, 254, 259, 272n104, 272n112, 272n117
    "Glass Mountain, The" 1-12, 18, 43, 120, 121, 263
    "Policeman's Ball, The" xvii, 11, 12, 14, 18, 28
    Snow White 22-36, 46, 115, 270n57
Barthes, Roland 3, 190, 191, 268n16, 285n3
Bell Jar, The 62, 98
Bettelheim, Bruno 30, 270n72
Blithedale Romance 121
Blood Oranges, The 121
Brownmiller, Susan 43, 65, 164, 272n108, 275n45

Camus, Albert 69
Cannibal, The 121, 162, 163
Catch – 22 112

Chopin, Kate 275n49
Cixous, Hélène xxiii, xxiv, xxvii, 40, 43, 47, 71, 113, 190, 246, 275n62, 276n73

Daly, Mary xxiii, 138, 169, 282n52
Davis, Angela Y. 208, 287n47
de Beauvoir, Simone xxiii, 56, 274n24
Derrida, Jacques 4, 24, 25, 47, 71
Descartes 124, 276n71
Didion, Joan
    Book of Common Prayer, A xviii, xxvii, 37, 52, 55, 56, 57, 68, 71, 80-94, 96, 97, 99, 100, 110, 274n43, 277n91
    Democracy xviii, xxvii, 7, 38, 40, 51, 52, 56, 68, 70, 71, 81, 89, 94-114, 119, 274n43, 278n112, 279n136
    Play It As It Lays xxvii, 37, 51, 52, 55, 56, 66-80, 87, 170, 254, 273n2, 275n55, 275n57, 275n58
    Run River xxvii, 37, 51, 52, 55, 56, 58-66, 67, 78, 80, 87, 101, 116, 274n30
    Salvador 38, 89, 97, 98, 99, 100, 108, 109, 110, 278n126, 279n129
    Slouching Towards Bethlehem 67, 68, 95, 97, 273n14
    White Album, The 24, 53, 66, 273n11
Dynasts, The 120

Eliot, T.S. 28, 80, 140, 190
Ellison, Ralph 204-207, 287n43
Euripedes 32, 250

Faludi, Susan xxii, 267n41
Faulkner, William 28, 29, 121
Fitzgerald, F. Scott 118
French, Marilyn xvii, 124, 266n23, 280n26,
Freud, Sigmund 21, 27, 30, 35, 60, 148, 151,
Friedan, Betty xxiii, 61, 66, 274n34

Gilbert, Sandra M. xiv, xxv, xxii, xxiii, 5, 14, 23, 24, 25, 31, 40, 47, 61, 75, 140, 148, 155, 204, 232, 250, 254, 265n8, 271n103, 276n73, 287n39
Gilman, Charlotte Perkins 98, 275n49
Ginsberg, Allen 160, 284n106
Great Gatsby, The 82, 120, 121
Grimm Brothers 23, 28, 29, 270n55
Gubar, Susan xiv, xxii, xxv, 5, 14, 24, 31, 40, 47, 61, 75, 140, 148, 155, 204, 232, 250, 254, 265n8, 276n73, 287n39, 271n103
Gyn/Ecology: The Metaethics of Radical Feminism 282n52

Habermas, Jürgen xiii
Hardy, Thomas 120
Hawkes, John 121, 122, 162
Heller, Joseph 112
Hemingway, Ernest 26, 28, 277n77
Howl and Other Poems 160, 284n106
Husserl, Edmund 27, 124

Invisible Man 205, 287n43
Irigaray, Luce xxiii, xxiv, 40, 43, 47, 48, 49, 150, 190, 272n120

Kesey, Ken 71
Kristeva, Julia xxiii, xxiv, xxvii, xxix,

Kristeva, Julia (*continued*) 216, 239, 246, 288n61, 288n62, 288n74, 290n127

Last Exit to Brooklyn 77, 121, 277n76
Lawrence, D.H. 28, 31
Light in August 121
Lime Twig, The 121
Long Day's Journey Into Night 275n49
Lost in the Funhouse 121
Lyotard, Jean-François xiii, xxiii, xxiv, xxv, 8, 33, 47, 55, 134, 273n19

Macbeth, Lady 17
Mailer, Norman xxiii, 31, 43, 117, 118, 121, 122, 126, 277n77
Marcuse, Herbert 128, 281n37
Medea 32, 250
Melville, Herman 140, 269n47
Miller, Henry 31, 42, 43, 118, 121, 178, 270n74, 272n106
Millett, Kate xxiii, 31, 270n76
Moby Dick 82
Morrison, Toni
  Beloved xxix, 48, 116, 118, 190, 192, 194, 229-231, 238, 246-261, 267n63, 271n103, 279n132, 285n4, 286n19, 289n104, 290n114
  Bluest Eye, The xxix, 192, 197-210, 211, 214, 224, 226, 286n22
  Jazz xxix, 189-192, 197, 198, 210, 211-230, 242, 245, 246, 248, 285n1
  Song of Solomon 190, 193, 194, 195, 279n132, 286n11
  Sula xxix, 32, 192-195, 229, 230, 231-245, 246, 250, 256, 286n18, 289n78, 289n80
  Tar Baby 192, 217, 286n22

Native Son 117, 204, 205, 287n40

Index 305

Nausea 126

O. Henry 15
O'Connor, Flannery 208
O'Neill, Eugene 275n49
Oates, Joyce Carol 80, 277n85
One Dimensional Man 128, 281n37
One Flew Over the Cuckoo's Nest 71
Outsider, The 117
Owl, The 121

Plath, Sylvia 62, 98, 274n42
Plato 124, 125
Pynchon, Thomas
 "Entropy" 149, 150
 "Small Rain" 149
 Gravity's Rainbow xxviii, xvi, xviii, xxi, 72, 90, 112, 113, 116, 118, 119, 134, 141, 154, 155, 158-187, 192, 195, 228, 254, 281n44, 282n64, 283n89, 284n104, 284n107, 284n111
 Slow Learner xi, 265n1
 V. xxi, xxviii, 116, 118, 119-157, 161, 162, 164, 165, 167, 170, 172, 252, 280n4, 280n11, 280n19
 Vineland 119, 186, 285n150

Rich, Adrienne xxiii, 73, 164, 184, 275n59, 276n66

Sadker, Myra and David xix, 266n31, 279n141
Sanctuary 121
Sartre, Jean-Paul 13, 27, 69, 124, 126, 129, 136
Scarlet Letter, The 20, 21, 119, 270n51
Second Sex, The 274n24
Selby, Hubert Jr. 77, 121, 122, 277n76
Sexus: The Rosy Crucifixion I 42, 272n106
Shilts, Randy xviii, 266n29

Sophie's Choice 250
Styron, William 250

Thurber, James 14-15
Tropic of Cancer 31, 126, 178, 270n74
Tropic of Capricorn 31
Twain, Mark 10

Vonnegut, Kurt Jr. xxii

West, Cornel 195, 286n23
West, Nathaniel 28
Why Are We In Vietnam? 126
Wife of Bath 17
Williams, William Carlos xxiii
Wittig, Monique 184
Wright, Richard 117, 204, 205, 287n40

Yeats, W.B. 67, 95
Yellow Wallpaper, The 98, 275n49